HANDBOOK OF ORGANIZATIONAL AND MANAGERIAL INNOVATION

Handbook of Organizational and Managerial Innovation

Edited by

Tyrone S. Pitsis

Reader in Strategic Design and Director, Strategy, Organization and Society (SOS) Group, Newcastle University, UK

Ace Simpson

Australian Postgraduate Award (APA) Scholar, University of Technology, Sydney (UTS) Business School, Australia and member, Centre for Management & Organisation Studies (CMOS)

Erlend Dehlin

Associate Professor, Trondheim Business School, Norway and Associate Professor II, Norwegian University of Science and Technology

Edward Elgar
Cheltenham, UK • Northampton, MA, USA

Published by
Edward Elgar Publishing Limited
The Lypiatts
15 Lansdown Road
Cheltenham
Glos GL50 2JA
UK

Edward Elgar Publishing, Inc.
William Pratt House
9 Dewey Court
Northampton
Massachusetts 01060
USA

A catalogue record for this book
is available from the British Library

Library of Congress Control Number: 2012940993

ISBN 978 1 84980 257 4 (cased)

Typeset by Servis Filmsetting Ltd, Stockport, Cheshire
Printed and bound by MPG Books Group, UK

Contents

PART III   INNOVATION AS NARRATIVE

Contributors

Renu Agarwal, UTS Business School, University of Technology, Sydney, Australia; renu.agarwal@uts.edu.au

John Bessant, University of Exeter, UK; j.bessant@exeter.ac.uk

Julian Birkinshaw, London Business School, UK; jbirkinshaw@london. edu

Kjersti Bjørkeng, SINTEF, Trondheim, Norway; kjersti.bjorkeng@sintef. no

Christina Boedker, University of New South Wales, Australia; c.boedker@ unsw.edu.au

Arne Carlsen, Department of Leadership and Organizational Behavior, BI Norwegian Business School, Norway; arne.carlsen@bi.no

Holly H. Chiu, Department of Management and Global Business, Rutgers University, NJ, USA; haochiu@pegasus.rutgers.edu

Stewart Clegg, UTS Business School, University of Technology, Sydney, Australia and Nova School of Business and Economics, Portugal; stewart. clegg@uts.edu.au

Miguel Pina e Cunha, Nova School of Business and Economics, Portugal; mpc@novasbe.pt

Fariborz Damanpour, Department of Management and Global Business, Rutgers University, NJ, USA; damanpour@business.rutgers.edu

Erlend Dehlin, Trondheim Business School, Norway; erlend.dehlin@hist. no

Roy Green, UTS Business School, University of Technology, Sydney, Australia; roy.green@uts.edu.au

Richard Hall, Business School, University of Sydney, Australia; richard. hall@sydney.edu.au

Katja Hydle, BI Norwegian Business School, Norway; katja.hydle@ bi.no

Emmanuel Josserand, CMOS, University of Technology, Sydney, HEC, Université de Genève; Emmanuel.josserand@unige.ch

Máire Kerrin, Work Psychology Group, UK; m.kerrin@workpsychology group.com

Richard Lamming, University of Exeter, UK; R.C.Lamming@exeter.ac.uk

Catherine Magelssen, Department of Management and Global Business, Rutgers University, NJ, USA; catiem@pegasus.rutgers.edu

Michael Mol, Warwick Business School, UK; michael.mol@wbs.ac.uk

Richard Northcote, Head of Communications and Public Affairs, Member of the Executive Committee of Bayer MaterialScience, Germany; richard.northcote@bayer.com

Fiona Patterson, University of Cambridge, UK; fcp27@cam.ac.uk

Tyrone S. Pitsis, Newcastle University Business School, UK; tyrone.pitsis@ncl.ac.uk

Nigel Rapport, University of St Andrews, UK; rapport@st-andrews.ac.uk

Arménio Rego, Universidade de Aveiro, Portugal; armenio.rego@ua.pt

Jonathon Mark Runnalls, Macquarie University, Australia; mark.runnalls@mq.edu.au

Lloyd Sandelands, University of Michigan, USA; lsandel@umich.edu

Ace Simpson, Australian Postgraduate Award (APA) Scholar, University of Technology, Sydney (UTS) Business School, Australia and a member, Centre for Management & Organisation Studies (CMOS); ace.simpson@uts.edu.au

G.M. Peter Swann, Nottingham University Business School, UK; gmps2011@yahoo.co.uk

Satu Teerikangas, University College London, UK; s.teerikangas@ucl.ac.uk

Patrick Thomas, CEO of Bayer MaterialScience AG, Member of the Executive Committee of Bayer MaterialScience, Germany; patrick.thomas@bayer.com

Ignacio G. Vaccaro, BTS Amsterdam, Netherlands; Ignacio.Vaccaro@bts.com

Liisa Välikangas, Aalto University, Finland; liisa.valikangas@aalto.fi

Frans A.J. Van Den Bosch, Rotterdam School of Management, Erasmus University, Netherlands; FBosch@rsm.nl

Florence Villesèche, HEC, Université de Genève, Switzerland; Florence.Villeseche@unige.ch

Henk W. Volberda, Rotterdam School of Management, Erasmus University, Netherlands; HVolberda@rsm.nl

Lara Zibarras, City University London, UK; Lara.Zibarras.1@city.ac.uk

Introduction: an entrée to organizational and managerial innovation

Tyrone S. Pitsis, Ace Simpson and Erlend Dehlin

Innovate: to make changes in something established, especially by introducing new methods, ideas, or products.

Innovation: the action or process of innovating.

(Oxford Dictionary Online)

The Oxford definitions of *innovate* and *innovation* present innovation as altering the nature or state of something that already exists. Hidden in the definition but often missed in innovation work are the political, power-relational complexities inherent in what is seemingly a benign word in the innovation process: specifically the word 'to make'. Making innovation is never free of its social context, its resistors, enablers, recalcitrants, champions and the like. Indeed, innovation can be thought of as the very stuff of social relations, as in the case of Hannah Arendt's (1958) idea of innovation being integral to democracy and vice versa. Wherever there is an absence of democracy, Arendt argued, there is also the decline of innovation. Without wishing to sound too clichéd, innovation is the cornerstone of human progress and of a free and democratic world. Unlike what is presented in a large body of the mainstream economic literature on innovation (see Swann, 2009), innovation is as much about process and practice innovation, as it is about the innovation of technology or product.

While the term *innovation* is often touted as an underlying value within society and as a core aim in the rhetoric of many organizations, the reality is that innovation is a slippery concept. Innovation cannot be fully understood unless the phenomenological properties of innovation are accounted for: its temporal-spatial properties, its pragmatic elements as part of the evolution of knowledge and its essence as a quality of experience and action, and therefore life. First, as a temporal concept, innovation is about a change or adaptation involving 'a before', 'a now' and 'an after': a past, present and future so to speak. Second, innovation is spatial and occurs in a context bound by unique stocks of knowledge, ways of knowing and ways of making sense of the world. As such, how it is defined and made sense of is a function of the people experiencing it as an innovation: by experience we are referring to how people act upon and make sense of

1

objects and events in their social world. In many ways, then, innovation is an essential and necessary component of human action. To put it succinctly, innovation is the norm of everyday life; it is not simply a metaphor or some rare product of human action but an essential language tool and human action in and of itself (see Lakoff and Johnson, 1999).

At the organizational level, innovation has been seen as something that organizations do, rather than as an essential part of organizational life. In many ways, there are parallels in how geneticists used to view junk DNA. It took innovative and entrepreneurial scientists to explore the idea that all the treasure of DNA is to be found in that 'junk'. Clearly, the focus of innovation has predominately been on technological innovations, and their subsequent impact and transformation of human behaviour. Underpinning this view is a bias privileging technology – especially information technologies – over that of the human spirit. Such an idea, while dominant, reinforces a technological determinism that glosses over the rich, exciting, sometimes mundane, and sometimes extraordinary humanity of innovation.[1]

While innovation is everywhere, everything cannot realistically be labelled innovation (in practice). What is clear to us, however, is that innovation is concomitant with social practices. That is, innovation is a function of human relations, and as such it is as much about the power inherent in human relations as much as it is about the emergent qualities of such relations. Innovation is about altering the tools of human relations: how we consume, how we communicate, how we work, how we relate, how we eat, sleep and even make love and war. Innovation is social in that it does not easily occur as a stated and pre-planned outcome but as emergent in the social relations and contexts within which they occur. It is also recursive, in that innovation is conceived and nurtured through human practices, just as human practices are conceived and nurtured through innovation (Clegg et al., 2012). Such an idea is central to pragmatic philosophy of course, and so the innovation of knowledge, about how we do things, how we make sense of them, is integral to any technological innovation. Process and practice innovation is as much an innovation within and between organizations as any other form of innovation. We unashamedly place humans, their acts, practices, processes and fantasies at the core of innovation.

The *Handbook of Organizational and Managerial Innovation* brings together some of the world's leading thinkers, academics and professionals, both established and emerging. Their combined contributions provide practitioners, students and academics with a comprehensive picture of the vibrant and engaging field of organizational and managerial innovation. Overall, organizational and managerial innovation is shown as a complex concept underpinned by varied ontological and epistemological traditions and disciplines. Innovation exists and occurs at multiple levels of analysis (individual, group, organizational, inter-organizational and social), and from multiple zones of experience – that is, the experience of managers, workers, psychologists, philosophers, economists and so on.

In compiling and editing this book we were surprised by a number of things. First, we became lost in the wonderful work being done on organizational and managerial innovation, partly by its simplicity, and especially by its potential as a dominant and important domain of theory, research and practice. Our initial inspiration came from Birkinshaw et al.'s (2008) paper in the *Academy of Management Review*, because they gave a name and a sense of unity to something that has been a focus for many theorists and researchers of management and organizations. It should be pointed out that the term 'managerial innovation' is not a new concept. Relatively speaking it is, but one need only look at the field of economics, economic history and medical sociology and management to find works dealing with the idea of managerial innovation (see Hannah, 1974; McFarland, 1979; Damanpour, 1987). Second, we could see such strong connections between what has been occurring within the disciplines in the social sciences, arts and humanities, and how important and fruitful multidisciplinary approaches to organizational and managerial innovation can be. With this in mind, and quite naively and with some self-indulgence, we decided to invite contributions from all the authors whose work we enjoy; in so doing we ignored the battles between the various methodological, ontological and epistemological traditions. Third, we could not find a similar book currently on the market that specifically addresses and offers ideas, innovations and inspiration for studying organizational and managerial innovation, at least not since Mol and Birkinshaw's (2007) work. The closest is William Lazonick and David J. Teece's (2012) essays on management innovation in the spirit of Alfred D. Chandler Jr. Definitely an interesting read, but a very different animal to our book.

The rich diversity displayed by the different contributions to this book gives some idea about the complexity and complicatedness that characterizes the field of organizational and managerial innovation (OMI). As a result of this diversity we have found it difficult, and counterproductive, to come up with a structure dividing the contributions into clear-cut categories. Rather, much like the emergence of contemporary musical forms and genres of today, it seems like the field of OMI is incessantly making itself up and defining its own parameters as it unfolds. Our strategy is therefore not to attempt to tame or restrict the exciting developments in the field into clearly demarcated sections, such as individual versus organizational or theory versus practice. Nonetheless, as an attempt to provide a space (a tool as it were) to unravel the complex constitution of OMI, we have chosen to organize the book around three key ideas that have emerged from our readings of each chapter. These are not mutually exclusive nor are they meant to restrict your own interpretation Simply stated, this is how we made sense of them. 'Part I: Innovation as Managerial Technique(s)' mostly assumes innovation as a stable technique that managers can institute within an organization as long as they understand the factors that facilitate such innovation. Most of the chapters in this section consider the various strategic, environmental, psychological or educational factors that facilitate organizational innovation.

'Part II: Innovation as (Practical) Emergence' emphasizes innovation as an ongoing and fluid process that organizations can learn to recognize and harness. Here there is also a warning that innovation is limited or dies when it is assumed to be a managerial technique rather than a process of learning and becoming.

'Part III: Innovation as Narrative' presents chapters with case studies of organizations and innovative organizational practices through the discourses practitioners adopt when inventing new ideas and new meanings.

Each of the chapters of this book presents a unique insight into organizational innovation, and each offering a different perspective. Some of the perspectives create tension with others: are happy employees with free minds more likely to be creative and innovative or, is 'necessity the mother of invention' as per the popular saying? In the context of this book, are organizational innovations more likely to occur under a supportive or a restrictive work place environment? Are organizational structures and managerial involvement likely to aid or obstruct innovation in practice? The handbook presents chapters that argue the case for one or the other of these positions, and some that argue all of them. As such, innovation 'depends' with regard to context, contents and quality, and in many ways the chapters provide insights into the array of factors upon which innovation depends. What underpins all these chapters is that they are grounded in scholarly literature and provide a foundation upon which scholarship can expand. They also offer suggestions for further study.

THE STRUCTURE

Part I: Innovation as Managerial Technique(s)

Part I opens with Mol and Birkinshaw's work on 'Relating management innovation to product and process innovation: private rents versus public gains' (pp. 13–35). The authors focus on the effects of management innovation on product and process innovation outcomes. They find that the association between management innovation with product and process innovation is limited. The association only holds true for product innovations new to the market, and for process innovations new to the industry. Surprisingly it does not hold for product and process innovations that are merely new to the firm. Their finding indicates the importance of management innovation to market- and industry-level effects.

Bessant and Lamming's chapter 'Network innovation' (pp. 36–53) suggests that innovation management has evolved to the point that it is now essentially about organizational dynamic capabilities in revising approaches and routines to meet changes in the environment. They propose that the future of organizational innovation will require a network-based and technology-enabled open environment, with multiple knowledge sources and participants.

Teerikangas and Välikangas's chapter 'Engaged employees! An actor perspective on innovation' (pp. 54–97) reports the findings of several empirical studies into the association between engagement and innovation. The authors offer a model of the engagement process involving a balance of mental states described as 'edging' and 'retreating'. Managers can facilitate or inhibit these states through the quality of the environment they create.

Continuing with this idea of facilitating innovation, Boedker and Runnalls's chapter 'Making innovation happen using accounting controls' (pp. 98–114) uses two lenses to explore the relationship between accounting controls as managerial innovation and innovation more broadly. The *ostensive* lens views innovation as the predictable and coherent engagement of senior executives. The contrasting *performative* lens views accounting controls as flexible and amenable to change depending on movements and shifts in actor networks, their logic always being open to questioning and interpretation.

Swann's chapter 'Innovation and the division of labour' (pp. 115–37) is written from an economic perspective. Swann portrays innovation as an intricate and complex matter and argues for a mutually constitutive relationship between innovation and the division of labour. A challenging and thought-provoking conclusion with implications for both theoreticians and practitioners is that there can be no one *best* organizational form or *best* division of labour to maximize innovation. While there is no one best path to innovation, fostering an internal environment for innovation is possible.

With this in mind, Vaccaro, Volberda and Van Den Bosch's chapter 'Management innovation in action: the case of self-managing teams' (pp. 138–62) discusses the role of internal change agents within self-managed teams. They conclude that managers play a key role through attention to issues relating to innovative leadership, knowledge exchange and trust.

Writing from a psychological perspective, Patterson, Kerrin and Zibarras seek to synthesize research on the factors associated with employee innovation and its contribution to innovation in organizations. In their chapter on 'Employee innovation' (pp. 163–88), they argue that managers seeking to nurture innovation would benefit from paying attention to traits such as openness to experience, motivation to change, and surprisingly, those who show some 'antisocial' traits such as challenging the status quo or questioning authority.

Finally, Agarwal, Green and Hall's chapter 'Management education for organizational and managerial innovation' (pp. 189–216) considers the role of education in innovation. They suggest that business schools have a contribution to offer organizational innovation through a refocusing of the practices of business schools as well as through the nurturing of specific skills and competencies in management training programmes.

Part II: Innovation as (Practical) Emergence

One way of making sense of the chapters in this section is by deploying a practice perspective of innovation, presenting it as ongoing processes that organizations can learn from, harness, create and innovate through practice. The section begins with the chapter 'Living ideas at work' by Carlsen and Sandelands (pp. 219–35), which stresses the importance of keeping ideas alive and continually emerging through participation, connection and wonder. The authors provide a metaphor of emergent innovation as a rose on a vine, and suggest that once the rose has been picked (by management) it quickly starts to die. As such, the authors concern themselves with the idea of how to keep innovation alive and breathing.

Taking a similar approach, Dehlin's chapter 'Fleshing out everyday innovation: phronesis and improvisation in knowledge work' (pp. 236–55) studies innovation in the tension between reified technical rationality (techne) and organic, everyday practice. He suggests that improvisation can be a fruitful concept for unravelling and sparking creative insight and wisdom (phronesis) in knowledge work. Like Carlsen and Sandelands, Dehlin stresses the value of technical-rational models as tools of innovative practice, which should not be allowed to become restraint jackets that are followed blindly.

Josserand and Villesèche's chapter 'Communities of practice: from innovation in practice to the practice of innovation' (pp. 256–74) also approaches innovation from a practice perspective. The focus of their chapter is the tension between the order provided by organizational bureaucracy and the need for openness to support learning and innovation. Referring to anthropology, the authors focus on the idea of informal communities of practice (crafts, apprentices, workshops) as traditional sites of learning and innovation. In their natural setting, such communities are composed of self-selecting members who share a common passion. The challenge of institutionalizing and commoditizing such informal communities of practice within organizational structures is that the project by necessity changes the orientation of innovation in informal communities of practice. That is, they are transformed to formalized and institutionalized communities attempting to practise innovation, thus losing their emergent and organic nature. Damanpour, Chiu and Magelssen's chapter 'Initiation, implementation and complexity of managerial innovation' (pp. 275–94) explains that attributes of implementation have a more pronounced impact on innovation than those of initiation. To understand the complexity of adoption of innovation in organizations, they argue that more is needed than a sole focus on management decision-making and the mere initiation of innovation processes.

In their chapter 'Surprising organization' (pp. 295–316), Cunha, Clegg and Rego discuss organizational innovation as an organizational response to surprises. They suggest that rather than striving to avoid or ignore surprises as threatening or unpleasant, organizations can learn to play with the unexpected and can innovate using surprises as discursive sources of novelty.

Part III: Innovation as Narrative

In this section we present works exploring the relationship between organizational innovation and the narratives ascribed to them. First, Rapport's chapter 'Managing the Łódź ghetto: innovation and the culture of persecution' (pp. 319–37), reconstructs the innovativeness of Rumkowski, the Nazi-appointed Jewish Elder of the Łódź ghetto. Rumkowski's managerial 'achievement', Rapport argues, is owed to the innovative way in which he represented his intentionality both to the Nazis and the Jewish population by appropriating to himself two established discourses – one from the Nazi ideology and the other from Jewish history. This chapter deals with a controversial subject matter to 'innovate' the way we might make sense of 'innovativeness'.

Bjørkeng and Hydle's chapter 'Innovating professionalism in a communication consultancy' (pp. 338–62), describes a process whereby organizational narratives are constantly being constructed and reconstructed to make sense of and legitimize past and future codes of organizational practice. Three common mechanisms are involved in this process. First, narratives are entangled within the contexts in which they are constituted – blending the professional and private lives of the employees. Second, the norms of narrative construction are constantly being tested as new narratives breach boundaries of appropriateness. Finally, the constructed narratives centre on displays of accomplishment and competency in the reclaiming of power. Conjointly, these three mechanisms enable the continuous innovative construction of professionalism within the organization.

The final contribution to the book is by Thomas and Northcote. Their chapter 'Storytelling in transforming practices and process: the Bayer case' (pp. 363–75) differs from the other contributions in that it is written not by academics, but by a CEO and a Head of Communications and Public Affairs of Bayer Material Sciences. We have noticed, that very few, if any, academic handbooks actually engage a strong practice focus. We would therefore like to begin innovating a process that overemphasizes the dualistic tradition of keeping academic storytelling separate from practitioner storytelling in handbooks. From our perspective, the stories of researchers, theorists and practitioners belong together. We are therefore excited about including this chapter written by practitioners who tell the story of how the management at Bayer has united the organization not by killing dissensus, but through the co-production of artwork to sell a change initiative. Each year the organization has commissioned and widely distributed an annual cartoon depicting the organization's current opportunities and obstacles, as well as progress towards the attainment of defined objectives. You will notice that the chapter includes colour images of the actual artwork created by managers to promote the changes in practices that the CEO was seeking to innovate through strong narratives of innovation. The authors report how the story has united the organization around a common vision, as well as to nurture a culture that is enthusiastic about innovation and change.

AN INVITATION

As you may be able to glean from this introductory chapter, the field is replete with ideas about managerial and organizational innovation processes and practices. From people operating under Nazi rule, through to industries innovating how they do things through artwork, you will see that the research, theory and breadth of innovation as a process are tremendously complex and diverse. Notice that we did not attempt to synthesize these chapters into one idea or definition of what managerial and organizational innovation is. We leave that to you, the community of students, scholars and practitioners in this space to do that through your ongoing research, theorizing and practising. Indeed, our aim here was not to suggest which we think are right or wrong, what theories are better or worse, or what methodological, epistemological and ontological orientation should be privileged over others. Rather, what we hope you are able to appreciate as a student of the field, which in the end is what all of us are, is that it is rich in diversity and in variety of approaches; there are multiple ways of making sense of organizational and managerial innovation and so it is an exciting, vibrant but also challenging field. Ultimately, we trust the readers will immerse themselves in this exciting field, from the purely *academic*, through to the purely *practice* oriented, and come away inspired, provoked and informed.

NOTE

1. This, however, is by no means to imply that innovation is solely a human process; animals are quite innovative. More importantly, artificial life forms are increasingly being designed to 'be' innovative. There will come a time when artificial intelligence will out-innovate us in both extraordinarily positive and disastrous ways. This possibility is not as far away as you might think (see http://singularity.org/).

REFERENCES

Arendt, H. (1958), *The Human Condition*, Chicago: University of Chicago Press.
Birkinshaw, J., G. Hamel and M.J. Mol (2008), 'Management innovation', winner of *Academy of Management Review* best article award, *Academy of Management Review*, **33**(4), 825–45.
Clegg, S.R., M. Kornberger and T.S. Pitsis (2012), *Managing and Organizations: Theory and Practice*, Thousand Oaks, CA: Sage.
Damanpour, F. (1987), 'The adoption of technological, administrative, and ancillary innovations: impact of organizational factors', *Journal of Management*, **13**(4), 675–88.
Hannah, L. (1974), 'Managerial innovation and the rise of the large-scale company in inter-war Britain', *The Economic History Review*, **27**(2), 252–70.
Lakoff, G. and M. Johnson (1999), *Philosophy in the Flesh: The Embodied Mind and its Challenge to Western Thought*, New York: Basic Books.
Lazonick, W. and D.J. Teece (2012), *Management Innovation: Essays in the Spirit of Alfred D. Chandler*, Oxford: Oxford University Press.
McFarland, D.E. (1979), *Managerial Innovation in the Metropolitan Hospital*, New York: Praeger.
Mol, M.J. and J. Birkinshaw (2007), *Giant Steps in Management: Innovations that Change the Way You Work*, Harlow/London: Prentice Hall/Financial Times.
Swann, G.M.P. (2009), *The Economics of Innovation: An Introduction*, Cheltenham, UK and Northampton, MA, USA: Edward Elgar.

PART I

INNOVATION AS MANAGERIAL TECHNIQUE(S)

1 Relating management innovation to product and process innovation: private rents versus public gains
Michael Mol and Julian Birkinshaw*

INTRODUCTION

It is argued that management innovation has a major impact on the competitive advantage of firms (Hamel, 2006). Anecdotal evidence suggests that well-known management innovations like Toyota's lean production system, 'six sigma' at General Electric and brand management at Procter & Gamble, have provided some firms with lasting performance gains. There is also a broader argument on the role of innovation in producing economic and societal progress. Baumol (2002) has argued convincingly that innovation is at the very heart of economic growth. Thus, management innovation has the potential to produce both private rents, generally interpreted in strategy research as above average returns, and public utility, which we define as the creation of positive outcomes for society at large.

In an earlier paper we defined management innovation as 'the invention and implementation of a new management practice, process, structure or technique that is intended to further organizational goals' (Birkinshaw et al., 2008, p. 825). In that paper, our focus was primarily on new to the state of the art and often well-known innovations. By contrast, in this study we focus on a wider, and perhaps more pedestrian, set of management innovations among less well-known and generally much smaller firms. We also focus on the implementation of management innovations, and not so much on how innovations are first created. It is quite possible that some of the innovations we study here are radically new and will in fact become well known in future but investigating that is not the purpose of our study. A final contrast is that while the Birkinshaw et al. (2008) paper is aimed at (re-) conceptualizing management innovation, here we are much more oriented towards making an empirical contribution to the understanding of management innovation.

The academic literature suggests that management innovation can potentially be a very valuable form of innovation in terms of its effects on economic growth (Teece, 1980; Kimberley, 1981), and there are occasional studies, such as Chandler's (1962) account of the emergence of the M-form structure and Low and Fullerton's (1994) analysis of the origins of brand management, that attest to its competitive and economic benefits for innovating firms. Management innovation has also been recognized as a useful approach to increasing the competitiveness and productivity of firms as they seek to differentiate themselves from their competitors (Gruber and Niles, 1972; Hamel, 2006).

Yet academics have commented that 'most studies address only one category of innovation, that is, technical innovations. All too often, studies neglect administrative innovations, which are equally essential to the growth and effective operation of an organization' (Damanpour and Evan, 1984, p. 392). And more recently it has been suggested that 'it still appears as if there is little systematic knowledge available about the determinants of the diffusion of organizational innovations and, indeed, about their effects' (Alänge et al., 1998, p. 3). Undoubtedly, progress has been made in recent years through the investigation of the diffusion patterns of specific management innovations like quality circles (Abrahamson, 1996), ISO 9000 (Guler et al., 2002), and total quality management (Zbaracki, 1998), often through the management fashion lens (Abrahamson, 1996; Abrahamson and Fairchild, 1999). And in a recent study (Mol and Birkinshaw, 2009), we found broader evidence that the use of different types of management innovation improves a firm's future productivity.

Although this literature is insightful, particularly regarding how specific management innovations diffuse across populations of firms, there is a range of potential questions it does not address sufficiently. In this chapter we will focus on one question in particular, which is: does being a management innovator make it more likely that a firm is also going to be a product and process innovator and, if so, are those product and process innovations simply adoptions of innovations created elsewhere or are they are innovations new to the market and industry a firm operates in? This latter aspect matters a great deal, from the perspective of practising managers but certainly also in terms of setting public policy. Innovations copied from elsewhere may help a firm to catch up with its competitors, and thus produce some form of private benefit by reducing the gap to what economists might call the efficient frontier, that is, the leading firms in a market and industry. But they will not provide much of a benefit to society if only applicable to a single firm. By contrast, we believe that the introduction of a new product into a market provides consumers with additional choice, while the introduction of a new process into an industry may lead to better ways of producing goods and services, which can then spread to other firms. Thus, such new to the market product innovations and new to the industry process innovations can create significant public utility, not just private rents. Thus, in a sense, while we are not interested in new to the state of the art management innovations here, we are contrasting new to the state of the art product and process innovations with innovations that are only new to the firm.

In this chapter we seek to address this question both conceptually and empirically. We proceed by putting forward a number of hypotheses linking management innovation to product and process innovation. We then test these using data from the fourth version of the UK Community Innovation Survey on a large number of firms operating in the United Kingdom. We conclude that there is substantial evidence that management innovation is positively associated with product and innovation outcomes, which suggests there is some form of organizational innovativeness that extends beyond a single form of innovation, and that, perhaps more interestingly, this association can be found only for product innovations new to the market and process innovations new to the industry.

RESEARCH QUESTIONS

The relationship between management innovation; the related terms of administrative, organizational and managerial innovation; and 'technological' innovation, or one of its constituent parts of product and process innovation, has been the subject of some interest in the academic literature. Various theories have been put forward to argue for such a relationship. As we have argued elsewhere (Birkinshaw et al., 2008), there are some similarities between management innovation and technological innovation but there are also important differences, other than the obvious fact that they deal with different objects. First, management innovations are more tacit in nature (Teece, 1980), which means that social and political processes play a greater role in how they come about and are implemented. Second, it is generally difficult to pinpoint where inside organizations the management innovation function is located and who has skills conducive to this type of innovation, which implies that external change agents are more likely to be involved in management innovation. Third, the higher levels of ambiguity and uncertainty associated with management innovation make it harder to effectively undertake this type of innovation.

One key argument on the relationship between these two types of innovation centres on the need for management innovation to take place in order to unlock the real benefits of technological innovation. For instance, it has been argued that the true benefits that accompanied the introduction of personal computers in organizations were not realized until after innovative new structures and practices had been implemented in these organizations to allow for the level of decentralization and autonomy required for optimal use of the PC (Arnal et al., 2001). And there are examples from military history that suggest that certain new technologies required a reorganization of armies before they proved to be effective. Important management innovations such as the industrial research laboratory at General Electric and elsewhere, skunkworks at Lockheed and, much more recently, open innovation at Procter & Gamble, have all helped to improve levels of technological innovation in the firms creating these management innovations (Mol and Birkinshaw, 2008).

Research on the link between management innovation and technological innovation has shown that management innovation often triggers technical innovation, but the process of invention and uptake of management innovation is typically slower (Kimberly and Evanisko, 1981; Damanpour and Evan, 1984; Georgantzas and Shapiro, 1993; Boer and During, 2001). Ettlie (1988) dubbed the simultaneous use of management innovation and technological innovation 'synchronous innovation' and argued that the use of appropriate forms of management innovation made technological innovation more effective in manufacturing firms in the United States in the 1980s. His point was confirmed in follow-up research undertaken by Georgantzas and Shapiro (1993) who looked at a range of management innovations in the field of operations management. Recently, Battisti and Stoneman (2010) found that management innovation and product/process innovation tend to complement one another. They also discuss the types of organizations that are most likely to undertake both forms of innovation. We follow the above literature by arguing that there is likely to be some positive relationship between the presence of management innovation and two important forms of technological innovation, namely product and process innovation, in a firm:

Hypothesis 1a: Being a management innovator is positively associated with successfully undertaking product innovation.

Hypothesis 1b: Being a management innovator is positively associated with successfully undertaking process innovation.

However, none of the studies cited above, nor any conceptual argument that we know of, has explicitly distinguished products and processes based on the degree of novelty when considering their relationship with management innovation. The degree of novelty of an innovation implemented by a firm can range from simply being new to that firm (but having previously been seen elsewhere) via new to the state of the art (such as a firm's industry and country context) to new to the world (not seen anywhere else previously).

This distinction has major implications for the possible benefits produced by an innovation. Of course, not all innovations end up producing benefits, and some in fact destroy value, but we would argue that by innovating, a firm at least tries to produce some private rents, that is, competitive advantage for the firm. The public gains produced by a single firm taking up a product or process innovation initiated by another firm, however, is relatively limited. By contrast, if a firm invents a product new to the market or a process new to the industry, and this innovation is successful, it can change its entire market or industry by doing so. For instance, without wanting to quantify this, the first large-scale introduction of hybrid technologies in the car industry by Toyota through its Prius model in 1997 has clearly produced larger societal benefits than the uptake of the technology by General Motors in 2006. If we were to consider the societal benefits of all later adoptions of the hybrid technology they may very well outpace the societal benefits produced by Toyota's move, but any individual later adoptions are unlikely to do so, unless they significantly alter the innovation (in which case it actually becomes a significantly different product and the adapting firm creates another new to the state of the art innovation). In other words, innovations new to the state of the art, which Toyota's hybrid technology was, are more likely to not only produce private rents but also significant public gains, while new to the firm innovations are primarily focused on private rents (or to be more precise, on allowing firms to catch up with their industry competitors).

If we consider new to the world innovations this is even more true, since new to the world innovations can spread to a variety of contexts, and then in a next step to a variety of firms within those contexts. In other words, new to the world product or process innovations will trickle down through two discrete steps and the potential societal gains they produce are therefore even larger. Ferdinand Porsche's first hybrid electric engine came almost 100 years before Toyota introduced its Prius, and Porsche's ideas found their way outside of the car industry, for instance in the production of trains and Boeing's Lunar Rover. Likewise, the introduction of the moving assembly line by Henry Ford was preceded by similar designs in the Chicago meatpacking industry. Thus, there is a hierarchy in terms of potential societal gains produced by innovations, starting with new to the firm innovations at the bottom, through new to the state of the art innovations in the middle, to new to the world innovations at the top. Also note that the private rents from these new to the world innovations do not necessarily correlate well with public gains. Hybrid technology was not really exploited by Porsche; in fact, it has only very recently resulted in mass produced hybrid models. Nor were the Chicago meat packers able to appropriate rents from the uptake of their designs in the car industry.

We argue that the presence of management innovation is most beneficial for new to the world product and process innovations, followed by new to the state of the art innovations, and finally new to the firm innovations, because these levels of newness indicate the complexity of inventing and commercializing each of these types of product and process innovation. If a product has been commercialized by another firm, or if a production process has been taken up elsewhere previously, its implementation will be less complex because more is known about the product or process itself and how best to implement it. For instance, existing products produced by competitors may be reverse engineered or studied in other ways, which makes their replication inside another firm much less problematic. And existing processes may spread to other firms through the intervention of third parties like consultants, industry associations or gurus. But if a product or process innovation is relatively unknown it is more likely to require adaptations in patterns of organizing, marketing, financing and managing before it can be taken to the market or implemented internally. If this is the case, a successful commercialization of a product new to the market or an implementation of a process new to the industry may be preceded by management innovation.

Combining these points, we argue that the (simultaneous) use of management innovations alongside product or process innovation is more likely to occur where these product and process innovations produce not only private rents but also public gains. Since we cannot actually empirically test this argument separately for new to the world innovations due to a lack of clearly identifiable observations of this type in our data, we will restrict the hypothesis to a comparison between new to the firm and new to the state of the art (i.e., industry and country) innovations:

Hypothesis 2a: Being a management innovator is more positively associated with successfully undertaking product innovation new to the market than it is associated with successfully undertaking product innovation that is only new to the firm.

Hypothesis 2b: Being a management innovator is more positively associated with successfully undertaking process innovation new to the industry than it is associated with successfully undertaking process innovation that is only new to the firm.

METHODS

There are not many existing data sources that document the implementation of management innovation by firms, and even fewer that simultaneously provide measures of product and process innovation. For these reasons, we decided to focus on the Community Innovation Survey (CIS). Although we acknowledge that its measures for management innovation are clearly imperfect from a theoretical point of view, lacking, for instance, specificity on what is being measured or an overall conception of what management innovation is about, we believe it still represents the best measure available to us, particularly for large numbers of firms. The UK CIS, commonly referred to as UKIS, has been used previously to study management innovation, particularly by Battisti and Stoneman (2010) and ourselves (Mol and Birkinshaw, 2009).

We discussed Battisti and Stoneman's work above. Our own paper, based on the third version of the UKIS, applies the reference group framework put forward in organization theory by Cyert and March (1963) and applied by among others Massini et al. (2005), and argues that management innovation comes about as a consequence of two factors: active managerial search and being part of a reference group, and a negative interaction (substitution effect) between these two factors. Through matching the UKIS to another data source, we also found evidence that management innovation leads to improvements in a firm's future productivity, unlike either product or process innovation (Mol and Birkinshaw, 2009).

We focus here on the fourth version of the UKIS, which covers the 2002–04 time period. Other than being more recent, this version also has the dual advantages of containing a larger number of responses and a higher response rate compared to the third version. The survey is administered by the Office for National Statistics. Robson and Ortmans (2006) discuss the stratified sampling procedure and some of the basic findings of the survey. We briefly describe the key measures below.

Product innovation
The survey states that:

> [a] product innovation is the market introduction of a new good or service or a significantly improved good or service with respect to its capabilities, such as quality, user friendliness, software or subsystems. The innovation must be new to your enterprise, but it does not need to be new to your market. It does not matter if the innovation was originally developed by your enterprise or by other enterprises. During the three-year period 2002–2004, did your enterprise introduce: New or significantly improved goods? (Exclude the simple resale of

new goods purchased from other enterprises and changes of a purely cosmetic nature). New or significantly improved services (0 = no; 1 = yes)?

For those firms that responded positively to this question, the survey then splits this into innovations new to the firm and innovations new to the market as follows:

Were any of your product innovations during the three-year period 2002–2004: New to your market? Your enterprise introduced a new good or service onto your market before your competitors (0 = no; 1 = yes). Only new to your enterprise? Your enterprise introduced a new good or service that was essentially the same as a product already available from your competitors in your market (0 = no; 1 = yes)?

This latter split is the basis for our analysis around hypothesis 2a.

Process innovation
Here the survey states that:

Process innovation is the use of new or significantly improved methods for the production or supply of goods and services. The innovation must be new to your enterprise, but it does not need to be new to your industry. It does not matter if the innovation was originally developed by your enterprise or by other enterprises. Purely organisational or managerial changes should not be included – these are covered at question 23. During the three-year period 2002–2004, did your enterprise introduce any new or significantly improved processes for producing or supplying products (goods or services) which were new to your enterprise (0 = no; 1 = yes)?

And for those firms that responded positively to this question, that is, stated they had engaged in process innovation, there was again a follow-up question:

During the three-year period 2002–2004, did your enterprise introduce any new or significantly improved processes for producing or supplying products (goods or services) which were new to your industry (0 = no; 1 = yes)?

While this question does not provide as clear-cut a measure for hypothesis 2b as is the case for product innovation, where new to the firm and new to the market are separated explicitly, it follows logically that if a firm introduced a process innovation that was not new to the industry, it must have been new to that firm only. In other words, if we find a positive relation between management innovation and process innovation new to the industry, we can also assume that there is no such relation for process innovation new to the firm only.

Management innovation

There is a question on 'wider innovation' in UKIS4. Respondents were asked:

> [d]id your enterprise make major changes in the following areas of business structure and practices during the three-year period 2002–2004? This section seeks to investigate new or significantly amended forms of organisation, business structures or practices, aimed at step changes in internal efficiency of effectiveness or in approaching markets and customers. Implementation of a new or significantly changed corporate strategy; implementation of advanced management techniques within your enterprise e.g. knowledge management systems, Investors in People; implementation of major changes to your organisational structure e.g. introduction of cross-functional teams, outsourcing of major business functions; implementation of changes in marketing concepts or strategies, e.g. packaging or presentational changes to a product to target new markets, new support services to open up new markets (0 = not used; 1 = used).

Following Mol and Birkinshaw (2009), we did not use the item on changed corporate strategies. In order to capture the breadth of management innovation undertaken in each firm, a single scale is applied with the value of 0 for no management innovation activity, and 1 added for each type of management innovation the firm engaged in, such that the maximum value is 3. For all practical purposes the measure can be thought of as a count measure that provides an indication of the number of areas of innovation a firm engages in. This measure reveals actual implementations, helping to overcome the decoupling problem Zajac and Fiss (2001) identify as common to some studies of management practices and performance (e.g., Staw and Epstein, 2000).

Control variables

We apply a range of control variables, each of which could potentially influence levels of product or process innovation. Because the distribution of firm size is often very skewed, the *'firm size'* variable is calculated as the logarithm of the number of employees in 2002. The *'degrees'* variable measures the number of employees with degree-level education or above, as a percentage of all employees of the firm. *'Alliances'* with other firms is a dummy variable that takes on the value of 1 if the firm has any innovation cooperation arrangements with other enterprises or institutions. *'Market scope'* looks at the firm's largest market. The survey asks:

> [i]n which geographic markets did your enterprise sell goods and/or services during the three-year period 2002–2004: Local/regional within the UK; UK; Other Europe; All other countries?

We then coded these options from 1 to 4.

'*Innovation inhibitors*' is a count variable and measures the number of factors inhibiting a firm's ability to innovate. Respondents were asked:

> please rate the importance of the following constraints during the period 1998–2000: (a) Excessive perceived economic risks, (b) Direct innovation costs too high, (c) Costs of finance, (d) Availability of finance, (e) Organizational rigidities within the enterprise, (f) Lack of qualified personnel, (g) Lack of information technology, (h) Lack of information on markets, (i) Impact of regulations or standards, (j) Lack of customer responsiveness to new goods or services.

Respondents were asked to specify 'no effect' or 'low', 'medium', 'high' for each item. The number of cases where the respondent gave a positive response is summed, resulting in a measure varying from 0 to 10.

'*Market sources*' is measured as:

> [s]ources of information and co-operation for innovation. How important to your enterprise's innovation activities during the three-year period 2002–2004 were each of the following information sources: Suppliers of equipment, materials, services, or software; Clients or customers; Competitors or others enterprises in your industry; Consultants, commercial labs, or private R&D institutes?

Similarly, '*other sources*' asks about 'Conferences, trade fairs, exhibitions; Scientific journals and trade/technical publications; Professional and industry associations; Technical, industry or service standards'. '*Business customers*' and '*government customers*' are both dummies with a value of 1 if the firm's largest customer was another business or government respectively, and 0 otherwise. '*New firm*' is a dummy with a value of 1 if the firm was established during the period under study and 0 otherwise. '*Corporation*' is a dummy with a value of 1 if the firm was part of a larger corporation and 0 otherwise.

We also control for a range of expenditures that could potentially increase product and process innovation levels. Firms were asked:

> [d]uring the three-year period 2002–2004, did your enterprise engage in the following innovation activities? (0 = no; 1 = yes).

We use such measures for the variables '*internal R&D*' ('[c]reative work undertaken within your enterprise on an occasional or regular basis to increase the stock of knowledge and its use to devise new and improved goods, services and processes'), '*external R&D*' ('[s]ame activities as above, but purchased by your enterprise and performed by other companies [including other enterprises within your group] or by public or private research organisations'), '*hardware & software*' ('[a]cquisition of advanced machinery, equipment and computer hardware or software to produce new or significantly improved goods, services, production processes, or delivery methods'), and '*licensing*' ('[p]urchase or licensing of patents and non-patented inventions, know-how, and other types of knowledge from other enterprises or organisations'). Each of these variables is a dummy with value 0 if there was no expenditure and value 1 if there was any expenditure. Finally, an industry dummy variable is included for each of the 43 2-digit industries.

RESULTS

Given the nature of the various dependent variables, we apply a probit analysis. The number of observations in the different analyses varies significantly. The most important and obvious reason for this is that the question whether an innovation is new to the market/industry or only new to the firm can only be answered by the subsample of firms that innovates. These large drops in numbers of observations are also the reason why the correlation table, Table 1.1, is based on pairwise rather than listwise correlations. Table 1.1 shows that a slight majority of firms is engaged in at least one of the three forms of management innovation (new management techniques, organizational structures, or marketing methods). By contrast, only a relatively small percentage of firms successfully produced a product or process innovation. The table also shows that the different forms of innovation are positively correlated, except for the association between new to the firm product innovations on the one hand and new to the industry process innovations/new to the market product innovations on the other. This demonstrates these forms of innovation are different, in line with our hypotheses.

Table 1.2 produces the results of the various analyses on product innovation while Table 1.3 contains the results for process innovation. Following recent discussion in the strategic management literature (Hoetker, 2007), we include the marginal effects with all variables at the mean. These were obtained using Stata's mfx command. There are no substantial differences when applying marginal effects. The second and third columns in Table 1.2 confirm the expected effect in hypothesis 1a, which is that product innovation is more likely to occur inside a firm when it also undertakes management innovation (significant at 0.1 per cent). The second and third columns in Table 1.3 likewise prove the same is true for process innovation, as per hypothesis 1b (significant at 0.1 per cent).

The evidence for hypothesis 2 is obtained in a slightly more complex manner. Hypothesis 2a is confirmed in the fourth, fifth, sixth and seventh

Table 1.1   Means of and pairwise correlations between variables

	Mean	1	2	3	4	5	6	7	8
1 Degrees	13.6	1							
2 Firm size	8.1	0.02	1						
3 Alliances	0.15	0.07	0.10	1					
4 Market scope	2.21	0.11	0.32	0.20	1				
5 Innovation inhibitors	5.55	0.07	0.13	0.19	0.24	1			
6 Market sources	2.37	0.08	0.18	0.26	0.26	0.64	1		
7 Other sources	2.10	0.09	0.21	0.25	0.27	0.59	0.77	1	
8 Business customers	0.62	0.05	0.09	0.24	0.33	0.13	0.13	0.11	1
9 Government customers	0.11	0.02	−0.07	0.01	−0.12	−0.01	−0.01	0.00	−0.36
10 New firm	0.08	0.01	−0.07	−0.01	−0.03	0.01	0.01	−0.01	−0.01
11 Corporation	0.33	0.05	0.41	0.12	0.27	0.17	0.17	0.19	0.10
12 Internal R&D	0.31	0.09	0.16	0.29	0.34	0.42	0.42	0.38	0.11
13 External R&D	0.12	0.06	0.15	0.28	0.19	0.27	0.27	0.24	0.05
14 Hardware & software	0.47	0.03	0.09	0.20	0.18	0.47	0.47	0.40	0.12
15 Licensing	0.14	0.06	0.09	0.22	0.12	0.27	0.27	0.25	0.04
16 Management innovation	0.60	0.10	0.23	0.27	0.23	0.37	0.37	0.37	0.09
17 Product innovation	0.28	0.10	0.14	0.33	0.31	0.38	0.38	0.32	0.13
18 New to market	0.56	0.09	0.06	0.15	0.17	0.15	0.15	0.14	0.05
19 New to firm	0.83	−0.05	0.04	0.00	−0.03	0.14	0.14	0.08	0.02
20 Process innovation	0.20	0.07	0.13	0.28	0.21	0.30	0.30	0.26	0.11
21 New to industry	0.26	0.08	0.02	0.10	0.08	0.10	0.14	0.08	0.05

Note: Industry dummies are not reported to save space but are available upon request.

columns of Table 1.2. In particular, the results show that the presence of management innovation is positively associated with product innovations new to the market (significant at 0.1 per cent), but not with product innovations new to the firm (insignificant). As noted above, for process innovation we cannot repeat the exact same analysis but columns 4 and 5 in

9	10	11	12	13	14	15	16	17	18	19	20	21
1												
0.01	1											
−0.06	0.00	1										
−0.01	−0.01	0.16	1									
−0.01	0.00	0.13	0.42	1								
−0.02	0.00	0.07	0.38	0.26	1							
−0.01	0.02	0.07	0.27	0.33	0.32	1						
−0.01	0.01	0.20	0.36	0.26	0.28	0.25	1					
0.00	0.01	0.15	0.47	0.29	0.32	0.25	0.35	1				
0.00	0.01	0.05	0.23	0.15	0.07	0.10	0.14	0.22	1			
−0.03	−0.01	0.03	0.05	0.02	0.11	0.05	0.06	0.42	−0.17	1		
−0.01	0.00	0.12	0.34	0.24	0.35	0.23	0.33	0.43	0.14	0.08	1	
0.06	0.01	0.02	0.15	0.09	0.03	0.08	0.10	0.19	0.33	−0.11	0.18	1

Table 1.3 demonstrate that the presence of management innovation is positively associated with undertaking process innovations new to the industry (significant at 5 per cent), and by extension not for process innovation only new to the firm. Note though that the statistical models employed explain relatively more variance for product and process innovation in

Table 1.2 Results of robust probit regressions on various forms of product innovation showing coefficients and standard errors

	Product Innovation	Marginal Effect	New to the Market	Marginal Effect	New to the Firm	Marginal Effect
Degrees	0.00(0.00)	0.00(0.00)	0.00(0.00)**	0.00(0.00)**	−0.00(0.00)**	−0.00(0.00)**
Firm size	−0.01(0.01)	0.00(0.00)	−0.01(0.01)	−0.01(0.01)	0.02(0.02)	0.00(0.00)
Alliances	0.62(0.04)***	0.22(0.02)***	0.25(0.05)***	0.10(0.02)***	−0.03(0.06)	−0.01(0.01)
Market scope	0.14(0.02)***	0.05(0.00)***	0.09(0.02)***	0.03(0.01)***	−0.06(0.03)*	−0.01(0.00)*
Innovation inhibitors	0.03(0.00)***	0.01(0.00)***	0.01(0.01)	0.00(0.00)	0.03(0.01)**	0.01(0.00)**
Market sources	0.15(0.02)***	0.05(0.01)***	0.03(0.03)	0.01(0.01)	0.11(0.03)***	0.03(0.01)***
Other sources	−0.06(0.01)***	−0.02(0.00)***	0.02(0.02)	0.01(0.01)	0.00(0.02)	0.00(0.01)
Business customers	0.01(0.04)	0.00(0.01)	−0.06(0.06)	−0.02(0.02)	−0.04(0.07)	−0.01(0.02)
Government customers	0.12(0.05)*	0.04(0.02)*	−0.03(0.08)	−0.01(0.03)	−0.14(0.10)	−0.03(0.02)
New firm	0.07(0.05)	0.02(0.02)	0.09(0.08)	0.03(0.03)	−0.05(0.10)	−0.01(0.02)
Corporation	0.05(0.03)	0.02(0.01)	−0.04(0.05)	−0.02(0.02)	0.02(0.06)	0.00(0.01)
Internal R&D	0.66(0.03)***	0.22(0.01)***	0.33(0.05)***	0.13(0.02)***	−0.08(0.06)	−0.02(0.01)
External R&D	0.06(0.05)	0.02(0.02)	0.11(0.06)*	0.04(0.02)*	−0.08(0.07)	−0.02(0.02)

Hardware & software	0.29(0.03)***	0.09(0.01)***	0.00(0.05)	0.00(0.02)	0.16(0.06)	0.04(0.01)*
Licensing	0.14(0.04)***	0.05(0.01)***	0.07(0.05)	0.03(0.02)	0.04(0.07)	0.01(0.01)
Management innovation	0.19(0.02)***	0.06(0.01)***	0.08(0.02)***	0.03(0.01)***	0.02(0.03)	0.01(0.01)
Constant	−1.99(0.08)		−0.65(0.14)***		0.45(0.16)	
Wald Chi squared	3315.89***		352.11***		120.02	
Log pseudo-likelihood	−4968.91		−2214.01		−1433.67	
Pseudo R^2	0.296		0.077		0.043	
N	11273		3514		3501	

Note: *** Significant at 0.001; ** significant at 0.01; * significant at 0.05. Industry dummies are not reported to save space but are available upon request.

27

Table 1.3   Results of robust probit regressions on various forms of process innovation showing coefficients and standard errors

	Process Innovation	Marginal Effect	New to the Industry	Marginal Effect
Degrees	0.00(0.00)	0.00(0.00)	0.00(0.00)*	0.00(0.00)*
Firm size	0.02(0.01)***	0.01(0.00)*	0.00(0.02)	0.00(0.01)
Alliances	0.48(0.04)***	0.13(0.01)***	0.12(0.06)*	0.04(0.02)*
Market scope	0.05(0.02)	0.01(0.00)***	0.04(0.03)	0.01(0.01)
Innovation inhibitors	0.00(0.00)	0.00(0.00)	0.00(0.00)	0.00(0.00)
Market sources	0.11(0.02)***	0.02(0.00)***	0.06(0.04)	0.02(0.01)
Other sources	−0.03(0.01)*	−0.01(0.00)*	0.00(0.02)	0.00(0.01)
Business customers	0.14(0.04)***	0.03(0.01)***	0.07(0.07)	0.02(0.02)
Government customers	0.13(0.06)*	0.03(0.02)*	0.21(0.10)*	0.07(0.04)
New firm	0.04(0.06)	0.01(0.01)	−0.04(0.10)	−0.01(0.03)
Corporation	0.00(0.03)	0.00(0.01)	−0.02(0.06)	−0.01(0.02)
Internal R&D	0.29(0.04)***	0.07(0.01)***	0.30(0.07)***	0.10(0.02)***
External R&D	0.08(0.05)	0.02(0.01)	0.08(0.07)	0.03(0.02)
Hardware & software	0.74(0.04)***	0.18(0.01)***	−0.08(0.08)	−0.03(0.03)
Licensing	0.11(0.04)**	0.03(0.01)*	0.09(0.06)	0.03(0.02)
Management innovation	0.23(0.02)***	0.06(0.00)***	0.06(0.03)*	0.02(0.01)*
Constant	−2.27(0.08)***		−1.14(0.18)***	
Wald Chi squared	2513.37***		141.60***	
Log pseudo-likelihood	−4567.70		−1440.13	
Pseudo R^2	0.241		0.049	
N	11 280		2595	

Note: *** Significant at 0.001; ** significant at 0.01; * significant at 0.05. Industry dummies are not reported to save space but are available upon request.

general, and less for the subgroups we investigate in hypothesis 2, which also contain fewer observations.

Post hoc Analysis

One interesting question, which our cross-sectional data do not shed any light on, is what the nature of causality is in the relationship between

Table 1.4   Bivariate correlations between different innovation variables for UKIS3 and UKIS4 panel (N = 797)

	1	2	3	4	5	6
1 Product innovation UKIS3	1					
2 Process innovation UKIS3	0.350	1				
3 Management innovation UKIS3	0.314	0.179	1			
4 Product innovation UKIS4	0.274	0.146	0.187	1		
5 Process innovation UKIS4	0.201	0.198	0.159	0.426	1	
6 Management innovation UKIS4	0.160	0.109	0.260	0.370	0.344	1

management innovation on the one hand and product and process innovation on the other. In particular, it potentially matters quite a lot whether management innovation occurs simultaneously with product and process innovation, is a consequence of these types of innovation, or is actually a driver (antecedent) of them. We firmly believe that all three possibilities are potentially feasible and in a large sample of firms each of them may be found. But which will tend to dominate?

By combining UKIS4 with the earlier UKIS3 survey we were able to obtain a relatively small panel of firms for which data are available for both surveys. We then ran a correlation analysis between each of the three types of innovation for both versions of the survey. Table 1.4 contains these bivariate correlations.

We apply a logic somewhat similar to that behind Granger causality here. Specifically, we are interested in whether the predictive value of management innovation (UKIS3) for future product/process innovation (UKIS4) is greater than the predictive value of product/process innovation (UKIS3) for future management innovation (UKIS4). If that is the case, we can argue that the strength of relationship is indicative of a causal relationship, given the time lag applied. Even so, it is of course plausible that all three types of innovation are determined by another, as yet unmeasured variable, so we cannot draw any final conclusions on causality. This is, in other words, a very exploratory analysis.

As could be expected, given our earlier argument around organizational innovativeness, all the correlations in this table are positive. Management innovation from the UKIS3 correlates with the other types of innovation in UKIS4 on average with a strength of 0.173. Management innovation from the UKIS4 correlates with the other types of innovation in UKIS3 on average with a strength of 0.135. Although both are positive and significant correlations, this seems to imply on the surface at least that for this sample of firms management innovation should more often be thought of as preceding product and process innovation than of following it. In other words, among these firms it is more likely that they first engage in management innovation and then in product or process innovation than the other way around. This in turn suggests that management innovation may be an effective means to help firms overcome problems they face in their other innovation activities. We of course acknowledge that it would be preferable to undertake this analysis through a multivariate analysis but with this particular data panel the number of observations becomes quite small once additional (control) variables are included. Future versions of UKIS, containing a large panel of observations or similar data sources could be employed for this purpose though. This is also how a true test of Granger causality can take place, which would lend credence to the idea that management innovation causes future product and process innovation, but not the other way around.

Incidentally, also note that the correlations between various types of innovation within the same survey version are stronger than correlations to the same type of innovation in the other survey. It is arguable whether that is an artefact of the method or reflects a real change in the firm over the time period. If it is an artefact of the method, this implies that the single-respondent approach of UKIS may produce some biases. If it reflects true change, there are various possible explanations. It could be that firms are not as consistent in pursuing different forms of innovation as one might believe or hope for. If that is the case, it would support our belief (Birkinshaw and Mol, 2006) that few firms are conscious and consistent management innovators and that management innovation in many ways remains an underutilized form of innovation. But, alternatively, firms that were management innovators in UKIS3 had already done their bit of innovation and hence did not need to innovate as much during the time period of measurement of UKIS4. That would imply that management innovation is more of an episodic event, which only needs to take place when firms face particular problems (like substantial organizational change). This issue warrants further research, as the current data do not allow us to establish which of these explanations makes most sense.

DISCUSSION AND IMPLICATIONS

We found the expected link between management innovation and two forms of technological innovation, product and process innovation. We also confirmed that, among innovating firms, management innovation is most likely to be found in those firms that produce new to the market product innovations and/or new to the industry process innovations.

And we found some initial evidence that management innovation is more likely to be associated with future product and process innovation than vice versa. How can we make sense of these findings and what are their implications?

From the perspective of academic research, this chapter provides some preliminary answers, and raises some additional questions. Like Battisti and Stoneman (2010), Ettlie (1988), Damanpour (1987) and others, we demonstrated the importance of jointly considering management innovation and technological innovation. Where our research proceeds beyond those sources is by showing that this link is particularly strong for new to the state of the art (industry and market) technological innovations. New to the state of the art technological innovations may produce additional private rents, especially where they are hard to replicate, but stand out particularly in terms of their ability to produce public gains. Strategic management theory typically focuses on the former and not the latter but they are both important to consider. Some interesting research questions that come to mind based on this study include the following. What strategies produce the organizational innovativeness that allows firms to undertake both types of innovation effectively? Under what conditions does management innovation precede technological innovation, when does technological innovation lead to future management innovation, and when do the two truly occur simultaneously? What types of management innovation are most strongly associated with technological innovation, for instance new processes more than new structures, or radical management innovations more than incremental ones? Further conceptualization and empirical research should help to shed more light on such and other questions around the relationship between management innovation and technological innovation.

For practising managers, the implications of this research are relatively straightforward. The research confirms that management innovation often goes hand in hand with product and process innovation. This suggests there is an overarching factor called 'organizational innovativeness' that benefits firms in more than one type of innovation. Firms like Google and W.L. Gore are prototypical examples of innovators that not only come up with new products and processes consistently, but have also created new management practices. Another outcome of the research is that this joint occurrence of different types of innovation takes place most often when the type of technological innovation pursued by a firm is more complex (i.e., new to the market or industry). This has clear implications in terms of the need to undertake management innovation: it is greatest among firms that are trying to be innovative within their operating context. In such firms investments in management innovation, in the form of more experimentation and assignment of additional resources, will produce greater pay-offs than elsewhere. A deeper understanding of what produces organizational innovativeness and how firms can best create management innovations will help in producing better evidence-based managerial advice. We believe that the emerging stream of academic literature on management innovation, and real-world experimentation that is under way, will help to produce that understanding.

Finally, we believe the findings presented here hold important lessons for public policy-makers. As noted above, strategic management scholars typically tend not to pay much attention to policy debates unlike economists or sociologists. But this research indicates that particularly for those technological innovations that produce the greatest societal benefits, namely truly new (to the market or industry context) innovations that could spread to other firms in future and thereby have a multiplier effect, it helps to have management innovation in place too. That surely is important from a public policy perspective. Policy-makers typically have not paid much attention to management innovation, perhaps because of its tacit and ambiguous nature, with some exceptions. In the UK for instance, the Department of Trade and Industry (now BIS) has in the past paid some attention to the spread of best practices, and to furthering the role of consultants in working with companies around these practices. Other organizations have been involved in similar initiatives. There may be market failure when it comes to management innovation. The presence of market failure could be a reason for more active and direct governmental action. We did not have the right type of data available to assess this, nor are we particularly specialized in answering this type of question, but based on our research we can suggest some directions and options.

More focus on the creation of management innovation, rather than adopting what appears to be best practice and often comes from elsewhere, could help increase the competitiveness of an economy. An example of the latter category might be lean manufacturing methods. The introduction of these methods may help firms to keep up with others, but it perhaps does not provide them with a competitive edge, that is, the state of the art in technological innovation. If firms are to operate at the state of the art, they should sometimes be actively involved in creating that state of the art. When it comes to innovation in services and goods we tell firms that coming up with something new is a worthwhile exercise. There is no reason why this would not be the case for management innovation. To stimulate the creation of new management innovations further, public policy-makers might want to consider the proven positive effects of having a highly trained workforce, and of encouraging the spread of information about management innovations between firms but also between firms and universities or public research institutes. This 'external knowledge sourcing' is a proven tool in stimulating levels of technological innovation but the use of external knowledge sourcing for the purposes of management has not received equivalent attention.

If firms are better informed about management innovation, and do not just restrict their attention to product and process innovation, they will be in a better position to produce and exploit it. Spreading information by policy-makers can of course take many forms, so further thought would have to go into the question of how to implement this. And policy-makers could encourage further and more detailed studies of the effects of management innovation on individual firms as well as on sector and overall productivity. This study of the CIS provided some useful insights but in many ways only scratches at the surface of this important issue.

CONCLUSION

In this chapter we explored the linkage between management innovation and two forms of technological innovation: product and process innovation. We find these different forms are linked but also, perhaps more surprisingly, that this link only holds true for product innovations new to the market and process innovations new to the industry, and not for product and process innovations that are merely new to the firm. This suggests that the occurrence of management innovation is most likely to coincide with that of technological innovations that not only produce private rents but also public gains, because product innovations new to the market and process innovations new to the industry create ripple or multiplier effects as they get taken up (disperse) across a wider set of firms. New to a market product innovations offer consumers further choices. New to the industry process innovations help to increase the efficiency of the industry as a whole in a certain country. We discuss the implications of these findings for academic research but also for managers and policy-makers. We conclude by calling for more attention to the effects of management innovation not just for firm performance but equally in terms of measures such as the satisfaction of a firm's key stakeholders, and of societal progress more broadly.

NOTE

* The authors would like to thank the Department of Trade and Industry (now BIS – Department for Business Innovation & Skills) for making the CIS data available to them. The usual disclaimer applies.

REFERENCES

Abrahamson, E. (1996), 'Management fashion', *Academy of Management Review*, **21**(1), 254–85.

Abrahamson, E. and G. Fairchild (1999), 'Management fashion: lifecycles, triggers, and collective learning processes', *Administrative Science Quarterly*, **44**(4), 708–40.

Alänge, S., S. Jacobsson and A. Jaryehammar (1998), 'Some aspects of an analytical framework for studying the diffusion of organizational innovations', *Technology Analysis & Strategic Management*, **10**(1), 3–22.

Arnal, E., W. Ok and R. Torres (2001), 'Knowledge, work organisation and economic growth', OECD Labour Market and Social Policy, Occasional Paper No. 50, Paris: OECD.

Battisti, G. and P. Stoneman (2010), 'How innovative are UK firms? Evidence from the Fourth UK Community Innovation Survey on synergies between technological and organizational innovations', *British Journal of Management*, **21**(1), 187–206.

Baumol, W.J. (2002), *The Free-market Innovation Machine: Analyzing the Growth Miracle of Capitalism*, Princeton, NJ: Princeton University Press.

Birkinshaw, J. and M.J. Mol (2006), 'How management innovation happens', *MIT Sloan Management Review*, **47**(4), 81–8.

Birkinshaw, J., G. Hamel and M.J. Mol (2008), 'Management innovation', *Academy of Management Review*, **33**(4), 825–45.

Boer, H. and W.E. During (2001), 'Innovation, what innovation?: a comparison between product, process and organizational innovation', *International Journal of Technology Management*, **22**(1–3), 83–107.

Chandler, A.D. (1962), *Strategy and Structure: Chapters in the History of the Industrial Enterprise*, Cambridge, MA: MIT Press.

Cyert, R.M. and J.G. March (1963), *A Behavioral Theory of the Firm*, Englewood Cliffs, NJ: Prentice-Hall.

Damanpour, F. (1987), 'The adoption of technological, administrative, and ancillary innovations: impact of organizational factors', *Journal of Management*, **13**(4), 675–88.

Damanpour, F. and W.M. Evan (1984), 'Organizational innovation and performance: the problem of "organizational lag"', *Administrative Science Quarterly*, **29**(3), 392–409.

Ettlie, J.E. (1988), *Taking Charge of Manufacturing: How Companies are Combining Technological and Organizational Innovations to Compete Successfully*, San Francisco: Jossey-Bass.

Georgantzas, N.C. and H.J. Shapiro (1993), 'Viable theoretical forms of synchronous production innovation', *Journal of Operations Management*, **11**(2), 161–83.

Gruber, W.H. and J.S. Niles (1972), 'Put innovation in the organization structure', *California Management Review*, **14**(4), 29–35.

Guler, I., M.F. Guillén and J.M. MacPherson (2002), 'Global competition, institutions, and the diffusion of organizational practices: the international spread of ISO 9000 quality certificates', *Administrative Science Quarterly*, **47**(2), 207–32.

Hamel, G. (2006), 'The why, what and how of management innovation', *Harvard Business Review*, **84**(2), 72–84.

Hoetker, G. (2007), 'The use of logit and probit models in strategic management research: critical issues', *Strategic Management Journal*, **28**(4), 331–43.

Kimberly, J.R. (1981), 'Managerial innovation', in P.C. Nystrom and W.H. Starbuck (eds), *Handbook of Organizational Design, Volume 1*, New York: Oxford University Press, pp. 184–104.

Kimberly, J.R. and M.J. Evanisko (1981), 'Organizational innovation: the influence of individual, organizational, and contextual factors on hospital adoption of technological and administrative innovations', *Academy of Management Journal*, **24**(4), 689–713.

Low, G.S. and R.A. Fullerton (1994), 'Brands, brand management, and the brand manager system: a critical-historical evaluation', *Journal of Marketing Research*, **31**(2), 173–90.

Massini, S., A.Y. Lewin and H.R. Greve (2005), 'Innovators and imitators: organizational reference groups and adoption of organizational routines', *Research Policy*, **34**(10), 1550–69.

Mol, M.J. and J. Birkinshaw (2009), 'The sources of management innovation: when firms introduce new management practices', *Journal of Business Research*, **62**(12), 1269–80.

Robson, S. and L. Ortmans (2006), 'First findings from the UK Innovation Survey, 2005', *Economic Trends*, No. 628, March, 58–64.

Staw, B.M. and L.D. Epstein (2000), 'What bandwagons bring: effects of popular management techniques on corporate performance, reputation, and CEO pay', *Administrative Science Quarterly*, **45**(3), 523–56.

Teece, D.J. (1980), 'The diffusion of an administrative innovation', *Management Science*, **26**(5), 464–70.

Zajac, E.J and P. Fiss (2001), 'The diffusion of ideas over contested terrain: the (non)adoption of a shareholder value orientation among German firms', *Administrative Science Quarterly*, **49**(4), 501–34.

Zbaracki, M.J. (1998), 'The rhetoric and reality of total quality management', *Administrative Science Quarterly*, **43**(3), 602–38.

2 Network innovation
John Bessant and Richard Lamming

INTRODUCTION

It is a truism to say that innovation matters to organizations – unless they change what they offer the world and the ways in which they create and deliver those offerings they risk being overtaken and may not survive in hostile and turbulent environments. Any organization might get lucky once but configuring ways of making innovation happen on a continuing basis – innovation capability – requires deliberate and systematic action. Learning and embedding such routines forms a key part of the innovation challenge – but a second component is developing the ability to reconfigure these routines. Dynamic capability requires that an organization continuously reviews and adapts its routines – in essence, it *innovates* its innovation process (Teece and Pisano, 1994).

For established players this raises the challenge of constantly reviewing their approaches to organizing and managing innovation – and for entrepreneurs this opens up opportunities for using their different models and approaches to create new innovation space. As Christensen (1997) highlighted, 'disruptive' innovation emerges when established incumbents continue to view new developments through an old lens – and these conditions represent a major opportunity for new entrant entrepreneurial players with a fresh perspective.

Innovation today takes place in a significantly new context to even a decade ago, enabled by globalization, social change and technological change; Table 2.1 summarizes these shifts. Under such 'fluid' conditions established organizations need to review their approaches and develop alternative or complementary approaches to innovation management.

Such experiments involve considerable modification of innovation routines, experimenting with new approaches whilst also letting go of others that are no longer appropriate for the emerging conditions. Examples include making extensive use of web-based approaches, exploring the role of social networking and user communities, mobilizing R&D from outside the firm, and so on (Berger et al., 2005; West et al., 2006; Bessant and Von Stamm, 2007; Reichwald et al., 2007; Bessant et al., 2009).

Table 2.1   Changing context for innovation management

Context Change	Indicative Examples
Acceleration of knowledge production	The OECD estimates that $750 billion is spent each year (public and private sector) in creating new knowledge – and hence extending the frontier along which 'breakthrough' technological developments may happen
Global distribution of knowledge production	Knowledge production is increasingly involving new players especially in emerging market fields like the BRIC nations – so the need for search routines to cover a much wider search space increases
Market fragmentation	Globalization has massively increased the range of markets and segments – putting pressure on search routines to cover much more territory, often far from 'traditional' experiences – such as the 'bottom of the pyramid' conditions in many emerging markets (Prahalad, 2006) or 'the long tail' (Anderson, 2006)
Market virtualization	Increasing use of the internet as a marketing channel means different approaches need to be developed. At the same time emergence of large-scale social networks in cyberspace poses challenges in market research approaches – for example, Facebook currently has over 500 million subscribers
Rise of active users	Although user-active innovation is not a new concept there has been an acceleration in the ways in which this is now taking place (Von Hippel, 2005). In sectors like media the line between consumers and creators is increasingly blurred – for example, YouTube has around 100 million videos viewed each day but also has over 70 000 new videos uploaded every day from its user base
Development of technological and social infrastructure	Increasing linkages enabled by information and communications technologies around the internet and broadband have enabled and reinforced alternative social networking possibilities. At the same time the increasing availability of simulation and prototyping tools have reduced the separation between users and producers (Schrage, 2000; Dodgson et al., 2005)

Source: Bessant and Venables (2008).

CHANGING EXPLANATORY MODELS

In his pioneering work on innovation management, Rothwell (1994) drew attention to models of innovation that policy agents and practitioners make use of – how they think the innovation process works – and the limitations of these. Such mental models are important because they shape what decision-makers pay attention to, what they commit resources to and how they manage the process. He suggested five generations of thinking about innovation management, moving from simplistic linear 'push' or 'pull' models, through increasingly sophisticated 'coupling' models that recognize the need for intra- and inter-organizational links, predicting a fifth generation that would involve extensive use of ICT, rich and diverse networking, and globally distributed activity. Within such a highly net-worked, multi-actor environment the emergent properties of the innovation system are likely to require different approaches.

In particular, the locus of attention has moved from the lone inventor to the organization and it is now increasingly moving to the inter-organizational network level. In the process, significant 'management innovation' (MI) has emerged as experiments towards new ways of organizing and managing the innovation process are explored, diffused and eventually become a widely used template for innovation capability (Birkinshaw et al., 2008).

The idea of innovation as a multi-player game is, of course, not new. Whilst the current fashion for exploring 'open innovation' has highlighted the importance of linkages and emphasized knowledge flows rather than knowledge production, this is not a new insight. For example, Carter and Williams's (1957) pioneering study of 'technically progressive' firms in the UK identified that the degree of 'cosmopolitan' orientation (as opposed to 'parochial') was a significant determinant of innovation success. In other words, those organizations with rich networks of connections were more likely to be successful innovators. This theme emerged in the many major studies of innovation throughout the 1960s and 1970s – for example, Project SAPPHO stressed linkages as a critical factor, whilst the Manchester 'Wealth from knowledge' research provided extensive case examples of award-wining innovators who shared a common external orientation (Langrish et al., 1972; Rothwell, 1977)

Innovation researchers have been working for some time on the theoretical development of models that recognize the shifting boundaries and the engagement of an increasingly diverse number of players. These include:

- distributed innovation processes (Howells et al., 2003);
- innovation systems (Lundvall, 1990; Metcalfe and Miles, 1999);

- user-led innovation (Von Hippel, 2005; Piller, 2006);
- globalization (Santos et al., 2004);
- high-involvement innovation (Boer et al., 1999; Bessant, 2003; Schroeder and Robinson, 2004);
- complex product systems (Gann and Salter, 2000; Davies and Hobday, 2005);
- 'recombinant innovation' (Hargadon, 2003);
- communities of practice (Wenger, 1999; Brown and Duguid, 2000);
- clusters and innovation (Best, 2001).

NETWORK EFFECTS AND INNOVATION

Arguably, an underlying principle in this emerging pattern is increasing 'openness' in terms of both the variety of knowledge sources and the participation/involvement of multiple stakeholders. Elsewhere we have termed this 'open collective innovation' (OCI), implying that the innovation process has – particularly through significant shifts in both the technological and social context – begun to evolve into a Rothwell-type of new, fifth-generation model (Bessant and Moeslein, 2011).

In particular, OCI involves the convergence of three key trends – opening up search, employee engagement and stakeholder participation, as indicated in Figure 2.1.

It will be helpful to expand briefly on these three spheres and the trends within them:

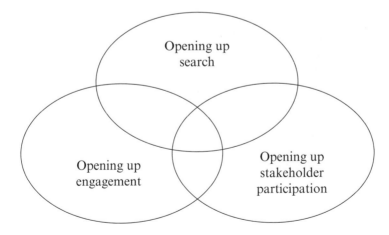

Figure 2.1   Convergence towards OCI

Opening Up Search

Whilst the core idea of open and distributed innovation has been around in innovation studies for a long time, the key aspect that Chesbrough (2003) drew out is that in an information-rich environment where multiple technological and social channels exist for the flow of knowledge it becomes an imperative to search beyond the boundaries of the organization and to manage those complex knowledge flows. The famous example of Procter & Gamble and its 'Connect and develop' programme was driven by concerns about internal R&D productivity – even in an organization with a $3 billion R&D spend and 8000 scientists it was becoming impossible to generate the volume and variety of ideas needed to grow the business (Lafley and Charan, 2008).

The emphasis since the publication of Chesbrough's book has been on finding ways to make open innovation work in a variety of different practical contexts. Organizations as diverse as the BBC, Lego and the UK Ordnance Survey are increasingly engaging communities of software developers, sharing source code and inviting them to 'use our stuff to build your stuff'. This is the highly successful open model used by Apple in building the iPhone platform where thousands of developers create applications that make the core product more attractive. 'Crowdsourcing' is another variant on this, where companies open up their innovation challenges to the outside world, often in the form of a competition and usually web enabled. A famous example here is Goldcorp – a struggling mining company that threw open its geological data and asked for ideas about where it should prospect. Tapping into the combined insights of 1200 people from 50 countries helped it find 110 new sites, 80 per cent of which produced gold. The business has grown from $100 million in 1999 to over $30 billion today. Such approaches engage an increasing range of players in a variety of ways – for example, companies like Swarovski have deployed crowdsourcing to expand their design capacity, whilst Audi and BMW use it to prototype and explore new features. The model has been applied in a variety of settings including public sector and social enterprise – for a detailed review see Bullinger et al. (2010).

Another variant – 'recombinant innovation – uses ideas developed in one world to good effect in another. Cross-sector learning throws some unlikely partners together and opens up new ways of looking at old problems. For example, low-cost airlines like Ryanair learned about rapid turnaround in airports by watching pit stop teams in Formula 1, whilst the UK National Health Service is learning some powerful lessons about patient safety from oil rigs, chemical plants and aircraft cockpits.

Successful open innovation strategies require new ways of accessing a wide and diverse set of ideas and connecting these to sites within the organization that can make effective use of them. In turn, this raises questions of networking and knowledge management, issues identified by Allen back in the 1970s but coming to the fore in an era of social networking and enabling technologies (Allen, 1977; Dahlander and Gann, 2010). Much of the new challenge is about combining and creating communities of practice around key themes that transcend traditional organizational boundaries (Wenger, 1999; Brown and Duguid, 2000; Lafley and Charan, 2008).

Open innovation of this kind shifts emphasis from knowledge creation to knowledge *flows* – and facilitating it requires increasing connectivity across the innovation system. Characteristic of the move towards open innovation has been the growing roles of intermediaries and significantly increased use of advanced networking and communication technologies.

Opening Up Engagement

Extensive research on 'high involvement innovation' – engaging employees in organized innovative activities across an organization – suggests that this offers a powerful source of ideas (Imai, 1987; Pfeffer, 1994; Boer et al., 1999; Bessant, 2003; Schroeder and Robinson, 2004). Until recently this emphasized incremental improvements – *kaizen* – but recent work, enabled by corporate intranets and the trend towards social networking have shifted the focus to more radical innovation, tapping into internal entrepreneurship through innovation competitions and so on. These effectively bring the traditional 'suggestion box' into the twenty-first century but also add the important dimension of interactivity. Within such systems there is the possibility for sharing and building on ideas and for voting and mobilizing support for strong ones – a feature that appears to engage and motivate employees.

Models of this kind are finding widespread application not only within the private sector but also across large public sector organizations (Murray et al., 2010). Mobilizing internal entrepreneurship, especially around social issues, is becoming a central element in the innovation strategies being deployed in the search for both efficiency savings (incremental innovation) and more radical service development.

An important variant on this theme can be observed in the growing number of 'quasi-organizations' represented by formally constructed networks. Examples of these might include:

- supply chains and networks;
- sectoral clusters;

- regional clusters;
- topic clusters.

In each of these there is a commitment to building a network within which shared, cooperative activity takes place and through which emergent properties can be generated. For example, active management of supply chains through various kinds of supplier development programmes is a well-established feature of many sectors. They arise from a recognition that the performance of large firm 'owners' of these supply chains depends on their ability to orchestrate improved performance from all the links in that chain (which may involve small and managerially inexperienced players). It is worth them investing a variety of development resources in order to upgrade performance across the entire network – and in doing so can generate system effects in which the whole becomes greater than the sum of its parts.

Studies of 'collective efficiency' have for some time explored the phenomenon of clustering in a number of different contexts (Piore and Sabel, 1982; Humphrey and Schmitz, 1996; Porter, 1997). From this work it is clear that the model is widespread – not just confined to parts of Italy, Spain and Germany but diffused around the world – and under certain conditions, extremely effective. Recent examples from China, for example, provide continuing support for the power of local networking – for example, the highly successful motorcycle cluster around the city of Chongquing (Brown and Hagel, 2005).

'Learning networks' of this kind can be found in a variety of contexts but they share the same principles of open engagement – bringing in actors already in the system more actively into the innovation process. But they do not emerge by accident – and the process of forming and then enabling performing requires active management. The conditions under which effective networking takes place are less clearly identified, but it is becoming clear that simple factors such as proximity do not, of themselves, explain the complexities of networking.

Opening Up Stakeholder Participation

Exemplified in the research of Eric Von Hippel, user-led innovation highlights the active role played by users as active initiators of change (Von Hippel, 1988, 2005; Herstatt and Von Hippel, 1992). The emergence of powerful communication technologies that enable active cooperation of user communities in co-creation and diffusion, whilst already a well-documented and important source of innovation, has accelerated the innovation trend.

Companies like Lego, Threadless, Adidas and Muji engage with users as front-end co-creators of new products and services. Importantly this doesn't stop at the private sector – there is growing use of these approaches to create innovative and more successful public services. Hospitals are increasingly focusing on patients as a source of 'experience-based design' input, and innovative partnerships like Nokia's Living Lab aim to work closely with users co-developing services for long-term care. At the limit, innovation of this form takes place entirely within the user community as a cooperative enterprise – the examples of Linux, Mozilla and Apache underline the potential of such emergent properties as an alternative to firm-centred R&D.

At the limit this involves communities creating innovation amongst and for themselves and the resulting innovations only then being appropriated by the traditional corporate agents in the public and private sectors – a significant reversal of the traditional innovation model (Murray et al., 2010).

This links with observed shifts at the 'fuzzy front end' of innovation and particularly the locus of design activity (Koen et al., 2001; Reid and Brentani, 2004). Traditional models of innovation implied a separation between design and adoption but there is growing use of increasingly sophisticated techniques to collect intelligence about user concerns and wishes. Further work has demonstrated the potential contribution of users as active co-creators of innovation, a trend reflected in much of the work on 'mass customization' (Piller, 2006; IJIM, 2008; Pickles et al., 2008; Bessant and Maher, 2009).

THE MODEL IN PRACTICE

Underpinning OCI is significant management innovation around learning to organize and manage networks for innovation. The enabling context is present and the *potential* for new forms of innovation is clear, based on several key systems theory principles:

- The whole can be greater than the sum of the parts – emergent properties.
- More nodes = more potential connections – but there is a risk of drowning in noise.
- Organized rich connectivity allows for higher levels of innovation – fluency and flexibility.

But exploiting this potential will require extensive learning and configuration of innovation routines at both organization and inter-organization level. As we suggested earlier, experiments around OCI are just that – probes into potentially rich innovation management space but without a clear map of where such exploration will lead.

In the following section we will look in more detail at one emerging example of network-level innovation – that of 'learning networks' – in a number of different contexts. They share these underlying design principles but the variation in the ways that they are being exploited suggests that considerable learning – exercise of dynamic capability – is involved.

LEARNING NETWORKS

Networks of any kind offer many opportunities for learning to take place – by sharing ideas, trying out experiments, and so on. Such learning takes place essentially as a by-product of some other activity or purpose within the network. But it might be possible to use the network concept as a vehicle whose *primary* purpose is to enable learning (Bessant and Tsekouras, 2001). This definition implies a number of features:

- Such networks are formally established and defined.
- They have a primary learning target – some specific learning/ knowledge that the network is going to enable.
- They utilize the principle of 'open engagement' – bringing many different perspectives to the innovation challenge.
- They have a structure for operation, with boundaries defining participation.
- They involve processes that can be mapped on to the learning cycle.
- They involve measurement of learning outcomes that feed back to the operation of the network and eventually determine whether or not to continue with the formal arrangement.

Examples of such learning networks might include:

- a formal club whose members have come together to try to understand and share experiences about new production concepts – for example, a 'best practice' club or forum;
- a regional grouping of small firms with the challenge of achieving and sustaining growth;
- a shared pre-competitive R&D project – 'co-laboratories';
- a supplier association or development programme where the aim is to upgrade levels of capability;

- a professional institution where the aim is to upgrade and update members' knowledge;
- a trade or sectoral research organization where the aim is to upgrade sectoral knowledge;
- an online user community where the aim is to share and develop knowledge – for example, in the Linux or Propellorhead communities;
- an online innovation contest where the aim is to capture and build on ideas and accumulate knowledge towards a dedicated target – for example, the Netflix prize.

Such networks can be formally promoted, with a clear focus and organizing 'hub', whilst others are largely cooperative and based on mainly informal mechanisms. And networks can also be hybrids; for instance, it is possible to find examples of networks that are both government promoted and also topic based.

A good and long-standing example of such arrangements in operation is the case of Toyota where an active supplier association has been responsible for sustained learning and development over an extended period of time (Dyer and Nobeoka, 2000). Hines reports on other examples of supplier associations that have contributed to sustainable growth and development in a number of sectors, particularly engineering and automotive (Hines et al., 1999). Case studies in the Dutch and UK food industries, the construction sector and aerospace provide further examples of different modes of learning networks organized around supply chains (Fearne and Hughes, 1999; Dent, 2001). Data from six UK supply chain learning networks studied in depth indicated improvements both for the main customer and its suppliers, confirming that supply chain learning programmes can, in principle, be 'win-win' programmes (Bessant et al., 2003).

As many authors have commented, there is considerable scope in geographically proximate networks (Piore and Sabel, 1982). Regional development programmes have increasingly used networking models of this kind – for example, in the Kent region of the UK a programme has been deployed to create learning clubs to support SME growth and development; this programme now involves 35 learning networks based around geographical, sectoral or topic lines. Morris reports on the active development of a cluster in the Durban area of South Africa using learning network principles as its core design (Morris et al., 2006).

The potential benefits of shared learning include the following:

- Challenge and structured critical reflection from different perspectives.

- Different perspectives can bring in new concepts (or old concepts that are new to the learner).
- Shared experimentation can reduce perceived and actual costs risks in trying new things.
- Shared experiences can provide support and open new lines of inquiry or exploration.
- Shared learning helps explicate the systems principles, seeing the patterns – separating 'the wood from the trees'.
- Shared learning provides an environment for surfacing assumptions and exploring mental models outside of the normal experience of individual organizations – helps prevent 'not invented here' and other effects.

Importantly these are not simply the by-products of network or supply chain activities; as one report comments, 'learning is not a natural feature of business networks. It is unlikely to thrive unless it is part of the emergent new models for inter-company collaboration which stress trust, cooperation and mutual dependence' (see DTI, 2000 and DTI and Office, 2000).

A good example of such an approach was the UK 'Industry Forum' (IF) programme, which originated as a sector-level activity in the automotive components field. Coordinated by the Society of Motor Manufacturers and Traders and backed by the then UK Department of Trade and Industry (now BIS), IF developed an approach to facilitating learning about and adoption of 'world class manufacturing' (WCM) involving core metrics of performance (cost, quality and delivery) and multiple approaches to facilitating learning about and experimentation with the new practices. Its success in the automotive sector led to more widespread promotion as a policy option and in the 2000 government White Paper on Competitiveness, provision was made to launch up to 13 other programmes in different sectors, all with the aim of promoting WCM.

IF and its derivatives operate on the basis of multiple mechanisms to engage and enable adoption of new ideas. Typically there is a core framework that involves some form of 'benchmarking' that creates a motivation for change in order to close performance gaps in key areas like cost, quality and delivery. Although such data is widely available outside of peer assist schemes, we would argue that it is the exposure to such benchmarking in the company of peers that creates a strong isomorphic pressure for change that underpins the adoption decision. Enabling learning and configuration involves demonstrations and exposure to others' experience together with a phase of facilitated learning by doing that enables local configuration to suit particular contexts and that deals with many of the perceived compatibility questions raised by WCM. These mechanisms include a high level of people-based support, for example through the loan of engineers and other experienced personnel as transfer agents.

There is growing evidence to support the use of such 'open engagement' modes of intervention. For example, in South Africa the domestic auto-motive components sector faced significant performance gaps as it moved into the post-apartheid era. Catching up to the 'world class' frontier became an urgent priority and central to it was the need to adopt WCM rapidly and widely. One approach was the formation of a series of 'bench-marking clubs' in key regions where the sector was a significant element in the local economy – around Durban, along the Eastern Cape seaboard and in the areas between Pretoria and Johannesburg. These clubs oper-ated in similar fashion to IF, using a mixture of benchmarking to develop shared motivation for change allied to extensive inter-firm support for experimenting with and learning about WCM and particularly how it could be adapted and configured to suit very different educational, social and cultural conditions (Bessant et al., 2006).

A key theme in OCI is the opening up of the innovation process to wider stakeholders and this can involve the construction of new networks or wider networks of participation to enrich the learning underpinning innovation. Such inclusive approaches have long been a feature of design methods but there is evidence of their wider adoption as part of the experi-mental routines by public and private sector organizations.

An example is in health care that has traditionally been dominated by an expert-driven linear model of innovation but which is now opening up to a much wider range of stakeholders. In recent years 'improvement collaboratives' – where members of multidisciplinary health teams work together both within and across organizations with a commitment to improving services – have emerged as a popular method for change within health care. Their impact includes significantly reducing waiting times and streamlining services (Kerr et al., 2002). Typically, such approaches – for example, deployed in improving outpatient care – involve a range of staff including nurses, clinic clerks, diagnostic services staff, doctors, secretaries and managers. Whilst they try to collect and integrate users' views into the redesign of services, there are fewer examples where *patients* and staff are jointly involved in a co-design process.

Experience-based design (EBD) of this kind involves identifying the main areas or 'touch points' where people come into contact with the service, and tries to identify areas where systems and processes need to be redesigned to create a better patient experience of health services. For example, work in the UK at the Luton and Dunstable (L&D) hospital involves using design methods to create a user-led solution to the challenge of improving patient care amongst neck and head cancer sufferers. The approach involves patients and carers telling stories about their experience of the service; these stories provide insights that enable the team of co-designers to think about designing *experiences* rather than designing services (Pine and Gilmore, 1999). Importantly the role of 'designer' includes all of those involved in the collaborative process: patients, staff, researchers, improvement leaders as well as design professionals (Bate and Robert, 2006).

The range of people involved as co-designers makes for an unusual mix of expertise in the context of traditional health care improvement efforts (Pickles et al., 2008). In the L&D such co-design has led to changes – for example, patients and carers have changed project documentation so that it better reflects their needs, and clinic staff and patients have worked together to redesign the flow of outpatients in the consulting room. The initial co-design group identified 38 different actions to be taken, all based on user experience.

LEARNING TO MANAGE OCI

The above examples give a flavour for the experiments going on within the 'open engagement' space and they are mirrored by others in the 'open search' and 'open stakeholder involvement' spheres. They represent a shift to network-level organization and management of the innovation process – but in doing so require development of new and complementary skills within and across participating organizations. Amongst the emerging challenges are the following:

- *Finding, forming, performing* – given that a key driver for OCI is to extend the search space and bring in new inputs the question is raised of how to find suitable network partners – and having found them, engage with them in ways that offer mutual benefit. This may involve searching in very new areas and ways and imply formation of 'weak ties' rather than the 'strong ties' traditionally associated with innovation success (Birkinshaw et al., 2007).
- What is the *extent* of open engagement – within OCI networks, are participants involved only in incremental, *kaizen* activities or also in more radical, 'intrapreneurial' developments?
- What is the *timing* of stakeholder involvement – at which stage in the innovation process and for how long is OCI relevant?
- What are the *targets* for OCI – is this capacity deployed to facilitate (in March's terms) richer exploitation or to engage in broader exploration, or combinations of the two (March, 1991)?

- What is the extent of, and what are mechanisms for, *involvement* in OCI? For example, how are 'peripheral innovators' (non-R&D members of the organization, external innovators, users, experts and other players) engaged in innovation processes?
- What are the *roles* within OCI? For example, we can distinguish between *initiators* (e.g., firms such as Adidas or Swarovski), *contributors*, and *intermediaries* who enable OCI in terms of technology or social interaction space. A more general issue relates to 'governance' of OCI networks – who is responsible and how might this process work?
- What are relevant *skills for OCI*? In order to operate effectively in an OCI environment organizations are likely to need new skills around broking and managing connections, network facilitation, and so on. How will these skills be articulated and developed – and is there a role for a growing service sector enabling OCI connectivity?
- *Tools for OCI* – in parallel there is a need for a new 'toolkit' of systems design and intervention tools enabling working at this network level.

As we suggested at the outset, innovation management is essentially about dynamic capability, requiring organizations to review their approaches and revise their routines in the face of a constantly shifting environment. The process whereby new routines are generated is, as Nelson and Winter (1982) originally observed, one of trial and error, and involves considerable experimentation and learning. Our argument is that the current shift towards OCI represents a significant step change in environmental conditions that will require a new version of the underlying model for innovation management – a fifth-generation, network-based and technology-enabled approach of the kind that Rothwell foresaw.

Of the many metaphors that we could use to represent this challenge we can conclude with two. First is the idea of creating a communications network – whereas the twentieth century began with telegraph systems, lines of poles stretched beside railway tracks and providing fixed line communication between clearly identified and planned points, the twenty-first century will require a wireless network, invisible and covering a wide area. Whilst telecommunications networks became richer and employed more forms of wiring, higher capacity cables and sophisticated switching and routing, their limit is in their fixed line nature. By contrast, wireless communications cater for mobility – information can flow across cellular networks in any direction and connect actors in reconfigurable ways.

The second metaphor is the human brain. Recent developments in neuroscience have begun to show the significant interconnectedness of our neural systems – the idea of particular 'modules' processing speech or vision has given way to models that are based on networks that can share and co-process information. But more significant is the growing understanding of 'plasticity' – the ability to remake those connections and find new pathways to meet new challenges – whether in the early experience of an infant learning about the world for the first time or in the case of stroke victims and others for whom damage in one part of the brain may be compensated for by re-establishing alternative connections.

For the wave of new organizations that are riding the waves of OCI the opportunities are significant – instead of concentrated and relatively bureaucratic structures there is an opportunity to exploit network effects that build on their agility and ability to form and manage relationships. And for established players the challenge is one of reconnecting their extensive internal knowledge bases and linking up to the rich potential set of additional players outside the organization's boundaries. Doing so may require significant capacity for letting go of old routines that have served well but that may no longer be relevant and that may get in the way of new approaches.

ACKNOWLEDGEMENTS

We gratefully acknowledge the support for the research reported here from the Theo and Friedl Schoeller Foundation – through its Dr Theo and Friedl Schoeller Research Center for Business and Society at the University of Erlangen-Nuremberg, Germany.

REFERENCES

Allen, T. (1977), *Managing the Flow of Technology*, Cambridge, MA: MIT Press.
Anderson, C. (2006), *The Long Tail: Why the Future of Business Is Selling More for Less*, New York: Hyperion.
Bate, P. and Robert, G. (2006), 'Experience-based design: from redesigning the system around the patient to co-designing services with the patient', *Quality and Safety in Health Care*, **15**(5), 307–10.
Berger, C. et al. (2005), 'Co-designing modes of cooperation at the customer interface: learning from exploratory research', *European Management Review*, **2**(1), 70–87.
Bessant, J. (2003), *High Involvement Innovation*, Chichester: John Wiley and Sons.
Bessant, J. and L. Maher (2009), 'Developing radical service innovations in health care – the role of design methods', *International Journal of Innovation Management*, **13**(4), 1–14.
Bessant, J. and K. Moeslein (2011), 'Learning to manage open collective innovation', AIM Executive Briefing, London: Advanced Institute of Management Research.
Bessant, J. and G. Tsekouras (2001), 'Developing learning networks', *AI and Society*, **15**(2), 82–98.

Bessant, J. and T. Venables (2008), *Creating Wealth from Knowledge: Meeting the Innovation Challenge*, Cheltenham, UK and Northampton, MA, USA: Edward Elgar.

Bessant, J. and B. Von Stamm (2007), 'Twelve search strategies which might save your organization', AIM Executive Briefing, London: Advanced Institute of Management Research.

Bessant, J., R. Kaplinsky and R. Lamming (2003), 'Putting supply chain learning into practice', *International Journal of Operations and Production Management*, **23**(2), 167–84.

Bessant, J., M. Morris and J. Barnes (2006), 'Creating innovative clusters – the view from below', in J. Bessant and D. Francis (eds), *Proceedings of the CINet Conference, Brighton*, Brighton, UK.

Bessant, J., B. Von Stamm and K. Moeslein (2009), 'Looking for innovation', *Wall Street Journal*, 22 June, 12.

Bessant, J., B. Von Stamm, K.M. Moeslein and A.-K. Neyer (2010), 'Backing outsiders: selection strategies for discontinuous innovation', *R&D Management*, **40**(4), 345–56.

Best, M. (2001), *The New Competitive Advantage: The Renewal of American Industry*, Oxford: Oxford University Press.

Birkinshaw, J., J. Bessant and R. Delbridge (2007), 'Finding, forming, and performing: creating networks for discontinuous innovation', *California Management Review*, **49**(3), 67–83.

Birkinshaw, J., G. Hamel and M.J. Mol (2008), 'Management innovation', *Academy of Management Review*, **33**(4), 825–45.

Boer, H. et al. (1999), *CI Changes: From Suggestion Box to the Learning Organisation*, Aldershot: Ashgate.

Brown, J.S. and P. Duguid (2000), 'Knowledge and organization: a social-practice perspective', *Organization Science*, **12**(2), 198–213.

Brown, J.S. and J. Hagel (2005), 'Innovation blowback: disruptive management practices from Asia', *McKinsey Quarterly*, No. 1, 34–45.

Bullinger, A.C. et al. (2010), 'Community-based innovation contests: where competition meets cooperation', *Creativity and Innovation Management*, **19**(3), 290–303.

Carter, C. and B. Williams (1957), *Industry and Technical Progress*, Oxford: Oxford University Press.

Chesbrough, H.W. (2003), *Open Innovation: The New Imperative for Creating and Profiting from Technology*, Boston, MA: Harvard Business Press.

Christensen, C. (1997), *The Innovator's Dilemma*, Boston, MA: Harvard Business School Press.

Dahlander, L. and D. Gann (2010), 'How open is innovation?', *Research Policy*, **39**(6), 699–709.

Davies, A. and M. Hobday (2005), *The Business of Projects: Managing Innovation in Complex Products and Systems*, Cambridge, UK: Cambridge University Press.

Dent, R. (2001), *Collective Knowledge Development, Organisational Learning and Learning Networks: An Integrated Framework*, Swindon: Economic and Social Research Council.

Dodgson, M., D. Gann and A. Salter (2005), *Think, Play, Do: Technology and Organization in the Emerging Innovation Process*, Oxford: Oxford University Press.

DTI (2000), *Learning Across Business Networks*, London: Department of Trade and Industry.

DTI & Office, C. (2000), *Learning Across Business Networks*, London: Department of Trade and Industry.

Dyer, J. and K. Nobeoka (2000), 'Creating and managing a high-performance knowledge-sharing network: the Toyota case', *Strategic Management Journal*, **21**(3), 345–67.

Fearne, A. and D. Hughes (1999), 'Success factors in the fresh produce supply chain; insights from the UK', *Supply Chain Management*, **4**(3), 120–31.

Gann, D. and A. Salter (2000), 'Innovation in project-based, service-enhanced firms: the construction of complex products and systems', *Research Policy*, **29**(7–8), 955–72.

Hargadon, A. (2003), *How Breakthroughs Happen*, Boston, MA: Harvard Business School Press.

Herstatt, C. and E. von Hippel (1992), 'Developing new product concepts via the lead user method', *Journal of Product Innovation Management*, **9**(3), 213–21.

Hines, P. et al. (1999), *Value Stream Management: The Development of Lean Supply Chains*, London: Financial Times Management.

Howells, J., A. James and K. Malik (2003), 'The sourcing of technological knowledge: distributed innovation processes and dynamic change', *R&D Management*, **33**(4), 395–409.

Humphrey, J. and H. Schmitz (1996), 'The Triple C approach to local industrial policy', *World Development*, **24**(12), 1859–77.

IJIM (2008), 'Special issue on user-led innovation', *International Journal of Innovation Management*, **12**(3).

Imai, K.(1987), *Kaizen*, New York: Random House.

Kerr, D. et al. (2002), 'Redesigning cancer care', *British Medical Journal*, **324**(20), 164–6.

Koen, P. et al. (2001), 'Providing clarity and a common language to the "fuzzy front end"', *Technology Management*, **44**(2), 46–55.

Lafley, A. and R. Charan (2008), *The Game Changer*, New York: Profile.

Langrish, J. et al. (1972), *Wealth from Knowledge*, London: Macmillan.

Lundvall, B. (1990), *National Systems of Innovation: Towards a Theory of Innovation and Interactive Learning*, London: Frances Pinter.

March, J. (1991), 'Exploration and exploitation in organizational learning', *Organization Science*, **2**(1), 71–87.

Metcalfe, S. and I. Miles (1999), 'Innovation systems in the service economy', *ICAIL, Volume 13*, Amsterdam: Kluwer.

Morris, M., J. Bessant and J. Barnes (2006), 'Using learning networks to enable industrial development: case studies from South Africa', *International Journal of Operations and Production Management*, **26**(5), 557–68.

Murray, R., J. Caulier-Grice and G. Mulgan (2010), *The Open Book of Social Innovation*, London: The Young Foundation.

Nelson, R.R. and S.G. Winter (1982), *An Evolutionary Theory of Economic Change*, Cambridge, MA: Belknap Press of Harvard University Press.

Pfeffer, J. (1994), *Competitive Advantage Through People*, Boston, MA: Harvard Business School Press.

Pickles, J., E. Hide and L. Maher (2008), 'Experience based design: a practical method of working with patients to redesign services', *Clinical Governance*, **13**(1), 51–8.

Piller, F. (2006), *Mass Customization: Ein wettbewerbsstrategisches Konzept im Informationszeitalter* (4th edition), Frankfurt: Gabler Verlag.

Pine, J. and J. Gilmore (1999), *The Experience Economy*, Boston, MA: Harvard Business School Press.

Piore, M. and C. Sabel (1982), *The Second Industrial Divide*, New York: Basic Books.

Porter, M.E. (1997), 'Location, knowledge creation and competitiveness', in D. Monisha (ed.), *Proceedings of Academy of Management Symposium on Knowledge Capitalism: Competitiveness Re-evaluated*, Boston, MA.

Prahalad, C.K. (2006), *The Fortune at the Bottom of the Pyramid*, New Jersey: Wharton School Publishing.

Reichwald, R., K. Moeslein, A. Huff, M. Kolling and A. Neyer (2007), *Services Made in Germany – A Travel Guide*, Leipzig: CLIC, HHL University.

Reid, S.E. and U. de Brentani (2004), 'The fuzzy front end of new product development for discontinuous innovations: a theoretical model', *Journal of Product Innovation Management*, **21**(3), 170–84.

Rothwell, R. (1977), 'The characteristics of successful innovators and technically progressive firms', *R&D Management*, **7**(3), 191–206.

Rothwell, R. (1994), 'Towards the fifth-generation innovation process', *International Marketing Review*, **11**(1), 7–31.

Santos, J., Y. Doz and P. Williamson (2004), 'Is your innovation process global?', *MIT Sloan Management Review*, **45**(4), 31–7.

Schrage, M. (2000), *Serious Play: How the World's Best Companies Simulate to Innovate*, Boston, MA: Harvard Business School Press.

Schroeder, A. and D. Robinson (2004), *Ideas Are Free: How the Idea Revolution Is Liberating People and Transforming Organizations*, New York: Berrett Koehler.

Teece, D. and G. Pisano (1994), 'The dynamic capabilities of firms: an introduction', *Strategic Management Journal*, **3**(3), 537–55.

Von Hippel, E. (1988), *The Sources of Innovation*, Cambridge, MA: MIT Press.

Von Hippel, E. (2005), *The Democratization of Innovation*, Cambridge, MA: MIT Press.

Wenger, E. (1999), *Communities of Practice: Learning, Meaning, and Identity*, Cambridge, UK: Cambridge University Press.

West, J., W. Vanhaverbeke and H. Chesbrough (2006), 'Open innovation: a research agenda', in H. Chesbrough, W. Vanhaverbeke and J. West (eds), *Open Innovation: Researching a New Paradigm*, Oxford: Oxford University Press, pp. 285–308.

3 Engaged employees! An actor perspective on innovation
Satu Teerikangas and Liisa Välikangas

INTRODUCTION

Today's world is increasingly characterized by turbulence in many forms (Ansoff and McDonnell, 1990). Thriving in such a landscape requires ever more novel ways of sustaining one's advantage over a global pool of competition (Porter, 1980). A parallel, pervasive shift, shaping the competitive landscape over the past decades has been the emergence of 'knowledge-based societies'. This shift has gained critical significance at the dawn of the twenty-first century especially for companies from developed economies: how to otherwise deal with the aggressive entry of lower-cost market players from emerging markets, whilst simultaneously leveraging opportunities provided by technological advances (Bartlett and Ghoshal, 1998)?

What makes the emergence of the 'knowledge era' particularly pertinent is that it has essentially come to revolutionize the way of working that has been in place since the Industrial Revolution. In knowledge-based societies, the core ingredients of competition take new forms: instead of a focus on efficiency and production only, innovation and creativity have become the strategic cornerstones of the successful modern organization. The recent examples of Apple with the iPhone and the iPad, or Google attest to the ways in which one organization can revolutionize the use of mobile handsets, computers or the internet, and in so doing shape entire industries. Both companies provide prime examples of succeeding with an innovative outlook and an engaged approach.

In a competitive context, where success and survival are based on an organization's ability to be innovative on an ongoing basis, organizations have become increasingly dependent on human capital (Davenport et al., 2002). In essence, in an 'innovation era', the effective utilization of talent emerges as a prerequisite to corporate success. The key question becomes – how to unleash the creative potential residing in an organization's employee base? Moreover, how to manage an organization wherein human talent takes center stage? Essentially, how to link the employee and an organization's ability to be innovative?

Though defined in many ways, we adopt here the view of Van de

Ven (1986, p.9), who defines innovation as 'a new idea, which may be a recombination of old ideas, a scheme that challenges the present order, a formula, or a unique approach'. Existing research on innovation can be categorized with regard to the level of analysis adopted, be it the study of the individual, a team/group, an organization, an industry, a region or a country (Gupta et al., 2007). Surprisingly, whilst the study of innovation has burgeoned over the past decades (ibid.), criticism has been voiced from within the field as to a relative lack of research on *the individual employee* engaged in innovative work (Scott and Bruce, 1994; Gupta et al., 2007; Birkinshaw et al., 2008). In so doing, it can be argued that the *act of innovating itself* seems to have been given lesser attention.

So what is it that we do know about the individual engaged or involved in innovative work? Research on innovation at the individual level has focused on the factors that predict individuals' creativity (Gupta et al., 2007). One stream has studied creativity as an outcome of the individual's personality traits (Kirton, 1994; Boden, 2003), temporary psychological states such as positive affect (Isen et al., 1987), or systematic problem-solving styles (Scott and Bruce, 1994). Another stream has studied the role that the work context plays in enabling creativity at work (Amabile, 1983; Scott and Bruce, 1994). Here, the quality of the supervisor–subordinate relationship in terms of trust, support and autonomy is not only meaningful, but has been found to mediate the subordinate's perception of the extent to which the organization supports innovation (Scott and Bruce, 1994). In parallel, in the area of management innovation, the individual has been treated from the perspective of either the 'change agent' or the 'recipient' of innovation (Birkinshaw et al., 2008), that is, not the 'inventor' him or herself.

If research on innovation can be regarded as having been slow to expand on the individual engaged in innovative work, on the side of organizations the need remains dire. Organizations are seeking ways in which they can relate to their employees and involve them in the organization's innovation quest. This has also been emphasized in the trendy literature on open innovation, following Chesbrough (2003), where the aim is to harness innovative ideas residing within and beyond the organization.

It is in this respect that over recent years, the term 'employee engagement' has been gaining currency (Macey and Schneider, 2008a). It has been welcomed as one means of approaching the employee–innovation dilemma. Globally reputed, high-performing organizations such as Nokia are taking engagement seriously: in the renewal of their corporate values in 2007, 'engaging you' emerged as one of the four new corporate values (source, Nokia corporate website).

Despite an acute need for engaged employees, the current situation as regards employee engagement in many an organization remains potentially alarming. Despite the many calls for 'open innovation' (e.g., Chesbrough, 2006; Fleming and Waguespack, 2007; Von Hippel and Von Krogh, 2009), there is serious concern over employee engagement, reported at low levels in corporate surveys (despite the same organizations possibly reporting positive financial results; see, e.g., Towers Watson's yearly employee engagement surveys). As an example, a survey by the Hay Group reported in the *Financial Times* found that 41 percent of employees in 3100 organizations feel demotivated by their managers (Stern, 2008). Not only is this situation unsustainable for the employees, having to work in jobs that are unengaging or demotivating, a deficit in employee engagement also bears dire performance consequences. A lack of employee engagement has been evidenced to represent corporate-wide potential losses in creativity (Gilson and Shalley, 2004), safety (Harter et al., 2002), customer satisfaction (Harter et al., 2002; Salanova et al., 2005), customer loyalty (Harter et al., 2002), and ultimately productivity and corporate performance (Harter et al., 2002; Britt et al., 2005; Salanova and Schaufeli, 2008). It has also been found to affect employee work performance (Harter et al., 2002; Sonnentag, 2003; Britt et al., 2005; Salanova and Schaufeli, 2008), turnover intentions (Harter et al., 2002; Schaufeli and Bakker, 2004), individual health (Sonnentag, 2003), and employees' extra-role behaviors (ibid.).

At the heart of the matter would seem to be the fact that for individuals in developed economies, the trend is increasingly to seek meaningful life paths and careers (Pratt and Ashforth, 2003; Cartwright and Holmes, 2006), whether by immersing oneself into one's career, hobbies, special causes, philanthropy or family (Baumeister, 1991). In other words, current bases of motivation have changed. Employees increasingly seek 'self-actualization' (Maslow, 1954), as in the modern developed economy their other needs have been met. Today's employees want to be engaged; they are actively seeking means of occupying themselves in a meaningful way. In contrast, it would appear that employing organizations have been slower to respond to this demand. Not surprisingly, then, engagement scores are not soaring.

It would seem that Frederick Taylor's dictum (2008) that we should not misuse human talent in organizations has led to building robotic, 'automaton-like' organizations focused on productivity that many of today's 'knowledge workers' do not approve of or wish to work in. This echoes Henry Ford's often-cited words: 'every time I ask for a pair of hands, a brain comes with them'. Today, smart employees want to use their brains; they want to get satisfaction out of their work, and use their creative capacities. Following Taylor, the issue for modern organizations is moving from the present 10 percent to utilizing the dormant 90 percent potential within the organization's workforce (Figure 3.1). These

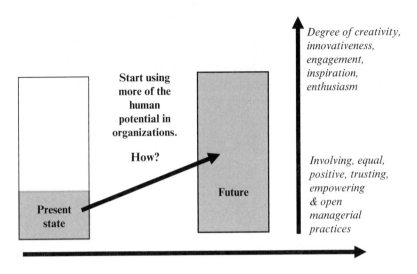

Figure 3.1   The future challenge of organizations: drawing from and appreciating human potential

changes are forcing managers to move further away from traditional authoritative hierarchy-based management styles toward empowerment and employee-engaging management styles (Conger and Kanungo, 1998). As an example, it has been argued that a global organization such as IBM cannot be managed (from the top) by giving people detailed orders as to what to do (see Bjelland and Wood, 2008).

These considerations leave us with the following overall conclusion – how can organizations thrive in a context wherein (1) the name of the game is innovation and a competition based on ideas, (2) the role of human agency, human capital, and creativity is of increasing importance, and (3) wherein meaningfulness and empowerment matter to employees? It seems that this dawning era calls for new ways of seeing, being, and organizing, new ways of perceiving organizations and their managerial function (cf. Hamel, 2007). It seems, provocatively speaking, that the traditional schools of theorizing have left managers with a toolkit fitting the Middle Ages, whereas the present era calls for a toolkit of an altogether different kind. In light of the parallel trends of employees' search for meaning and organizations' striving for innovativeness, we explore 'employee engagement' as a lens to approaching the individual, micro-dimension of organizations facing pressures to thrive in this new era.

In this chapter, we propose to gaze through the lens of employee engagement into the seeming 'black box' of the individual employee undertaking innovative work. Based on an inductive, explorative approach using a theory-building research design in five distinct research settings (Glaser and Strauss, 1967; Eisenhardt, 1989), we argue that employee engagement is an important antecedent of modern innovation work. In other words, we claim that an individual employee engaged in his or her work activity is more likely to come up with novel insights, new solutions to work problems than a non-engaged employee. In order to further our understanding of employee engagement as a key antecedent to innovation, we develop a grounded model of 'the engagement process'. Our findings highlight the performance consequences of being 'highly engaged', the characteristics of high-engagement experiences, as well as individual, interpersonal and spatial factors that enable engagement. In a broader perspective, we argue that our findings offer not only a means to understand the individual actor engaging in innovative work, but also a means to identify the prerequisites of organizational routines in an innovation-geared corporate landscape. We posit employee engagement as an 'actor'-based perspective to innovation. This is a challenge for the future of managerial innovation.

Our chapter is structured as follows. We start with an overview of the current state of the art as regards research on employee engagement. In the next section we briefly detail our methodological approach and research setting. The following sections present our findings, before we finally present our conclusions.

WHAT IS KNOWN ON EMPLOYEE ENGAGEMENT

Whilst research on employee engagement emerged in the early 1990s with the work of Kahn (1990, 1992), thereafter it has been fed for a long time by a practitioner interest (see Macey and Schneider, 2008a). Led by social psychologists and scholars of organizational behavior, since the early twenty-first century the field has seen a rapid burgeoning and rebirth. However, at present, the field remains criticized for lacking appropriate conceptualizations of 'what' engagement is (Little and Little, 2006; Macey and Schneider, 2008a). Macey and Schneider state that 'engagement is a concept with a sparse and diverse theoretical net – the relationships among potential antecedents and consequences of engagement as well as the components of engagement have not been rigorously conceptualized, much less studied' (2008a, pp. 3–4).

In order to begin to appreciate what engagement is about and its wide usage in popular parlance, let us draw on the *Oxford English Dictionary*. Its definitions of engagement fall into two camps. The *first* category relates to more superficial facets and uses of the term, seeing engagement as a 'contract', whereas the second category calls for deeper levels of emotional and cognitive commitment and presence. It is this second connotation that we refer to and discuss in this chapter. Here, engagement is defined, among others, as 'being engaged to be married; betrothal', a 'moral or legal obligation; a tie of duty or gratitude', or 'the state of being engaged in fight; a battle, conflict, encounter; also formerly, a single combat'. What these definitions share is a reference to 'engagement' as a personal, deeper-level, formal, moral involvement, promise or agreement to a serious undertaking, such as a long-term relationship in the example of being engaged to be married; or as a serious short-term instance requiring immediate presence and action, as in the example of a combat or a fight.

Defining employee engagement in this way raises questions though. Can organizations expect to gain this level of employee commitment to their tasks and the organization? What are the risks involved; what is the promise in return? As the lifelong employment guarantee no longer holds, companies must find new returns on employees spending their intellectual, emotional and career resources on the company (Cartwright and Holmes, 2006). And is it possible to be highly engaged in a job, purpose, or organization, and then move on, or do such shorter-term commitments contradict the fundamental quality of what engagement is all about?

Three Approaches to Engagement

In contrast to the term 'employee engagement' having gained societal and corporate currency, the term has to date received scanter, though increasing research attention (Macey and Schneider, 2008a). The study of engagement has been strongest in the areas of applied psychology and sociology, with an increasing interest from organization scientists. In defining engagement and its antecedents, three broad approaches can be identified.

Though individual experiences of engagement have occurred throughout history, the seminal academic study on engagement in organizations is that of Kahn (1990), who coined the terms 'personal engagement' vs. 'personal disengagement' during work role performances. Kahn argues that prior literature has taken a static view on a person's fit to one's job, be it in the job involvement, commitment to work, or work alienation literatures. In contrast, Kahn considers engagement from a dynamic, constantly changing lens. Basing himself on Goffman (1961), Maslow (1954) and Alderfer (1972), Kahn defines personal engagement as 'the extent to which employees harness themselves in their work roles, i.e. employing and expressing oneself physically, cognitively and emotionally during work role performances' (Kahn, 1990, p. 701). This is contrasted with personal disengagement, likened to automatic or robotic behaviors, effortlessness, defensive, unexpressive, impersonal or closed behaviors, that is, situations wherein one does not fulfill one's role with authenticity (Harter, 2002).

Kahn (1990) further identifies psychological meaningfulness, safety and availability as defining one's capability for becoming engaged. These factors can be further broken down into psychological, interpersonal and organizational antecedents. In May et al.'s (2004) study, meaningfulness appeared to have the greatest predictive impact on engagement. Also, the fit between one's job and one's personality has been found of central importance (Maslach and Leiter, 1997). Despite the seminal nature of Kahn's (1990) work, it has nevertheless been scantly developed further in academic research. In contrast, it has gained a wider audience in the consulting community (including Towers Watson, Gallup or CIPD), as exemplified in the study of Harter et al. (2002) on the performance effects of employee engagement.

A second approach to engagement has its roots in research on burnout (see Maslach and Jackson, 1981; Maslach et al., 2001), where engagement initially emerged as the conceptual opposite of burnout (Maslach and Leiter, 1997; González-Romá et al., 2006), though the nature of this relationship has thereafter been subject to debate (Schaufeli and Bakker, 2004). As a result of this work, today an individual's psychological relationship to their job has come to be conceptualized as a continuum between the negative experience of burnout and the positive experience of engagement (Maslach and Leiter, 2008). In this stream, engagement is defined as 'a positive, fulfilling, work-related state of mind characterized by vigor, dedication, and absorption' (Schaufeli et al., 2002, p. 74).

With its origin in burnout studies, this research stream has developed the 'job resources–job demands' model of engagement (Bakker and Demerouti, 2007). This is the most empirically tested model in the field (Demerouti et al., 2001). The model assumes that each occupation has its own risk factor, defined either as a job resource or a job demand. While job resources (be they organizational, social, work or task related) and personal resources (e.g., optimism, efficacy, resilience, self-esteem) create motivation, job demands (whether physical, social, psychological, organizational) create strain. Work engagement results from the ongoing negotiation between job resources and demands. Job resources supportive of engagement include social support, feedback, skill variety, autonomy and opportunities for learning (Bakker and Demerouti, 2007). Job demands, on the other hand, related to workload and reorganizations, do not affect engagement but affect burnout by creating exhaustion and cynicism (Bakker et al., 2003). The significance of sufficient job resources increases with the demands of the job (Hakanen et al., 2005). Instead of being a state to be achieved, engagement is considered as a process requiring constant attention (Maslach and Leiter, 1997).

A third approach has aimed to deconstruct engagement. To this end, Saks (2006) distinguishes between job (or work) engagement and organizational engagement. Tyler and Blader (2003) find that group engagement has psychological and behavioral components. Most recently, Macey and Schneider (2008a) divide engagement into trait (i.e., positive stance to life and work), psychological state (i.e., absorption, pride, alertness), and behavioral engagement (i.e., extra-role behaviors). The model has been subject to a heated debate (see, e.g., Macey and Schneider, 2008b). In parallel, the relative independence and uniqueness of engagement as a concept and its links to other related concepts, especially commitment, has been raised (Hallberg and Schaufeli, 2006; Macey and Schneider, 2008a).

Despite differences between these three approaches to engagement, it is generally agreed that engagement is manifested in a flow of positive emotions, extra-role behaviors, vigor and energy. Yet, the ways in which these manifestations are defined and operationalized vary from one study to the next. In addition to defining engagement in different ways, the three approaches differ further with regard to their views as to the temporal nature of engagement: is engagement temporary and dynamic (Kahn, 1990), permanent (e.g., Schaufeli et al., 2002), or possibly both (e.g., Macey and Schneider, 2008a)? Moreover, the approaches differ as to the nature of engagement: is engagement related to work role (Kahn, 1990), is it a psychological state and related to work activity (Schaufeli et al., 2002), or does it have multiple components (Macey and Schneider, 2008a)? As a result, the issue of 'what' engagement is, 'what' it consists in, and 'how' it differs from related concepts remains disputed.

All the while, it would seem that engagement is a capability available to all: neither age, gender nor race have been found to affect reported levels of engagement (e.g., Storm and Rothmann, 2003). In contrast, previous (work) experiences, for example, help to predict one's current level of engagement (Koyncu et al., 2006). It has to be noted though that most research on engagement has been quantitative in nature, seeking to assess rather than understand. Studies approaching engagement using a qualitative approach remain rare.

Performance Effects

The positive performance effects of engagement have received confirmation in a number of studies. Engagement has been found to be positively related to employee performance (Britt et al., 2005, Salanova and

Schaufeli, 2008), firm performance, customer satisfaction (Salanova et al., 2005) and team creativity (Gilson and Shalley, 2004). In terms of corporate performance, a recent meta-analysis of the Gallup industry database found employee engagement and satisfaction to strongly correlate with employee turnover, customer satisfaction and safety, and also to correlate with productivity and firm profitability (Harter et al., 2002). In a study on the predictors of service climate and its impact on employee performance and customer loyalty, Salanova et al. (2005) find that service climate mediates the relationship between (1) work engagement and organizational resources on the one hand, and (2) employee performance and customer loyalty on the other hand.

As regards individual-level outcomes, Kahn (1992) suggests that engagement results in an improved quality of one's work and a positive experience of undertaking the work. In their model of burnout, Maslach et al. (2001) consider engagement to mediate the relationship between work conditions and individual-level work outcomes, including job satisfaction, withdrawal, performance and commitment. Engagement has been evidenced to relate negatively to turnover intention (Schaufeli and Bakker, 2004) and positively to job performance, extra-role behavior, good health and positive work affect (Sonnentag, 2003). Engaged individuals have further been found to experience overall greater happiness in their lives than non-engaged individuals (Schaufeli et al., 2006).

Interestingly, similar positive performance effects have been found as regards concepts close to engagement such as the meaning of work (Pratt and Ashforth, 2003), work as calling (Hall and Chandler, 2005), job involvement (Brown and Leigh, 1996), and intrinsic motivation (Grant, 2008). In essence, the more one is attuned and emotionally attached to one's job, the better not only one's own, but also one's team's and ultimately the organization's performance. Judging from these findings, we start to understand why it may appear that engaged employees are the 'ultimate goal' in present-day organizations. Engaged workers are creative, alert, energetic, present, available, happy all the while, and what is best, very effective at their work. Through this narrative we understand why engagement has become the 'de rigueur' managerial goal. In an era geared toward innovation, engaged employees offer the promise of better returns.

Current State

In practice, though, we are far from being there yet. Cartwright and Holmes (2006) position the prevailing managerial challenge as *re*gaining employee engagement; they argue that factors causing a lack of employee

Table 3.1   An engagement audit

Contributing to Engagement Deficit?	Contributing to Engagement Surplus?
Radical restructuring and programmatic change	Interesting work, a feeling of accomplishment, friendly and helpful colleagues, adding something to people's lives (Bibby, 2001)
Break up of the traditional commitment and loyalty	A greater sense of meaning and purpose in working lives (Guevara and Ord, 1996) (alignment with one's values)
Lack of work–life balance and more demanding work conditions	A source of community and a place to feel connected (Conger, 1994)
Lack of interpersonal relationships and social support	
A purely transactional work contract	A source of feeling of self-worthiness (Seligman, 2002)
	Achieve a 'sort of immortality' (Handy, 1998)
Lack of trust in the leadership and/or lack of transparency	Emotional engagement ('a type of positive arousal') and passion
Lack of integrity in living the company values	(i.e., the work is enjoyable and meaningful) (Boverie and Kroth, 2001)

engagement have gained an upper hand. There is increasing employee cynicism, as demands for work increase at the expense of personal life. What is more, transactional employment contracts offer little in return in terms of opportunities for self-expression and emotional rewards. Perceptions of companies lacking integrity and authenticity further contribute to such disenchantment. The lack of alignment of one's personal values with those of the company purpose (Ghoshal and Bartlett, 1997) and hurtful management practices grounded in 'bad management theory' (Ghoshal, 2005) arguably also lead to disengagement. Reasons for employees distancing from the company they work for are therefore many (Table 3.1). Many of these reasons have to do with the basic decency of corporate management, the perceived lack of authenticity (or perhaps integrity) of leaders, and the lack of a meaningful purpose for the occasionally fragmented toil at work. In sum, the positive effects of engagement would seem to remain distant from many an organization's reality (Cartwright and Holmes, 2006). This is rather paradoxical, given the simultaneously increasing corporate hype on the need for an engaged workforce. It would seem that developing an engagement capability is much needed if organizations wish to thrive in a hypercompetitive landscape (e.g., Ilinitch et al., 1996; Wiggins and Ruefli, 2005). Engagement would seem to offer the promise of not only being a hygiene factor behind employee satisfaction and performance, but more importantly, to be a key factor at the very source of corporate innovativeness.

RESEARCH METHOD AND SETTINGS

Given the relative lack of empirical, qualitative fieldwork on engagement at work, we decided to embark on an explorative journey seeking to unearth the nature of (high) engagement and ways of enabling it. In the design of our research approach, we were inspired by Alvesson and Kärreman's (2007) recent work on 'constructing mystery': while issues such as work meaningfulness have been long known to affect employee engagement, nevertheless many recent in-company assessments suggest that actual employee engagement is declining.[1] The mystery is: why and how, despite the assumed managerial knowledge, is it so hard to build engagement?

Our research approach draws from the inductive theory-building tradition (Glaser and Strauss, 1967). As there are a variety of approaches toward grounded theory (see Charmaz, 2000 for an excellent overview), the grounded theory-building approach that we saw as best fitting our work was the approach of Glaser (1978, 1992, 1998, 2001). Glaser's work differs from Strauss's work (Strauss, 1987; Strauss and Corbin, 1990) and Charmaz's (2000) work in that it advocates the significance of 'emergence' vs. 'forcing' when conducting grounded theory research. By this Glaser (1978, 1992, 1998, 2001) refers to the ideal of aiming to base as much of one's findings and reasoning on the emerging reality from the studied settings and data, instead of aiming to force-fit one's findings onto extant literature too early on. The second tenet that distinguishes Glaser's work is his emphasis on the use of the constant comparative method of analysis on one's data, instead of forcing a pre-empted analysis technique.

We approached engagement by taking a positive deviance perspective to seek to understand what '*high* engagement' is, that is, what happens when individuals are 'highly engaged' in their work. This is in contrast to a lot of research on engagement that has sought to disassociate it from burnout (e.g., Maslach and Leiter, 1997). Our focus was to further study employee engagement in contexts requiring innovativeness.

In order to ensure diversity in our research setting, our study is based on five consecutive empirical data-gathering moments:

1. highly engaged employees and their work environment in an IT corporation (performed by the authors);
2. a study of highly engaged individuals across different professions in the arts and economy (Rikkinen, 2010);
3. a study of Chinese and Finnish young professionals regarding their experiences of high engagement and their future expectations of engagement at work (Yang, 2010);
4. a research-based design of a work space that invites, initiates and enables high engagement (Lönngren, 2010); and
5. an ethnography of engagement in the context of blue-collar workers (Paananen, 2010).

The aim through these five studies was to create a cross-disciplinary perspective appropriate to the study of engagement in that we draw on management studies, psychology and design in our exploratory research.

In the first two sub-projects, we sought to understand what 'high engagement' is, that is, what are the experiences of individuals who are 'highly engaged' in their work? We began our empirical work by conducting interviews of highly engaged engineers working in the research and development subsidiary of a Swedish multinational firm in Finland. The interviewees were selected by our contact persons in the company, who headed the Finnish innovation management operations at the time. Through discussions and feedback from their colleagues (by peer review), they sampled a set of six 'highly engaged' engineers for our study. These engineers represented diversity in terms of research work, work experience, current task, managerial experience, age and gender. Interviews conducted by the first author lasted between one and two hours. Interviews were taped and transcribed. The findings from the interviews were fed back onto our contact persons in the company. This discussion has resulted in not only an ongoing dialogue but moreover, the decision to launch a joint university–company cooperation project, where we will study the implementation of one particular engagement approach in one part of the company.

The second sub-project extended the first one. Here, we were interested in understanding the experiences of individuals across professions as regards engagement, and high engagement in particular. The individuals, who were recognized as positive outliers in their reference group (cf. McKelvey and Andriani, 2005), were selected based on their strong reputation in their respective work communities as being 'highly engaged' (that is, known to give their very best to their work and excelling in it). The research was conducted using open-ended questions in the spirit of dialogue (by Petri Rikkinen). A total of 16 interviews were conducted.

The interviewees were theoretically sampled (Glaser and Strauss, 1967; Eisenhardt, 1989) to represent various professions, ranging from entrepreneurs, scientists, successful executives and business angels to artists and writers in Finland. Also, an unusually dedicated blue-collar worker involved in cleaning work was interviewed. Interviews were taped and transcribed.

In order to tap into the future of organizations and managerial work, our third sub-project focused on the younger generation's experiences of engagement and their career expectations. A total of 24 interviews were conducted (by Luyi Yang). Half of the interviewees were Finns, half Chinese. Half of both national samples were students at the Master's level, half were recent graduates (having graduated one to three years ago). Further, half of the sample were vocational students in arts or medicine, whilst the other half were non-vocational students in engineering and business. Interviews were taped and transcribed.

The fourth sub-project was conducted through an architectural design-based research project. The aim was to study and design an office environment inciting high engagement. In a first phase, a literature review and interviews of six informants in research, management, or designer roles in multinational firms and design companies were performed. Thereafter, the researcher – a graduate student at the University of Art and Design in Helsinki (Mats Lönngren) – organized a 'co-design' workshop wherein the participants were able to assess these views as well as get involved in co-creating the ideal high-engagement office environment. This had been termed 'Design Lab – a space for engagement' (Lönngren, 2010). In the fifth sub-project, an ethnography of blue-collar workers involved in cleaning and maintenance work was conducted (by Harri Paananen).

The analysis of the findings was undertaken in two parallel phases. In the first phase, each of the researchers undertook the analysis of the findings rising from their own work. All the while, monthly feedback and discussion sessions amongst the research team ensured links between the sub-projects, with each researcher receiving feedback for his or her work. In a second phase, when all of the sub-projects' data gathering and within-project analyses had been completed, we proceeded to a cross-project analysis of the overall themes and relationships emerging across the five projects. This phase resembled a cross-case analysis (Eisenhardt, 1989; Miles and Huberman, 1994; Yin, 2009). When engaged in this cross-project analysis exercise, we noticed that the emerging core findings from the sub-projects bore similarities, in that emerging commonalities (discussed in the next section) across the five studies became visible.

Inspired by our empirical, exploratory studies, in the next sections

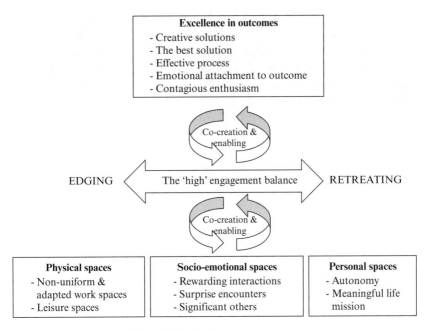

Figure 3.2   A grounded model of high engagement

we move onto presenting our findings on the characteristics and means of enabling engagement. We start by addressing the outcomes of high engagement. Thereafter, we identify characteristics of highly engaged individuals. Third, we explain how the process of becoming engaged and maintaining one's level of engagement requires a dyadic tension between 'edging' and 'retreating'. Fourth, we discuss physical, interpersonal and personal factors that enable engagement. In a final section, we summarize our findings by proposing four scenarios ranging from low to high degrees of engagement depending on the extent to which individuals and the organization attend to engagement-critical factors. Throughout the following section, readers are encouraged to refer to Figure 3.2, which summarizes the findings.

OUTCOMES OF HIGH ENGAGEMENT

We start the overview of our empirical findings by focusing on the question – why does engagement matter? How does a high degree of employee engagement affect performance? More specifically, what is the link between a high degree of employee engagement and firm innovativeness? Extant research has used numerical evidence to link employee engagement with the employee's individual performance at work (Britt et al., 2005; Salanova and Schaufeli, 2008), a team's level of creativity (Gilson and Shalley, 2004), and firm performance and customer satisfaction (Salanova et al., 2005). In the following, we provide a succinct overview of the results from our qualitative studies. We first focus on answering the question: what are the results or outcomes of high engagement?

Previous research has evidenced that engaged teams are more creative in the solutions they come up with (Gilson and Shalley, 2004). This baseline was confirmed in our study of research and development engineers. The interviewees highlighted how a research project, wherein the team members were engaged, ended up with outcomes that were more creative than projects where engagement was lacking. In other words, the quality of the team's creative outcome was higher when the team members were engaged in the activity at stake. Interviewees highlighted how in these instances the team would 'go beyond' current solutions in search of novel ones. This leads us to posit:

Proposition 1.1:   High engagement feeds creative solutions.

Interviewed engineers further noted that research projects characterized by high degrees of engagement would generally result in an outcome that was of high quality and highly elaborate. Also, the work process itself was praised in that engineers would find the solution more rapidly, they would take initiative to find new methods and approaches of working, and they would overall make less errors in their work. In sum:

Proposition 1.2:   High engagement nurtures high-quality outcomes and effective work processes to reach such an outcome.

Interviewed research and development engineers in the first sub-project highlighted how projects with a high degree of engagement tended to result in outcomes that the entire team's members were emotionally committed to even after the project was over. All team members wanted to 'own' the result, and to claim overtly that 'I was part of that team'. As a result, team members would effortlessly defend the team's outcome, if faced with opposition. Their belief in the outcome was so high that they would do their best not to let the outcome be sabotaged by unnecessary criticism. It would seem that the degree of immersion, authenticity and fullness of the experience results in a strong emotional attachment to the outcome of the project. We propose:

Proposition 1.3: High engagement results in outcomes to which those involved in their making are attached and committed to emotionally.

Bakker et al. (2006) find that a team's level of engagement depends on its members' engagement levels; in other words, engagement is contagious. Engagement has further been found to transfer from work to home life and vice versa (see Rikkinen, 2010), and between spouses (Bakker et al., 2005). In our study, highly engaged interviewees (in Rikkinen, 2010) noticed how they were able to attract motivated highly qualified team members to work with them, owing to their own inspirational engagement. These findings parallel the work of Losada (Losada, 1999; Losada and Heaphy, 2004) on the effect of positive interactions on the degree of member connectivity and performance of high-performing teams. The findings also relate to Wrzesniewski (2003) on the transfer effects of persons who have a 'work as calling' attitude toward the entire group. Basing ourselves on this evidence, we claim that engaged individuals radiate enthusiasm into their immediate surroundings:

Proposition 1.4: High engagement results in contagious enthusiasm; it engages others.

In summary, the above overview starts to draw a picture as to the significance of an engaged workforce in the present knowledge era, wherein innovation and creativity are critical for corporate success. Interviewed research and development engineers as well as highly engaged individuals across professions all agreed on the positive effects of high engagement on work outcomes. In particular, our findings highlight that engaged individuals and teams come up with work outcomes that (1) are creative, (2) exhibit high quality in terms of outcome and work process, (3) result in emotional attachment and commitment toward the outcomes. Moreover, engaged individuals and teams tend to radiate enthusiasm, this serving to attract other like-minded members to join the team, thus furthering the potential for future high-quality work outcomes. In essence, it would seem that securing a strong degree of engagement in today's workforce is critical if organizations are to aim for creative outcomes and an innovative outlook.

THE EXPERIENCE OF HIGH ENGAGEMENT

If engagement is performance- and innovation-critical, then how does one know whether someone is engaged? What are characteristics of *high engagement as an experience or an activity?* In this section, basing ourselves on the existing literature and supported by our empirical insights, we put forward a set of tentative propositions that highlight instances of *engagement surplus*, instances wherein an individual is (more than) fully engaged in his or her activity.

In his seminal work on engagement, Kahn (1990, p. 694) defined engagement as the 'harnessing of a person's self to her work role; in engagement, people employ and express themselves physically, cognitively, and emotionally during role performances'. He distances engagement from 'disengagement', seeing the difference between the two in the degree to which an individual brings his or her own self into the work activity or role being undertaken. In essence, in high-engagement situations, an individual is fully present in one's role, in harmony with oneself and his or her own person; in low-engagement or disengagement situations the individual brings in a robot-like facet of oneself, keeping one's true identity and desires hidden deep within. Kahn (1990) reflects this onto Goffman's (1961) work on role attachment vs. detachment as well as onto social scientists' work on 'self-in-role' (Freud, 1922; Goffman, 1961; Smith and Berg, 1987). The latter discuss individuals' parallel needs to both belong to and retreat from the groups they belong to. In essence, being fully in a role means authenticity (Baxter, 1982), that is, being genuinely oneself in a given situation. To reflect these established streams of research, we offer a first proposition on the nature of high engagement as follows:

Proposition 2.1:   People are fully engaged when they are authentic and bring their true selves and personalities into the activity and roles that they are performing.

Image I: Opera singer, e.g., Pavarotti singing vs. factory worker on an assembly line

This idea relates closely to recent work in the domain of systems thinking, wherein Senge et al. (2005), echoed in Jaworski (2002), launched the notion of 'presence' as qualifying those instances of stillness that characterize the creative work of successful and award-winning inventors, scientists and entrepreneurs. Based on their research, Senge et al. (2005) claim that the most successful creative workers are ones who are able to link in and draw from the present moment as a source of authentic inspiration. This brings us to our second proposition:

Proposition 2.2:   People are fully engaged when they are creatively present during their work performance.

Image II: *A researcher in a lab vs. people working in Dilbert-like cubicles*

Given the novelty of such creative presence though, individuals involved do not have a ready, pro forma behavior to cope with the situation. They do not have time to rely on rational reasoning; rather, they act instinctively, and in so doing rely on their gut feeling and intuition (Isaack, 1978; Dane and Pratt, 2007). This brings us to propose:

Proposition 2.3: Engaged individuals act out of their gut feeling and intuition rather than relying solely on rational (or calculative) reasoning.

Image III: *Expressing passion in action vs. relying on Excel spreadsheets as a justification for a decision*

A seeming paradox relates to the relationship between intensity vs. effortlessness characterizing high-engagement instances. Indeed, whilst engagement means being intensively focused on one's activity, in parallel engaged persons appear to act effortlessly. In a philosophical discourse, this would be close to a 'zen'-type attitude and presence. Hence, our next proposition:

Proposition 2.4: People are fully engaged when they are intensively focused on their activity whilst the performance appears seemingly effortless (to observers).

Image IV: *Ice skater doing difficult pirouettes (without falling)*

In summary, we concur with many of the prior researchers, extending their findings, that when highly engaged, individuals (1) are authentic, (2) are creatively present in the activity at stake, (3) act out of their gut feeling and intuition, (4) whilst, despite its intensity, their performance appears effortless. We note a similarity with findings on highly creative and innovative individuals (e.g., Senge et al., 2005). In light of the positive effect of high engagement on work performance, innovation and creativity, the above characteristics of high-engagement instances would seem to have desirable features for organizations seeking to thrive in a knowledge-based era geared toward innovation. We start to understand the corporate hype on engagement.

REACHING AND MAINTAINING HIGH DEGREES OF ENGAGEMENT

If high degrees of engagement are innovation-critical to the (post)modern organization, and further present the above-introduced characteristics, what can be done to enable and sustain high degrees of engagement over time? Further, are there limits to high engagement?

Based on our study of high engagement in five diverse settings, we see the maintenance of a high degree of engagement as essentially consisting of an inherent, creative tension between seeking extreme experiences, or 'edging', on the one hand and the need to savor the present moment through calming down, or 'retreating' on the other hand. We term this the 'dynamics of renewable engagement'. We claim that this dyadic tension is characteristic of engagement to the extent that neither full 'edging', nor continuous 'retreating', by themselves, are enough to sustain high degrees of engagement in the long term. Instead, the maintenance and rhythm of this dynamic tension enables one to sustain a high level of engagement over time. Engagement, as a psychological state of mind, is strongly linked with the person's (best) self (Kahn, 1990) as well as intensive presencing in the moment (Schaufeli et al., 2002). Hence, we are reminded of the fragility of engagement at any moment in time. This is why a too strong focus on either edging or retreating can offset this balance. We propose:

Proposition 3.1:   Engagement is a fragile state of mind renewed over time by an ongoing movement between experiences of 'edging' on the one hand and 'retreating' on the other hand.

Engaging by 'Edging'

Our findings provided support for the argument that high-engagement instances occur when individuals experience an 'on the edge' situation. Here, we borrow the metaphor 'on the edge' from chaos and complexity theory (see, e.g., Brown and Eisenhardt, 1998; Stacey, 2001), where the term refers to a boundary state, situated at the point of transfer as a system moves from a stable to a fully chaotic state. Chaos and complexity theorists argue that natural systems have been found to reorganize and self-organize when faced with a close-to-chaos state, that is, 'being on the edge' (see, e.g., Prigogine and Nicolis, 1977; Burgelman, 1991).

Meaning as a means to edge
Our findings suggest that high engagement occurs when one's work, task or activity bears meaning toward others. High engagement activities might

be created in isolation, but their longer-term objective is often concerned with a larger-scale impact. Here, we can draw from examples of many a scientist, entrepreneur, executive, or artist who wishes to make a long-lasting (though occasionally highly traumatic or detrimental) impact on the world. Human history has been populated by these figures, famed in world history books, namely Napoleon, Churchill, or Mao Tse Tung. In our sample of high-engagement studies, edging experiences referred to individuals who were highly engaged because they had a meaningful work or mission to accomplish (Rikkinen, 2010). Our highly engaged professionals saw their work as sustained by a mission to help others, create and improve, bring forth concrete results, make things visible (ibid.). Our younger-generation Finnish and Chinese interviewees experienced high engagement when occupied with a meaningful or inspiring activity (Yang, 2010).

This finding underlines the significance of meaningfulness (Vecchio, 1980; Baumeister, 1991; Pratt and Ashforth, 2003) to high-engagement activities. It further echoes prior findings on aspiration and inspiration as drawn from a 'higher' source, a deeper value, a more intense commitment. Already, Maslow (1954), in his classic pyramid of fundamental human needs, highlighted the growing need for self-expression in (post)industrialized societies. Seen thus, engagement could be the natural longing of the (post)modern individual, whose more basic needs (ibid.), have already been met. Zohar and Marshall (2001) call this 'spiritual intelligence'; they argue that in the developed world the Maslow pyramid should be reversed, given that the prevailing most fundamental need has become that of self-expression.

Survival as a means to edge
We further find that people are fully engaged when they are involved in something of utter urgency or importance, such as survival or a competitive victory. At the extreme, people in war zones can be regarded as being 'engaged' owing to the high stakes at play. Research and development teams in our case company noted that the prerequisite for a highly engaging work experience was a mission impossible so challenging that it forced the team members to stretch. Interviewees reported that high engagement occurred in instances of (team) survival threatened by a particularly demanding project at the brink of failure. Thus, experiences of potential failure were also significant as building conditions for team engagement. Further, these interviewees noted that highly engaging work experiences were identified when a team member was experiencing a significant shift in his or her personal life (see, e.g., Carlsen, 2006), thus described as being more open toward novel try-outs and creative solutions. High engagement

further took place during a performance requiring a high degree of alertness and vigilance, such as training, acting, or teaching.

Insights as a means to edge
Third, instances that allow for novel insights to emerge provided experiences of edging. In our study of engagement across physical space, it was noted that engagement levels peaked in times of travel, movement becoming the key stimulant (not entering a particular place as thought in the beginning of the study, or being stationary) (Lönngren, 2010). The Chinese younger generation, in their interviews, mentioned traveling to a new country as an experience of high engagement. Likewise, good books, museums and movies that spark our inspiration were identified as means for reaching (or preparatory antecedents for) high levels of engagement (Yang, 2010).

***

What these perhaps evident moments of 'meaning', 'survival' and 'insights' have in common is a need to be 'open to the opportunity'. These examples of high engagement share the idea of having to be fully alert, vigilant, present in the moment owing to the inspirational nature of the task (e.g., meaningful work, interesting book, movie or museum visit), the intensity of task (e.g., survival, or acting), or the novelty of the task (e.g., travel to a new country). In essence, experiences of high engagement would seem to exhibit a characteristic of being in a 'non-space', that is, a space in between, that we term being 'on the edge', or 'edging'. A non-space experience occurs, for example, as one stretches toward an impossible goal or travels to a new country, as we move beyond our habitual daily practices, routines and boundaries toward unknown, novel, untraveled territory.

In such instances, using the metaphors of chaos and complexity theory (e.g., Stacey, 2001), we are 'at the edge of chaos'. Systems, when confronted with extreme situations in which everyday rules do not work have been found to self-organize and emerge into new, improved, or at least different forms (ref. to Prigogine's Nobel-winning work on dissipative structures in the field of chemistry, 1977). Such rewriting of the rules presumably requires total system engagement. In human organizations, a similar example is shown in Weick's (1993) analysis of fire-fighters in the midst of a disastrous fire where the firemen dropped their tools, and hence their identities, and sought escape (though many perished).

Just like natural systems have been found to self-organize at the edge of chaos (Stacey, 2001), we find that individuals' engagement levels peak in these moments of 'edging'. As individuals self-organize, they find a likely creative, a more adapted solution to the context at hand. We see this 'edging' moment as a ritual transfer from one static, known state toward a currently unknown state. As long as the future state remains unknown, one remains highly engaged. In essence, these situations require high degrees of cognitive, emotional and physical vigilance. We can make a metaphorical link to wild animals in the tropical forest or savannah, hunting for game. A lion engaged in hunting is 'highly engaged' as long as the hunt still continues, that is, the kill is not yet foretold.

In his seminal work on engagement, Kahn (1990) defines engagement as the extent to which an individual is fully him- or herself in the work role he or she is performing, that is, the extent to which one portrays one's authentic self (Harter, 2002) to the situation at hand. While for Kahn this is a definitional matter, an essence of engagement, for us authenticity occurs and is awakened when 'edging', which, as a highly demanding state between the known and the unknown, cannot be sustained by means that do not reflect one's innermost capabilities and natural inclinations (so-called 'best self'). We bring authenticity forth here as a prerequisite to high-engagement instances. Authenticity is critical for high engagement to occur, because of the travel between the known and the unknown, and the novel context that a high-engagement experience represents. Owing to the ensuing stress and vigilance required to thrive in such a situation, one can attempt survival by relying on what comes naturally and effortlessly. In other words, the novelty of the high-engagement, 'edging' situation cannot afford the usual defenses and thus forces the everyday habitual masks off, inviting the mere person, or the authentic self, to emerge. Of course, this nakedness may not always suffice, and in such demanding situations a failure may be just as likely as success (March, 1991).

In sum, we posit that high engagement occurs in contexts, situations, or instances that are experienced as 'on the edge' for the individual in question. Such contexts force the individual to remove their non-authentic masks, become their authentic selves in the situation as well as to self-organize to find the solution likely fitted for that context. In formal terms, this brings us to propose:

Proposition 3.2: 'Edging', the experience of being in a boundary state, is a prerequisite for an experience of high engagement, as it forces the individual(s) involved to exhibit their authentic selves and to self-organize to find the solution likely fitted to that situation.

Engaging by Retreating

Given the high-presence, high-intensity nature of engagement experiences, our findings bring forth the significance of 'retreating' as a means of maintaining healthy and sustainable engagement on a long-term basis. This parallels recent work in the literature on engagement, where the significance of recovery has been brought to attention (Sonnentag, 2003). Extant research on well-being at work has highlighted the significance of vacations and periods of rest as helping to reduce stress (e.g., Westman and Etzion, 2001) and to increase life satisfaction (Lounsbury and Hoopes, 1986). As the effect of vacations has been found to dissolve soon after return to work (Westman and Eden, 1997), Sonnentag (2003) argues that day-level recovery is also critical to the maintenance of work engagement on a daily basis. Sonnentag et al. (2010) further find that psychological detachment from work during off-time is an important factor protecting employee well-being.

Our findings support and extend this exciting literature. Our findings lead us to argue for a mature, yet complex, conceptualization of engagement; interviewees acknowledged a need to nurture their levels of engagement by ensuring retreats, relaxing and recovering following periods of high, intensive engagement. Our sample of highly engaged interviewees confirmed that recovery, be it in the form of daily breaks, yearly holidays, or detaching from work, is significant with regard to maintaining a high level of engagement (Rikkinen, 2010). Our interviews and ongoing ethnographic work in a high-tech global organization's research and development department provide a constant reminder of the need to wind down, of the impossibility of being constantly highly engaged, and sustaining high levels of energy, concentration, or presencing. Our empirical work on the design of work spaces (Lönngren, 2010) points to the need for environments of retreat at the workplace and outside the workplace to counter the intensity of modern work. It would appear that retreating is a necessity if one is to seek engagement in the long term instead of burning out. We propose:

Proposition 3.3: 'Retreating' enables the maintenance of renewable and healthy engagement on a long-term basis through occasional rhythmic withdrawal and detachment from work.

Intriguingly, we find retreat instances to hold a dual role. Not only do they enable retreats from the intensity of high engagement, but they also enable high engagement moments to occur whilst one is 'on retreat'. Interviewees also experienced high-engagement moments when being on an apparent retreat from daily work, for example, walking in a forest, relaxing after gym, or when being in places where they perform physical activities, for example, at the swimming pool. These experiences provided a sense of detachment from daily issues. This was considered important as a means of maintaining an active interest in one's work. Also, such instances opened up immersive and perhaps breakthrough thought patterns. This finding might explain why Sonnentag et al. (2010) did not find a direct link between psychological detachment and engagement; this relationship has more complexity to it than the present literature attests.

This surprising finding relates to work in systems thinking, wherein Senge et al. (2005), echoed in Scharmer (2007), coined the notion of 'presencing' as qualifying those instances of stillness that characterize the creative heed of successful and award-winning inventors, scientists and entrepreneurs. Based on their research, Senge et al. (2005) claim that the most successful creative workers are ones who are able to link in and draw from the present moment as a source of deep inspiration. Here, we see that retreats offer an occasion for engaged individuals to move away from the hectic routines of daily life, thereby offering an opportunity for 'presencing' (ibid.), exploring the momentary, being mindful (Weick and Sutcliffe, 2006), drawing from one's intuition (Isaack, 1978; Dane and Pratt, 2007), and in so doing, being creative. This brings us to propose:

Proposition 3.4: 'Retreating' provides opportunities for presencing, for drawing from the moment to reach creative insights.

In summary, if organizations wish to find ways of engaging their employees in the pursuit of better and more innovative work outcomes, the present findings remind us of the fragile nature of engagement. High degrees of engagement, according to our findings, can only be maintained when individuals are able to fluctuate between (1) states of 'edging' on the one hand, and (2) states of 'retreating' on the other. Whilst too much edging can lead to overload, or at worst burnout, too much retreating has the potential of lowering one's degree of engagement. We thus argue that for high degrees of engagement to be maintained on a renewable basis, individuals need to consider what is the rhythmic balance that he or she needs as regards edging vs. retreating to sustain her or his level of engagement. Only by respecting this dyadic nature of high engagement can a long-term flow of positive, creative outcomes be expected.

SPACES THAT ENABLE HIGH ENGAGEMENT

In this section, we focus on a spatial perspective to enabling high engagement. Our findings lead us to argue that for high degrees of engagement to be sustainably nurtured over time, the physical, social and personal contexts in which individuals find themselves on a daily basis matter. For this purpose, we posit that high engagement emerges from an ongoing, continuous co-creation between the individual and the physical environment on the one hand, and the individual and the social environment on the other hand. We term these: (1) the physical space, (2) the socio-emotional space, and (3) the personal space enabling engagement.

Engaging Physical Spaces

Rather intriguingly, the influence of the physical work environment on creativity and innovation has to date received relatively little emphasis (Moultrie et al., 2007), whilst research effort has accrued on developing a creative and innovative atmosphere (Steiner, 2006), or the productivity effects of physical spaces (Becker, 2004; Haynes, 2008). Moreover, empirical studies of physical work environments have received little attention in extant engagement literature, though frameworks for such studies have been developed (Moultrie et al., 2007) and prevail in architecture. A consulting report on workplaces confirms that leading organizations do use high-quality physical environments combined with a supportive management culture to generate high degrees of engagement (Gensler, 2008).

Our study on the effect of physical office space on the ensuing levels of engagement for creative workers (Lönngren, 2010) found renewed evidence for a link between physical space and high engagement. We hence agree that physical space needs to be considered as a critical external factor affecting engagement. Interviewees saw that uniform environments (long, straight corridors, standardized elements, 'one size fits all'-type office environments), commonly used as work spaces, were perceived to decrease possibilities for creative activity. This reflects extant work, where uniform office environments have been found to have little positive effect on creativity and innovation, as they tend to support a focus on single activities instead of a variety of activities (Haner, 2005). The use of uniform environments has further been found to have negative effects on well-being, creativity and productivity (Ehlers et al., 2004). Interviewees saw that there was a need for diversity, hybridity in the use of office space, that is, different types of spaces of work are required (cf. Jacobs, 1961).

Interestingly, there was variance in the importance that the interviewees placed on the impact of physical space on engagement. Whilst some considered it to be of primary importance, for others it was a secondary matter. For the former, the environment tended to be perceived as a form of expression of their personal selves, as the following quote exemplifies: 'ideally, the physical environment should express my personality, just as my clothing does'. In connection with Kahn's (1990) definition of engagement as harnessing oneself fully to one's role, it would seem that the extent to which the physical space is considered a part of the continuum of one's authentic, full self, differs from one person to another. The intriguing finding here is that the way of defining, feeling and expressing one's authentic self does reach out to the physical space, though more for some than for others.

Further, the interviewees agreed that there is a need to better adapt environments according to the type of work, processes, people, and their values. In essence, there would appear to be a need to design workplaces that cater for varying purposes: meeting points, retreats, intense work, teamwork spaces and open office spaces (Lönngren, 2010). Work spaces should also allow for customization of individual expression, instead of seeking uniformity.

Interestingly, most interviewees described the environments that they perceive as most engaging as being situated outside of the day-to-day office environments. Hence, meetings in public spaces such as cafés were provided as examples of highly engaging work contexts. These contexts provided the interviewees a sense of movement and freedom that did not normatively force them to work, but instead invited them to do so. The incentive to voluntarily choose the space in which to engage seems to be shared by the interviewees. In formal terms, this leads us to propose:

Proposition 4.1:   High engagement depends on surrounding and changing physical spaces and the ability to habit off-work environments in ways that vary between individuals in nature and requirements.

Engaging Socio-emotional Spaces

What are the characteristics of the socio-emotional space that enable engagement? Our findings sustain the argument that engagement is continuously co-created in one's daily work- and non-work-related interactions. Engagement appears to be an activity that is highly sensitive to other people's reactions and behaviors: emphatically it is an interplay between the individual and the collective. First, our work on office spaces enabling engagement pointed to the fact that physical office spaces geared toward and enabling social, informal interaction are critical (Lönngren, 2010). Second, in our study of the younger generation's engagement patterns in Finland and China (Yang, 2010), high engagement was defined by interviewees as having both an individual and interpersonal component, leading one to argue that engagement occurs in interaction, not solely through solitary activity. More specifically, we found that high engagement is best enabled via rewarding social interactions and being acknowledged for one's work. On the contrary, negative or no feedback was seen as an engagement 'killer', as were unpleasant interactions (ibid.). Third, in our study of highly engaged professionals (Rikkinen, 2010), interactions with colleagues, managers as well as important individuals in one's life were found to be significant. Colleagues with whom one shared a sense of similarity perceived easiness in mutual interactions, and with whom interactions were characterized by feedback, encouragement and appreciation helped gear an individual toward higher levels of engagement. Managers who provide correcting and repairing feedback, help employees to be at ease at work, behave consistently, trust and believe in employees' capabilities, and stop corporate misbehavior, were found to support engagement (ibid.). Similarly, in our study of a research and development unit, we found that respectful, open and trusting managerial behaviors positively affected employee engagement.

In sum, these findings lead us to concur that engagement is continuously co-created in one's work- and non-work interactions. This finding is aligned with existing engagement literature. Kahn (1990) found that engagement occurs as a result of personal, interpersonal and organizational factors. In formal terms, this leads us to propose:

Proposition 4.2: Engagement is a shared state of mind that is co-created on an ongoing basis through one's work- and non-work related social interactions.

Positive and rewarding interactions enable engagement

What the studied experiences of high engagement share is that they have occurred in instances where there has been a social space that has supported rather than distracted or destroyed the emergence of high engagement. We see hence that for high engagement to occur, in addition to the use of supportive work- and non-work-related physical spaces, there needs to be a social/emotional space that is conducive to one's being one's authentic self, that is, conducive to personal opening and presence in the moment. Indeed, the role of emotional space has been found to be a critical factor behind successful high-performance teams (Losada, 1999; Losada and Heaphy, 2004).

The reason why a supportive emotional/social space is critical for high engagement to occur can be traced back to the fragility of the high-engagement instance occurring 'on the edge' that we discussed earlier. Think of suggesting radical, perhaps even highly personal and dear ideas to a group of peers, whose first reaction may be: 'It won't work. It is a (more or less) stupid idea'. This common innovation workshop experience regularly kills engagement. The fragile, often painful insight bears cognitive, emotional and physical intensity, and also risk in terms of outcome and exposure. The degree of intensity and exposure involved in a high engagement instance requires a supportive emotional context. Indeed, one would not wish to be in a state of risky 'self-organizing', without emotional support from one's family, friends and colleagues. People talking about 'being in a particular space' is descriptive of this spatial need. This brings us to propose:

Proposition 4.3: The high-engagement moment, a fragile, fleeting, exposed, authentic, risky and intense experience, is enabled, sustained, nurtured and developed by a supportive, positive and rewarding socio-emotional space.

Serendipitous element in co-creation enables engagement

Our findings further lead us to argue that there is an inherent serendipity element in co-creation that enables engagement. All of our empirical studies brought support for the finding that accidental and sporadic meetings bear significance for high engagement to occur and for engagement to be sustained long term. This finding relates to the importance of serendipity (e.g., Cohen et al., 1996; Becker, 2004). We find that random encounters withhold surprising potential to occasion inspiration, and in so doing enable high engagement:

Proposition 4.4: High engagement experiences are enabled serendipitously by accidental sporadic co-creation encounters.

Further, our findings pointed to so-called 'important individuals' in enabling and sustaining engagement; these individuals might come from one's family, be highly valued by the individual, or emerge from random encounters – persons whose role is to sustain the individual's engagement. Such relationships were captured by the highly engaged interviewees we met (Rikkinen, 2010). In our study of the research and development engineers we found that these important individuals might also be senior managers acting as role models for the younger engineers. In formal terms, this brings us to propose:

Proposition 4.5: Sustainable, lasting engagement benefits from 'significant others', that is, the supportive presence of individuals who are important to the person in question.

Engaging Personal Spaces

In addition to being affected by the surrounding physical and socio-emotional spaces, we find that high degrees of engagement are sustained when the individual has enough 'personal' space. We posit that this relates to having (1) the sufficient degree of autonomy, as well as (2) identified a meaningful life mission that guides one's actions.

Autonomy enables engagement

Research on employee autonomy, involvement and empowerment at work finds that the degree to which employees are allowed to involve themselves in the activity being performed impacts their willingness to engage in performing this activity well. Here, we do not refer to the civic empowerment literature (Putnam, 1995), but to the more recent employee empowerment literature (Conger and Kanungo, 1998). The focus of this research stream has been on studying the impacts of empowerment on individuals and the organizational consequences of empowerment as regards, for example, creativity, flexibility and performance (Feldman and Khademian, 2003). We argue that given the positive individual and organizational benefits of empowerment, employees are likely to become engaged in their work, if and when they are involved in it. One of our field studies concerned the engagement of blue-collar workers, who were found to be most engaged when provided with autonomy in their work (Paananen, 2010). We posit:

Proposition 4.6:   Engagement benefits from individuals empowered by involvement in work-related decisions and working autonomously on their task.

The reason why autonomy turns out to be as critical to engagement would seem to be linked to the fact that when working independently on a task individuals are allowed to create the immersive 'space' that they need for completing that particular task. This 'space' is not predetermined by the organization or by one's supervisor. As renewable, sustainable engagement is about maintaining a balance between edging and retreating, then autonomy would seem to be a means of creating the individual space at work that enables the person to find his or her way for edging and retreating. This autonomous, self-created space seems to emerge as critical for high-engagement instances to occur, as the latter requires high degrees of openness to presencing, to exploring the opportunities in the moment. As an example, let us consider the work of writers – they tend to work in a solitary mode, for example, from home or a far-away location. As the work of writers is highly dependent on their creative mind, writers tend to nurture this need by creating an autonomous space around them that allows them to draw from their personal sources of inspiration. We propose:

Proposition 4.7: When working creatively, individuals need to possess the immersive space they require to best organize for and complete their work task.

Meaningful life mission
A defining characteristic of engaged individuals would appear to be that they have made a conscious choice and have reasoned with regard to their purpose in life. In essence, what they do bears meaning. This links in with an ongoing debate about the meaning of work (Vecchio, 1980), the meaning of life (Baumeister, 1991) and meaningfulness in work and at work (e.g., Pratt and Ashforth, 2003). The seminal work of Kelman (1958) studied attitude change. Three distinct ways of accepting external influence, resulting in attitude change, were identified: (1) compliance to gain a favorable reaction from a social group, (2) identification to gain a means to define oneself through this group, and (3) internalization, as the outcome is considered intrinsically rewarding and fits the individual's value base. A later study (O'Reilly and Chatman, 1986) found that this categorization predicts one's degree of psychological attachment (and commitment) to an organization. Moreover, when attachment was based on identification and internalization, individuals exhibited a greater degree of pro-social behaviors and a far lesser intent to leave the organization. A recent orientation is the link between positive psychology and the meaning of work. Here, Bellah et al. (1985) identify three dominant orientations to work, these being (1) work as a job, (2) work as a career, and (3) work as calling. The way we see engaged individuals at work comes close to the notion of 'work as calling', where work is not an end in itself, but associated with the idea that by working one contributes to a greater good and to the improvement of the world. In her review, Wrzesniewski (2003) shows that a calling orientation toward work is related with a higher workload, high job satisfaction, and results in top-performing individuals. This leads us to posit:

Proposition 4.8: Engaged individuals have identified a meaningful life mission they are actively fulfilling (in part) through their work.

***

In summary, our findings lead us to posit that for high degrees of engagement to emerge and be sustained over time, the physical, socio-emotional and personal spaces that individuals are surrounded by, matter. In essence, high degrees of engagement are being co-created on an ongoing basis in the interactions between one's personal space and the surrounding physical and socio-emotional spaces.

As regards physical spaces, non-uniform office environments and non-work-related physical spaces (e.g., cafés, laboratories, museums, travel to foreign countries, etc.) were experienced as particularly conducive to high engagement. Socio-emotional spaces that (1) exhibited positive and rewarding characteristics, (2) allowed for sporadic and serendipitous encounters, and (3) included 'significant' mentors and others, were experienced as particularly conducive to high degrees of engagement. At an individual level, personal spaces that allow the rhythmic balancing of edging and retreating and that can be characterized by (1) autonomy, and (2) a meaningful life mission, were experienced as offering individuals the opportunity to engage. These are the enablers of high engagement that organizations need to consider if they wish to develop into high-engagement, high-innovation organizations.

WHERE IS THE 'ENGAGED' ORGANIZATION? FOUR SCENARIOS

In this section, we move onto proposing a conceptual framework that allows for organizations to judge what their current engagement capability is, and subsequently, which engagement scenario they are presently enacting. Our findings lead us to argue that both individual- and organizational-level capabilities are required. These two capability types are present, to different degrees, in the four engagement scenarios we propose. We further argue that each scenario can be related to the organization's innovation outcomes.

By focusing on the individual and organizational components of an engagement capability, we follow the Abell et al. (2008) approach to social science explanations (see p. 491), where macro-level 'social facts and outcomes' are juxtaposed with micro-level 'conditions of individual action' and the actions themselves. Where these actions take place (i.e., the work space) also matters. We seek to connect these two levels based on our research observations to develop four scenarios that build engagement capability (or lack thereof). We thus seek to fill in the otherwise empty box of explanation (ibid., p. 494).

In Figure 3.3, we identify four alternative engagement scenarios depending on where the capability for engagement is located: at the individual and/or the organizational level. These scenarios draw our attention to the interplay between individual and collective in organizations – which comes first: the individual finding her or his engagement or the organization inviting it and/or supporting it? And (how) can management move the organization between these states?

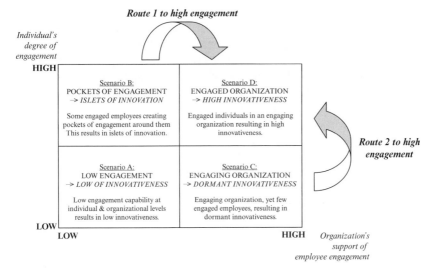

Figure 3.3   Scenarios of engagement for organizations

Scenario A: Low Engagement; Low Innovativeness

In the first scenario, the individual employees are to a large extent disengaged. Moreover, the practices, structures and culture of the employing organization do not support the engagement of its employees. This results at worst in robot-like organizations consisting of disengaged, apathetic employees. We argue that this scenario is likely to represent the situation in many a modern larger-sized organization today (as argued by Cartwright and Holmes, 2006). This scenario is the allegory of the bureaucratic, machine-like organization that treats its employees as mere resources or work tools without seeing that the employees have inner goals and a willpower of their own. In this example, there is a lacking capability to engage at both the level of individual employees as well as the organization at large. As a result, this organization type is not likely to be a strong performer innovation-wise.

Scenario B: Pockets of Engagement; Islets of Innovation

In this second scenario, some or many of the individual employees are engaged in their work roles, yet the employing organization has not yet realized its role in supporting its employees in this pursuit. As a result, engaged individuals either (1) exit the organization in due time, or (2) develop personal adaptation strategies to avoid being discouraged by the organization's lack of engagement support mechanisms. In so doing, they have potential to create atmospheres of positive organizational engagement in their immediate organizational vicinity that then, as positivity spirals, enthuse engagement in others (Wrzesniewski, 2003). 'Pockets' of engagement emerge within the organization. We claim that this scenario represents the present reality in many an organization facing turbulence, where some individual employees have become engaged by their own initiative, yet the organization has not yet awakened to the need for novel, emphatic managerial practices to support employee engagement. The capability to engage is strong at the level of individual employees, but weak at the level of the organization. The outcome innovation-wise is a set of islets of high innovation potential located in the vicinity of the pockets of high engagement.

Scenario C: Engaging Organization; Dormant Innovativeness

In this scenario the individual employee is not yet engaged. However, the employing organization is realizing its role in supporting its employees' engagement; it is seeking to actively engage its employee base. In so doing, it develops and nurtures an organizational-level engagement capability. In such an organization, employees have great potential to flourish and become engaged if they so wish, yet for some reason (perhaps due to cynicism stemming from prior poor management) the employees have not responded to the engagement call. The organization portrays dormant potential for future innovations, provided it can convey credibility and sincerity in its ways of supporting its employees' engagement journey.

Scenario D: Engaged Organization; High Innovativeness

In this scenario, high engagement occurs as both the individual is engaged and the employing organization supports his or her efforts. The microclimate effect (see scenario B) further enriches the existing organizational engagement efforts, as positive, contagious engagement spirals are created on a continuous basis. This results in increasingly flourishing individuals, who intuitively self-organize for creative outcomes. We wonder, where are the organizations that operate in this way? In this scenario, the capability to engage rests both at the level of the individual employee as well as at the level of the organization and its management. Engagement is constantly co-created in their interactions. Subsequently, high levels of innovativeness are to be expected.

Having presented these four scenarios, we now turn our attention to the alternative routes that organizations can undertake in order to reach the supposedly ideal scenario combining high engagement with high innova-tiveness. We identify two alternative routes:

First route

We term the first route 'revolution' through individual action and indi-vidual engagement. This refers to situations wherein high levels of engage-ment capability at the level of individual employees gradually radiate and transform toward higher levels of employee engagement across the organization. We claim that in quadrants B and D, that is, high engage-ment scenarios, engaged individuals radiate enthusiasm into their immedi-ate surroundings, thereby increasing the performance of the workplace, potentially indirectly causing an engagement-supportive microclimate in the entire organization. Hence, larger organizations could be argued to consist of nests that are to different degrees implicitly engaged, depend-ing on the degrees of personal engagement amidst their leaders and key personnel. This mirrors earlier findings. In his work on high-performing teams, Losada (Losada, 1999; Losada and Heaphy, 2004) found that posi-tive interactions bore the greatest effect on the degree of member connec-tivity, and thus performance. Wrzesniewski (2003) draws attention to the 'transfer effects' of persons who have a 'work as calling' attitude toward the larger social group.

Second route

We term the second route 'revolution' through 'orchestrated action'. This refers to situations wherein high levels of engagement capability in the employing organization, when practiced over time, result in high degrees of employee engagement across the organization. Our suggestion is that rather than attempting to 'manage' or 'force-induce' engagement, manag-ers, through their understanding of the micro-level foundations of engage-ment, should learn to *invite* and enable engagement-supportive conditions. Our findings, discussed in the preceding sections, regarding the nature of engagement as a phenomenon and its spatial characteristics may provide an agenda for management innovation in this regard (Birkinshaw et al., 2008). In addition to developing dependence (addiction) or dominance (ideology), high engagement is voluntary and fragile. Clearly, if they are used wrongly or superficially, engagement encouragement efforts can con-tribute to employee cynicism.

***

In summary, if organizations are to develop a capability for high engage-ment they first need to start by identifying their current positioning on the engagement scenario map. Each engagement scenario relates to a predicted innovation outcome for the organization. Our conjecture is that individual and organizational engagement capabilities together and in interaction are required to create the most conducive context for innovativeness. Thus, as suggested, *management* innovation is also required to create the potential for edging and retreating for employees and for the whole organization. We further identify two alternative routes to high engagement, either through engaged individual action or through orchestrated organizational action.

DISCUSSION

In this chapter, our aim has been to explore employee engagement, a (post)modern source of human capital-based competitive advantage for firms competing in the knowledge era (Lynch, 2008). Based on an inductive, explorative approach using a theory-building research design in five distinct research settings (Glaser and Strauss, 1967; Eisenhardt, 1989), we presented findings based on our research on experiences of high engagement in these settings. We argue that our findings bear three types of implications for research and practice. First, they offer a means to discover the role of the individual employee as a driver and locus of innovative work. Second, they allow the identification of the types of organizational routines required to enable employee engagement in a knowledge-based era, defining an aspirational agenda for management innovation. Third, they call for management innovation if organizations are to take engagement and innovation seriously.

An Actor-based View on Innovation

Despite the significance and centrality of innovation to the modern corporation, we note a seeming lack of attention to the individual employee engaged in innovative work (Scott and Bruce, 1994; Gupta et al., 2007; Birkinshaw et al., 2008). In other words, there is much written and known about innovation itself, yet seemingly less so on the actors involved in this endeavor (beyond common hero stories of lone innovators working against all odds).

The present findings offer one lens to approach the individual actor engaged in innovative activity in an organizational context. Throughout this chapter we explored the notion of 'employee engagement', and focused more particularly on 'high engagement' as an antecedent to innovativeness. The premise underlying our argument was the significance of a person to an organization's innovation performance. Whilst the academic discourse has been less vocal with regard to the individual's role vis-à-vis innovativeness, in parallel there has been a rising interest in the practitioner world toward the notion of 'employee engagement'. Based on our empirical findings, we argue that the concept of 'employee engagement' – once shed from its instrumental notion of an employee as a mere resource or tool – has potential to bring forth an actor-based perspective to the literature on innovation. We thus posit employee engagement as one lens to approach the individual or micro-dimensions in innovative work.

We find that when people are highly engaged, their work outcomes tend to exhibit higher degrees of creativity, quality, commitment and contagious enthusiasm. In essence, it would seem that securing a strong degree of engagement in today's workforce is critical if organizations are to aim for creative outcomes and an innovative outlook.

We posit that when highly engaged, individuals are authentic, creatively present and rely on their intuition, all this in an intensive yet seemingly effortless way. We note that the causal direction is likely to be both ways: whereas engagement both requires and leads to authenticity and innovation, innovation likely also leads to engagement. However, given the intensity of the experience, for high degrees of engagement to be sustained over time, individuals need to learn to effectively balance between (1) states of 'edging' and (2) states of 'retreating'. The high engagement experience is enabled by immersive and inviting physical, socio-emotional and personal spaces. In essence, high degrees of engagement are being co-created on an ongoing basis in the interactions between one's personal space and the surrounding physical and socio-emotional spaces. In particular, we highlight the significance of (1) non-uniform office environments and non-work-related physical spaces, (2) positive socio-emotional spaces that also allow for sporadic, serendipitous encounters and (3) personal spaces characterized by their immersive availability, autonomy and a meaningful life mission.

Finally, we identified a set of four scenarios that distinguish an organization's positioning with regard to employee engagement. It is expected that an organization, in which the workforce is engaged, and which itself exhibits engaging characteristics, is likely to exhibit higher degrees of innovativeness. In order to further develop their engagement capability, organizations need to secure the latter at both individual and organizational levels. This is also the opportunity and challenge for management innovation. Only then can the organization expect a truly innovative culture to develop, notwithstanding a likely rise in its innovative performance.

A Dynamic Perspective to Organizational Routines

Assuming that employee engagement is a capability that modern organizations seek in order to enhance their innovativeness, what kinds of routines are required to enable engagement? Our findings show that engagement-enabling organizational routines are dynamic and active, as they relate to creating 'on the edge' situations whilst allowing for retreat, and as they are co-created on an ongoing basis with one's physical, socio-emotional and personal environments.

Such a perspective diverts from the habitual usage of the term 'routines' that tends to refer to routines as 'patterns' of action at either the individual or collective levels (Becker, 2004; Felin and Foss, 2009), or to seeing routines as 99 percent of what an organization does, whereas the interesting 1 percent are the exceptions that managers really spend their time on (Felin and Foss, 2009). Further, existing research has been criticized for lacking an ability to explain *how* routines are created and *where* they come from (see discussion in Felin and Foss, 2009, p.163). In this respect, we argue that our findings bring forth a novel perspective to organizational routines and capabilities in that they offer micro-level insights into the ways in which routines and capabilities emerge in organizations.

Our findings show an agent- and interpersonal interaction-based view to routines that, moreover, is rhythmic and active. We see that, to be successful in an innovation-geared era, organizations need to develop capabilities to engage their employees. Such a task is supported by dynamic, micro-level routines. These routines refer to engagement-enabling physical spaces at work and outside work, interpersonal interactions, sporadic interactions, autonomy, meaningful work, retreating and opportunities to 'edge'. Such routines are intriguing, because by enabling engagement, they de facto help gear an organization toward higher levels of self-organization and renewal, and thus, potentially higher levels of creativity and innovativeness.

This view of routines diverts from the prevailing view, and actually makes routines closer to what Felin and Foss (2009) called 'exceptions' (rather than 'routines'). We see that such routines represent a critical component of the future organization's engagement capability. Indeed, if organizations are faced with ongoing change and turbulence, it can be argued that tomorrow's routines should be dynamic, emergent, active and evolving instead of being static and non-amenable to change. We see that the rhythmic pattern of work between intense concentration and loose detachment becomes critical. We argue that organizations can thrive amidst turbulence, if they take a micro-level interactional approach to routines, this making routines active, dynamic and evolving.

By enabling employee engagement, these routines likely allow for creative organizational outcomes to emerge. We argue that such a stance is critical if one is to enable high engagement in today's organizations. We see engagement, enabled by dynamic and active micro-level routines, as having the potential to become the organizational capability of the future that enables organizations to naturally surf and co-create on the creative edge. We see that the concept of engagement, by taking the person as an active agent shaping his or her environment to center stage, offers opportunities to explore the co-evolutionary dynamics of organizations, in particular, in the holistic renewal of the organization (Volberda and Lewin, 2003). We suggest high employee engagement, and its related passion for work, to be constitutive of all innovation capabilities.

Finally, we suggest that managerial innovation is needed to develop managerial practices that can answer the call of engagement in its motivational, spatial and rhythmic characteristics, combining individual aspects with organizational complements. The trade-off between individual enthusiasm and organizational efficiency is long past its prime. The growing literature on ambidexterity has acknowledged the issue (e.g., Raisch et al., 2009), yet is still short of a solution. The tension between exploitation and exploration in many organizations remains acute (March, 1991) and invites specific management innovation (Hamel, 2006) to enable the renewable dynamics of high engagement as described in this chapter. This quest for management innovation, in our view, must start from an actor perspective to innovation, then travel the first or the second route to sustaining high-engagement organizational capabilities (see Figure 3.3).

CONCLUSION

Based on our research on high-engagement experiences across professions, generations and work spaces, we develop propositions and a model on the dynamics of employee engagement in the organizational context. Our findings suggest that for high degrees of engagement to be maintained renewably over time, there needs to be a balance between 'edging' and 'retreating' instances on the one hand, and supportive physical, socio-emotional and personal spaces on other. We see that our findings bring forth an actor-based perspective to innovation, in addition to proposing a rhythmic micro-level perspective to organizational routines. We call for managerial innovation for this view to become rooted in the modern organizational practice.

NOTE

1. Based on personal communications with a number of HR professionals in large multi-national corporations. Similar findings are also reflected in the Towers Perrin's (today Towers Watson) report on employee engagement (2008).

REFERENCES

Abell, P., T. Felin and N. Foss (2008), 'Building micro-foundations for the routines, capabilities, and performance links', *Managerial and Decision Economics*, **29**(6), 489–502.
Alderfer, C.P. (1972), *Human Needs in Organizational Settings*, New York: Free Press.
Alvesson, M. and D. Kärreman (2007), 'Constructing mystery: empirical matters in theory development', *Academy of Management Review*, **32**(4), 1265–81.
Amabile, T.M. (1983), *The Social Psychology of Creativity*, New York: Springer-Verlag.
Ansoff, A. and P. McDonnell (1990), *Implanting Strategic Management*, New York: Prentice-Hall.
Bakker, A.B. and E. Demerouti (2007), 'The job demands-resources model: state of the art', *Journal of Managerial Psychology*, **22**(3), 309–28.
Bakker, A.B., E. Demerouti and W.B. Schaufeli (2005), 'The crossover of burnout and work engagement among working couples', *Human Relations*, **58**(5), 661–89.
Bakker, A.B., H. Van Emmerik and M.C. Euwema (2006), 'The crossover of burnout and engagement in work teams', *Work and Occupations*, **33**(4), 464–89.
Bakker, A.B., E. Demerouti, E. De Boer and W.B. Schaufeli (2003), 'Job demands and job resources as predictors of absence duration and frequency', *Journal of Vocational Behavior*, **62**(2), 341–56.
Bartlett, C.A. and S. Ghoshal (1998), *Managing Across Borders: The Transnational Solution*, New York: Random House.
Baumeister, R.F. (1991), *Meanings of Life*, New York: Guilford.
Baxter, B. (1982), *Alienation and Authenticity*, London: Tavistock.
Becker, F.D. (2004), *Offices at Work: Uncommon Workplace Strategies That Add Value and Improve Performance*, San Francisco: Jossey-Bass.
Becker, M. (2004), 'Organizational routines: a review of the literature', *Industrial and Corporate Change*, **13**(4), 643–77.
Bellah, R.N., R. Madsen, W.M. Sullivan, A. Swidler and S.M. Tipton (1985), *Habits of the Heart: Individualism and Commitment in American Life*, New York: Harper & Row.
Bibby, R.W. (2001), *Canada's Teens: Today, Yesterday and Tomorrow*, Toronto: Stoddart.
Birkinshaw, J., G. Hamel and M. Mol (2008), 'Management innovation', *Academy of Management Review*, **33**(4), 825–45.
Bjelland, O. and R. Wood (2008), 'An inside view of IBM's "Innovation Jam"', *MIT Sloan Management Review*, **50**(1), 32–40.
Boden, M. (2003), *The Creative Mind: Myths and Mechanisms*, London: Routledge.
Boverie, P.E. and M. Kroth (2001), *Transforming Work: The Five Keys to Achieving Trust, Commitment and Passion in the Workplace*, Cambridge, MA: Perseus Books.
Britt, T.W., C.A. Castro and A.B. Adler (2005), 'Self-engagement, stressors, and health: a longitudinal study', *Personality and Social Psychology Bulletin*, **31**(11), 1475–86.
Brown, S. and K. Eisenhardt (1998), *Competing on the Edge: Strategy as Structured Chaos*, Boston, MA: Harvard Business School Press.
Brown, S.P. and T.W. Leigh (1996), 'A new look at psychological climate and its relationship to job involvement, effort and performance' *Journal of Applied Psychology*, **81**(4), 358–68.
Burgelman, R. (1991), 'Intraorganizational ecology of strategy making and organizational adaptation: theory and field research', *Organization Science*, **2**(3), 239–62.

Carlsen, A. (2006), 'Organizational becoming as dialogic imagination of practice: the case of the indomitable Gauls', *Organization Science*, **17**(1), 132–49.

Cartwright, S. and N. Holmes (2006), 'The meaning of work: the challenge of regaining employee engagement and reducing cynicism', *Human Resource Management Review*, **16**(2), 199–208.

Charmaz, K. (2000), 'Grounded theory: objectivist and constructivist methods', in N.K. Denzin, K. Norman and Y.S. Lincoln (eds), *Handbook of Qualitative Research* (2nd edition), Thousand Oaks, CA: Sage Publications, pp. 509–35.

Chesbrough, H. (2003), *Open Innovation: The New Imperative for Creating and Profiting from Technology*, Boston, MA: Harvard Business School Press.

Chesbrough, H. (2006), *Open Business Models: How to Thrive in the New Innovation Landscape*, Boston, MA: Harvard Business School Press.

Cohen, M., R. Burkhart, G. Dosi, M. Egidi, L. Marengo and M. Warglien (1996), 'Routines and other recurrent action patterns of organizations: contemporary research issues', *Industrial and Corporate Change*, **5**(3), 653–98.

Conger, J.A. (1994), 'Introduction: our search for spiritual community', in J.A. Conger (ed.), *Spirit at Work: Discovering the Spirituality in Leadership*, San Francisco: Jossey-Bass, pp. 1–18.

Conger, J.A. and R.N. Kanungo (1998), 'The empowerment process: integrating theory and practice', *Academy of Management Review*, **13**(3), 471–82.

Dane, E. and M.G. Pratt (2007), 'Exploring intuition and its role in managerial decision-making', *Academy of Management Review*, **32**(1), 33–54.

Davenport, T.H., R.J. Thomas and S. Cantrell (2002), 'The mysterious art and science of knowledge-worker performance', *MIT Sloan Management Review*, **44**(1), 23–30.

Demerouti, E., A.B. Bakker, F. Nachreiner and W.B. Schaufeli (2001), 'The job demands-resources model of burnout', *Journal of Applied Psychology*, **86**(3), 499–512.

Ehlers, I.L., A. Greisle, G. Hube, J. Kelter and A. Rieck (2004), 'Crucial influences on office performance', in D. Spath and P. Kern (eds), *Office 21 – Push the Future. Better Performance in Innovative Working Environments*, Cologne/Stuttgart; Egmont VGS, pp. 54–168.

Eisenhardt, K (1989), 'Building theories from case study research', *Academy of Management Review*, **14**(4), 532–50.

Feldman, M.S. and A.M. Khademian (2003), 'Empowerment and cascading vitality', in K.S. Cameron, J.E. Dutton and R.E. Quinn (eds), *Positive Organizational Scholarship*, San Francisco: Berrett-Koehler, pp. 343–58.

Felin, T. and N. Foss (2009), 'Organizational routines and capabilities: historical drift and a course-correction toward microfoundations', *Scandinavian Journal of Management*, **25**(2), 157–67.

Fleming, L. and D. Waguespack (2007), 'Brokerage, boundary spanning, and leadership in open innovation communities', *Organization Science*, **18**(2), 165–80.

Freud, S. (1922), *Beyond the Pleasure Principle*, London/Vienna: International Psycho-analytical Press.

Gensler (2008), *2008 Workplace Survey United Kingdom*.

Ghoshal, S. (2005), 'Bad management theories are destroying good management practices', *Academy of Management Learning*, **4**(1), 75–91.

Ghoshal, S. and S. Bartlett (1997), *The Individualized Corporation: A Fundamentally New Approach to Management*, New York: Harper Business.

Gilson, L.L. and C.E. Shalley (2004), 'A little creativity goes a long way: an examination of teams' engagement in creative processes', *Journal of Management*, **30**(4), 453–70.

Glaser, B.J. (1978), *Theoretical Sensitivity*, Mill Valley, CA: Sociology Press.

Glaser, B.J. (1992), *Basics of Grounded Theory Analysis: Emergence vs. Forcing*, Mill Valley, CA: Sociology Press.

Glaser, B.J. (1998), *Doing Grounded Theory: Issues vs. Discussions*, Mill Valley, CA: Sociology Press.

Glaser, B.J. (2001), *The Grounded Theory Perspective: Conceptualization Contrasted with Description*, Mill Valley, CA; Sociology Press.

Glaser, B.J. and A.L. Strauss (1967), *The Discovery of Grounded Theory*, Chicago: Aldine Publishing Company.

Goffman, E. (1961), *Encounters: Two Studies in the Sociology of Interaction*, Indianapolis: Bobbs-Merrill Co.

González-Romá, V., W. Schaufeli, A. Bakker and S. Lloret (2006), 'Burnout and work engagement: independent factors or opposite poles?', *Journal of Vocational Behavior*, **68**(1), 165–74.

Grant, A.M. (2008), 'Does intrinsic motivation fuel the prosocial fire? Motivational synergy in predicting persistence, performance, and productivity', *Journal of Applied Psychology*, **93**(1), 48–58.

Guevara, K. and J. Ord (1996), 'The search for meaning in a changing work context', *Futures*, **28**(8), 709–22.

Gupta, A.K., P.E. Tesluk and M.S. Taylor (2007), 'Innovation at and across multiple levels of analysis', *Organization Science*, **18**(6), 885–97.

Hakanen, J.J., A.B. Bakker and E. Demerouti (2005), 'How dentists cope with their job demands and stay engaged: the moderating role of job resources', *European Journal of Oral Sciences*, **113**(6), 479–87.

Hall, D.T. and D.E. Chandler (2005), 'Psychological success: when the career is a calling', *Journal of Organizational Behavior*, **26**(2), 155–76.

Hallberg, U.E. and W.B. Schaufeli (2006), '"Same, same", but different? Can work engagement be empirically separated from job involvement and organizational commitment?', *European Psychologist*, **11**(2), 119–27.

Hamel, G. (2006), 'Why, what and how of management innovation', *Harvard Business Review*, **84**(2), 72–84.

Hamel, G. (2007), *The Future of Management*, Boston, MA: Harvard Business School Press.

Handy, C. (1998), *The Hungry Spirit*, London: Arrow Books Ltd.

Haner, U.-E. (2005), 'Spaces for creativity and innovation in two established organizations', *Creativity and Innovation Management*, **14**(2), 88–298.

Harter, J.K., F.L. Schmidt and T.L. Hayes (2002), 'Business-unit-level relationship between employee satisfaction, employee engagement, and business outcomes: a meta-analysis', *Journal of Applied Psychology*, **87**(2), 268–79.

Harter, S. (2002), 'Authenticity', in C.R. Snyder and S.J. Lopez (eds), *Handbook of Positive Psychology*, Oxford: Oxford University Press, pp. 382–94.

Haynes, B.P. (2008), 'The impact of office layout on productivity', *Journal of Facilities Management*, **6**(3), 189–201.

Ilinitch, A., R. D'Aveni and A. Lewin (1996), 'New organizational forms and strategies for managing in hypercompetitive environments', *Organization Science*, **7**(3), 211–20.

Isaack, T. (1978), 'Intuition: an ignored dimension of management', *Academy of Management Review*, **3**(4), 917–22.

Isen, A.M., K.A. Daubman and G.P. Nowicki (1987), 'Positive affect facilitates creative problem solving', *Journal of Personality and Social Psychology*, **52**(6), 1122–31.

Jacobs, J. (1961), *The Death and Life of Great American Cities*, New York: Random House.

Jaworski, J. (2002), *Synchronicity – The Inner Path of Leadership*, San Francisco: Berrett-Koehler.

Kahn, W.A. (1990), 'Psychological conditions of personal engagement and disengagement at work', *Academy of Management Journal*, **33**(4), 692–724.

Kahn, W.A. (1992), 'To be fully there: psychological presence at work', *Human Relations*, **45**(4), 321–49.

Kelman, H.C. (1958), 'Compliance, identification, and internalization: three processes of attitude change', *Journal of Conflict Resolution*, **2**(1), 51–60.

Kirton, M.J. (1994), *Adaptors and Innovators: Styles of Creativity and Problem Solving* (2nd edition), New York: Routledge.

Koyuncu, M., R.J. Burke and L. Fiksenbaum (2006), 'Work engagement among women managers and professionals in a Turkish bank: potential antecedents and consequences', *Equal Opportunities International*, **25**(4), 299–310.

Little, B. and P. Little (2006), 'Employee engagement: conceptual issues', *Journal of Organizational Culture, Communication and Conflict*, **10**(1), 111–20.

Lönngren, M. (2010), '"Design Lab" – a place for engagement', Master's thesis, Aalto University School of Arts and Design, Helsinki.

Losada, M. (1999), 'The complex dynamics of high performance teams', *Mathematical and Computer Modelling*, **30**(9–10), 179–92.

Losada, M. and E. Heaphy (2004), 'The role of positivity and connectivity in the performance of business teams', *American Behavioral Scientist*, **47**(6), 740–65.

Lounsbury, J.W. and L.L. Hoopes (1986), 'A vacation from work: chances in work and non-work outcomes', *Journal of Applied Psychology*, **71**(3), 392–401.

Lynch, R. (2008), *Strategic Management* (5th edition), Harlow/London: Financial Times/Prentice Hall.

Macey, W.H. and B. Schneider (2008a), 'The meaning of employee engagement', *Industrial and Organizational Psychology*, **1**(1), 3–30.

Macey, W.H. and B. Schneider (2008b), 'Engaged in engagement: we are delighted we did it', *Industrial & Organizational Psychology*, **1**(1), 76–83.

March, J. (1991), 'Exploration and exploitation in organizational learning', *Organization Science*, **2**(1), 71–87.

Maslach, C. and S.E. Jackson (1981), 'The measurement of experienced burnout', *Journal of Occupational Behavior*, **2**(2), 99–113.

Maslach, C. and M.P. Leiter (1997), *The Truth About Burnout: How Organizations Cause Personal Stress and What To Do About It*, San Francisco: Jossey-Bass.

Maslach, C., W.B. Schaufeli and M.P. Leiter (2001), 'Job burnout', *Annual Review of Psychology*, **52**(1), 397–422.

Maslow, A. (1954), *Motivation and Personality*, New York: Harper and Row.

May, D.R., R.L. Gilson and L.M. Harter (2004), 'The psychological conditions of meaningfulness, safety and availability and the engagement of the human spirit at work', *Journal of Occupational and Organizational Psychology*, **77**(1), 11–37.

McKelvey, B. and P. Andriani (2005), 'Why Gaussian statistics are mostly wrong for strategic organization', *Strategic Organization*, **3**(2), 219–28.

Miles, M.B. and M.A. Huberman (1994), *Qualitative Data Analysis: An Expanded Sourcebook* (2nd edition), Thousand Oaks, CA: Sage Publications.

Moultrie, J., M. Nilsson, M. Dissel, U.-E. Haner, S. Janssen and R. Van der Lugt (2007), 'Innovation spaces: towards a framework for understanding the role of the physical environment in innovation', *Creativity and Innovation Management*, **16**(1), 53–65.

O'Reilly, C. and J. Chatman (1986), 'Organizational commitment and psychological attachment: the effects of compliance, identification, and internalization on prosocial behavior', *Journal of Applied Psychology*, **71**(3), 492–9.

Paananen, H. (2010), 'Fiercely independent? How autonomy affects the experience of engagement in manual labour', unpublished Master's thesis, Aalto University School of Economics, Helsinki.

Porter, M. (1980), *Competitive Strategy: Techniques for Analyzing Industries and Competitors*, New York: Free Press.

Pratt, M.G. and B.E. Ashforth (2003), 'Fostering meaningfulness in working and at work', in K. Cameron, J.E. Dutton and R.E. Quinn (eds), *Positive Organizational Scholarship*, San Francisco: Berrett-Koehler, pp. 309–27.

Prigogine, I. and G. Nicolis (1977), *Self-organization in Non-equilibrium Systems*, New York: Wiley.

Putnam, R. (1995), 'Bowling alone: America's declining social capital', *Journal of Democracy*, **6**(1), 65–78.

Raisch, S., J. Birkinshaw, G. Probst and M. Tushman (2009), 'Organizational ambidexterity: balancing exploitation and exploration for sustained performance', *Organization Science*, **20**(4), 685–95.

Rikkinen, P. (2010), 'Head, hands and heart – highly engaged employees as a phenomenon and ways of enabling it', unpublished Master's thesis, Aalto University, School of Science and Technology, Helsinki.

Saks, A.M. (2006), 'Antecedents and consequences of employee engagement', *Journal of Managerial Psychology*, **21**(6), 600–619.

Salanova, M. and W.B. Schaufeli (2008), 'A cross-national study of work engagement as a mediator between job resources and proactive behavior', *International Journal of Human Resource Management*, **19**(1), 116–31.

Salanova, M., S. Agut and J.M. Peiro (2005), 'Linking organizational resouces and work engagement to employee performance and customer loyalty: the mediation of service climate', *Journal of Applied Psychology*, **90**(6), 1217–27.

Scharmer, O. (2007), *Theory U, Leading from the Future as it Emerges: The Social Theory of Presencing*, Cambridge, MA: Society for Organizational Learning.

Schaufeli, W.B. and A.B. Bakker (2004), 'Job demands, job resources, and their relationship with burnout and engagement: a multi-sample study', *Journal of Organizational Behavior*, **25**(3), 293–315.

Schaufeli, W.B., A.B. Bakker and M. Salanova (2006), 'The measurement of engagement with a short questionnaire: a cross-national study', *Educational and Psychological Measurement*, **66**(45), 701–16.

Schaufeli, W.B., M. Salanova, V. González-Romá and A.B. Bakker (2002), 'The measurement of engagement and burnout: a two sample confirmatory factor analytic approach', *Journal of Happiness Studies*, **3**(1), 71–92.

Scott, S.G. and R.A. Bruce (1994), 'Determinants of innovative behavior: a path model of individual innovation in the workplace', *Academy of Management Journal*, **38**(5), 1442–65.

Seligman, M.E. (2002), *Authentic Happiness*, London: Nicholas Brealey Publishing.

Senge, P., O. Scharmer, J. Jaworski and B.S. Flowers (2005), *Presence: An Exploration of Profound Change in People, Organizations, and Society*, Cambridge, MA: Society for Organizational Learning.

Smith, K.K. and D.N. Berg (1987), 'A paradoxical perspective on group dynamics', *Human Relations*, **40**(10), 633–57.

Sonnentag, S. (2003), 'Recovery, work engagement, and proactive behavior: a new look at the interface between non-work and work', *Journal of Applied Psychology*, **56**(2), 518–28.

Sonnentag, S., C. Binnewies and E.J. Mojza (2010), 'Staying well and engaged when demands are high: the role of psychological detachment', *Journal of Applied Psychology*, **95**(5), 965–76.

Stacey, R. (2001), *Complex Responsive Processes in Organizations: Learning and Knowledge Creation*, London: Routledge.

Steiner, G. (2006), *Innovative Performance of Organizations as a Result of their Physical Environment*, paper presentation, XVIth World Congress of Sociology, 23–29 July, Durban, South Africa.

Stern, S. (2008), 'Keep up motivation levels through long summer days', *Financial Times*, 5 August, 10.

Storm, K. and S. Rothmann (2003), 'A psychometric analysis of the Utrecht work engagement scale in the South African police service', *SA Journal of Industrial Psychology*, **29**(4), 62–70.

Strauss, A.L. (1987), *Qualitative Analysis for the Social Scientist*, Boston, MA: Cambridge University Press.

Strauss, A.L. and J.R. Corbin (1990), *Basics of Qualitative Research: Techniques and Procedures for Developing Grounded Theory*, Newbury Park, CA: Sage Publications.

Taylor, F.W. (2008), *The Principles of Scientific Management* (reprint), Stilwell, available at: Digireads.com.

Towers Perrin (2008), *Closing the Engagement Gap: A Road Map for Driving Superior Business Performance*, Towers Perrin Global Workforce Study 2007–2008, Global Report.

Tyler, S.L. and T.R. Blader (2003), 'Testing and extending the group engagement model: linkages between social identity, procedural justice, economic outcomes, and extra-role behavior', *Journal of Applied Psychology*, **94**(2), 445–64.

Van de Ven, A. (1986), 'Central problems in the management of innovation', *Management Science*, **32**(5), 590–607.

Vecchio, R.P. (1980), 'The function and meaning of work and the job: Morse and Weiss (1955) revisited', *Academy of Management Journal*, **23**(2), 361–600.

Volberda, H. and A. Lewin (2003), 'Guest editors' introduction: co-evolutionary dynamics within and between firms: from evolution to co-evolution', *Journal of Management Studies*, **40**(8), 2111–36.

Von Hippel, E. and G. Von Krogh (2003), 'Open source software and the "private-collective" innovation model: issues for organization science', *Organization Science*, **14**(2), 209–23.

Weick, K.E. (1993), 'The collapse of sensemaking in organizations: the Mann Gulch disaster', *Administrative Science Quarterly*, **38**(4), 628–52.

Weick, K.E. and K.M. Sutcliffe (2006), 'Mindfulness and the quality of organizational attention', *Organization Science*, **17**(4), 514–24.

Westman, M. and D. Eden (1997), 'Effects of a respite from work on burnout: vacation relief and fade-out', *Journal of Applied Psychology*, **82**(4), 516–27.

Westman, M. and D. Etzion (2001), 'The impact of vacation and job stress on burnout and absenteeism', *Psychology and Health*, **16**(5), 595–606.

Wiggins, R. and T. Ruefli (2005), 'Schumpeter's ghost: is hypercompetition making the best of times shorter?', *Strategic Management Journal*, **26**(10), 887–911.

Wrzesniewski, A. (2003), 'Finding positive meaning in work', in K. Cameron, J.E. Dutton and R.E. Quinn (eds), *Positive Organizational Scholarship*, San Francisco: Berrett-Koehler, pp. 296–308.

Yang, L. (2010), 'Patterns of engagement in Generation Y – comparing Chinese and Finnish students and graduates in vocational and non-vocational careers', unpublished report, Aalto University School of Science and Technology, Helsinki.

Yin, R.K. (2009), *Case Study Research* (4th edition), Thousand Oaks, CA: Sage Publications.

Zohar, D. and I. Marshall (2001), *Spiritual Intelligence, the Ultimate Intelligence*, New York: Bloomsbury.

4 Making innovation happen using accounting controls

Christina Boedker and Jonathon Mark Runnalls

1 INTRODUCTION

The aim of accounting controls has traditionally been to ensure conformity to plans and targets and this requires elimination of deviations, and protection from unexpected events or disturbances. Accounting controls do this job very well; they make the organization predictable by reducing uncertainty and by promoting clarity. They are associated with routine, conformance and the close monitoring of progress towards predefined goals and intents. Yet, organizations also need to innovate, to develop new products, services and processes in order to ensure long-term survival. Since innovation is not an orderly process that moves smoothly towards predefined intents, some researchers have questioned the suitability of accounting controls for innovation purposes (Ouchi, 1979; Amabile et al., 1996; Davila, 2005).

When one takes a closer look at the literature on management accounting controls, it transpires that accounting controls can play a significant role in orienting firms to pursue innovation outcomes. Financial targets and budgets can, for example, help organizations to appreciate when innovation should be extended or reduced (Mouritsen et al., 2010). Formal controls can also shape cognitions and actions that favour creativity and idea generation; managers, when pushed for profit and deprived of resources, become imaginative and creative (Roberts, 1990; Dent, 1991; Simons, 2010), they 'fiddle' with resources and key performance indicators and new ideas and solutions emerge (Ahrens and Chapman, 2007; Jørgensen and Messner, 2010; Revellino and Mouritsen, 2010), sometimes with unanticipated consequences, resulting, for example, in new company strategies (Skaerbaek and Tryggestad, 2010).

This chapter illustrates and discusses different ways in which accounting controls can enable innovation. Specifically, it reviews two different approaches that describe how organizations can use accounting controls to innovate. Drawing on Latour (1986; see also Mouritsen et al., 2005; Mouritsen, 2006; Boedker, 2010), we label these the ostensive and performative approaches. By contrasting these two approaches, we are able to illustrate how different conceptual framings and assumptions lead to different insights into the control–innovation relationship. The aim is to encourage researchers, managers and others to reflect on the dominant assumptions that they share and to ask 'How do controls enable innovation differently when viewed through different lenses?'

The ostensive approach is represented here by North American research. For the purposes of this chapter, we draw specifically on the work of Robert Simons (1987, 1990, 1991, 1994, 1995, 2000, 2005, 2010), who has written extensively on controls and innovation. The second approach, the performative approach, is represented by the growing body of work primarily by European researchers on innovation and controls (e.g., Ahrens and Chapman, 2007; Boedker and Chua, 2010; Mouritsen et al., 2010; Revellino and Mouritsen, 2010; Skaerbaek and Tryggestad, 2010; Skaerbaek and Vinnari, 2010). We draw here on the work of Jørgensen and Messner (2010) on new product development (NPD) to provide an alternative perspective to the prevailing North American view and to illustrate how controls enable innovation differently. Two themes are found that describe the agency of accounting controls in innovation: (1) enabling conversations and (2) creating boundaries.

The chapter is structured is as follows. The next section outlines the two approaches. The third section summarizes key differences between the two approaches and concludes the chapter.

2   ENABLING INNOVATION: THE OSTENSIVE VERSUS PERFORMATIVE APPROACHES

Latour's (1986, pp. 272–3) discussion of two approaches, the ostensive versus performative, illustrates different paradigms (or worldviews) brought to bear by social scientists and their prevailing assumptions. Discussing these assumptions is important because they circumscribe what is 'worthwhile' and 'acceptable' research and practice. Chua (1986) argues that ostensive accounting scholars share a particular worldview that emphasizes hypothetico-deductivism and technical control. She explains (p. 602):

> accounting research has been guided by a dominant, not divergent, set of assumptions. There has been one general scientific world-view, one primary disciplinary matrix. And accounting researchers, as a community of scientists, have shared and continue to share a constellation of beliefs, values and techniques. These beliefs circumscribe definitions of 'worthwhile problems' and 'acceptable scientific evidence'. To the extent that they are continually affirmed by fellow accounting researchers, they are often taken for granted and subconsciously applied.

McCloskey (1983) similarly illustrates how the official rhetoric subscribed to in economics declares people to be scientists: 'Modernism is influential in economics, but not because its premises have been examined carefully and found good. It is a revealed, not a reasoned, religion' (p. 172).

Latour's (1986) *performative approach* is defined by a variable ontology, dispersion of power to many agents (some human, some not), and preoccupation with actor networks as the path to knowledge discovery. This approach suggests that actors, whatever their size, define in practice what society is. 'Society is not the referent of an ostensive definition discovered by social scientists despite the ignorance of their informants. Rather it is performed through everyone's efforts to define it. . . . what is at stake is the practical definitions made by actors' (ibid., p. 273). This contrasts to the *ostensive approach*, which is defined by a stable ontology, centralization of power to only a few agents or universal ideals, and attempts at knowledge discovery through deductive reasoning and predefined building blocks. Whilst the performative approach is concerned with the practical definitions of actors, the ostensive approach is concerned with universal laws and what is 'ideal' as opposed to 'real'. This can be helpful to managers in defining 'best fit' solutions and orderliness. In contrast, the performative approach offers descriptions, not prescriptions, and grants insights to the messiness and complexity that is inevitably found in organizations.

Performativity is considered to be one in a range of 'practice approaches'. Shatzki (2001) discusses four broad areas of practice theory:

- philosophers, for example, Wittgenstein and Dreyfus;
- social theorists, for example, Bourdieu and de Certau;
- cultural theorists, for example, Foucault and Giddens, and finally;
- theorists of science and technology, for example, Latour and Pickering.

Practice theorists sought to find a middle ground between the opposing views that first 'social phenomena must be explained by showing how they result from individual actions' and the antithetical position that society can be explained by means of structures and social wholes. Social phenomena manifest through the actions of people (bodies), which form an 'array of activity' (ibid., p. 2) that is constituted and kept together by several elements, such as human bodies, things, rules, knowledge or emotions. In a nutshell, practice theorists claim that social action and order are best explained with reference to the existence of social practices that span across time and space.[1]

The following subsection analyses and compares the logic of two illustrative papers (Simons, 2010; Jørgensen and Messner, 2010) that have these qualities (ostensive versus performative). The comparison of the two papers helps to develop claims about the nature of innovation when seen in the context of accounting.

Drawing on 102 case studies, Simons (2010) discusses how accountability and control can be catalysts for strategic exploration (e.g., innovation) in addition to exploitation (e.g., the effective use of existing resources). Simons recommends that 'managers deliberately hold subordinates accountable for measures that are wider than their span of control to foster exploration activities' (ibid., p. 30). By deliberately withholding resources, managers become creative in 'figuring out how to turn opportunities into results even though he or she does not control the resources to get the job done' (ibid., p. 12). Setting the 'spans of accountability' wider than 'spans of control'[2] helps managers to tilt people's efforts towards exploration. This creates an 'entrepreneurial gap' that is said to heighten innovation performance.

In contrast, Jørgensen and Messner look at a single company and chart the progress of a new product development (NPD) initiative called the modularization project. They examine the many competing demands and high levels of uncertainty about outcomes inherent in any innovation project. Their findings suggest that when reviewing NPD initiatives, actors make decisions not just based on the numbers revealed by accounting but also by mobilizing different strategic objectives to which the NPD practices are supposed to contribute. They demonstrate that accounting controls are flexible and can be overridden in cases where management deems it appropriate to do so. Used in such a manner, controls become a guide that assists in making decisions rather than erecting boundaries that must be followed. The study highlights the pluralistic, sometimes competing, demands of complex organizations and sheds light on the unpredictable directions of innovation and the many actors that take part in its designs.

2.1 Enabling Conversations

In both the ostensive and the performative approach, accounting controls heighten innovation performance by enabling conversations between sometimes disparate actors. Table 4.1 summarizes how controls operate differently in the ostensive and the performative approach.

In the ostensive approach, innovation is often seen to be a task charged to senior executives located at the 'top of organizational hierarchies'. Executives debate and decide what to do and which strategy the firm must pursue (e.g., a cost, quality or innovation strategy). It is senior management who can choose to proceed with a particular innovation strategy, or not. Whilst interaction and conversations about innovation may also take

Table 4.1   Enabling conversations

	Ostensive	Performative
How do accounting controls enable innovation?	Controls are put in place by 'top management' to implement innovation strategy. Once an innovation strategy has been decided on, controls can be 'fitted' to ensure its proper implementation. Lower-level employees are charged with implementing the innovation strategy but are not necessarily involved in its design (unitary and centralized approach); this is the so-called 'diagnostic use' of accounting controls. Controls are also used in conversations between managers and subordinates to detect strategic uncertainties in the external environment (e.g., competitive moves, shifting customer needs etc.), the so-called interactive use. Here, it is the responsibility of subordinates to 'channel up' information and learnings to executives, who can then make decisions about what to do	Controls are mediators, which bring diverse actors together. Through accounting controls, many people ('inside' and 'outside' the company, lay people and others) are drawn into relationships to participate in the innovation process and innovation design. Innovation is a network effect, an anti-heroic affair made possible by accounting controls. Anyone in a company's network can participate and many perspectives are given consideration, sometimes resulting in disputes and tension (pluralistic and dispersed approach). Innovation is sometimes a surprise, even an accident, made possible by a diverse range of actors. Translation happens when ideas and tokens travel through the hands of many and are transformed along the way

place lower down organizational hierarchies, ultimately senior leaders are in charge of the process and the direction of innovation is 'top-down'. At later stages, subordinates and lay people may be tasked with its implementation, but they are not necessarily involved in its design and have little say in how and when innovation should take place. Consensus is high and power is centralized to senior executives, who, after all, have superior knowledge. Accounting controls are important because they are used during the implementation process to monitor progress, align staff behaviour to strategic intent and promote clarity. They ensure that any given innovation strategy is successfully implemented and realized. This is the so-called diagnostic use of accounting controls (Simons, 1987, 1990, 1991, 1994, 1995, 2000, 2005, 2010), where controls assist to reduce uncertainty and deviations through the close monitoring of progress against stated targets. A key aim of controls is to 'help managers track the progress of individuals, departments or production facilities towards strategically important goals' (Simons, 1995, p.81). Controls are necessary because employees, in this view, cannot always be trusted and if left unsupervised might deviate from the path chosen for them by management. Simons (2010, p.18) illustrates this in a case on innovation strategy at a China-based computer company where senior executives wanted to 'increase innovation in their R&D unit'. To do so, they introduced a range of new accounting controls that would ensure the proper implementation of the new strategy. They changed the performance measures and targets of managers, as follows:

> Managers of the R&D unit, who had previously been accountable only for meeting corporate funding allocations, were now accountable for the number of new models launched, the number of design awards won, successful market introduction of new software, and the number of models ranked as top sellers in the market. (Simons, 2010, p.18).

Simons offers a second account of how accounting controls can heighten innovation performance. He calls this 'interactive use'. Whereas diagnostic use seeks to eliminate deviation from stated goals, interactive use seeks to explore emerging opportunities and threats. It is concerned with an aspiration to identify and learn about external changes in technological developments, customer relations and socioeconomic conditions, and is generally said to encourage innovation and stimulate the emergence of new strategies (Simons, 1987, 1995; see also Naranjo-Gil and Hartmann, 2007; Bisbe and Malagueño, 2009), particularly if innovation levels are low (Bisbe and Otley, 2004). Conversations feature strongly in the interactive use of accounting controls in that controls demand more face-to-face interaction and require managers 'to involve themselves regularly and personally in the decisions of subordinates' (Simons, 1995, p.86). This makes the interpretation of information a broad and collective affair (Simons, 1987, 1991, 1994), and can break down functional and hierarchical barriers that may inhibit information flows and the sharing of ideas (Abernethy and Brownell, 1999). Yet, whilst possibly conducive to detecting change in the external market and facilitating learning and information exchange, also in this approach the role of subordinates remains limited to channelling information 'up' to the senior managers (who decide what to do), rather than to involve themselves in innovation design or the crafting of creative solutions to emerging problems and opportunities. Again, accounting controls assist to direct the attention of subordinates and ensure they focus on the 'right things'. Simons (1995, p.139) tells the story of a newly promoted company president at a health aids company who introduced a new accounting control (a profit planning control system) that was used interactively to 'promote a deeper understanding of market conditions, competitor actions, brand profitability, and the timing and effect of line extensions and new product introductions', as follows:

> Under the new system, profitability for each brand was revised and discussed from the bottom of the organization to the top on a monthly basis. Through face to face meetings with operating managers, the senior manager and executive committee focused attention on data from the new profit planning system and thereby sent a clear signal throughout the organization about what strategic uncertainties the organization should collect data and respond to. (Ibid.)

By way of contrast, Jørgensen and Messner (2010) suggest that while senior managers and boards of directors are involved in many conversations about innovation, they are not the only ones to decide how to develop or implement innovations. The performative-based approach contrasts with the ostensive approach by suggesting that there are many (often competing) interests in organizations and also many strategic options. Indeed, compared to the somewhat heroic nature of innovation design in the ostensive approach, Jørgensen and Messner (ibid.) suggest that surprises can happen when diverse actors are involved in the design process and that innovation sometimes happens by accident. In this view, innovation is rather messy, even unpredictable, and takes place in many spaces, also outside executive meetings and boardrooms. In addition, ideas change as they travel through the hands of many and this makes any given implementation process less predictable and less certain.

By tracing the NPD process across time and space, Jørgensen and Messner (ibid.) illustrate that the initial idea behind a particular innovation came from a customer with whom the company had a very close relationship. This customer 'poured wine into an instrument originally developed to measure levels of different constituents in milk to "see what happened"' (p. 192). This led engineers to realize that an opportunity existed for an adaptation to the existing product and they started the process of developing a new product, which later was successfully sold to wine producers, who in turn suggested an adaptation that would work for grape must.[3] Sales people saw opportunities for product development and so spoke to their senior manager, who in turn talked to Finance about the business case. Over time, the CEO and the board became involved and suggested building a modular new product.

In this example, the innovation began outside the company, travelled through various departments and individuals before it eventually reached senior managers who suggested further investment. It then travelled back and forth through various departments and potential customers with many amendments and adaptations along the way until it finally became a new product available for sale. In this case, innovation started off as an accident and was not entirely anticipated in its origins or consciously planned by heroic leaders. Rather, lay people and a wider array of diverse actors had a say in its design as it travelled through the hands of many. Translation happened and the NPD transformed along the way as more people got involved. The direction of innovation was not necessarily 'top-down' and predictable (as in the ostensive approach); rather it was multi-directional, iterative and often uncertain, even unplanned. It followed a rather unpredictable and 'messy' path as actors drew on external data sources and started conversations with customers, consultants, major producers and universities in search for advice on market size, functionality requirements, competitive products, specifications and so on. Furthermore, in Jørgensen and Messner's (2010) case study, accounting controls were not necessarily used to restrict people's choices or reduce deviations. Rather, they were used to provide forums for discussing and possibly resolving different views, objectives and options. Competing views were taken into consideration, and a singular focus was disputed, for example:

> the fact that there were more than several competing, strategic objectives (a fact that the Ranking Report had criticized) indicates that there was at least no focus on one particular strategy. As a consequence of the variety of strategic objectives associated with modularity, there was considerable leeway regarding the interpretation and evaluation of NPD practices. (Jørgensen and Messner, 2010, p. 201)

The performative approach suggests, in this regard, that rather than being passive actors who require close monitoring, employees have the potential to make a useful and constructive contribution to the innovation process. Accordingly, a range of actors are given voice and their views on the innovation and roles in it are heard and given visibility. This spans from the CEO, finance director, production director, R&D director, group controller to various middle managers, R&D strategists, project coordinators, production planners, marketing analysts and development engineers (p. 191). The following quote (from an internal document at the case study organization) is illustrative of a more collaborative tone:

> It is important to declare a common business focus and to diminish the differences between the departments by, for instance, meetings, discussions and education. To be able to benefit from all the advantages of modularization, all departments and employees have to be involved and it should be high priority to increase the knowledge and understanding of modularization and customer needs. (Company Ranking Report, p. 34, Jørgensen and Messner, 2010, p. 196)

Whilst Simons talks predominantly to senior managers and executives, thus implying that their views are the ones that matter, Jørgensen and Messner (2010) interview a wider range of employees and managers. They take into consideration a wider range of actors and the network and the relations that exist between actors to draw insights about innovation and from where it may arise. They let the data speak and do not ex ante draw artificial divides between who can legitimately participate in the innovation process and design.

In summary, accounting controls define who can be part of the innovation process and participate in conversations and debates about innovation. The ostensive approach sees innovation as a centralized, somewhat heroic affair that can be managed with a high degree of certainty. In contrast, the performative approach recognizes the existence of many diverse actors, each of whom can potentially participate in the innovation process and disturb and mould it along the way. This co-production of innovation by many actors makes innovation less predictable and opens up the possibility that surprises and accidents can happen. Accounting controls, in the ostensive approach, define how innovation should be done. In contrast, in the performative approach, controls act as mediators that draw in diverse actors to discuss and debate different perspectives and interests.

2.2   Creating Boundaries

It is generally agreed that organizations use accounting controls to set boundaries in order to guide and monitor innovation efforts. Yet, how those boundaries are set and how they are taken up and followed is what separates the ostensive and the performative approaches. Table 4.2 summarizes key differences in the role of accounting in setting boundaries to enable innovation.

In the ostensive model, the boundaries set by accounting controls are seemingly rigid, even fixed; it is generally argued that tight boundaries are required for innovation to take place. Simons (1995, p. 39) defines boundary systems as a means to manipulate employee behaviours and to 'delineate the acceptable domain of activity for organizational participants'. He refers to an 'entrepreneurial gap' (2010), which can be achieved if executives reduce the breadth of resources available to the job holders, for example, people, assets and infrastructure (called the span of control), whilst simultaneously widening the type of goals the job holder is expected to achieve (called the span of accountability). 'With span of accountability wider than span of control, an individual is accountable for figuring out how to turn opportunities into results even though he or she does not control the resources to get the job done' (Simons, 2010,

Table 4.2   Creating boundaries

	Ostensive	Performative
How do accounting controls enable innovation?	Tight boundaries are required for innovation to take place. For example, by depriving people of resources and by making them accountable for factors outside their control, people become innovative. While this may appear (to some) to be overtly manipulative or coercive, it is considered to be an effective and necessary stimulus for innovation to result. Controls, once set, are deemed to be fixed and not a topic of much debate or movement	Boundaries are flexible and act as a guide in decision-making rather than an 'answer machine'. They can be set aside and overridden, if required. For example, controls can produce accounting calculations that challenge the viability of an innovation. Rather than rejecting it outright, managers use this as an opportunity to debate the assumptions behind a project, question its strategic value to the organization, and even challenge the validity of the control that might transform it. This approach acknowledges that continual movement is to be expected in the network and that assumptions or controls that once were useful may no longer hold valid

p. 12). This fixing of boundaries results in an 'entrepreneurial gap', which forces people to become more innovative (see Figure 4.1). Simons (ibid., p. 13) explains: 'there may, in fact, be good reason for managers to hold subordinates accountable for variables outside their control if they want them to act as entrepreneurs, exploring new possibilities for creating value for customers'.

Examples from 11 organizations with an entrepreneurial gap (11 per cent of the sample) are provided by Simons (2010). Managers did the same thing in all of these situations: they widened the 'entrepreneurial gap' by either widening the span of accountability, narrowing the span of control, or both (see again Figure 4.1). Simons says: 'this was the only way to unlock people and force them to be more entrepreneurial' (ibid., p. 17); 'they have no choice but to figure out how to be accountable' (ibid., p. 23). By depriving people of resources and making them accountable for variables outside their control, they become innovative. Simons (2010) goes on to provide a practical example from executives of a European investment firm, who changed the span of control and span of accountability to force innovation in the delivery of products and services to larger clients:

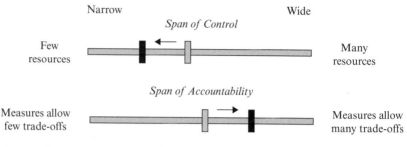

Source: Simons (2010, p. 18).

Figure 4.1   Widening the entrepreneurial gap

> To support the change in strategy, span of control for managing directors was narrowed by assigning each director access to only five client companies instead of the twenty or more clients they had served under the previous strategy. At the same time, their span of accountability was widened by adding both cross-selling and overall company performance to their previous accountability for revenue. Collectively, these changes widened the entrepreneurial gap substantially. (Ibid., p. 19)

The ostensive approach suggests, in this regard, that innovation results by setting tight boundaries. Managers put pressure on employees and 'force' them to become entrepreneurial by tightening controls and by heightening levels of accountability. In the ostensive model, controls ought not to be overridden or bent. They are seemingly rigid.

By way of contrast, the performative view assumes that less rigidity and notional boundaries do not exist in the same way. The performative approach suggests that there are no fixed boundaries, only the transfer, exchange and adaptation of ideas, initiatives and technologies between disparate actors in the network. Jørgensen and Messner (2010, p. 199) describe several instances where employees adapt controls to suit the situation at hand. For this to happen, controls need to be amendable and flexible to absorb and adjust to movements and changes in actor networks. The process appears to be both iterative and cooperative. The emphasis on controls, in the performative approach, is not to coerce or manipulate by erecting tight boundaries but rather to engage and mobilize a wider network of actors and actants.

Jørgensen and Messner (ibid., p. 193) illustrate that accounting controls help managers deal with uncertainty in new product development projects, yet generally they cannot 'serve as an answer machine'. Managers at various levels of the organization used a range of criteria that had a relationship to accounting numbers and financial considerations in their deliberations and sense-making. The new innovation, for example, the modularization project, was problematic for a number of reasons when viewed from the point of the existing accounting tools used to evaluate NPD projects. First, the existing financial model for NPDs did not find the suggested modularization project to be financially viable. The problem with the spreadsheet model was that it was based on a generic NPD project. However, each NPD project demonstrated quite different characteristics, and therefore it was difficult to apply the model in a generic way. For users, translating an NPD project into the terms of the model was often an act of 'creativity' (p. 10). It meant that profitability calculations produced by the spreadsheet were considered unreliable by its users and that predicted profitability was regarded 'with some scepticism' (p. 9). The second problem arose because the spreadsheet model was designed to deal with only one product initiative at a time. In contrast, the modularization project would share several of the modules under consideration and thus required the evaluation of more products or variants at the same time. Essentially, the accounting criteria traditionally used to evaluate NPD projects did not work in the case of the modularization project. This represented a change to what had been considered appropriate in the past and this should be expected in networks where continuous movement and change is common. The Senior Manager, who was championing the project with great persistency, lobbied strongly in favour of the innovation and pointed out the inadequacy of the spreadsheet. In the end, the CEO 'overruled' the control and requested that the NPD project proceed:

> Finally, after one of my numerous presentations to the Management Board trying to get them to follow my idea of modularization [the CEO] cut through the talk and said that he was fed up with this discussion. He believed in the idea [of modularization] and the project [Alpha] was hereby authorized! If he had not done that, the idea would have been scrapped. Senior Manager, Team Greenhouse. (Jørgensen and Messner, 2010, pp. 9–10)

The case illustrates, in this regard, that innovation was not made possible because of the existing spreadsheet model used to estimate the financial profitability of NPD projects; rather, it became viable because the CEO believed in the idea. Indeed, to make the innovation work, the CEO had to 'overrule' the spreadsheet, which deemed the innovation 'financially unviable'. In contrast to the ostensive view where controls are seemingly rigid and erect tight boundaries, in the performative view, controls are flexible and create notional boundaries. This is a view that suggests that boundaries can be set aside and 'bent' if required. Controls guide the organization but decisions can still displace the accounting representations contained therein.

In summary, accounting controls enable innovation by erecting boundaries that define what is acceptable and permissible behaviour by employees. The ostensive approach suggests that boundaries ought to be rigid and fixed. The performative approach sees boundaries as flexible, even malleable and suggests that these can be set aside if required. Within the ostensive approach, boundaries dictate what is deemed to be appropriate to work on whereas in the performative view, accounting controls can be overridden if they are misrepresenting the potential of an innovation or delivering an incorrect calculation, for example, profitability. A performative approach acknowledges that things change in networks over time and that sometimes it may be necessary to 'bend' an accounting control because it is no longer capable of acting effectively due to movements in the network. As networks constantly change (due to changing ideas and new knowledge being produced and passed between actors), so do controls.

3   DISCUSSION AND CONCLUSION

This chapter has discussed the relationships between accounting controls and firm innovation. Despite earlier work that questioned the suitability of accounting controls for innovation purposes, it transpires from this and other papers that accounting controls have much to do with orienting firms to pursue innovation outcomes. Specifically, the chapter has illustrated that different conceptual framings (ostensive and performative) can lead to different insights into and understandings of the control–innovation relationship. By asking 'How do controls enable innovation differently when viewed through different lenses?' the chapter has shown that controls affect innovation in more than one way. The control–innovation relation is a multi-faceted phenomenon defined in part by the framing chosen by managers, researchers and others. By reflecting on the dominant assumptions that we make about how relationships work and are formed, new insights and understandings can be achieved.

In the ostensive approach, accounting controls assist managers to ensure the correct implementation of predefined intents. An innovation strategy, in such a view, is 'seemingly stable and coherent, and somehow "ready made"' (Boedker, 2010, p. 596). Its implementation is linear and 'top-down', perhaps even predictable. Accounting controls, in this approach, are important because they shield out unwelcome disturbances, orient employee behaviour and promote clarity. They reduce uncertainty and deviations through the close monitoring of progress against stated targets. In this view, innovation is largely a heroic affair, confined to executive directors and boardroom conversations. Lay people and others are charged with implementation tasks or, at best, act as conduits for feedback of information to executives who can then decide what to do and how to act. Executives encourage entrepreneurial behaviour in the organization by creating entrepreneurial gaps, whereby people are deprived of resources and held accountable for goals outside their direct influence. This is a view where tight boundaries need to be set, as employees need strong guidance and because they cannot always be trusted.

The performative view, by contrast, challenges the assumptions of 'best fit' and suggests that the world is often a messy place where prediction and linear pathways are not always possible. In this view, innovation is emergent and unpredictable as many actors, lay people and others, participate in innovation design. Ideas and innovations change as they travel along often bumpy pathways in actor networks. Sometimes they are disputed and sometimes they fail, depending on locality-specific interests and needs. Diverse actors throughout the network play a role in helping innovations succeed (or not). In this view, there is no 'right fit' or ideal solution; there are only the actions and relationships between actors in the network and each situation is unique, requiring specific solutions and adaptation. Superior knowledge does not reside at the 'top' of an organization; nor do ideas, technologies and innovations only flow 'top-down'. Instead, innovations and ideas move in many directions. This opens up the possibility of surprise and suggests that innovation cannot always be planned or predicted beforehand. Indeed, innovation can be an accident. Accounting controls in the performative view inform debates and assist actors to question viable options rather than follow a blueprint or become an 'answer machine' for decision-making. In other words, they guide management decision-making, not replace it. Their logic is always open for questioning and interpretation and, as such, they are flexible rather than fixed. Controls can be 'set aside', 'bent' and even 'overridden' depending on the situation at hand and their usefulness in any given event. They are able to change depending on movements and shifts in actor networks. Because it is expected that the network is always changing, the way the controls are designed and applied is challenged from time to time to ensure they are still appropriate.

It is evident that the two views, ostensive and performative, both have merit and offer benefits to managers and others in pursuit of innovation outcomes. The ostensive view is, at present, the more dominant in management accounting research; yet the performative view holds much promise in that it helps us make sense of a sometimes surprising world where change is constant and predictability is in short supply. To managers, the ostensive search for 'best fit' solutions makes the world more accessible. Prescriptions and blueprints with five-step solutions reduce the complexity of organizational life and grant opportunities for management intervention and a sense of being in control. They can play a comforting role for managers in search of certainty and may act as coping mechanisms to deal with the messiness that is inevitably part of organizational life. The performative view is more sceptical of 'best fit' solutions. It acknowledges that tokens change as they move through the hands of many and indicates, in this regard, that the ostensive approach might be more 'ideal' than 'real'. Managers can learn from the performative approach to better deal with the shifts that inevitably occur in organizational networks. This is a view of management that is more supportive of the participation of many and that suggests that unexpected movement and surprises in actor networks can be opportunities for knowledge creation rather than things that should be done away with.

In conclusion, managers and scholars have a choice to make, and debate. Like ostensive scholars, they may opt to approach the innovation–control relationship as a linear top-down affair, assuming that stability and orderliness characterize social life. Yet, they may also opt for a less prescriptive approach and discuss the shifting nature of social life and embrace the messiness and complexity that it offers as opportunities for learning and progress. Whilst the former views accounting controls as a means by which uncertainty can be reduced and predictability enhanced, the latter offers managers and others the possibility to be surprised by accounting controls and their many possible configurations and effects. Historically the ostensive position has been widely viewed as useful and relevant. We suggest, however, that the performative approach, with its nuanced and anti-heroic tenets may in future provide a more fruitful and practical framing of accounting controls and their relation to innovation management within organizations.

NOTES

1. Jorgensen and Messner (2010, p. 186) use practice theory to study accounting controls. They see it as similar to performativity in that it is concerned with what people do in practice, but differentiate it by looking at how practices can be theorized as ontological phenomena.
2. Spans of accountability are defined as 'the range of tradeoffs inherent in the measure(s) for which a manager is accountable' (Simons, 2010, p. 9). Span of control is defined as the 'total resources under a manager's direct control' (ibid.).
3. Freshly pressed fruit juice contains the seeds, skins and stems of the fruit, the first stage of turning grapes into wine.

REFERENCES

Abernethy, M.A. and P. Brownell (1999), 'The role of budgets in organizations facing strategic change: an exploratory study', *Accounting, Organizations and Society*, **24**(3), 189–204.

Ahrens, T. and C. Chapman (2007), 'Management accounting as practice', *Accounting, Organizations and Society*, **32**(1–2), 1–27.

Amabile, T.M., R. Conti, H. Coon, J. Lazenby and M. Herron (1996), 'Assessing the work environment for creativity', *Academy of Management Journal*, **39**(5), 1154–84.

Bisbe, J. and R. Malagueño (2009), 'The choice of interactive control systems under different innovation management modes', *European Accounting Review*, **18**(2), 371–405.

Bisbe, J. and D. Otley (2004), 'The effects of the interactive use of management control systems on product innovation', *Accounting, Organizations and Society*, **29**(8), 709–37.

Boedker, C. (2010), 'Ostensive versus performative approaches', *Accounting, Auditing and Accountability Journal*, **23**(5), 595–625.

Boedker, C. and Chua, W.F. (2009), 'Visualising, disciplining and seducing, the performativity of accounting in strategizing in a global network', submitted to *Accounting, Organizations and Society* special issue on accounting and strategy, working paper under final review.

Chua, W.F. (1986), 'Radical developments in accounting thought', *The Accounting Review*, **61**(4), 601–34.

Davila, A. (2005), 'The promise of management control systems for innovation and strategic change', in C. Chapman (ed.), *Controlling Strategy: Management, Accounting and Performance Measurement*, Oxford: Oxford University Press, pp. 37–61.

Dent, J.F. (1991), 'Accounting and organizational cultures: a field study of the emergence of a new organizational reality', *Accounting, Organizations and Society*, **16**(8), 705–32.

Jørgensen, B. and M. Messner (2010), 'Accounting and strategising: a case study from new product development', *Accounting, Organizations and Society*, **35**(2), 184–204.

Latour, B. (1986), 'The powers of association', in J. Law (ed.), *Power, Actions and Belief – A New Sociology of Knowledge*, London: Routledge and Kegan Paul, pp. 264–80.

McCloskey, D.N. (1983), 'The rhetoric of economics', *Journal of Economic Literature*, **21**(2), 481–517.

Mouritsen, J. (2006), 'Problematising intellectual capital research: ostensive versus performative IC', *Accounting, Auditing and Accountability Journal*, **19**(6), 820–41.

Mouritsen, J., A. Hansen and C.O. Hansen (2010), 'Short and long translations: management accounting calculations and innovation management', *Accounting, Organizations and Society*, **34**(6–7), 738–54.

Mouritsen J., H. Thorsgaard Larsen and P.N. Bukh (2005), 'Dealing with the knowledge economy: intellectual capital versus balanced scorecard', *Journal of Intellectual Capital*, **6**(1), 8–27.

Naranjo-Gil, D. and F. Hartman (2007), 'Management accounting systems, top management team heterogeneity and strategic change', *Accounting, Organizations and Society*, **32**(1–2), 735–56.

Ouchi, W.G. (1979), 'A conceptual framework for the design of organizational control mechanisms', *Management Science*, **25**(9), 833–48.

Revellino, S. and J. Mouritsen (2010), 'The Chronoprogramme – capital budgeting and motorway construction', working paper, Copenhagen Business School.

Roberts, J. (1990), 'Strategy and accounting in a UK conglomerate', *Accounting, Organizations and Society*, **15**(1–2), 107–26.

Shatzki, T.R. (2001), 'Introduction. Practice theory', in T.R. Shatzki, K. Knorr Cetina and E. Von Savigny (eds), *The Practice Turn in Contemporary Theory*, London and New York: Routledge, pp. 1–14.

Simons, R. (1987), 'Accounting control systems and business strategy: an empirical analysis', *Accounting, Organizations and Society*, **12**(4), 357–74.

Simons, R. (1990), 'The role of management control systems in creating competitive advantage: new perspectives', *Accounting, Organizations and Society*, **15**(1–2), 127–43.

Simons, R. (1991), 'Strategic orientation and top management attention to control systems', *Strategic Management Journal*, **12**(1), 49–62.
Simons, R. (1994), 'How top managers use control systems as levers of strategic renewal', *Strategic Management Journal*, **14**(3), 69–189.
Simons, R. (1995), *Levers of Control: How Managers Use Innovative Control Systems to Drive Strategic Renewal*, Boston, MA: Harvard Business School Press.
Simons, R. (2000), *Performance Measurement and Control Systems for Implementing Strategy*, Upper Saddle River, NJ: Prentice Hall.
Simons, R. (2005), *Levers of Organization Design: How Managers Use Accountability Systems for Greater Performance and Commitment*, Boston, MA: Harvard Business School Press.
Simons, R. (2010), 'Accountability and control as catalysts for strategic exploration and exploitation: field study results', *Harvard Business School Working Papers*, No. 10-051.
Skaerbaek, P. and K. Tryggestad (2010), 'The role of accounting devices in performing corporate strategy', *Accounting, Organizations and Society*, **35**(1), 108–24.
Skaerbaek, P.A. and E. Vinnari (2010), 'The role of risk management technologies in the public sector', presented at the Sixth Asia Pacific Interdisciplinary Research in Accounting (APIRA) Conference, Sydney, Australia, 12 July 2010.

5 Innovation and the division of labour
G. M. Peter Swann

1 INTRODUCTION

The purpose of this chapter is to summarize the relationships between innovation and the division of labour. These relationships operate in both directions: from innovation to the division of labour and from the division of labour to innovation. Moreover, these relationships are not *monotonic*.[1] For example, as the division of labour increases, this may lead to more innovation (of certain types). But eventually, the further division of labour may be dysfunctional, and get in the way of innovation. As a result, the relationship between the division of labour and innovation is better described as an inverted 'U'.

To motivate the chapter, we start with a brief summary of the history of economic thought about the division of labour and its relationship to innovation. This shows that the bi-directional nature of these relationships was well known to earlier writers, and so also was the idea that excessive division of labour would be dysfunctional. Then, in Sections 3 and 4, we distinguish various forms of innovation and various aspects of the division of labour. We do this because it will become clear that the nature of the relationships to be described here depend on which form of innovation and which aspect of the division of labour is being considered. Next, in Section 5 we summarize the relationship from innovation to the division of labour. We make a distinction here between organizational innovations (where one of the explicit objectives is to redesign the division of labour) and other innovations (where effects on the division of labour are more indirect). Then in Section 6, we consider one aspect of the relationship from the division of labour to innovation: which division of labour is best for incremental innovation, and which is best for radical innovation? Section 7 concludes.

Lam (2005) offers an excellent review of recent literature, and this chapter is not intended to be a further literature review. Rather, as the objective of this chapter is to provide a brief summary of the relationships at work here, we have limited the references to a few essential sources.

2   HISTORY OF THOUGHT

Here we give a brief review of the history of economic thought about the relationship between the division of labour and innovation. A natural place to start is the writings of Adam Smith (1776) and John Rae (1834), because the different perspectives taken by Smith and Rae bring out a fundamental distinction that is essential to this chapter.

We turn to Smith in a moment, but the reader should be aware that he was by no means the first to write about the division of labour. Roll (1973) and Thomas (1999) note some early writings about the division of labour, from the Old Testament, in the works of Plato and Xenophon, in William Langland's *Piers Plowman*, in Shakespeare, and in the writings of early economists such as William Petty, David Hume and Adam Ferguson. We should add to that list Mandeville's *Fable of the Bees*, as Mandeville anticipates Smith in observing that the division of labour would deliver 'much greater improvements', and indeed Smith used some examples from this book in his own work. Before Smith, however, writings on the economics of innovation were scarcer. Mumford (1934, 1966) lists some writings about technology, economy and society before Smith – including Agricola, Appier and Thybourel, Bacon, Hooke, della Porta and Zonca. Recent historians of technology, moreover, have shown the role of technology in economic and social development from 3000 BC onwards (Lilley, 1948; Singer et al., 1954, 1956, 1957, 1958).

Adam Smith's *Wealth of Nations* was, however, probably the first book to put the division of labour at the centre of a discussion of wealth creation. He argued that the division of labour played an essential role in productivity growth ([1776] 1904a, p. 5): 'The greatest improvement in the productive powers of labour, and the greater part of the skill, dexterity, and judgment with which it is anywhere directed, or applied, seem to have been the effects of the division of labour.' Smith illustrated this with a famous passage about pin manufacturing. He could also have chosen the example of watch-making, which had already made a huge impression on Mandeville.

While, to Smith, the division of labour is the underlying force leading to productivity growth, one important implication of the division of labour is that it gives rise to invention and innovation (ibid., p. 11):

> The invention of all those machines by which labour is so much facilitated and abridged, seems to have been originally owing to the division of labour. Men are much more likely to discover easier and readier methods of attaining any object, when the whole attention of their minds is directed towards that single object, than when it is dissipated among a great variety of things.

The argument has something in common with the idea of 'learning by doing'. Repeated specialization in a particular task gives the worker an intimate knowledge of what is involved, and the experience from which to come up with improvements. In short, invention stems from a *prior* division of labour; the direction of causation runs from the division of labour to the invention.

John Rae (1834) saw this the other way around. Referring to Smith's *Wealth of Nations*, he put his alternative perspective as follows (Rae, 1834, Appendix to Book II): 'In the Wealth of Nations, the division of labour is considered the great generator of invention and improvement, and so of the accumulation of capital. In the view I have given it is represented as proceeding from the antecedent progress of invention.' Here, invention leads to a *subsequent* division of labour; the direction of causation runs from invention to the division of labour to the invention. Indeed, Brewer (1998) has argued that Rae (1834) was perhaps the first economist to put invention at the heart of economic growth.

Why did he think that the direction of causation should run from invention to the division of labour? His explanation centres around economies of scale and specialization. Suppose an invention creates a new piece of capital equipment, which can offer a substantial productivity gain. But suppose this piece of capital is expensive and it is only really economically viable for a firm to buy one if it is in regular use. Rae's argument is that such productivity-enhancing inventions will only be adopted and used if a specialist worker puts the invention to constant use.

Some subsequent debates have asked, who is right? Smith or Rae? The correct answer to this is *not* one or the other, but *both*. Certainly, some invention and innovation stems from a prior division of labour. But equally, some inventions and innovations lead to a change in the division of labour. Both effects can be at work and we need to look out for both. It is for this reason that this chapter looks at both directions of causation: how does innovation influence the division of labour, and how does the division of labour influence innovation?

Many subsequent economic writings on the division of labour took their lead from Smith, and saw it as an important influence on productivity. Charles Babbage (1835) went further and showed how the division of labour would allow the employer to find workers to fulfil a variety of tasks even if few individual workers had the requisite combination of talents to carry out all these tasks (ibid., pp. 175–6):

The master manufacturer, by dividing the work to be executed into different processes, each requiring different degrees of skill or of force, can purchase exactly that precise quantity of both which is necessary for each process;

whereas, if the whole work were executed by one workman, that person must possess sufficient skill to perform the most difficult, and sufficient strength to execute the most laborious, of the operations into which the art is divided.

Thanks to this 'Babbage effect', for example, it is possible to assemble a world-class cricket team, even if very few players are able to perform at a world-class level with *both* bat and ball.

By 1849, belief in the power of the division of labour was so strong that Prince Albert spoke of, 'the great principle of division of labour, which may be called the moving power of civilisation'.[2] Not all writers saw it this way, however. One of the most vocal critics was John Ruskin ([1853] 1996, p. 196):

We have much studied and much perfected, of late, the great civilized invention of the division of labour; only we give it a false name. It is not, truly speaking, the labour that is divided; but the men: – Divided into mere segments of men.

Indeed, Adam Smith – though much impressed with the power of the division of labour as an engine of productivity growth – also had some harsh words to say on the subject ([1776] 1904b, p. 267):

The man whose whole life is spent in performing a few simple operations, of which the effects are perhaps always the same, or very nearly the same, has no occasion to exert his understanding or to exercise his invention . . . [he] generally becomes as stupid and ignorant as it is possible for a human creature to become.

Marx developed these arguments further. He used the term 'alienation' to describe the sentiments of workers when their work becomes ever more specialized and repetitive. He (1844) argued that:

With this division of labour on the one hand and the accumulation of capital on the other, the worker becomes ever more exclusively dependent on labour, and on a particular, very one-sided, machine-like labour at that. Just as he is thus depressed spiritually and physically to the condition of a machine and from being a man becomes an abstract activity and a belly, so he also becomes ever more dependent on every fluctuation in market price, on the application of capital, and on the whim of the rich.

If the division of labour has such damaging consequences, how can that support creativity and innovation? This thinking lay behind William Morris's scathing attack on the division of labour (1879, p. 82): 'the division of labour, once the servant, and now the master of competitive commerce, itself once the servant, and now the master of civilization'.

Some have argued that the negative claims about the division of labour are exaggerated. Ludwig von Mises (1951) maintained that the benefits from the division of labour far exceeds the costs, and that alienation is an exaggeration, because even the labourer restricted to monotonous work can develop as a person with judicious use of leisure time. Jevons (1878, p. 41) had taken a similar view: 'There are certainly some evils which arise out of the great division of labour now existing in civilized countries. These evils are of no account compared with the immense benefits which we receive; still it is well to notice them.' Some optimists asserted that the damaging effects only arose from the most monotonous manual labour. Durkheim ([1893] 1984, p. 307) argued, however, that the damage from repetitive work would apply equally to a 'brain worker' (such as a researcher) as to a manual worker.

It is interesting to note that probably the greatest writer on innovation, Joseph Schumpeter, also recognized that the relationship between division of labour and innovation was not straightforward. He suggested two theories, at different stages of his career. In the first (often called Mark I), and a product of his early works, Schumpeter argued that innovation comes from entrepreneurs, or *wild spirits*. In the second, Mark II, he recognized the role of R&D in innovation, and noted that in the main, it is only big companies that have the resources to invest in R&D (Schumpeter, 1954).

We can summarize what we have learnt from this review as follows. The division of labour can deliver huge gains in productivity. It can also lead to innovation, and, in addition, a reverse effect from innovation to a division of labour is also found. Sometimes, however, an extreme division of labour may be in conflict with creativity and innovation, and as a result it is unlikely that all organizational innovations will lead invariably to an ever narrower and more specialized division of labour. As we shall see below, some organizational innovations (such as flexible team-working) move in a different direction.

In what follows, we shall examine both the linkage from innovation to the division of labour and the linkage from the division of labour to innovation. First, however, it is helpful to have a simple way to classify different features of innovation and the division of labour, and the next two sections (respectively) are concerned with this.

3 INNOVATION – A SIMPLE CLASSIFICATION[3]

The scholar of innovation will consider that the simple classification used here is too simplistic. That is inevitable, given the constraints of this short chapter. But we can show that to understand the relationships between innovation and the division of labour, it is essential to consider *at least* the following distinctions. First, we need to consider the different locations of the innovation within an organization or in relation to an organization. Second, we need to consider what sort of challenge the innovation represents to the organization.

3.1   Where it is Located Within (or in Relation to) the Organization

A simple classification would distinguish (at least) five areas in which the innovation can take place:

1. The environment within which the organization operates. This includes the infrastructure around the organization, including *physical* infrastructure (such as road, rail, airports, telecoms, high-speed ICT infrastructure) and the *technology* infrastructure (such as universities, research labs, libraries, metrology institutes, testing facilities and standards institutions). It also includes formal institutions (such as legal systems, contract law, IPR), and those informal institutions (such as political and social culture, and values) that help to support business.
2. The inputs to the organization's work. These would include: raw materials and utilities, tools, machinery and other equipment, business and other services, and so on.
3. The processes, management procedures, routines and organizational forms used within the organization.
4. The products, services and other outputs produced by the organization.
5. The markets in which the organization buys its inputs and sells its outputs.

3.2   How it Challenges the Organization

The other dimension to innovation we must include in this classification is the extent to which an innovation challenges an organization. Here the conventional distinction between *radical* and *incremental* innovation is useful.

Some writers use this distinction to differentiate between small changes (incremental) and large (radical). But that misses the point, somewhat. The key importance of the distinction is not so much the size of the technological change involved, but whether or not innovation challenges the organization.

A better use of this distinction is to differentiate between those technological changes with which an organization is comfortable (incremental) and those that pose a greater challenge (radical). Some incremental innovations may be large steps, but if they are consistent with the organization's vision, culture, routines and structure, then the organization will cope with them easily enough. And, from the other side, it is not so much the *size* of a radical change that makes it a challenge to the organization, but the fact that it is not consistent with the organization's vision, culture, routines and structure.

4   DIVISION OF LABOUR – A SIMPLE CLASSIFICATION

Once again, the scholar of organization will consider that the simple classification used here is too simplistic, but again this is inevitable. But, as a minimum, it is essential to consider *at least* the following distinctions. First, we need to consider the character of the division of labour when viewed from the micro-perspective of the individual employee. Second, we need to consider the character of the division of labour when viewed from the broader perspective of the organization or the economy as a whole.

4.1   Micro Level – The Employee

A simple classification of the character of the division of labour from the perspective of the employee would include, at least, the following. It would consider:

- the variety of tasks performed;
- the variety of settings in which work is done;
- the variety of 'colleagues' with whom work is done;
- the proportion of value chain for which one employee is responsible;
- the relationship with those on either side in the value chain (e.g., fellow team member; colleague from the same organization, but separated physically and socially; anonymous market transactions);
- the working environment experienced by the employee (e.g., member of a team; a 'cog' in a machine).

These factors amongst others will influence: the employee's attitude to work; job satisfaction; the scope for career development; the degree of mental stimulation and scope creativity; the degree of 'alienation', if relevant, and so on.

4.2   Meso Level – The Organization

At the level of the organization, there is a mapping from division of labour to organization structure. Burns and Stalker (1961) famously illustrated two points on that spectrum. At one end is the *mechanistic* structure: a very hierarchical organization, with a well-defined organizational structure and a well-used organizational chart, with well-defined job descriptions and promotion paths, and with clear norms about the expected channels of communication and those that are expected to remain closed. At the other end is the *organic* structure, which is in very many respects the antithesis: a flat organization, not hierarchical, without a stable organizational structure or an organizational chart, where job descriptions are fluid and promotion paths are rather ad hoc, and with all or most channels of communication open and none expected to be closed.

The literature on organizational forms has identified several leading 'types' on the above spectrum. These are the M-form (or multidivisional), U-form (or unitary form), the matrix organization, the network firm and the organic form (often a small start-up).

4.3   Macro Level – The Economy

At a more macroeconomic level, there is a mapping from national or global division of labour to interregional and international trade flows. While globalization was not a new phenomenon to the late twentieth century, nonetheless that period saw a very rapid growth in the international division of labour. One of the most striking examples of this is found in the computer industry (see Section 5.2) where the components within an ordinary PC, for example, come from a very wide variety of countries.

5   FROM INNOVATION TO THE DIVISION OF LABOUR

Here we explore John Rae's perspective as described above. How do the different types of innovations described in Section 3 influence the different aspects of the division of labour described in Section 4? In what follows, it is helpful to distinguish between those innovations where there may be an explicit intent that the innovation should change the division of labour, from those innovations where the effect may be incidental rather than explicitly intended.

The first category would often include those listed in Section 3.1(1): the processes, management procedures, routines and organizational forms used within the organization. The others may often fall in the second category. However, we should bear in mind that sometimes when organizations adopt a particular innovation that requires a consequent change in organizational structure and the division of labour, such changes are by no means incidental and unintended, but were fully intended. Some organizations see innovations of that sort as a good occasion to implement change. But even if this distinction between intentional and unintentional rearrangements in the division of labour is not hard and fast, it is still useful to organize our discussion.

5.1 Explicit Organizational Innovations and the Division of Labour

Here we show that many organizational innovations can be analysed in terms of their effects in rearranging the division of labour. However, we should stress that that this classification does not generally offer a *complete* description of the important effects of the innovation, nor may all organizational innovations be amenable to such classification.

Table 5.1 selects 32 well-known organizational innovations, and notes briefly some of the implications these may have for the division of labour – at a macro, meso and micro level. The reader requiring a description of what these innovations mean in practice is referred to Swamidass (2000) and Lam (2005). The absence of an entry in a particular cell does not imply that there is no effect, but rather that it is hard to generalize about it.

In most cases, it is easy enough to comment on the *meso* (or organization) level implications of the innovation. If *Taylorism* represents the ultimate limit of the division of labour, then some of the organizational innovation listed in the table represent some steps *short* of that – to avoid some of the dysfunctional implications and, for example, to exploit the benefits from certain types of cross-functional collaboration. In those cases, we can often say that the innovation implies, at a micro level, a *more varied* job description. But in some cases, the innovation does not represent a greater or a lesser division of labour, but instead a *different* design of the division of labour, on different lines. In those cases, all we can usually say is that the innovation implies, at a micro level, *different* job description.

Turning to the macro implications, it is often harder to comment on these conclusively, because that outcome depends on other factors as well, but the two most common are probably: globalization, where the labour involved in creating a particular output is dispersed over a larger geographical area; and concentration, where the outcome of the innovation is a greater concentration of production (and labour) within a smaller number of organizations.

Table 5.1   Analysis of effects of organizational innovations on the division of labour

Organizational Innovation	Implications for Division of Labour		
	Macro level (economy)	Meso level (organization)	Micro level (employee)
Agile logistics	Globalization: ever finer and ever more unstable division of labour	Hollowing-out to core activities	Some job descriptions will change to involve more spot transactions
Business process re-engineering (BPR)		Fundamental re-think and re-design in division of labour in organization to optimize process as a whole	Will change the job description and working environment of some employees
Cellular manufacturing		Breaks up a U-form into something more like an M-form	Will change the job description and working environment of some employees
Concurrent engineering		May not change total workload but requires more frequent communication between departments	More employees will have more frequent communication with colleagues in other departments
Cross-functional teams		A distinct innovation for both an M-form or U-form organization	Teams made up of employees from various functions. Employee no longer works with functional peers but across functions. Work more varied and challenging
Decentralization of functions		A less hierarchical organization	More individuals are empowered to make decisions
Decentralization to customer-oriented departments		Changes a U-form into an M-form	Functional employee works with fewer of his or her functions and more from other functions

Term		
Flexible job design	Need be no underlying change in division of labour, but different workers fill some of the functions	Some employees will have greater variety of work, with scope for personal development
Flexible manufacturing	Possible horizontal concentration as firms diversify to wider range of products	Increased economies of scope in an organization
Flexible working	More flexible working arrangements within the same division of labour	Individual employees have more autonomy to decide their working hours
Hoshin kanri	Hoshin kanri may not have an explicit objective to change division of labour, but such changes will occur if strategy changes require new daily control activities	As left, some job descriptions will change if strategy changes require changes in daily control activities
'Just in time' (JIT)	Increased and/or changed communication between employees will require new organizational structure	Some job descriptions will change as employees have to react to kanban (signals)
Kaizen	Continual improvement of functions that span organizational boundaries, so requires new organizational form	Involves new activities that continually improve all functions, so implying change in individual job descriptions
Kanban – see JIT	Changed communication between employees requires organizational change	Some job descriptions will change as employees must react to kanban (signals)

Table 5.1 (continued)

Organizational Innovation	Implications for Division of Labour		
	Macro level (economy)	Meso level (organization)	Micro level (employee)
Lean production		Involves taking a customer-centred perspective on processes so as to eliminate waste	Some employees will become more customer-focused and other job descriptions will change as 'wasteful' activities are removed
Manufacturing resource planning (MRP)		A technique for planning an efficient division of labour. Will lead to organizational change if MRP identifies inefficiencies in existing division of labour	As left, may imply changes in job descriptions for some employees
Mass customization	Likelihood of horizontal concentration as large firms diversify into a wider range of products	Increased economies of scope in an organization	
Multi-function teams		New organizational form incorporating workers from many different functions	Individual job descriptions will change: less work with functional peers and more work with colleagues from other functions
Open innovation	Globalization: innovation involves collaboration with many other organizations in many different locations	Hollowing-out the organization: some activities will no longer be done in-house	Changing job descriptions for some workers. Some involved in communications with other organizations
Outsourcing	Globalization	Hollowing-out the organization	More arms' length transactions in the market

126

Technique			
Project evaluation and review technique (PERT)		Changes in organizational form will occur if the PERT identifies inefficiencies in processes	Some changes in job description
Poka-yoke	As some functions can be performed by less skilled staff, will increase importance of cost-competitiveness and hence increase concentration	Can increase capital intensity and may enable some functions to be performed by less skilled staff, thereby cutting costs	Some originally skilled work now demands less skill
Quality circles		Creation of new, self-managing work groups, to reverse the more extreme versions of the division of labour	Greater work variety, communication and collegiality
Quality management systems		Creating a quality management system requires organizational change to enable such a system	
Rapid prototyping			A great reversal in the division of labour. Can give one employee the tools to create objects as a craftsperson creates a sculpture
Self-managing work teams		A fully self-managed company may have no hierarchy (the ultimate 'organic form')	Workers decide the division of labour in their own team
Simultaneous engineering		May not change total workload but requires more frequent communication between departments	More employees with have more frequent communication with colleagues in other departments
'Six sigma'		Implementation of 'six sigma' requires a new infrastructure of 'black belt' and 'green belt' experts	New specialized jobs for quality management experts

Table 5.1 (continued)

Organizational Innovation	Implications for Division of Labour		
	Macro level (economy)	Meso level (organization)	Micro level (employee)
Strategic business units	May lead to internationalization of division of labour	Creation of new market-facing divisions for which a discrete business strategy can be defined	
Taylorism		Taylorism describes the organizational form that results when the division of labour is pushed to the ultimate	The ultimate degree of specialization in job descriptions
Total quality management (TQM)			Employees skills will be enhanced through training so that workers can minimize errors
Virtual organization	Globalization and regional dispersion	A temporary alliance of enterprises brought together to share skills and resources for a specific business objective	The employee in a virtual organization experiences a wide diversity of job descriptions and working environments

Source: Authors' own classification, based on material in Swamidass (2000), Lam (2005) and various other online resources.

5.2 Other Innovations and the Division of Labour

We can create the equivalent to Table 5.1 for other sorts of innovation, as listed in Section 3.1. To recap, these are:

- The environment within which the organization operates. This includes:
  - *physical* infrastructure (such as roads, rail, airports, telecoms, high-speed ICT infrastructure);
  - *technology* infrastructure (such as universities, research labs, libraries, metrology institutes, testing facilities and standards institutions);
  - *formal* institutions (such as legal systems, contract law, IPR);
  - *informal* institutions (such as political and social culture, and values) that help to support business.
- The inputs to the organization's work. These would include:
  - raw materials;
  - utilities;
  - tools, machinery and other equipment;
  - business and other services.
- The products, services and other outputs produced by the organization.
- The markets in which the organization buys its inputs and sells its outputs.

With these, it is usually easiest to comment on their effect on the division of labour at a macro and meso level, by reference to a simple model of the 'make or buy' decision – where 'make' means carrying out an activity in-house, and 'buy' means sourcing components or service inputs from the market.

First, innovations that improve the physical infrastructure reduce transport and communications costs. These can either make it easier to use the market (rather than make in-house) or make it easier to coordinate production activity that is geographically dispersed.

Second, innovations that improve the technology infrastructure can facilitate some of the organizational innovations listed in Section 5.1. So, for example:

- Innovations in universities and research labs may facilitate open innovation (Chesbrough, 2003).
- Innovations in metrology can facilitate the division of labour directly, because it is easier to ensure that the output from one link

of the supply chain is consistent with the requirements of the next link.

- Innovations in metrology can also facilitate those organizational innovations like TQM and 'six sigma' that depend on reducing errors by more accurate measurement (amongst other things).
- Innovations in testing facilities and standards (more or better standards) can reduce transaction costs, which tends to lead to a greater use of the market.[4]

Third, innovations that strengthen formal institutions may also reduce transaction costs and so lead to a greater use of the market (Besanko et al., 2010). It may seem strange to write that the use of lawyers reduces costs (!) but what this means is that the existence of well-developed legal systems reduces the risk of doing business.

Fourth, innovations that improve informal institutions help to build trust between trading partners, and that can also be seen as a mechanism that reduces transaction costs and so facilitates use of the market. Next, turning to innovations in inputs, it is hard to generalize about the effects of innovations in raw materials and utilities on the division of labour. But we can make some general comments about innovations in tools and equipment, and innovations in business services.

Fifth, those innovations in tools and equipment that increase capital intensity (e.g., an expensive new machine with features not found in existing machinery), will tend to increase concentration (and labour) within a smaller number of companies. Moreover, it was this sort of thing that Rae had in mind when he said that innovation can lead to greater specialization in labour.

Sixth, those innovations in tools and equipment that reduce capital intensity (e.g., a cheaper PC that replaces an existing mainframe system), will tend to have the opposite effect on concentration. Moreover, these innovations will often reduce the division of labour – for example, the use of PCs by university lecturers to type their own material, rather than use a typist.

Next, turning to innovations in the products, services and other outputs produced by the organization, it is hard to make any firm generalizations about how these innovations will impact on the division of labour. We have already listed in Section 5.1 those organizational innovations such as mass customization and flexible manufacturing that increase economies of scope and thereby make it easier for one organization to produce a wider variety of related products. The researcher who observes such product proliferation and growing concentration of production (and labour) might suspect that the link is between innovations such as product proliferation and the concentration of labour, but actually the chain of causation is from the organizational innovation to concentration, with proliferation as a by-product.

Finally, turning to innovations in the markets in which products and services are bought and sold, we can make two further generalizations. Seventh, innovations in input markets that make it easier to use the market to source cheap components (for example, B2B e-commerce) will tend to reduce transaction costs and lead to a greater use of outsourcing. Eighth, innovations in output markets (e.g., the opportunity for B2C e-commerce over the internet) may appear to level the playing field in favour of small and remote businesses, but the history of bookselling over the internet suggests otherwise, when the selling operation enjoys substantial economies of scale. For in that case, online bookselling has allowed a smaller number of large players (e.g., Amazon) to exploit economies of scale and has driven many smaller players out of the market.[5]

6 FROM DIVISION OF LABOUR TO INNOVATION

Now we turn to the reverse connection from the division of labour and organizational form to innovation. The broad question, 'How does the division of labour in particular organizational forms impact on innovation?', is too broad for this chapter. If we ask a narrower question, 'Which organizational forms and which designs for the division of labour are best for different types of innovation?', we can get closer to an answer. In what follows, we shall answer a narrower question still, which comes in two parts: (1) Which organizational forms and which designs for the division of labour are best for incremental innovation? (2) Which organizational forms and which designs for the division of labour are best for radical innovation? We shall take these two questions in turn.

6.1 Incremental Innovation

Smith's explanation, discussed in Section 2, gets quite close to the reason why specialization and incremental innovation may be related: 'men are much more likely to discover easier and readier methods of attaining any object, when the whole attention of their minds is directed towards that single object' Smith ([1776] 1904a, p. 11). It suggests a form of 'learning by doing', 'learning from mistakes', or 'practice makes perfect'.

It is unlikely that the detail of Smith's explanation (which operates at an individual level) is quite right for the incremental innovation of today. But the parallel with 'learning by doing' is still the right one. Even those organizational innovations (such as 'just in time', *kaizen*, lean manufacturing, PERT, quality circles, quality management systems, 'six sigma' and TQM) that seek continuous improvement and organizational learning from pooled experience, are still based on a fairly firm division of labour and specialization. This division of labour is modified to increase cross-functional sharing of experience, knowledge and understanding between experts in different functions. This is a significant step back from pure Taylorism. But the point is still that these are experts with much experience in their own function, gained through the division of labour.

So, we conclude that the best environment in which to develop incremental innovation is in the large, relatively hierarchical organization. Such organizations support a fairly high (though not extreme) division of labour and job specialism. One example of this would be the U-form organization, in which each unit of the firm manages a particular business function. Such a structure facilitates the division of labour, and hence allows the firm to exploit scale economies from specialization. It is best suited to stable market conditions, where job descriptions are stable and most decisions are routine. This is an environment in which operational efficiency (i.e., carrying out the task at the lowest cost) is the key element of business strategy.

Small, flat organizations are unlikely to be so well adapted to achieve a long stream of incremental innovations, because: (1) they have more modest opportunities for learning by doing; (2) they cannot support such an intricate division of labour, and indeed in the ultimate organic form, job descriptions are very broad indeed. Such organizations cannot therefore fit Smith's criterion for incremental innovation.

6.2   Radical Innovation

The roots of radical innovation are quite different. Radical innovations don't happen in steady streams, as a result of learning by doing and learning from errors within a relatively stable process. No, they arise from the radical and challenging fusion of distinct competencies, knowledge bases, and Smith's description really doesn't capture this. It is caught much better in the writings of Koestler and Simon. Koestler's (1964) work is concerned with creative thinking rather than industrial innovation, but he captured the essence of radical thinking very well. He made, 'a distinction between the routine skills of thinking on a single "plane". . . and the creative act which . . . always operates on more than one plane'. He coined the term *bisociation* to describe what happens in creative thinking: it is about perceiving an idea or situation, 'in two self-consistent but habitually incompatible frames of reference' (ibid., p. 35). Simon (1985) expressed a similar perspective, but now within the context of management and economics, and relating explicitly to innovation. He asserted that the process of learning from *diverse knowledge bases* is a highly important source of invention and innovation.

Now there is an unresolved issue here: if radical creativity requires learning from *diverse knowledge bases*, does that mean that it must be the work of cross-functional teams? Smith ([1776] 1904a, p. 12) thought not. He recognized that some inventions were made by: 'those who are called philosophers or men of speculation, whose trade it is not to do anything, but to observe everything; and who, upon that account, are often capable of combining together the powers of the most distant and dissimilar objects'. Smith, Carlyle, Mill, Ruskin, Marx, Morris and Marshall were shining examples of such philosophers with the powers to combine 'the most distant and dissimilar objects'. But these powers are very rare in the modern university. It is even rarer amongst companies and entrepreneurs.

So in practice, this combinatorial activity involves collaboration between people with multiple diverse knowledge bases. This approach to innovation requires a markedly different form of organization. Because *bisociation* involves combining the *habitually unfamiliar*, such innovation requires communication that cuts right across existing structures, and communications with many unfamiliar communities. These sorts of changes conflict with accepted norms and routines in the hierarchical organization. Moreover, such communication is not easy to develop in hierarchies, for the simple reason that such hierarchies were designed to prevent it, when it serves no purpose. For that reason, the required channels do not exist in a hierarchy, and to create them involves some of the organizational innovations described in Section 5.1 (cellular manufacturing, cross-functional teams, *hoshin kanri*, quality circles, etc.)

On the other hand, the communication required to support this combinatorial activity is easier to develop within an organic form or network organization. In these forms, the relationships among employees are not confined by strict lines of authority but can change to meet the requirements of common tasks, as they evolve. Indeed, the organizational form can be reconfigured and the division of labour recombined, as the tasks of the organization change.

A famous example of this was the pioneering study of firms in the electronics industry (Burns and Stalker, 1961, p. 92). They argued that:

> In the electronics industry . . . there is often a deliberate attempt to avoid specifying individual tasks, and to forbid any dependence on management hierarchy as a structure of defined functions and authority. The head of one concern, at the beginning of the first interview, attacked the idea of the organization chart

as inapplicable in his concern and as a dangerous method of thinking about the working of industrial management.

These structures are well adapted to cope with radical innovation, and well adapted to engage in open innovation, where some competencies are concentrated in-house, and others are found outside.

A good example of the disruptive character of radical innovation is found in the software industry. From the mid-1980s onwards, Microsoft emerged as the leader in the PC operating systems market, and then also as leader in the market for office software, during the 1990s. The business model was based on selling software that runs on every individual PC. Google's business model was rather different, however. Google was a software company, but it made its money from selling advertising rather than selling software. As more applications move to the 'Cloud', this can be seen as a *radical* innovation, because it is changing the structure of the market, and Google is replacing Microsoft as the dominant company in the software industry. Indeed, there is a saying in the software industry – to paraphrase: 'When you work on your PC, Microsoft makes money; when you work online, Google makes money.'

Some of the largest companies have tried to recreate the feel of a small organic firm for particular projects. A famous example was how IBM set up the 'Project Chess' team at IBM's Boca Raton labs in Florida, and charged them with developing the IBM PC in a very short timescale (Langlois, 1992). But the use of such 'start-up' ventures by the largest hierarchical organizations doesn't always work. To use a botanical metaphor, can small saplings thrive in the shadow of a great oak?

7   CONCLUSIONS

What have we learnt from the summary of the relationships between innovation and the division of labour? Six main points stand out:

1. The relationships definitely work in *both* directions: from innovation to the division of labour and vice versa.
2. The relationships are not *monotonic*: increasing division of labour may increase innovation for a while, but eventually the dysfunctional effects of an excessive division of labour sets in, and this gets in the way of innovation.
3. The relationship from innovation to the division of labour can be split into two categories. Organizational innovations have the explicit objective to change organizational form and the division of labour.

Other innovations may not have any such explicit objective, but will still impact on the division of labour. Two examples, for illustration: (a) innovations in the infrastructure and institutions around the organization can lead to greater outsourcing and a geographical dispersion of the division of labour; (b) some innovations in tools and equipment may lead to greater (or lesser) concentration of production across companies, and hence a change in the corporate division of labour.

4. We can make some reasonable generalizations about the ideal organizational form (and division of labour) for different types of innovation. Incremental innovation stems from intelligent learning by doing, and requires quite a well-developed division of labour, but augmented by some management initiatives to improve knowledge sharing between different functions. Radical innovation calls for a very different type of organization: an organic form or a network firm, where the division of labour is not so well developed and is not strict.

5. There is no one 'best' organizational innovation or 'best' rearrangement in the division of labour. The right organizational innovations depend entirely on strategic objectives.

6. And finally, there is no one 'best' organizational form or 'best' division of labour to maximize innovation. The right form will depend on the intended innovation.

NOTES

1. In mathematics, a monotonic function is one that preserves the given order. So, for example, if Y is a monotonically increasing function of X, then a graph of Y against X will be upward-sloping.
2. Here quoted from Pevsner (1960, p. 40).
3. A more detailed discussion of how to classify innovations is given in Swann (2009).
4. The most striking example of how standards have led to a greater international division of labour is in the personal computer market. If we open up a PC, we find that the constituent components come from many different countries. This is possible because the existence of well-known international standards allows producers to specialize in a particular small segment of the industry and sell their outputs to a worldwide market. For example, for some years the majority of hard disk drives in personal computers were made in Singapore.
5. This, at least, is the case with the sale of new books. Interestingly enough, however, when we look at the market for second-hand and antiquarian books, it does seem that the advent of B2C by e-commerce has made it easier for small-scale companies to improve their performance by exploiting the much larger marketplace accessible online.

REFERENCES

Babbage, C. (1835), *On the Economy of Machinery and Manufactures* (4th edition), London: Charles Knight.
Besanko, D., D. Dranove, M. Shanley and S. Schaefer (2010), *Economics of Strategy* (5th edition), Hoboken, NJ: John Wiley and Sons.
Brewer, A. (1998), 'Invention', in O.F. Hamouda, C. Lee and D. Mair (eds), *The Economics of John Rae*, London: Routledge.
Burns, T. and G. Stalker (1961), *The Management of Innovation*, London: Tavistock.
Chesbrough, H. (2003), *Open Innovation*, Boston, MA: Harvard Business School Press.
Durkheim, E. ([1893] 1984), *The Division of Labour in Society*, translated by W.D. Halls, New York: Free Press.
Jevons, W.S. (1878), *Political Economy*, London: Macmillan.
Koestler, A. (1964), *The Act of Creation*, London: Hutchinson.
Lam, A. (2005), 'Organizational innovation', in J. Fagerberg, D. Mowery and R.R. Nelson (eds), *The Oxford Handbook of Innovation*, Oxford: Oxford University Press, pp. 115–47.
Langlois, R.N. (1992), 'External economies and economic progress: the case of the micro-computer industry', *Business History Review*, **66**(1), 1–50.
Lilley, S. (1948), *Men, Machines and History*, London: Cobbett Press.
Marx, K. (1844), 'Wages and labour', in *Economic and Philosophic Manuscripts of 1844*, available at: http://www.marxists.org/archive/marx/works/download/pdf/Economic-Philosophic-Manuscripts-1844.pdf; accessed 28 March 2012.
Mises, L. von (1951), *Socialism: An Economic and Sociological Analysis*, New Haven, CT: Yale University Press.
Morris, W. ([1879] 1966), 'Making the best of it: paper read before the Trades' Guild of Learning and the Birmingham Society of Artists', in *The Collected Works of William Morris, Volume 22*, New York: Russell and Russell, pp. 81–118.
Mumford, L. (1934), *Technics and Civilization*, New York: Harcourt Brace and Company.
Mumford, L. (1966), *The Myth of the Machine*, New York: Harcourt Brace and Company.
Pevsner, N. (1960), *Pioneers of Modern Design*, Harmondsworth: Penguin Books.
Rae, J. (1834), *Statement of Some New Principles on the Subject of Political Economy*, available at: http://www.efm.bris.ac.uk/het/rae/; accessed 28 March 2012.
Roll, E. (1973), *A History of Economic Thought* (4th edition), London: Faber & Faber.
Ruskin, J. ([1853] 1996), *The Stones of Venice, Volume II: The Sea Stories*, in E.T. Cook and A. Wedderburn (eds), *The Works of John Ruskin, Volume 10*, CD-ROM Version, Cambridge: Cambridge University Press.
Schumpeter, J.A. (1954), *Capitalism, Socialism and Democracy* (4th edition), London: Unwin University Books.
Simon, H.A. (1985), 'What do we know about the creative process?', in R.L. Kuhn (ed.), *Frontiers in Creative and Innovative Management*, Cambridge, MA: Ballinger.
Singer, C., E.J. Holmyard and A.R. Hall (1954), *A History of Technology, Volume 1*, London: Oxford University Press.
Singer, C., E.J. Holmyard, A.R. Hall and T.I. Williams (1956), *A History of Technology, Volume 2*, London: Oxford University Press.
Singer, C., E.J. Holmyard, A.R. Hall and T.I. Williams (1957), *A History of Technology, Volume 3*, London: Oxford University Press.
Singer, C., E.J. Holmyard, A.R. Hall and T.I. Williams (1958), *A History of Technology, Volume 4*, London: Oxford University Press.
Smith, A. ([1776] 1904a), *An Inquiry into the Nature and Causes of the Wealth of Nations, Volume I*, London: Methuen.
Smith, A. ([1776] 1904b), *An Inquiry into the Nature and Causes of the Wealth of Nations, Volume II*, London: Methuen.
Swamidass, P.M. (ed.) (2000), *Encyclopedia of Production and Manufacturing Management*, Boston, MA and London: Kluwer Academic.

Swann, G.M.P. (2009), *The Economics of Innovation: An Introduction*, Cheltenham, UK and Northampton, MA: Edward Elgar Publishing.

Thomas, K. (ed.) (1999), *Work*, Oxford: Oxford University Press.

6 Management innovation in action: the case of self-managing teams

Ignacio G. Vaccaro, Henk W. Volberda and Frans A.J. Van Den Bosch

INTRODUCTION

The pursuit of management innovation is influenced by both internal and external change agents as new practices, processes or structures will be shaped by both employees of the innovating organization and third parties such as consultants and academics (Birkinshaw et al., 2008). Following Birkinshaw et al. we propose that internal change agents play a particularly relevant role as they are the individuals championing the introduction of management innovation in order to make organizations more efficient. This also espouses the rational view of management innovation, and in particular the role of human agency, as we study the deliberate actions of change agents within the organization.

In understanding the role of internal change agents we consider the case of self-managing teams at Royal DSM, a Dutch life sciences and material sciences company, which has been working with self-managing teams in its Anti-Infectives plant for ten years. In coping with the cost advantages that companies can achieve in Asian production sites and remain competitive, many firms have moved production to Asia and away from Europe and North America. Royal DSM, however, continues to produce in Europe while remaining competitive. One of the reasons for this is its use of self-managing teams in its Anti-Infectives plant in Delft, the Netherlands. In this chapter we seek to understand how self-managing teams work and what the role is of those involved to make them successful. Hence, our guiding research question is: 'What is the role of internal change agents in the functioning of self-managing teams?' In answering this question, and building on insights from previous research, we focus our attention on three key issues related to internal change agents in the context of self-managing teams: leadership, knowledge exchange and trust.

Our study contributes to the literature on management innovation in at least three ways. First, we present an in-depth case study of an instance of management innovation, which complements insights from conceptual (e.g., Birkinshaw et al., 2008) and large-sample studies (e.g., Vaccaro et al., 2012). Second, we analyze the role of leadership, trust and knowledge exchange within this instance of management innovation. Last, we analyze the period 2001–10 during which self-managing teams have been active at DSM, providing longitudinal insights into the process of self-managing.

SELF-MANAGING TEAMS AS MANAGEMENT INNOVATION

Self-managing teams are teams that regulate their own functioning without the direct intervention of a supervisor (Waterman, 1994). These teams typically have no internal hierarchy and are accountable for achieving the goals they set for themselves (Zárraga and Bonache, 2005). Members of these teams typically interact face to face, have control over a well-defined work area and have discretion over decisions regarding how to organize and structure their work (Cummings, 1978; Cohen and Ledford, 1994; Bunderson and Boumgarden, 2010).

Self-managing teams are an example of management innovation, as they represent a change in the way management work is performed (Hamel, 2006). In particular, self-managing teams trigger changes in three facets of management innovation: practices, processes and structures (Birkinshaw et al., 2008). Management practices refer to managerial day-to-day work, which may include setting objectives and procedures, developing talent and meeting demands from different stakeholders (Birkinshaw et al., 2008; Mol and Birkinshaw, 2009). Self-managing teams typically set their own production goals and decide on how those goals will be achieved by assigning responsibility for the different tasks amongst team members (Lawler, 1990). Management processes refer to the routines that govern the work of managers, drawing from abstract ideas and turning them into actionable tools, which typically include strategic planning, project management and performance assessment (Hamel, 2006; Birkinshaw et al., 2008). In self-managing teams, for instance, reward systems may be linked to the set of skills individuals possess, as this reflects the understanding and know-how team members have about the job their team is responsible for (Lawler, 1990). Organizational structure, that is, how organizations arrange communication, align and harness effort from their members (Hamel, 2007; Birkinshaw et al., 2008), is typically adapted to reflect the self-managing teams' autonomy and discretion. This usually involves the elimination of a foreman or supervisor position, making the structure flatter, and allowing for teams to report directly to management (Lawler, 1990; Bunderson and Boumgarden, 2010). Table 6.1 shows each of these facets illustrated by

Table 6.1   Illustrative quotes on management innovation facets

MI Facet	Illustrative Quotes from DSM	Notes
New Management Practices	'Operators who went to work in the early days, they did their work and nothing else, nowadays you have to think more about the job you are doing, you have to think better about it, can we improve? . . . In the early days we had to go to the technologist to solve the problems, and nowadays we have to do that ourselves. There has to be a change in the way you thought as process operator, and for most people that was a good thing to do'. (Operator)	This illustrates a shift in what is done by the operators and teams. Rules and procedures formerly precluded operators from addressing problems themselves, while now they have to do it
New Management Processes	'In the past, a shift leader was working and would come up and say: "You have to do that and you will do that". And if you have a problem you called the shift supervisor and say: "Ok, I have a problem". And then the supervisor had to come and help the shift leader out. That is the "old" way . . . . With the building of this [plant], if one technologist or a member of the group, they give you work to do. And if you had a problem, you'd have to try and solve it yourselves. Don't run back to the staff-group leader and come with a problem to solve, but solve it and report what you did (to solve it)'. (Operator)	This reflects changes in how people do things. Before, the management system emphasized the role of the operator as the executor of orders and the leader as the problem solver. After the introduction of self-managing teams, execution and problem-solving reside within the teams of operators
New management Structures	'They [operators] were looking for an anchor point, which used to be the shift supervisor, but this anchor was not there anymore, so they had to communicate directly with the staff, and the technologists in the staff in the past used to communicate via shift supervisors'. (Former Plant Manager)	Reducing hierarchical layers to allow self-managing teams to take control

quotes obtained during interviews at DSM Anti-Infectives regarding their use of self-managing teams.

THEORETICAL BACKGROUND: LEADERSHIP, KNOWLEDGE EXCHANGE AND TRUST

Leadership

Studies of leadership in the context of self-managing teams have often faced the paradoxical task of studying how leaders can lead others who are meant to lead themselves (Stewart and Manz, 1995). Some authors have proposed that self-managing teams may be fit to lead themselves (Manz and Sims, 1987), thus bypassing the need for external leadership. Similarly, others have studied the emergence of leadership within such teams (e.g., Wolff et al., 2002). Yet others, however, have focused on the role of leadership as a facilitator for self-managing teams. Authors in the latter stream propose, for instance, that leadership behavior characterized by guidance, encouragement and delegation (Stewart and Manz, 1995) as well as providing autonomy (Yukl and Yukl, 2002) is conducive to self-management within teams. Our view of the role of leadership regarding self-managing teams remains close to the latter view.

In studying the context in which self-managing teams develop and function, we draw on transactional and transformational leadership (Bass, 1990). Research suggests that both leadership behaviors are positively associated with management innovation (Vaccaro et al., 2012). Transactional leadership entails engaging followers by means of transactions between leaders and followers. This is commonly done by the clear establishment of goals and rewards as well as the active involvement of leaders when expected standards are not met (Bass, 1990; Yammarino and Bass, 1990; Bass and Avolio, 1993). Transformational leadership entails instilling a sense of purpose and identification in followers towards the achievement of common goals (Burns, 1978; Bass, 1985). Transformational leaders are usually admired and trusted by their followers and promote the questioning of assumptions. They also consider their followers' individual needs and inspire them by attaching meaning and challenge to what they do (Bass et al., 2003). In addition, research suggests that transformational leaders promote proactive behavior amongst followers (Belschak and Den Hartog, 2010), which relates to self-managing as it implies taking charge of one's work and also suggests putting forward ideas for new work methods to improve production and team processes (Parker et al., 2010). Moreover, teams led by transformational leaders may favor cooperation as opposed to competition when resolving conflict within the team, which may subsequently translate into better performance (Zhang et al., 2011).

Knowledge Exchange

At the core of self-managing teams is the notion that they are ultimately accountable for the organization of their work and its execution. Because of this, members of self-managing teams will see their work affected by that of others within or outside the team as knowledge is obtained from these different sources. The experience of individuals or groups that come into contact with the work of other units may affect the work of a self-managing team (Argote and Ingram, 2000). Self-managing teams are given the independence and the tools to collaborate and exchange the necessary knowledge to execute their work (Wageman, 1995). Yet, collaboration alone may be insufficient for a team to achieve higher levels of performance, needing also to exchange knowledge to achieve performance and implement innovative measures (Collins and Smith, 2006). Cummings (2004) shows that teams that exchange information across functions and geographical locations achieve better levels of performance.

Due to the fact that self-managing teams are highly interdependent, their need to share knowledge becomes essential in carrying out their work. This has been argued to lead to a higher sense of collective responsibility and promote cooperation (Wageman, 1995). Furthermore, research suggests that accountability for the way in which work is done in groups is associated with better decision quality (Scholten et al., 2007).

In order to achieve high levels of performance, group members need to have the ability to recognize and incorporate relevant knowledge from other members (Thomas-Hunt et al., 2003).

Trust

Trust implies the willing vulnerability of a party to another's actions, based on the expectation that the trustor will perform a valuable action the trustee may not be able to monitor or control (Mayer et al., 1995).

The implementation of self-managing teams means that individuals within these teams will have a high degree of independence and that their work will depend on others' work and vice versa. Because teams will operate in this way without supervision, making members vulnerable to the actions of others (Kiffin-Petersen and Cordery, 2003), trust will become particularly relevant (Mayer et al., 1995).

Trust relates to the development of self-managing teams as it increases with the successful completion of trust-based assignments (Gagnon et al., 2008). Research has proposed that trust plays a key role in the employee's willingness to accept his or her role within self-managing teams, the associated increase in cooperation with others and interdependence (Kiffin-Petersen and Cordery, 2003). Teams may benefit from the development of trust as they will regulate their functioning in the absence of direct supervision from a team manager. Because of this, their performance as a team will be related to their ability to effectively rely on the autonomous work of the different members and the competent execution of such work.

Kiffin-Petersen and Cordery (2003) and De Jong and Elfing (2010) find that trust amongst team members is positively related to their performance as a team. This suggests that trust aids the team in meeting the demands of increased interdependence and accountability within a self-managing team by engaging in productive interaction (De Jong and Elfring, 2010).

METHODS

In studying management innovation within an organization we are studying a dynamic process, which may include many different actors. In order to best capture these dynamics we chose to employ a case study methodology. This is an appropriate methodology as it suited our 'what' research question and allows for the investigation of a phenomenon in depth and within its context (Yin, 2009).

For our analysis we selected the case of DSM, which had implemented a management system centered on self-managing teams at one of its plants. By focusing on self-managing teams at DSM, we analyze a 'transparently observable' (Pettigrew, 1990) example of this management innovation in action. We employed this form of theoretical sampling as the organization was open to cooperating with our study, which enabled us to further understand this management innovation (Eisenhardt, 1989) while complementing other related studies.

Research Setting

Our study was carried out at the ZOR-f plant, a DSM Anti-Infectives plant that produces a key ingredient for a family of antibiotics through a biochemical process (see Box 6.1). DSM is a large life sciences and material sciences company founded in the Netherlands in 1902, which employs over 20 000 people worldwide and had net sales of €7.7 billion in 2009. The production of anti-infectives is a part of DSM's Pharma business group, which represents 9.39 percent of the company's operation by net sales.

BOX 6.1   BACKGROUND: BIOTECHNOLOGY AT
DSM ZOR-F ANTI-INFECTIVES PLANT
IN DELFT

DSM's ZOR-f plant is a purpose-built biochemistry-based facility, which since 2001 has been producing a type of antibiotic called cephalexin. Cephalexin is a type of cephalosporin C, which is more efficient at fighting gram-negative bacteria while being less toxic than penicillin. Over the years, semi-synthetic antibiotics based on cephalosporin C, such as cephalexin, have been developed.

Between 1975 and 1985, cephalexin was produced, employing traditional chemistry processes involving ten different steps. This, however, led to a relatively large amount of waste, reaching 30–40 kg per kg of product. In addition, these processes would be run at high temperatures and would involve the use of several solvents and toxic materials.

While improvements to the process were later achieved through recycling and optimization, the breakthrough came in 1995 when biocatalysis was used to produce cephalexin, yielding a six-step process that produced 10 kg of waste per kg of product. Further developments of this process at DSM have resulted in the production of the key raw material for cephalexin, 7-ADCA (7-aminodeacetoxy cephalosporanic acid), by direct fermentation, shortening the overall process to four steps. This process now yields between 2 and 5 kg of waste per kg of product. Additionally, the amount of toxic materials employed has been sharply reduced and production is carried out at lower temperatures.

Sources: DSM (2000), *DSM N.V. Annual Report 2000*; OECD (2001), *The Application of Biotechnology to Industrial Sustainability*, Paris: OECD.

DSM's ZOR-f plant

We focused our study on the DSM Anti-Infectives plant ZOR-f, where self-managing teams have been in place since the plant began production in 2001. In particular, we looked at the functioning of self-managing teams of process operators at ZOR-f. The ZOR-f plant, located within a DSM site in Delft, the Netherlands, specializes in the production of 7-ADCA through a biotechnology process (see Box 6.1) and is one of the largest producers worldwide as well as one of the last ones outside of Asia.

The ZOR-f plant employs 60 people, which includes process operators (28) in charge of running the production process, process technologists (four) overseeing the technical aspects of the biotechnology production, planners (three) in charge of logistics, as well as an operations manager, a maintenance manager and a plant manager. There are five self-managing teams of process operators with five operators each. These teams work in shifts of eight hours, keeping the production facility running 24 hours a day, seven days a week. Teams rotate shifts in cycles of two morning shifts, two afternoon shifts and two evening shifts.

While the teams are self-managing and have no formal supervisor, there is an *operations expert* who sits as an interface between the teams and management. This position has no formal authority, and in fact is at the same hierarchical level as process operators, however it is acknowledged by managers and operators alike as a key element in keeping the functioning of self-management at the plant.

In addition to this, a maintenance team services the plant. This team is the product of a joint venture between DSM and two maintenance companies, which means that some of the employees within the joint venture are DSM employees while others are not. The relationship between DSM and the maintenance joint venture is regulated by a contractual agreement between the parties. This agreement in itself represented a departure from the way that maintenance had been arranged in the past. Under this agreement, the joint venture has the obligation to deliver a functioning plant. However, it did not charge DSM by the hour, but rather participated in the savings it could produce beyond an established threshold. These savings could relate to both maintenance and operations. In this way, maintenance personnel were explicitly invited to get involved in all aspects of the plant, effectively broadening the span of their work beyond maintenance itself.

Data Collection and Data Sources

Primary data were collected by means of semi-structured interviews with key informants involved with self-managing teams at the ZOR-f plant during the second semester of 2009.

In order to have a better understanding of the phenomenon under study as well as the key individuals involved, before starting collecting data we had a series of meetings with members of the management at DSM. These interviews were carried out with managers from DSM corporate as well as with plant management at ZOR-f. In these initial meetings we obtained information regarding key individuals involved in self-managing teams at

ZOR-f (formerly and currently working at this plant) as well as information regarding self-managing teams we subsequently used in drafting questions for our semi-structured interviews.

During our research, we interviewed current plant management at ZOR-f as well as operators. Interviews with members of the plant management often led to referrals for other sources of evidence, typically former members of the plant management, now occupying management positions in other parts of the organization within DSM. This contributed to a richer understanding of the underlying logic of the phenomenon under study and enabled us to contrast the different accounts given by the interviewees (Pettigrew, 1990; Yin, 2009). Similarly, we interviewed the operators themselves working in self-managing teams. We ensured we interviewed at least one member of each team.

In carrying out the interviews we employed multiple researchers. Typically, two or three researchers would be present during the interviews, with one asking the questions and the other(s) taking notes and asking for clarification when needed. All interviews were recorded with the consent of interviewees and later transcribed. Overall, we had 864 minutes of recorded interviews, which represented 236 pages of transcripts plus field notes. For the analysis of the data, we also employed multiple researchers. In order to minimize the possibility of a biased interpretation of the data, three researchers independently analyzed the data. Furthermore, one of them had not been present during the interviews, so his or her analysis would not have been influenced by the collection of the data (Eisenhardt, 1989).

Each researcher analyzed the data and coded passages that illustrated actions and behaviors associated with self-managing, transactional and transformational leadership, knowledge exchange and trust. We then compared the results of the analysis and further discussed the instances in which there was disagreement.

In addition, secondary data was collected in order to supplement the longitudinal study of the implementation of self-steering teams as well as the competitive dynamics present during that time. For this we relied primarily on annual reports (1998–2009), but also drew from other sources such as financial newspapers (e.g., *Financieel Dagblad*) and industrial organizations (e.g., European Chemical Industry Council). These data were not only relevant in articulating the context in which the implementation of a management innovation took place, but also as a way of triangulating the data obtained through interviews on related topics.

BACKGROUND: COMPETITIVE DYNAMICS AND THE IMPLEMENTATION OF SELF-MANAGING TEAMS

DSM's participation in the global penicillin market was intensified in 1998 with the merger with Gist-Brocades, a Dutch producer of biotechnological products such as enzymes, penicillin and penicillin derivatives. As a part of DSM Anti-Infectives, this merger allowed DSM to develop the industrial production of the breakthrough technological innovation allowing 7-ADCA to be produced through biocatalysis in the purpose-built ZOR-f plant in Delft, opened in October 2001.

The global industrial production of penicillin is characterized by excess supply, most of which is produced in China, where DSM itself produces through a joint venture with a local partner. Over the last 15 years, this has put pressure on producers outside of China as prices have decreased considerably over the same period. Figure 6.1 shows the increasing share of global penicillin production coming out of China.

The growth of the Chinese producers and the decrease in the price of penicillin had serious implications for DSM Anti-Infectives in Delft and the viability of continuing production at the ZOR-f plant. Against this backdrop, the future of ZOR-f was unclear only a few years after its opening and the option of moving production entirely to China was being considered. In this environment, the management of ZOR-f decided to push forward with the concept of self-managing teams and

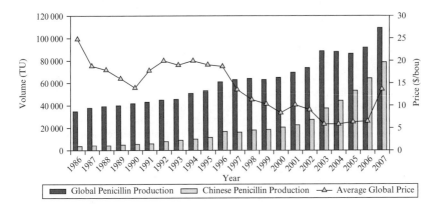

Note: TU = trillion units; $/bou = dollars per billions of units.

Source: European Fine Chemicals Group/CEFIC.

Figure 6.1 Global penicillin production and price (1986–2007)

achieving increased efficiency through smaller teams, more interaction between different constituencies and a larger, more active, involvement of maintenance.

Figure 6.2 presents a longitudinal view of the most significant milestones in the development of the ZOR-f plant. This illustrates the external and internal dynamics that affected the implementation of self-managing teams at DSM Anti-Infectives.

FINDINGS

Leadership

In our study of self-managing teams at DSM we observed that the leadership behavior displayed by different internal change agents showed traits of both transactional and transformational leadership. Each of these leadership behaviors, however, tended to be more strongly associated with different levels of hierarchy within the plant.

At the level of plant management, leadership behavior was predominantly transactional. In this way, while keeping to the principles of self-managing teams, managers were primarily concerned with gaining compliance from operators by clearly specifying targets and rewards and intervening when the achievement of these goals seemed compromised.

Managers focused largely on achieving results, typically around production targets. This can be associated with contingent reward, a dimension of transactional leadership, whereby managers seek commitment to fulfill 'contracts' with subordinates (Bass and Avolio, 1993; Avolio, 1999). Interviews with members of the plant management (past and current) illustrate this:

> Everything is fine with me, as long as the key performance indicators are booked. . . . If you are incapable of keeping that business within the KPIs [key performance indicators], and do not deliver on the contract, then you have one or two chances to do it, and then you will be replaced. (Interview with former site manager at DSM Anti-Infectives Delft, 18 August 2009)

> What we did (with managers) is to drill down their part of the organization into a set of key performance indicators. That was the contract we had. They were very detailed, not because they have to be detailed, but if because if you have detailed KPIs then you really start to understand your business. (Interview with site plant manager at DSM Anti-Infectives Delft, 18 August 2009)

These quotes show the contractual nature of the relationship between the site manager and managers at DSM Anti-Infectives. While the emphasis is

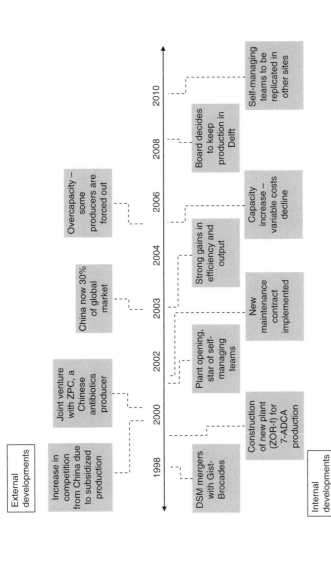

Sources: *Royal DSM Annual Reports* (1996–2009); *Financieel Dagblad* (2000), 'Het ruikt weer cyclisch bij DSM'; *Financieel Dagblad* (1999), 'DSM in Chinese antibiotica'.

Figure 6.2 *External and internal developments influencing the implementation of self-managing teams (2000–10)*

on the accomplishment of targets, the manner in which they are achieved is largely left to the subordinates to decide. In this way, contingent reward seems to serve as a means to set the targets that self-managing teams will strive for in the way they think best.

In a similar way, transactional leadership behavior, in particular contingent reward, is also present in the relationship between the operations manager and the operators. Rewards are a strong feature in motivating operators and ensuring goals are met:

> I've got 52 direct reports, attention is the first thing that will suffer. But I still think that . . . you need a reward, and you can reward and get reward from anyone else, but a reward from your boss is different from a reward from your colleague. (Interview with operations manager at DSM Anti-Infectives Delft, 29 September 2009)

Operators saw their relationship with management as being based on meeting these targets, with management intervening only to take corrective action when things did not go to plan. This reflects a second dimension of transactional leadership: active management by exemption. Active management by exemption implies the leader's intervention when standards seem compromised and rectification is needed to meet objectives. In the case of DSM Anti-Infectives, teams were free to decide how to organize their work and distribute the workload as they saw fit. However, management would intervene when problems arose:

> He (the plant manager) is responsible for everything at the end. He is the one looking down . . . he will come and tell somebody or the entire group 'it's going the wrong way, we have to do this or we have to do that'. (Interview with operator at DSM Anti-Infectives Delft, 15 September 2009)

> When there is a problem, then he (the plant manager) can talk about it at a higher level . . . or solve a huge problem. That's his thing I think. (Interview with operator at DSM Anti-Infectives Delft, 17 September 2009)

Traits of transformational leadership were also prominent at DSM Anti-Infectives. These traits, however, primarily concerned the relationship between operators and the operations expert. Through this kind of leadership behavior, leaders inspired operators to identify with the plant's goals, stimulating them to take charge of their jobs and be creative while also attending to their individual needs:

> I think the problem [of motivation] is here as well, but the lever or solution is also in the operations expert, because he stimulates people, in a positive way, to find their own solutions, and manage their problems. (Interview with operations manager at DSM Anti-Infectives Delft, 29 September 2009)

His [the operations expert] role is management too, but in a way of trying to give a message to operators. . . . It is not formal. It has its ups and downs, but in a way . . . you talk to him and go back to your seat and want to try and do it. (Interview with operator at DSM Anti-Infectives Delft, 17 September 2009)

This illustrates the role of the operations expert as a predominately transformational leader capable of inspiring and stimulating operators to look for new solutions, experiment and challenge assumptions. This is key in the development and functioning of self-managing teams, as leaders will rely, to a large extent, on their ability to self-regulate, organize their work and deliver results without close supervision:

I always try to approach people enthusiastically, because in organizations you always give a lot but don't get as much back. This, obviously, has its limits. It's all about emotions, really. If people feel good in their own skin and you give them the space to develop, it really helps them. (Interview with operations expert at DSM Anti-Infectives Delft, 08 October 2009)

The operations expert's predominately transformational leadership behavior was important in motivating and stimulating operators to identify with their work and the plant. Operators sought to perform well, largely because they felt ownership for their work and the results the plant achieved. This identification with their job was closely related with the leadership behavior exercised by their leader, the operations expert:

He [the operations expert] knows exactly how to talk to you. He knows how to 'massage' somebody to get him in the direction he wants, or to make him do something he actually didn't want to do. He knows how to do this in a good way. (Interview with operator at DSM Anti-Infectives Delft, 15 September 2009)

Both transformational and transactional leadership behaviors are found at DSM Anti-Infectives, which seem to provide the appropriate environment for the development of self-managing teams. On the one hand, leaders make goals and rewards clear, an example of extrinsic motivation. On the other hand, they inspire others to identify with their work and their self-managing team in order to achieve their goals, which is an instance of intrinsic motivation. This may imply, as Vera and Crossan (2004) suggest, that leaders may be able to display both transactional and transformational traits. In the case of the DSM's ZOR-f plant, leadership spans both transactional and transformational behaviors. Figure 6.3 illustrates along a continuum the presence of both transactional and transformational leadership behaviors at the ZOR-f plant.

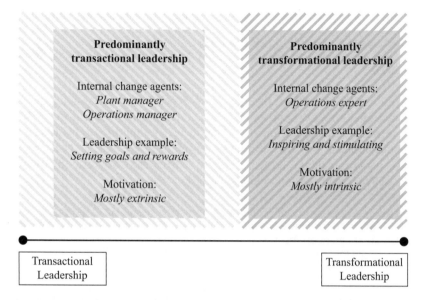

Figure 6.3   Both transactional and transformational leadership behaviors present at ZOR-f

Proposition 1: Employing both transactional and transformational leadership behaviors facilitates the pursuit of management innovation by allowing management to stress the achievement of results while stimulating experimentation with new practices, processes and structures.

Knowledge Exchange

The work of self-managing groups at DSM Anti-Infectives implied that these teams had a high degree of autonomy. In this way, teams decided on how to carry out their work without the intervention of a supervisor. Because of this, operators sought to exchange relevant information and knowledge not only as a way in which to stay current with new developments in the plant, but also in a bid to build on improvements introduced by other teams. In this way, exchange of knowledge took place within teams as well as between them:

> Before, you had an assistant chief and a chief. They would tell you what to do, and that's what you would do all day. Now we are part of team, we decide what people are going to do, when and how. . . . With this structure you will create specializations. For instance, if my specialization is fermentation, my colleagues will know. They know that, if something happens, they can always

ask me for information. (Interview with operator at DSM Anti-Infectives Delft, 15 September 2009)

We have, almost every day, a work meeting where we come together for half an hour and we talk about problems and solutions within the plant. All specialties are represented. (Interview with operator at DSM Anti-Infectives Delft, 22 September 2009)

Interestingly, knowledge exchange was also observed to take place between different constituencies. As team supervisors were not part of the organization at DSM Anti-Infectives, it was up to operators to exchange the necessary knowledge to complete tasks with others within the plant. In this way, it was common for teams to exchange knowledge with the maintenance teams.

Management encouraged the involvement of maintenance in knowledge exchange through the way in which their contract was arranged. Instead of being paid a fee for carrying out routine maintenance, they were asked to deliver a functioning plant and actively engage in suggestions for improvements (of which they would share the benefits). These suggestions could be around maintenance or operational cost reduction, explicitly inviting the maintenance team to become familiar with the job of process operators, and effectively expanding the scope of maintenance work. To further encourage this, the maintenance teams were also self-managing:

The main idea of the maintenance concept is that the service operators add to rather than optimize the process. These people are also self-managing. They picked it up quickly, they like the freedom. (Interview with Plant Manager at DSM Anti-Infectives Delft, 17 September 2010)

The scope of maintenance is wider than just maintenance. . . . Their job is not only to improve production, but also the whole way in which we work. (Interview with Maintenance Manager at DSM Anti-Infectives Delft, 17 February 2010)

They [maintenance] have the same goal as I do. Otherwise, we are pursuing two different goals. That's how we manage the whole process – by communicating at the same level. What we do here, they have to know about, and also think from our perspective. We coach them and they coach us. (Interview with operator at DSM Anti-Infectives Delft, 17 September 2009)

It is up to us to manage, take responsibility and make decisions about, not only our job, but also things that have do with maintenance and groups around it. This is strengthening everybody . . . so it is a kind of web. In the early days you were just a person working in a specific place in the plant, not knowing what happened around you. Now you know nearly everything. (Interview with operator at DSM Anti-Infectives Delft, 15 September 2009)

The quotes above illustrate how people from different functions, operations and maintenance engage in exchange of knowledge. Plant management attributes to this collaboration significant savings in maintenance cost and a decrease in production down-time due to maintenance. Initiatives from maintenance personnel have also led to more efficient use of energy, who in turn are more motivated by their involvement in the plant.

Similarly, operators were encouraged to interact with the technologists at the plant. As operators became more involved in the generation of improvements in the production process, exchange of knowledge with technicians became commonplace:

> The technologists across the hall, they are making plans and you try to find the way to make their plans happen. We are also free to do things the way we want to. Our ideas of how to produce more . . . we also give them to the technologists and they find out whether it would be a good way of producing. (Interview with operator at DSM Anti-Infectives Delft, 15 September 2009)

> A good part of self-managing is that you get your ideas across. Before you would just be working here and nobody actually listened to you. You had your task and that was it. If you thought you had a good idea, there was always a boss saying 'no'. Now, because we're all close to the technologists, everybody is talking, listening and getting knowledge from each other. In the end, that will have a positive result on the quality and quantity of your product. (Interview with operator at DSM Anti-Infectives Delft, 15 September 2009)

Management also encouraged this, as it was seen as a way to improve the knowledge of operators and bring a host of new ideas for improvement to the attention of technologists. One of the ways in which this was encouraged was to reward the high-performing operators who had ideas for improvements with the possibility to work with the technologists assisting in the development of projects or even working as internal consultants to improve processes. Figure 6.4 illustrates the knowledge exchange between the different teams of operators as well as the exchange of knowledge between operators and both technologists and maintenance.

Proposition 2:   The pursuit of management innovation requires both the presence of diverse knowledge as well as the conditions for that knowledge to be exchanged across the organization.

Trust

The implementation of self-managing teams within an organization carries with it a certain amount of trust associated with the level of auton-

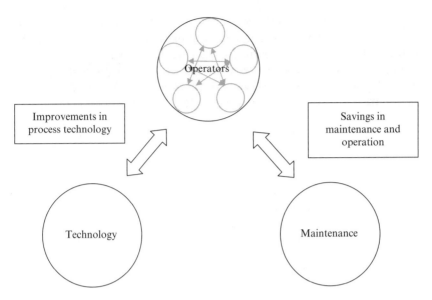

Figure 6.4   Knowledge exchange dynamics at ZOR-f

omy embedded in them. In the case of DSM Anti-Infectives, trust is seen within the teams, where members trust one another, between teams, where members of the different teams trust members of other teams with whom they share the running of the same continuous production process, and finally we see trust in teams from management, where management trusts the different teams to perform their job without intervening in the way teams organize themselves as well as how they carry out the work.

Teams of operators were completely in charge of the plant during their shift. They were trusted to run the plant in the way they thought best. In the absence of a shift supervisor, management relied entirely on the teams and had only a limited ability to control or monitor their actions:

> It's like they [management] says: It's your plant! You are here for eight hours with your group. You five people are the owners of the factory and you decide what is going to happen. (Interview with operator at DSM Anti-Infectives in Delft, 15 September 2009)

> You know that when you're here for eight hours, you have to produce . . . and take care of the quality of the product. It is something that you take for granted . . . 'I have to do it, but I have to do it right'. Nobody will tell you how to do it. (Interview with operator at DSM Anti-Infectives in Delft, 17 September 2009)

Trust dynamics between plant management and the different teams was primarily from management to teams, with the opposite trajectory, that is,

from teams to management, not characterized by a strong trusting relationship. Teams saw the managerial positions at the plant as a step in the
career of high potential, typically rotated every two years.

Because of the independence with which they carried out their work,
and the lack of a shift supervisor, operators at DSM Anti-Infectives also
had to trust their team mates to do their fair share of work and do it well:

> It's easy to write down some numbers and say 'I checked it' . . . that comes with
> the freedom I guess. (Interview with operator at DSM Anti-Infectives in Delft,
> 15 September 2009)

Trust between teams and management's trust in teams enabled them
to become more entrepreneurial. Teams were trusted and encouraged to
improve processes and try to become more efficient. In this way, teams
introduced many changes to the processes, albeit some of them were ultimately unsuccessful. However, this also facilitates learning and improvement of team capabilities:

> Trust people and give them a chance, also when it goes wrong. Give them the
> trust to manage the next time. Self-managing has a learning curve, you need to
> go step by step. (Interview with operator at DSM Anti-Infectives in Delft, 22
> September 2009)

Overall, trust at DSM Anti-Infectives plays an instrumental role in
enabling operators to pursue self-managing teams. Because management
shows trust in the different teams by being dependent on their actions to
complete tasks, yet largely unable to monitor and control the process,
operators enjoy the freedom to organize and carry out their work in the
way they consider best. This trust, ultimately, fosters innovation in teams
as they feel empowered to try new ways of doing things. Similarly, teams
trust one another to run the production of the plant to the same standard,
as teams depend on each other to meet the production goals established by
the plant management. Figure 6.5 illustrates the different trust dynamics
present at the ZOR-f plant.

Proposition 3:   Trust will contribute to an environment conducive to
management innovation.

DISCUSSION AND CONCLUSION

In this chapter we set off to understand what the role of internal change
agents is in the functioning of self-managing teams. For this, a longitudi-

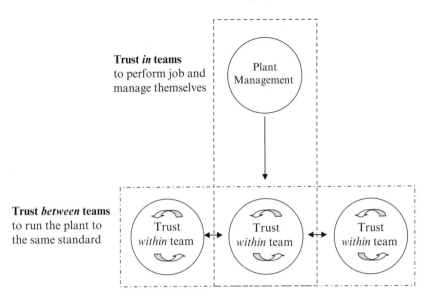

Figure 6.5   Trust dynamics at ZOR-f

nal study of self-managing teams was carried out at ZOR-f, a Royal DSM plant in Delft, the Netherlands. Overall, internal change agents at different hierarchical levels contributed to the pursuit of management innovation. While the plant management created a conducive environment, at the operational level, front-line employees and their supervisors were the key change agents implementing and operating within new practices, processes and structures.

Specifically, we focused on three key issues related to internal change agents that are particularly relevant for self-managing teams: leadership, knowledge exchange and trust. Our study suggests that both transformational and transactional leadership are present at the ZOR-f plant, though these leadership behaviors are each more strongly associated with different levels of hierarchy. Studies suggest that teams whose leaders display traits of transformational leadership will be more proactive (Belschak and Den Hartog, 2010) and will take a cooperative approach to resolving conflict, which in turn will improve team coordination and ultimately lead to better team performance (Zhang et al., 2011). In this way, this sort of leadership, shown at the ZOR-f plant by the teams' leader, relates to the teams' ability to efficiently organize and coordinate their functioning. We extend Vaccaro et al. (2012) by showing how both leadership behaviors contribute to an environment that is conducive to the development of self-managing teams, seemingly striking a balance between emphasizing the achievement of results and its associated rewards, and stimulating employees to identify and engage with their work. This resonates with studies that have proposed a guiding and encouraging role for leadership when organizing for self-managing teams (Stewart and Manz, 1995) and providing them with autonomy (Yukl and Yukl, 2002).

Our study also showed that both transactional and transformational leadership played a role in managing for self-managing teams. This complements Vaccaro et al. (2012) who reported the positive association between management innovation and both transactional and transformational leadership. In this study, we go beyond this association in showing that both leadership styles contribute to management innovation, but seem to be associated with leaders at different hierarchical levels. This means that the two leadership behaviors the operators are exposed to within the plant may encourage them to display attitudes of creativity and risk-taking – when transformational leadership is predominant– or risk aversion and accuracy –when transactional leadership is more prominent (Kark and Van Dijk, 2007). This relates to the notion that employees may be able to attend to both creativity and accuracy (Miron et al., 2004), implying that both types of leadership behavior may play a role in creating an environment for self-managing teams. This ability to consider both transformational and transactional leadership and meet creativity and accuracy needs, further underpins the self-regulatory nature of self-managing teams.

Regarding knowledge exchange, our study shows that knowledge was not only exchanged within teams but also, and perhaps most importantly, between different constituencies with different – yet related – tasks and backgrounds. Due to the autonomy and ownership that operators had over their work, knowledge exchange was the natural way of carrying out their work and ensuring that the process ran smoothly. The routine exchange of knowledge may make teams more efficient as the retrieval of information becomes more accurate as team members are familiar with the different knowledge stocks (Hinsz et al., 1997). During interviews carried out at the plant it was clear that operators found it essential to be able to communicate directly with the different parties involved in running the plant, be it from maintenance or technology. Besides the exchange of knowledge, this facilitates quick feedback regarding ideas, problems or solutions (ibid.) that may be beneficial in understanding the ramifications of actions beyond an employee's function, for example, operations, maintenance or technology. This in turn underscores the self-managing teams' discretion and control over their work. This may also contribute to implementing new ways of working within the plant, as operators know what knowledge is available within the plant and how to retrieve it (ibid.).

Trust was also found to play a prominent role in self-managing teams. Our interviews point to trust within teams, between different teams, and from management towards the teams. Team members display trust in one another in their taking on different, yet interrelated, roles without direct supervision and on which they depend. Such trust may contribute to the teams' ability to acquire new competencies and improve their functioning. De Dreu (2006) suggests that within-team trust may promote an environment in which task conflicts can be openly discussed and in this way stimulate creativity and innovation. In this way, teams may be better equipped to deal with issues related to work allocation, procedures and changes to the production processes they oversee that could improve their performance. Similarly to the dynamics we found between individuals (Serva et al., 2005), we also observed trust between teams, where individual teams relied and depended on other teams to run the production process to a similar standard. A team's perception that another team's competence to carry out their tasks may have contributed to increasing the team's trust (ibid.). The continuous nature of the studied production process lends itself to allowing teams to assess the quality of the work carried out by their peers as they take over production from the team overseeing the previous shift.

Lastly, we confirmed management's trust in the operators to run the production process and organize their functioning within their respective teams independently. While this is to be expected in a plant where self-managing teams have been put in place, it is not trivial. Support for trust and autonomy from management also signals support for innovative initiatives (Scott and Bruce, 1994), which contributes to an environment in which self-managing teams develop.

As a single case study, this study of self-managing teams as a management innovation introduced at a DSM plant is limited to the context of one firm. Future research may consider alternative methodologies, such as a multiple-case design, through which to assess the salience of the issues outlined in this chapter. Another limitation is analysis of internal knowledge exchange alone. Birkinshaw et al. (2008) clearly state a role for external knowledge to influence management innovation. Future research may consider the knowledge acquired from sources external to the organization or brought in by external personnel temporarily involved with the innovating organization such as consultants. While it is not a core argument of this study, this chapter offers a glimpse into the association and potential synergies of considering both technology and management innovation. As presented in the case study of the ZOR-f plant of DSM Anti-Infectives this plant was built specifically to house the production of a type of anti-infectives through a revolutionary process involving biotechnology instead of chemistry. The company management recognized that the new plant and new technology could operate in a more efficient way if changes to how management was performed were introduced as well. The result, as reported in this study, was the elimination of certain supervisory positions and the implementation of self-managing teams. In the context of a very specific technological advancement, this contributes to the role of human agency in providing an adequate organizational environment for management innovation to be pursued. Future study may explicitly target this kind of synergy between technological and management innovation. Last, in order to understand the introduction and functioning of self-managing teams we drew on archival data and carried out interviews with key informants involved in the process. Future studies may consider alternative approaches closer to ethnographic research and witness the introduction of such changes to an organization to gain a more detailed understanding of the challenges faced by innovating organizations and how these may be overcome.

Overall, this case study makes several contributions to the management innovation literature. In particular, it describes the introduction and development of self-managing teams over a ten-year period, it shows how complementary leadership behaviors coexist, and how trust and knowledge exchange processes affect the development of self-managing teams. In conclusion, this study shows that different internal change agents play a fundamental role in the functioning of self-managing teams. The ZOR-f plant at DSM shows that internal change agents such as plant management, but also the operators themselves, are key in setting up an environment that is conducive to the success of management innovation, underscoring the paramount role of human agency.

REFERENCES

Argote, L. and P. Ingram, 2000, 'Knowledge transfer: a basis for competitive advantage in firms', *Organizational Behavior and Human Decision Processes*, **82**(1), 150–69.
Avolio, B.J., 1999, *Full Leadership Development: Building the Vital Forces in Organizations*, Thousand Oaks, CA: Sage.
Bass, B.M., 1985, *Leadership and Performance Beyond Expectations*, New York: Free Press.
Bass, B.M., 1990, 'From transactional to transformational leadership: learning to share the vision', *Organizational Dynamics*, **18**(3), 19–31.
Bass, B.M. and B.J. Avolio, 1993, 'Transformational leadership and organizational culture', *Public Administration Quarterly*, **17**(1), 112–21.
Bass, B.M., D.I. Jung, B.J. Avolio and Y. Berson, 2003, 'Predicting unit performance by assessing transformational and transactional leadership', *Journal of Applied Psychology*, **88**(2), 207–18.
Belschak, F.D. and D.N. Den Hartog, 2010, 'Pro-self, prosocial, and pro-organizational foci of proactive behaviour: differential antecedents and consequences', *Journal of Occupational and Organizational Psychology*, **83**(2), 475–98.

Birkinshaw, J., G. Hamel and M.J. Mol, 2008, 'Management innovation', *Academy of Management Review*, **33**(4), 825–45.
Bunderson, J.S. and P. Boumgarden, 2010, 'Structure and learning in self-managed teams: why "bureaucratic" teams can be better learners', *Organization Science*, **21**(3), 602–24.
Burns, J.M.G., 1978, *Leadership*, New York: Harper and Row.
Cohen, S.G. and G.E. Ledford, Jr, 1994, 'The effectiveness of self-managing teams: a quasi-experiment', *Human Relations*, **47**(1), 13–43.
Collins, C.J. and K.G. Smith, 2006, 'Knowledge exchange and combination: the role of human resource practices in the performance of high-technology firms', *Academy of Management Journal*, **49**(3), 544–60.
Cummings, J.N., 2004, 'Work groups, structural diversity, and knowledge sharing in a global organization', *Management Science*, **50**(3), 352–64.
Cummings, T.G., 1978, 'Self-regulating work groups: a socio-technical synthesis', *Academy of Management Review*, **3**(3), 625–34.
De Dreu, C.K.W., 2006, 'When too little or too much hurts: evidence for a curvilinear relationship between task conflict and innovation in teams', *Journal of Management*, **32**(1), 83–107.
De Jong, B.A. and T.O.M. Elfring, 2010, 'How does trust affect the performance of ongoing teams? The mediating role of reflexivity, monitoring, and effort', *Academy of Management Journal*, **53**(3), 535–49.
DSM, 2000, *DSM N.V. Annual Report 2000*, available at: http://www.dsm.com/en_US/cworld/public/investors/downloads/annual_report_2000_en.pdf; accessed 20 June 2012.
Eisenhardt, K.M., 1989, 'Building theories from case study research', *Academy of Management Review*, **14**(4), 532–50.
Gagnon, M.A., K.J. Jansen and J.H. Michael, 2008, 'Employee alignment with strategic change: a study of strategy-supportive behavior among blue-collar employees', *Journal of Managerial Issues*, **20**(4), 425–43.
Hamel, G., 2006, 'The why, what, and how of management innovation', *Harvard Business Review*, **84**(2), 72–84.
Hamel, G., 2007, *The Future of Management*, Boston, MA: Harvard Business School Press.
Hinsz, V.B., R.S. Tindale and D.A. Vollrath, 1997, 'The emerging conceptualization of groups as information processors', *Psychological Bulletin*, **121**(1), 43–64.
Kark, R. and D. Van Dijk, 2007, 'Motivation to lead, motivation to follow: the role of the self-regulatory focus on leadership processes', *Academy of Management Review*, **32**(2), 500–528.
Kiffin-Petersen, S.A. and J.L. Cordery, 2003, 'Trust, individualism and job characteristics as predictors of employee preference for teamwork', *International Journal of Human Resource Management*, **14**(1), 93–116.
Lawler, E.E., 1990, 'The new plant revolution revisited', *Organizational Dynamics*, **19**(2), 4–14.
Manz, C.C. and H.P. Sims, 1987, 'Leading workers to lead themselves: the external leadership of self-managing work teams', *Administrative Science Quarterly*, **32**(1), 106–29.
Mayer, R.C., J.H. Davis and F.D. Schoorman, 1995, 'An integrative model of organizational trust', *Academy of Management Review*, **20**(3), 709–34.
Miron, E., M. Erez and E. Naveh, 2004, 'Do personal characteristics and cultural values that promote innovation, quality, and efficiency compete or complement each other?', *Journal of Organizational Behavior*, **25**(2), 175–99.
Mol, M.J. and J. Birkinshaw, 2009, 'The sources of management innovation: when firms introduce new management practices', *Journal of Business Research*, **62**(12), 1269–80.
OECD, 2001, *The Application of Biotechnology to Industrial Sustainability*, Paris: Organisation for Economic Co-operation and Development.
Parker, S.K., U.K. Bindl and K. Strauss, 2010, 'Making things happen: a model of proactive motivation', *Journal of Management*, **36**(4), 827–56.
Pettigrew, A.M., 1990, 'Longitudinal field research on change: theory and practice', *Organization Science*, **1**(3), 267–92.

Scholten, L., D. van Knippenberg, B.A. Nijstad and C.K.W. De Dreu, 2007, 'Motivated information processing and group decision-making: effects of process accountability on information processing and decision quality', *Journal of Experimental Social Psychology*, **43**(4), 539–52.

Scott, S.G. and R.A. Bruce, 1994, 'Determinants of innovative behavior: a path model of individual innovation in the workplace', *Academy of Management Journal*, **37**(3), 580–607.

Serva, M.A., M.A. Fuller and R.C. Mayer, 2005, 'The reciprocal nature of trust: a longitudinal study of interacting teams', *Journal of Organizational Behavior*, **26**(6), 625–48.

Stewart, G.L. and C.C. Manz, 1995, 'Leadership for self-managing work teams: a typology and integrative model', *Human Relations*, **48**(7), 747–70.

Thomas-Hunt, M.C., T.Y. Ogden and M.A. Neale, 2003, 'Who's really sharing? Effects of social and expert status on knowledge exchange within groups', *Management Science*, **49**(4), 464–77.

Vaccaro, I.G., J.J.P. Jansen, F. Van den Bosch and H.W. Volberda, 2012, 'Leadership and management innovation: the moderating role of organizational size', *Journal of Management Studies*, **49**(1), 28–51.

Vera, D. and M. Crossan, 2004, 'Strategic leadership and organizational learning', *Academy of Management Review*, **29**(2), 222–40.

Wageman, R., 1995, 'Interdependence and group effectiveness', *Administrative Science Quarterly*, **40**(1), 145–80.

Waterman, R.H., 1994, *What America Does Right: Learning From Companies that Put People First*, New York; W.W. Norton and Co.

Wolff, S.B., A.T. Pescosolido and V.U. Druskat, 2002, 'Emotional intelligence as the basis of leadership emergence in self-managing teams', *Leadership Quarterly*, **13**(5), 505–22.

Yammarino, F.J. and B.M. Bass, 1990, 'Transformational leadership and multiple levels of analysis', *Human Relations*, **43**(10), 975–95.

Yin, R.K., 2009, *Case Study Research: Design and Methods* (4th edition), Thousand Oaks, CA: Sage Publications, Inc.

Yukl, G.A. and G. Yukl, 2002, *Leadership in Organizations*, Upper Saddle River, NJ: Prentice Hall.

Zárraga, C. and J. Bonache, 2005, 'The impact of team atmosphere on knowledge outcomes in self-managed teams', *Organization Studies*, **26**(5), 661–81.

Zhang, X.a., Q. Cao and D. Tjosvold, 2011, 'Linking transformational leadership and team performance: a conflict management approach', *Journal of Management Studies*, **48**(7), 1586–611.

7 Employee innovation
Fiona Patterson, Máire Kerrin and
Lara Zibarras

INTRODUCTION

There is broad agreement in the research literature that an individual's ability to innovate at work is influenced by a multitude of factors, which can be classified into four levels of analysis: the *individual, group, managerial* and *organizational* level. However, research over the past few decades has generally lacked integration. Different academic disciplines, such as management, business, economics and organizational psychology have explored the concept of innovation from different vantage points and often regularly ignore findings arising from other disciplines. As psychologists, our primary approach to the study of innovation has been to start with an analysis at the individual (or employee) level, as we view this as the foundation for investigating managers, work groups and organizational-level innovation. In this chapter, we focus on the individual level of analysis – employee innovation as other contributors focus on work groups, managers, leadership and the organizational-level analysis of innovation. Our intention in this review is to analyze how best to understand the role of the individual, by exploring linkages between innovation and cognition, intellect, personality, emotions and mood states amongst other variables.

An individual's tendency to innovate is thought to be one of the least understood, but perhaps most important, aspects of human behavior in the workplace (Bunce and West, 1995). The research literature on the characteristics and behaviors associated with innovative people in organizations is immense, both in quantity and diversity. As a result, there has been a lack of a cohesive theoretical understanding of how employees create new ideas and apply those ideas in organizations. A key aim of this chapter is to synthesize the key research in this area and provide an understanding of how employee innovation contributes to managerial and organizational innovation.

In navigating the research literature at the individual level, we draw upon our previous review (see Patterson et al., 2009) where we adopt a resourced-based approach to understanding employee innovation in organizations. Figure 7.1 identifies the relevant resources at the level of the employee, including intelligence and cognition, knowledge, motivation,

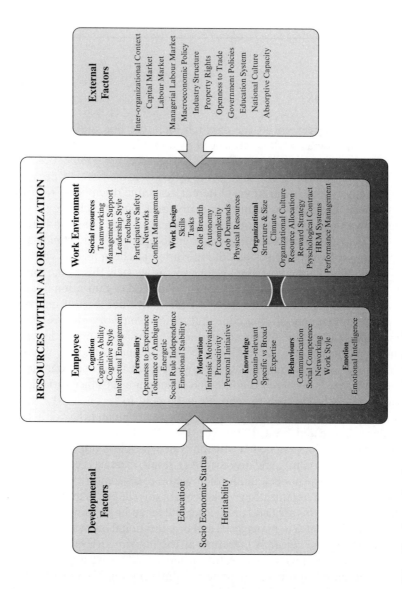

Figure 7.1 Employee-level resources associated with innovation

personality, behaviors, mood states and emotional intelligence. Hence, Figure 7.1 provides a broad structure for the research evidence presented in this chapter.

DEFINING INNOVATION

Definitions and terminology surrounding the concepts of creativity and innovation has proved troublesome over many years. Part of the problem relates to the fact that the terms 'creativity' and 'innovation' are often used interchangeably. Researchers agree that confusion remains over the definition of innovation (e.g., Patterson, 2002), although in general terms, creativity and innovation may be viewed as overlapping constructs (Axtell et al., 2000; Patterson, 2002). However, innovation is broader and more complex than creativity. Creativity generally refers to the generation of new ideas, whereas innovation also relates to idea implementation (Axtell et al., 2000). Furthermore, creativity concerns the generation of new and totally original ideas, whilst innovation could involve the application of novelty to generate something new and useful (West and Farr, 1990; West, 2000; Patterson, 2002). An accepted definition of innovation is offered by West and Farr (1990, p. 9), which will be used in the present chapter: 'the intentional introduction and application within a role, group or organization of ideas, processes, products or procedures, new to the relevant unit of adoption, designed to specifically benefit the individual, group, organization or wider society'.

Within the literature, researchers generally consider that innovation consists of at least two main stages – an idea generation phase followed by an idea implementation phase (Axtell et al., 2000). However, there is little evidence that innovations progress in a linear sequence of discrete stages; the innovation process is complex and iterative (Patterson et al., 2009) with an overlap of stages likely to be the norm (Rickards, 1996). Throughout this chapter we refer to innovation or the propensity to innovate although it is acknowledged that the literature also uses creativity-related terms.

INTELLIGENCE AND COGNITION

The relationship between innovation and intelligence has been explored by numerous researchers (e.g., Cattell and Butcher, 1968; Eysenck, 1995; Sternberg and O'Hara, 1999; Silvia, 2008a, 2008b). However, results are generally inconclusive in this area, with the exact nature of the association remaining unclear. Various researchers have suggested (e.g., Patterson, 2002; Patterson et al., 2009) that the research literature can be subdivided into four areas that conceive human innovation to be:

- a subset of general intelligence;
- an aspect of genius;
- a set of cognitive abilities and mental processes;
- related to observer judgments of intelligence (or perceived intelligence).

A brief overview of each is provided below.

Innovation as a Subset of General Intelligence

Early research suggested that creativity was equal to high intelligence (e.g., Spearman, 1923). However, several authors have questioned this view (e.g., Eysenck, 1995) since innovators may be intelligent, but high intelligence does not guarantee that an employee will innovate. In his theory of the structure of intellect (SI), Guilford (1950, 1988) claimed that creative thinking was a mental ability involving divergent production (that is, the generation of information emphasizing variety of output). Stemming from this, the notion of 'divergent thinking' (DT) emerged, and divergent thinking tests were viewed as a way to measure creative abilities (Harrington, 1975). However, review studies have criticized divergent thinking tests (Barron and Harrington, 1981; Weisberg, 2006), particularly because it is quantity, not quality, of ideas that are considered. Furthermore, the validity of DT tests has been questioned since they are influenced by the conditions under which they are administered: creative abilities increase significantly when participants are instructed to be creative (Harrington, 1975). Whilst reviewing the notion of divergent thinking tests, Simonton (2003, p. 216) offers the following critique of their validity:

> None of these [divergent thinking tests] can be said to have passed all the psychometric hurdles required of established ability tests. For instance, scores on separate creativity tests often . . . correlate very weakly among each other (that is, low convergent validity), and correlate very weakly with objective indicators of overt creative behaviors (that is, low predictive validity).

In sum, Guildford's model has received much criticism, highlighting doubt over whether divergent thinking tests measure abilities actually involved in creative thinking (e.g., Sternberg and O'Hara, 1999; Runco, 2006). As such, the notion of divergent thinking has largely lost support.

Innovation as an Aspect of Genius

From the 1970s onwards, Eysenck (1979) suggested that genius, a manifestation of high intelligence, is closely linked to the propensity to innovate. However, there has been a lack of evidence to support a direct relationship between innovation and high intelligence. Indeed, more recently, researchers including Eysenck (1994) himself have concluded that instead intelligence is a necessary, but not a sufficient, condition for innovation. Indeed, a recent meta-analysis (Kim, 2005), reported a mean correlation of $r = 0.17$, for the relationship between innovation and IQ, concluding that this relationship is almost negligible.

In overview, the research examining the precise associations between innovation and intelligence currently appears mixed. For example, some research (e.g., Silvia, 2008a) suggests that higher-order intelligence has a medium-large effect on innovation, whilst lower-order subsets of intelligence (fluidity, strategy, verbal fluency) have much smaller effects on innovation. Furthermore, findings suggest that openness to experience (explored later in this chapter) partly accounts for the relationship between intelligence and innovation. Conversely, other research (e.g., Batey et al., 2009) indicates that fluid intelligence has a stronger relationship with innovation, than does a broader measure of IQ. Still further investigations (e.g., Gilhooly et al., 2004) have tested the possibility of a curvilinear relationship between intelligence and innovation where intelligence may become less influential as intelligence increases beyond a certain level. For example, one study (e.g., Feist and Barron, 2003) suggests that there is a moderate relationship between intelligence and innovation, however above an IQ score of approximately 115–120 the relationship is near zero. This has been termed the 'threshold theory'. By contrast, other authors (e.g., Preckel et al., 2006) dispute this idea of a threshold theory since their school-based research showed similar associations between innovation and intelligence across different ranges of ability, including students who attended specialized schools for the gifted.

Cognitive Abilities

It has been suggested (e.g., Finke et al., 1992) that in order to understand the role of cognitive abilities in idea generation, models from cognitive psychology can be used, with experimental observations of the processes underlying idea-generative tasks. Finke and colleagues' work involves a framework called the 'geneplore model', which proposes that innovative activities can be described in terms of a preliminary generation of ideas that are then explored for their potential utility. The model assumes that individuals alternate between generative and exploratory phases, refining the ideas according to the demands or constraints of the specific task; an ongoing iteration of generative and exploratory steps with cognitive processes that are common to both. The emphasis of this 'creative cognition' approach is that generative capacity is part of normal human cognition. Furthermore, there are individual differences in capacity for generative thinking that stem from variations in the use and application of these generative processes, coupled with the sophistication of a person's memory and their knowledge of the relevant domain. In essence, capacity for creative cognition is normally distributed, implying that a highly creative person's mind does not operate in any fundamentally different way to other people. This suggests therefore that assessment techniques could be devised to assess an employee's capacity for generative thinking. However, generative thinking and contextual application are only a small part of the innovation process, and other resources are important such as motivation and personality (outlined later in this chapter).

Observer Judgments of Intelligence

Much of the early literature suggested that innovative individuals are perceived and rated by others as more intelligent than less innovative people. For example, in a study of architects (MacKinnon, 1960), innovative architects were rated as more 'intelligent' than less innovative architects by their supervisors. The author described these architects as having high 'effective intelligence', arguing that traditional measures of intelligence (that is, IQ) do not fully explain 'real-world' intelligence. More recently, in a 44-year longitudinal investigation, Feist and Barron (2003) showed that observer-rated intellect at age 27 was related to originality also at the age of 27 and also predicted lifetime innovation at 72. Furthermore, actual tested intelligence had a much weaker relationship with innovation at both ages 27 and 72.

Summary

Historically, the literature on innovation and its association with intelligence has lacked clarity. One drawback has been that intelligence is often viewed as a unitary concept with previous theories tending to overemphasize cognitive abilities and downplaying the role of knowledge-based or crystallized intelligence (Silvia, 2008a), explored in greater detail in the following sections. Indeed, in using modern paradigms of intelligence it may be possible to find greater clarity in the research findings since cognitive abilities and knowledge-based intelligence have been treated separately (e.g., Ackerman, 1996, 2000). Indeed, Ackerman's model of adult intellectual development might be useful since it suggests that knowledge is as important as intellectual processing abilities, particularly, for example, in its power to predict success in higher education as well professional success. In conclusion, intelligence comprising both cognitive abilities and knowledge are linked to the innovative process.

KNOWLEDGE

Researchers in the field, regardless of their theoretical viewpoint, have suggested that knowledge is important for both generative thinking and innovation (e.g., Amabile, 1988; Patterson, 2002). Indeed, domain-specific knowledge is considered a basic requirement since one needs an accurate sense of the domain before one can change or improve it. However, the literature also highlights that too much expertise in a particular area can be a *block* to innovating within that domain (Sternberg, 1982). Thus, it is suggested that an inverted U relationship exists between knowledge and innovation, where too much or too little knowledge hamper the innovative process. Findings from a widely cited study (Simonton, 1984), where the lives of over 300 eminent people were studied to explore lifespan development of innovation, suggest that both a lack, and an excess, of familiarity within a particular subject domain, can be detrimental to innovation. This view has been supported in other research (e.g., Frensch and Sternberg, 1989; Williams and Yang, 1999). Indeed, Sternberg (1997) suggests that 'expertise' may result in rigid thinking and reduced flexibility in problem-solving; and later claims: 'knowledge about a field can result in closed and entrenched perspective leading to a person not moving beyond the way in which he or she has seen problems in the past' (Sternberg, 1999, p. 11).

Thus, the research literature highlights the importance of being 'immersed' in domain-specific knowledge as a prerequisite for innovation, although the domain-specific knowledge does not need to be highly complex or detailed and can be broad (Amabile, 1988; Mascitelli, 2000). Thus, personal mastery and an accurate sense of the domain and context are necessary antecedents of innovation. However, domain-specific knowledge, like intelligence, is necessary, but not sufficient for innovation to occur.

MOTIVATION

High levels of motivation are necessary for innovation (Amabile, 1983, 1996). Indeed, even after training, participants' likelihood of generating ideas at work is mediated by their motivation to innovate (Birdi, 2007). One influential researcher in this area, Amabile (1996), presented a componential model of innovation entailing three components: *intrinsic task motivation*, *domain-relevant skills*, and *innovation-relevant process skills* (cognitive skills and work styles conducive to novelty). The model proposes five stages of the innovation process where the roles of these three components vary at each of the stages of innovation. The model implies that intrinsic motivation is conducive to innovation, and Amabile's work has been influential in promoting the importance of the role of motivation on innovation. Conversely, the model suggests that extrinsic motivation is detrimental to innovation.

Although innovation theories generally refer to intrinsic motivation as an important antecedent, few studies have tested this association empirically (Patterson et al., 2009). One exception (Shin and Zhou, 2003) reported that transformational leadership promoted employee's intrinsic motivation, which was conducive to creative performance. Similarly, in a laboratory-based study, Sosik et al. (1999) found that transformational leadership style encouraged 'flow', a psychological state characterized by intrinsic motivation, concentration and enjoyment, which in turn encourages idea generation. These studies support the notion that motivation may mediate the relationship between leadership style and creative performance.

Whilst intrinsic motivation is an important prerequisite for innovation (Amabile, 1988; Frese et al., 1999), the role of extrinsic motivators is less clear (Harrison et al., 2006). It is thought that extrinsic motivators may be detrimental to innovation because they divide attention between the task and the individual (Collins and Amabile, 1999). In exploring contextual and environmental influences on motivation, Collins and Amabile (ibid.) suggest that expected performance evaluation has a detrimental influence on innovation. The idea of freedom from external evaluation seems to be important in innovation research, articulated as a genuine passion and interest in innovation itself (ibid.). However, evidence suggests that in the workplace, informative evaluation (e.g., constructive, supportive, or recognizing accomplishments) can in fact enhance innovation (Amabile and Gryskiewicz, 1989; Amabile et al., 1996). Amabile and colleagues suggest that intrinsic motivation is important in tasks that require novelty and extrinsic motivators may be a distraction during early stages of the innovation process. However, later on in the innovation process, where evaluation of ideas and persistence are required, extrinsic motivators may help innovators to persist in solving the problem within a given domain.

Thus, any extrinsic motivators that improve an employee's sense of competence without undermining self-determination, should enhance intrinsic motivation and in turn should increase the propensity for innovation (Eisenberger and Cameron, 1996). It is also possible, as suggested by Mumford (2003), that intrinsic and extrinsic motivation might serve different functions: intrinsic motivation might be related to work on a task, whilst extrinsic motivation might influence choice of task, field, or implementation strategy. More recently, Sauermann and Cohen (2008) analyzed the impact of employee motivation on organizational innovation and performance. Findings suggested that intrinsic and extrinsic motivation influenced both employee effort and the overall quality of the innovative endeavors. They confirmed that extrinsic rewards, such as pay, were not as important as certain aspects of intrinsic motivation, such as the desire for intellectual challenge, in enhancing innovation. These findings have implications for how to best nurture innovation within the workplace. It seems that further research is necessary to investigate the part that different aspects of intrinsic motivation play in innovation, such as curiosity, improving feelings of mastery, and self-expression potential.

PERSONALITY

In general, it has been noted that personality plays a role in an individual's tendency to innovate (e.g., Barron and Harrington, 1981; Feist, 1999; Patterson, 2002; Zibarras et al., 2008). Over the past few decades the empirical work on the personality characteristics of innovators has revealed a fairly stable set of core characteristics that consistently relate to innovation (King et al., 1996; Oldham and Cummings, 1996; Patterson, 1999, 2002). These include: self-confidence, high energy, independence of judgment, autonomy and toleration of ambiguity (Barron and Harrington, 1981; Sternberg and Lubart, 1991). However, many early studies examined single personality traits (e.g., Barron and Harrington, 1981) in order to establish relationships between specific characteristics and creative outcomes. In order to integrate the findings, models of personality have been used to categorize the characteristics found in the innovation literature. Two such models of personality are the Five Factor Model (FFM) and Eysenck's Three Factor Model, outlined in further detail below.

Innovation and the Five Factor Model of Personality

The emergence of the FFM of personality (Goldberg, 1990; McCrae and Costa, 1999) has led to a better understanding of how creativity relates to broad personality domains. The FFM is a relatively well agreed-upon standardization of personality dimensions based on factor-analytic studies of personality structure. Common labels for the factors are: openness to experience, extraversion, conscientiousness, agreeableness and neuroticism (Barrick and Mount, 1991).

With regard to the factors within the FFM, diverse and sometimes conflicting associations have been made with innovation. However, of all the FFM factors, openness to experience is most often found to be positively related to innovation (McCrae, 1987; King et al., 1996; Kwang and Rodrigues, 2002). Open individuals are more curious about the world and have an interest in varied experience for its own sake (McCrae, 1987); and comparable characteristics are associated with both innovation and openness such as 'imaginative' and 'original' (Patterson, 2002). By definition, individuals high on openness are likely to have original ideas, which relate to innovation. Although recent findings suggest that the relationship might be moderated by contextual factors (Andrews and Smith, 1996; Burke and Witt, 2002; Baer and Oldham, 2006) researchers tend to agree that it is likely to be the most important personality dimension in predicting innovation potential (McCrae, 1987; King et al., 1996; Wolfradt and Pretz, 2001; Patterson 2002; Batey and Furnham, 2006; Harrison et al., 2006).

Empirical studies have revealed conflicting findings with regard to the relationship between innovation and extraversion. Although many researchers report a negative relationship (MacKinnon, 1962; Götz and Götz, 1979a; Feist, 1998, 1999), other studies have found a positive association (McCrae, 1987; Aguilar-Alonso, 1996; King et al., 1996; Martindale and Dailey, 1996; Kwang and Rodrigues, 2002). However, none of these studies have been conducted in organizational settings; most were student based, so currently there is a lack of clarity regarding the association between innovation and extraversion in organizations. Another possible reason for conflicting results in the literature relates to the differences in the nature of the studies, with some focusing on the idea generation phase of the innovation process (e.g., MacKinnon, 1962), and others on outcomes such as innovative accomplishments (e.g., King et al., 1996).

A further explanation for conflicting findings is that different facets of extraversion are linked to innovation in different ways. Feist (1998) notes two distinct sub-dimensions of extraversion: *assertiveness* and *sociability*, which although related to each other, are not synonymous since one can be assertive without being sociable and vice versa. Findings suggested that assertiveness had a small relation to innovation while sociability had none. However, Feist's review focused on artists and scientists, with no evidence from general working population contexts. Additionally, in meta-analytic studies of general occupational work performance (e.g., Barrick et al., 2001) extraversion is a positive predictor for many occupations. This is particularly the case for jobs where interpersonal factors are important for effective job performance (e.g., sales, managers and other professional occupations). Thus, it can be inferred that the association between extraversion and innovation may be context dependent. Introversion is likely to be important to real-life artistic endeavors whereas extraversion may predict performance measures of creativity and innovation (Patterson, 2002; Batey and Furnham, 2006). Clearly, further empirical research is needed to explore the association between extraversion and innovation in different occupational sectors and contexts.

The vast majority of research demonstrates that a lack of conscientiousness is related to innovation (e.g., King et al., 1996; Feist, 1999; Kwang and Rodrigues, 2002). Defined by terms such as fastidious, ordered, neat and methodical, the evidence shows that individuals high on conscientiousness do not challenge authority and are more likely to resist change (Costa and McCrae, 1992). So, at first glance conscientiousness may appear to be negatively related to innovation. However, within the personality literature, conscientiousness is considered to have a broad bandwidth (Barrick and Mount, 1991) since it entails two distinct facets: *dependability* and *achievement striving*. Innovation is known to be positively associated with achievement striving and persistence (Busse and Mansfield, 1984; Sternberg and Lubar, 1991; Feist, 1999) but negatively associated with being systematic and dependable (Patterson, 1999). Furthermore, King et al. (1996) found that self-discipline and hard work is vital for innovative achievement. Therefore, the broad bandwidth of conscientiousness may make it hard to determine its relationship with innovation, and so more research at the facet level of analysis is clearly needed.

Research shows that the organizational context is important in determining the influence of conscientiousness on innovative output. For example, George and Zhou's (2001) research suggests that high conscientiousness may inhibit innovative behavior but only when the workplace encourages the conformist and controlled tendencies of individuals who report high on conscientiousness. The authors suggest that it is not conscientiousness *per se* that is detrimental, but instead a combination of high conscientiousness and a work context that encourages conformity, self-controlling behavior, and also lacks support for innovative behavior.

Several studies have shown a negative association between agreeableness and innovation (Dudek et al., 1991; King et al., 1996; Gelade, 1997; Patterson, 1999; George and Zhou, 2001). That is, being disagreeable is linked to innovation. Findings are consistent with Eysenck's emphasis on the potentially negative dispositional characteristics of innovators, where innovators are often outspoken, uninhibited, quarrelsome, and sometimes asocial. Findings also show that agreeableness is negatively associated with creative achievement but not with creative thinking (King et al., 1996); this may indicate that lack of agreeableness is important in the implementation stage of innovation but not for idea generation (Patterson, 2002). This affords intuitive sense because implementation of new ideas is likely to be a group effort involving social processes and activities. Such findings have important implications for selecting and managing employees: how should employers reconcile the need for innovative employees who may display traits traditionally viewed as 'difficult to manage', and the need to select agreeable employees who will fit within a team and within the organization as a whole (Patterson, 2002: Zibarras et al., 2008)?

There is relatively little research examining an association between neuroticism (low emotional stability) and innovation. Of the literature that is available, there appears to be some inconsistencies depending on the domain of interest. For example, some researchers (e.g., McCrae, 1987; Aguilar-Alonso, 1996; King et al., 1996) have found no association between neuroticism and creative thinking or innovation. Conversely, other research literature suggests a positive association with neuroticism (Götz and Götz, 1979a; Mohan and Tiwana, 1987; Feist, 1998). An explanation for these inconsistencies is likely to be that the association between neuroticism and innovation is domain dependent. For example, in a meta-analytic review, Feist (1998) observed that artists appear to be more anxious, less emotionally stable and impulsive than the scientists he studied. A more thorough investigation in organizational settings is necessary, with a broader range of occupations. Meta-analytic studies of personality and work performance generally suggest a curvilinear association between emotional stability and performance, where too much or too little anxiety is detrimental (Barrick and Mount, 1991; Salgado, 1997), and this could be tested in the innovation arena. Perhaps a first step could be to examine possible links at the facet level since Costa and McCrae's (1992) conceptualization of neuroticism comprises six facets, including anxiety, hostility and impulsiveness. The innovation literature shows different associations with these facets: for example, innovation is associated with moderate levels of anxiety (Nicholson and West, 1988); hostility (Eysenck, 1995) and impulsiveness (Eysenck, 1994). Thus, testing these observations using samples within organizational settings is needed before conclusions can be drawn in this area.

Innovation and Psychopathology

Innovation has long been associated with psychoticism and many proponents have linked psychopathology with innovation (Eysenck, 1993; Burch, 2006). However, this gives rise to a paradox: psychopathology is evident in innovative individuals, but is known to suppress innovation. Eysenck (1993, 1995, 2003) therefore postulates a factor called psychoticism, which predisposes a person to psychotic illness under stress, but is also linked to innovation (Patterson, 2002). Individuals high on psychoticism are cold, egocentric, aggressive, impulsive and antisocial (Eysenck, 1993).

Eysenck's Three Factor Model of Personality

Eysenck's (1993) Three Factor Model of personality, includes three traits: neuroticism, extraversion and psychoticism. Within this model, Eysenck (1993, 1995) claims that psychoticism is most closely linked to the tendency to innovate. There are four lines of evidence that Eysenck (1995) uses to support his view that psychoticism and innovation are inextricably linked. The first line of evidence is genetic. Several well-controlled studies have shown that the descendants of psychotic parents show higher levels of innovation than do matched controls. For example, Heston (1966) studied the children of schizophrenic mothers who were raised by foster parents. As adults, about half showed psychosocial disability, whilst the others were notably successful, pursuing artistic talents and showing original adaptations to life to an extent not found in the control group. McNeil (1971) studied the occurrence of mental illness in highly innovative adopted children and their biological parents; he found that the mental illness rates in the adoptees and their biological parents were positively and significantly related to the level of innovation in the adoptees. These studies have been used to support Eysenck's opinion, particularly because they separate environmental and hereditary influences, suggesting either a genetic or pre-birth influence (Martindale and Dailey, 1996).

The second line of evidence is the association between psychoticism and measures of creativity/innovation. For example, Woody and Claridge (1977) found high correlations between the Wallach-Kogan Creativity Test and psychoticism scores. Additionally, psychoticism positively correlates with unusual and rare responses in word association tests (Merten, 1993; Eysenck, 1994; Martindale and Dailey, 1996) and preference for complexity on the Barron Welsh Art Scale (Eysenck, 1994). The third line of evidence is the correlation of psychoticism with creative achievement. For example, Götz and Götz (1979a) found that artists were lower on extraversion and higher on both neuroticism and psychoticism than non-artists; and in a second study (Götz and Götz, 1979b) the authors found that more successful artists had higher scores on psychoticism than less successful artists.

The final line of evidence relates to highly innovative individuals often responding to personality tests in ways that indicate lack of psychological adjustment or health (e.g., Mohan and Tiwana, 1987). On the Minnesota Multiphasic Personality Inventory (MMPI), innovative writers consistently appear to have more psychopathology than do representative members of the same profession (Barron, 1963). MacKinnon (1962) also found his architect participants to be abnormal on this inventory, with 'clear evidence of psychopathology, but also evidence of adequate control mechanisms, as the success with which they live their productive and creative lives testifies' (p. 488). Using these lines of evidence Eysenck (1995) identifies a set of characteristics that appear to be associated with innovation: 'unstable, irresponsible, disorderly, rebellious, uncontrolled, self-seeking, tactless, intemperate, rejecting of rules, uncooperative, impulsive and careless' (p. 233).

More recently, research has suggested a relationship between schizotypy and creativity/innovation. Burch (2006) discusses the concept of the 'creative schizotype' – a person who may have strange beliefs, thinking and odd behaviors, but it is thought that such factors may facilitate the generation of original ideas. However, the creative schizotype may also demonstrate anti-social behaviors, being impulsive, irresponsible and possibly hostile. Burch et al. (2006) explored differences in scores on measures of personality and creativity between non-artists and visual artists. Findings showed that visual artists scored higher than non-artists on three types of schizotypy: positive schizotypy (unusual experiences), disorganized schizotypy (cognitive disorganization) and asocial schizotypy (impulsive non-conformity). It is likely that unusual ideas (positive schizotypy) are particularly important in the generation of ideas in the process of innovation.

BEHAVIORS

Concepts such as *personal initiative* and *voice behavior*, may provide insight into our understanding of human innovation (Frese, 2000). For example, the concept of personal initiative (PI) describes a set of behaviors that have been positively linked to innovation and entrepreneurial orientation (Frese, 2000; Frese et al., 2007).

Personal Initiative and Self-efficacy

PI is comprised of three facets: *self-starting*, *proactivity* and *persistence* (Frese, 2000; Frese et al., 2007). A self-starting approach is characterized by setting context-specific goals and going beyond formal job requirements. Proactivity suggests that an employee anticipates opportunities and problems (as opposed to reacting to them), and prepares to deal with issues before they occur. Persistence is also involved in PI since it is required to overcome barriers in reaching goals. Frese and colleagues suggest that the three PI facets reinforce each other and tend to co-occur. Additionally, they can be used to understand how employees develop goals, collect information, make plans for executing goals, and also how individuals gather and use feedback. There is a growing body of research examining the association between PI and innovation. Indeed, Rank et al. (2004a) suggest that personal initiative plays an important moderating role in the innovation process. For example, recent studies (Baer and Frese, 2003; Rank et al., 2004b) suggest that personal initiative positively predicts employee- and team-level innovation and innovative ideas are more often implemented when personal initiative is high. Additionally, the relationship between PI and conservatism in the workplace has been studied (Frese et al., 2007). Results show that conservatives showed significantly less personal initiative than their less conservative counterparts; additionally, conservatives were less orientated towards growth and challenge, and were less innovative. Research also shows environmental influences on PI, for example increases in job complexity and job control can help enhance PI at work (Frese et al., 2007).

Personal initiative may be particularly important during the idea implementation phase of the innovation process, since it may often involve overcoming barriers and persistence. In a recent study (Parker et al., 2006) several predictors of innovation were examined, including employee-level variables (e.g., PI, self-efficacy, interest in innovation), work characteristics (e.g., control, complexity), motives (e.g., reward) and organizational factors (e.g., supervisor support). Results showed that being proactive, actively involved in one's work environment and confident that one is capable of thinking of good ideas were the most important predictors of innovation. Organizational factors were also important, indicating that innovation is maximized when organizational climates promote an active approach towards work and interpersonal risk-taking. Further, recent work (Judson and Patterson, 2010), showed that proactive personality significantly and positively influenced the generation and suggestion of new ideas in the workplace, accounting for significant variance over and above other employee factors such as motivation towards change.

A similar, yet distinct construct, self-efficacy has also been associated with innovative outputs. Bandura (1997) suggested that self-efficacy would be a necessary condition for innovative productivity and the ability to discover new knowledge. Tierney and Farmer (2002) considered the concept of 'creative self-efficacy', which is important in innovative work output. Their findings suggest that both creative self-efficacy and job self-efficacy have differential predictive effects on employee innovation. The authors suggest that their research enhances research on innovation by suggesting a new concept that is instrumental in innovation output. Further research (Jaussi et al., 2007) also supports the idea that self-efficacy is an important factor in predicting innovative outputs at work.

Voice Behavior and Further Skills

Voice behavior is an individual's willingness to speak up with suggestions for change (Van Dyne and LePine, 1998). This involves challenging the status quo, behavior that may play an important role in enabling the implementation of creative ideas (Rank et al., 2004b). Further research is needed to explore whether proactive behaviors may be developed through training (Frese, 2000). There has been a recent surge of interest in the transferrable skills, such as communication skills, that are important for innovation, especially during the implementation phase of innovation (Good et al., 2007). Although employees are the source of innovations, rarely does innovation occur in isolation. In order to innovate, employees are likely to have to relate and interact with other individuals – inside or outside the organization – hence the importance of communication, articulation and social networking skills. Other important skills may include conflict resolution, and collaborative problem-solving. Further research is needed in order to shed light on how innovative employees manage social interactions and on how they integrate social and intellectual demands.

EMOTIONS AND MOOD STATES

Examining the relationship between emotions, mood states and innovation is a new but rapidly growing research area. Moods are said to be relatively transient generalized affective states and are not typically directed to any particular object. They are experienced in the short term and are potentially influenced by contextual factors. Generally they are characterized by two dimensions, either positive or negative (George and Brief, 1992). A wide range of empirical studies have found links between positive mood states and aspects of innovation (George and Brief, 1992; Isen, 1999; Grawitch et al., 2003; Shalley et al., 2004; Amabile et al., 2005). For example, George and Brief (1992) proposed that positive mood facilitates voluntary behaviors relevant to both initiative and innovation, including making constructive suggestions, developing oneself, and helping co-workers. That is, individuals in positive moods are more likely to continue in self-development since they have more favorable self-perceptions, experience increased self-efficacy and develop higher aspirations.

Although Amabile and colleagues (2005) note that most studies indicate that positive mood facilitates creativity, they and other authors (e.g., Eisenberg and James, 2005) also point out that research has shown relationships between negative affect and creativity. For example, several studies (e.g., Heston, 1966) have identified a higher incidence of affective disorders (e.g., depression, bipolar disorder) among innovative individuals and their relations compared to the general population. Nevertheless, it should also be noted that this relationship seems to mainly apply to artistic creativity (Feist, 1999). Furthermore, the best creative work by individuals suffering from bipolar disorder seems to occur during the hypomanic phase rather than during the depressed state (Russ, 2000). However, the idea that negative affect may facilitate creativity and innovation has recently gained in popularity. In relation to creativity, authors have acknowledged that 'negative emotions may be necessary to break down old expectations and paradigms' (Higgins et al., 1992, p. 122). Similarly, Madjar and colleagues argued that tension and dissatisfaction may be important for creative problem-solving (Madjar et al., 2002). More recently, Anderson et al. (2004) presented a distress-related innovation model. They suggest that distress-related variables at the individual, group and organizational levels of analysis may be a trigger for innovation. To support their notion, they cited studies showing a positive influence of an individual's negative mood (George and Zhou, 2002) or job dissatisfaction (Zhou and George, 2001) and of external demand factors on the organization, including a turbulent environment (West, 2000). In fact, increasingly, field studies suggest that negative mood may sometimes facilitate innovative behavior (Fay and Sonnentag, 2002; George and Zhou, 2002).

To summarize, it appears that mood and creativity/innovation are linked in a number of studies, however, further research on this topic is warranted. Specifically, the relationship between emotions, moods and their association with different phases of the innovation process deserves more emphasis in future research.

EMOTIONAL INTELLIGENCE

The concept of emotional intelligence (EI) has become very popular in recent years, attracting a huge amount of interest from academics. EI is defined as 'the ability to perceive accurately, appraise and express emotion; the ability to access and/or generate feelings when they facilitate thought; the ability to understand emotion and emotional knowledge;

and the ability to regulate emotions to promote emotional and intellectual growth' (Mayer and Salovey, 1997, p. 10). In relation to innovation, some authors suggest that EI has a positive influence on organizational innovation, both for leaders and individual employees. For example, in a review of the role emotions have in transformational leadership, Ashkanasy and Tse (2000) suggested that EI involves the ability to utilize emotions in a way that allows flexible planning and creative thinking. Similarly, leaders' levels of EI are likely to accentuate the employees' inclination to engage in the innovation process (Zhou and George, 2003). From an employee perspective, researchers have suggested that employees who show high levels of EI are likely to benefit more from both positive and negative creativity-related feedback (Zhou, 2008). Furthermore, it is thought that EI may be beneficial when innovative employees have to persuade others to support them during the implementation phase of innovation (Rank and Frese, 2008). Specifically, being able to perceive others' emotions and to regulate them appears to be important.

IMPLICATIONS FOR FUTURE RESEARCH AND THE MANAGEMENT OF INNOVATION

Our review of the literature demonstrates the array of variables to account for when exploring employee innovation, not just within individuals but also the influence of variables in the work environment. In drawing together the literature it is clear that a multi-level analysis is required to fully understand the variables important in employee-level innovation. In this chapter, we focused in particular at the employee level of analysis by exploring the role of cognition, personality, intellect, motivation and affect. However, in exploring the resources important at this level of analysis, we also acknowledge the important role of work groups and teams, managers and leaders in predicting innovative outcomes. In this way, we suggest that further research should focus on exploring more fully the higher-order interactions between these domains, with the ultimate aim of understanding how best to design interventions to promote innovation in organizations. Here, multi-level analysis techniques could be used to define an evidence-based, integrative theoretical model to explain the causal associations between employee-level resources, work environment, organizational practices and innovation in organizations. For example, when innovation is assessed at the individual level, it is inappropriate to analyze the data with simple multiple regression, because an individual's contribution to outcomes is not statistically independent, but nested within teams (see, Kenny et al., 2002). Instead, one should use multi-level techniques (see, Snijders and Bosker, 1999), which are especially useful when several teams are investigated within one or more organization.

In a turbulent economic climate, with consequent uncertainty for many employees, a major challenge is how managers can best encourage employees to be creative and to innovate. Although our review suggests that an array of employee resources are important in promoting innovation, here we emphasize the relative importance of certain resources and the practical implications for corporate policy in terms of managing and advancing organizational innovation. Practically, we discuss these in terms of organizational practices relating to recruitment, management and management systems, and how to approach the development of employees to enhance the propensity for innovation to occur.

In order to advance organizational levels of innovation, organizations are seeking to attract and retain innovative employees. For individuals, research consistently shows that three key characteristics important for innovation are openness to experience (King et al., 1996), motivation (Amabile, 1996) and proactivity (Frese et al., 2007). We argue that if organizations are seeking to nurture innovation, recruiters would benefit from not focusing solely on the results of cognitive ability tests and conscientiousness (as many do in practice) and pay as much attention to other important traits, such as openness to experience. For example, the Innovation Potential Indicator (Patterson, 1999) is a useful selection and development tool for employees and managers, as it is a trait-based, multi-dimensional measure of innovative behavior in organizations. The measure captures self-reports of important behaviors associated with idea generation and idea implementation. Specifically, one aspect of the IPI measures 'motivation to change', which is an individual's intrinsic motivation for change and tolerance of ambiguity at work, characterized by persistence and ambition. Independent researchers have shown this dimension (motivation to change) to be the best of innovation outcomes for employees and teams (Burch et al., 2008).

Another stream of research, however, shows that some 'antisocial' behaviors are associated with innovative employees (e.g., Burch, 2006; Zibarras et al., 2008). If innovators are sometimes seen as 'disruptive troublemakers', it is understandable why Patterson (2002) has previously questioned whether organizations are '"ready" to recruit individuals that are likely to challenge the status quo, question authority and are less conforming' (p. 136). The association of innovative characteristics with some potentially dysfunctional traits suggests that those individuals who are responsible for managing innovative employees may be a challenging experience (Zibarras et al., 2008). So how can organizations assist managers in promoting innovation, especially in work groups and teams, when some employees demonstrate social rule independence? Furthermore, although organizations see innovation as key to their success (Bunce and West, 1995), the management systems employed may be actively reducing the likelihood for innovation to occur. For example, do managers prefer and reward employees that are conscientious, methodical, reliable, neat, punctual and dutiful? Here, Burch (2006) notes a paradox for organizations seeking to develop creativity and innovation: 'do organizations want people who, while being more likely to express original ideas, will probably be more anti-social . . . ? Or, do organizations want team members who may be more prosocial, and . . . may come up with less unique ideas?' (p. 48). Perhaps this implies that management styles need to be flexible in order to nurture an environment where innovation (both idea generation and idea implementation) is likely to occur.

Research shows that the motivational component of innovation explains a large proportion of the variance in innovative behaviors (Patterson, 1999). When a person is motivated they tend to seek out challenges and novelty (Amabile, 1996). In drawing together the research reviewed in this chapter, the evidence suggests that managers are likely to significantly influence (positively or negatively) an employee's motivation to innovate. Managers and leaders are fundamental in promoting employee motivation to innovate. In a recent policy report in conjunction with the UK Chartered Management Institute called 'Innovation for the Recovery' (Patterson and Kerrin, 2009) where over 850 UK organizations were surveyed, results showed that although many organizations wished to enhance innovation in their organization, many management practices used were likely to inhibit the likelihood for innovation to occur. For example, many of the human resource management (HRM) systems did not reward innovative behaviors in the workplace. Furthermore, in this report, Patterson and Kerrin suggest that the relationship an employee has with their immediate line manager is directly related to how the employee perceives and describes the working culture. Therefore, managers play an important 'gatekeeper' role in influencing innovation and such that specific development interventions can be used to enhance a manager's competence in enhancing employee innovation (such as how best to provide feedback to employees to promote innovation; see Tierney, 2008). In summary, researchers have identified evidence-based development interventions for managers in how best to promote innovative working in future. For organizations seeking to enhance innovation, unlocking the potential of employees through adopting appropriate management practices is a fundamental prerequisite. Future research should focus on developing an improved understanding of the contingent relationship between employee and manager to inform practical interventions to enhance innovation.

REFERENCES

Ackerman, P.L. (1996), 'A theory of adult intellectual development: process, personality, interests, and knowledge', *Intelligence*, **22**(2), 227–57.

Ackerman, P.L. (2000), 'Domain-specific knowledge as the "dark matter" of adult intelligence', *The Journals of Gerontology Series B: Psychological Sciences and Social Sciences*, **55**(2), 69–84.

Aguilar-Alonso, A. (1996), 'Personality and creativity', *Personality and Individual Differences*, **21**(6), 959–69.

Amabile, T.M. (1983), 'The social psychology of creativity: a componential conceptualization', *Journal of Personality and Social Psychology*, **45**(2), 357–76.

Amabile, T.M. (1988), 'A model of creativity and innovation in organizations', in B.M. Staw and L.L. Cummings (eds), *Research in Organizational Behavior, Volume 10*, 123–67.

Amabile, T. (1996), *Creativity in Context: Update to the Social Psychology of Creativity*, New York: Westview Press.

Amabile, T.M. and N.D. Gryskiewicz (1989), 'The creative environment scales: work environment inventory', *Creativity Research Journal*, **2**(4), 231–53.

Amabile, T.M., S.G. Barsade, J.S. Mueller and B.M. Staw (2005), 'Affect and creativity at work', *Administrative Science Quarterly*, **50**(3), 367–403.

Amabile, T.M., R. Conti, H. Coon, J. Lazenby and M. Herron (1996), 'Assessing the work environment for creativity', *Academy of Management Journal*, **39**(5), 1154–84.

Anderson, N., C.K.W. De Dreu and B.A. Nijstad (2004), 'The routinization of innovation research: a constructively critical review of the state-of-the-science', *Journal of Organizational Behavior*, **25**(2), 147–73.

Andrews, J. and D.C. Smith (1996), 'In search of the marketing imagination: factors affecting the creativity of marketing programs for mature products', *Journal of Marketing Research*, **33**(2), 174–87.

Ashkanasy, N.M. and B. Tse (2000), 'Transformational leadership as management of emotion: a conceptual review', in N.M. Ashkanasy, C.E.J. Haertel and W.J. Zerbe (eds), *Emotions in the Workplace: Research, Theory, and Practice*, Westport, CT and London: Quorum, pp. 221–35.

Axtell, C.M., D. Holman, K. Unsworth, T. Wall, P. Waterson and E. Harrington (2000), 'Shopfloor innovation: facilitating the suggestion and implementation of ideas', *Journal of Occupational and Organizational Psychology*, **73**(3), 265–85.

Baer, M. and M. Frese (2003), 'Innovation is not enough: climates for initiative and psychological safety, process innovations, and firm performance', *Journal of Organizational Behavior*, **24**(1), 45–68.

Baer, M. and G.R. Oldham (2006), 'The curvilinear relation between experienced creative time pressure and creativity: moderating effects of openness to experience and support for creativity', *Journal of Applied Psychology*, **91**(4), 963–70.

Bandura, A. (1997), *Self-efficacy: The Exercise of Control*, New York: Freeman.

Barrick, M.R. and M.K. Mount (1991), 'The Big Five personality dimensions and job performance: a meta-analysis', *Personnel Psychology*, **44**(1), 1–26.

Barrick, M.R., M.K. Mount and T.A. Judge (2001), 'Personality and performance at the beginning of the new millennium: what do we know and where do we go next?', *International Journal of Selection and Assessment*, **9**(1–2), 9–30.

Barron, F. (1963), 'The needs for order and for disorder as motives in creative activity', in C.W. Taylor and F. Barron (eds), *Scientific Creativity*, New York: John Wiley and Sons, pp. 153–60.

Barron, F. and D.M. Harrington (1981), 'Creativity, intelligence, and personality', *Annual Review of Psychology*, **32**(1), 439–76.

Batey, M. and A. Furnham (2006), 'Creativity, intelligence, and personality: a critical review of the scattered literature', *Genetic, Social, and General Psychology Monographs*, **132**(4), 355–429.

Batey, M., T. Chamorro-Premuzic and A. Furnham (2009), 'Intelligence and personality as predictors of divergent thinking: the role of general, fluid and crystallised intelligence', *Thinking Skills and Creativity*, **4**(1), 60–69.

Birdi, K. (2007), 'A lighthouse in the desert? Evaluating the effects of creativity training on employee innovation', *The Journal of Creative Behavior*, **41**(4), 249–70.

Bunce, D. and M.A. West (1995), 'Self-perceptions and perceptions of group climate as predictors of individual innovation at work', *Applied Psychology*, **44**(3), 199–215.

Burch, G.S.J. (2006), 'The "creative-schizotype": help or hindrance to team-level innovation?', *The University of Auckland Business Review*, **8**(1), 43–50.

Burch, G.S.J., C. Pavelis, D.R. Hemsley and P.J. Corr (2006), 'Schizotypy and creativity in visual artists', *British Journal of Psychology*, **97**(2), 177–90.

Burch, G.S.J., C. Pavelis and R. Port (2008), 'Selecting for creativity and innovation: the relationship between the innovation potential indicator and the team selection inventory', *International Journal of Selection and Assessment*, **16**(2), 177–81.

Burke, L.A. and L.A. Witt (2002), 'Moderators of the openness to experience–performance relationship', *Journal of Managerial Psychology*, **17**(8), 712–21.

Busse, T.V. and R.S. Mansfield (1984), 'Selected personality traits and achievement in male scientists', *Journal of Psychology*, **116**(1), 117–31.

Cattell, R.B. and H.J. Butcher (1968), *The Prediction of Achievement and Creativity*, Indianapolis: Bobbs-Merrill.

Collins, M.A. and T.M. Amabile (1999), 'Motivation and creativity', in R.J. Sternberg (ed.), *The Handbook of Creativity*, Cambridge, UK: Cambridge University Press.

Costa, P.T. and R.R. McCrae (1992), 'Normal personality assessment in clinical practice: the NEO personality inventory', *Psychological Assessment*, **4**(1), 5–13.

Dudek, S.Z., R. Bernèche, H. Bérubé and S. Royer (1991), 'Personality determinants of the commitment to the profession of art', *Creativity Research Journal*, **4**(4), 367–89.

Eisenberg, J. and K. James (2005), 'The relationship between affect and creativity in organizations: the roles of affect characteristics, neuro-cognitive mechanisms and task type', in N.M. Ashkanasy, W.J. Zerbe, C.E.J. Haertel (eds), *The Effect of Affect in Organizational Settings, Research on Emotion in Organizations, Volume I*, Bingley, UK: Emerald Group Publishing, pp. 241–61.

Eisenberger, R. and J. Cameron (1996), 'Detrimental effects of reward: reality or myth?', *American Psychologist*, **51**(11), 1153–66.

Eysenck, H. (ed.) (1979), *The Structure and Measure of Intelligence*, New York: Springer-Verlag.

Eysenck, H.J. (1993), 'Target article: creativity and personality: suggestions for a theory', *Psychological Inquiry*, **4**(3), 147–78.

Eysenck, H.J. (1994), 'Personality and intelligence: psychometric and experimental approaches', in R.J. Sternberg and P. Ruzgis (eds), *Personality and Intelligence*, New York: Cambridge University Press, pp. 3–31.

Eysenck, H.J. (1995), *Genius: The Natural History of Creativity*, New York: Cambridge University Press.

Eysenck, H. (2003), 'Creativity, personality, and the convergent-divergent continuum', in M.A. Runco (ed.), *Critical Creative Processes*, Cresskill, NJ: Hampton Press Inc., pp. 95–114.

Fay, D. and S. Sonnentag (2002), 'Rethinking the effects of stressors: a longitudinal study on personal initiative', *Journal of Occupational Health Psychology*, **7**(3), 221–34.

Feist, G.J. (1998), 'A meta-analysis of personality in scientific and artistic creativity', *Personality and Social Psychology Review*, **2**(4), 290–309.

Feist, G.J. (1999), 'The influence of personality on artistic and scientific creativity', in R.J. Sternberg (ed.), *Handbook of Creativity*, Cambridge: Cambridge University Press, pp. 273–96.

Feist, G.J. and F.X. Barron (2003), 'Predicting creativity from early to late adulthood: intellect, potential, and personality', *Journal of Research in Personality*, **37**(2), 62–88.

Finke, R.A., T.B. Ward and S.M. Smith (1992), *Creative Cognition*, Cambridge, MA: MIT Press.

Frensch, P.A. and R.J. Sternberg (1989), 'Expertise and intelligent thinking: when is it worse to know better?', *Advances in the Psychology of Human Intelligence*, **5**, 157–88.

Frese, M. (2000), 'The changing nature of work', in N. Chmiel (ed.), *Introduction to Work and Organizational Psychology: A European Perspective*, Oxford: Blackwell Publishing, pp. 424–39.

Frese, M., H. Garst and D. Fay (2007), 'Making things happen: reciprocal relationships between work characteristics and personal initiative in a four-wave longitudinal structural equation model', *Journal of Applied Psychology*, **92**(4), 1084–102.

Frese, M., E. Teng and C.J.D. Wijnen (1999), 'Helping to improve suggestion systems: predictors of making suggestions in companies', *Journal of Organizational Behavior*, **20**(7), 1139–55.

Gelade, G.A. (1997), 'Creativity in conflict: the personality of the commercial creative', *The Journal of Genetic Psychology*, **158**(1), 67–78.

George, J.M. and A.P. Brief (1992), 'Feeling good–doing good: a conceptual analysis of the mood at work–organizational spontaneity relationship', *Psychological Bulletin*, **112**(2), 310–29.

George, J.M. and J. Zhou (2001), 'When openness to experience and conscientiousness are related to creative behavior: an interactional approach', *Journal of Applied Psychology*, **86**(3), 513–24.

George, J.M. and J. Zhou (2002), 'Understanding when bad moods foster creativity and good ones don't: the role of context and clarity of feelings', *Journal of Applied Psychology*, **87**(4), 687–97.

Gilhooly, K., V. Wynn and M. Osman (2004), 'Studies of divergent thinking', *Proceedings of the British Psychological Society*, **12**(2), 146.

Goldberg, L.R. (1990), 'An alternative "description of personality"': the Big-Five Factor structure', *Journal of Personality and Social Psychology*, **59**(6), 1216–29.

Good, D., S. Greenwald, R. Cox and M. Goldman (2007), *University Collaboration for Innovation – Lessons from the Cambridge-MIT Institute*, Rotterdam: Sense Publishers.

Götz, K.O. and K. Götz (1979a), 'Personality characteristics of professional artists', *Perceptual and Motor Skills*, **49**(1), 327–34.

Götz, K.O. and K. Götz (1979b), 'Personality characteristics of successful artists', *Perceptual and Motor Skills*, **49**(3), 919–24.

Grawitch, M.J., D.C. Munz and T.J. Kramer (2003), 'Effects of member mood states on creative performance in temporary work groups', *Group Dynamics: Theory, Research, and Practice*, **7**(1), 41–54.

Guilford, J.P. (1950), 'Creativity research: past, present and future', *American Psychologist*, **5**(1), 444–54.

Guilford, J.P. (1988), 'Some changes in the structure-of-intellect model', *Educational and Psychological Measurement*, **48**(1), 1–4.

Harrington, D.M. (1975), 'Effects of explicit instructions to "be creative" on the psychological meaning of divergent thinking test scores', *Journal of Personality*, **43**(3), 434–54.

Harrison, M.M., N.L. Neff, A.R. Schwall and Zhao, X. (2006), 'A meta-analytic investigation of individual creativity and innovation', paper presented at the 21st Annual Conference for the Society for Industrial and Organizational Psychology, Dallas, Texas.

Heston, L.L. (1966), 'Psychiatric disorders in foster home reared children of schizophrenic mothers', *The British Journal of Psychiatry*, **112**(489), 819–25.

Higgins, L.F., S.H. Qualls and J.D. Couger (1992), 'The role of emotions in employee creativity', *Journal of Creative Behavior*, **26**(2), 119–29.

Isen, A.M. (1999), 'On the relationship between affect and creative problem solving', in S.W. Russ (ed.), *Affect, Creative Experience, and Psychological Adjustment*, London: Taylor & Francis, pp. 3–17.

Jaussi, K.S., A.E. Randel and S.D. Dionne (2007), 'I am, I think I can, and I do: the role of personal identity, self-efficacy, and cross-application of experiences in creativity at work', *Creativity Research Journal*, **19**(2–3), 247–58.

Judson, H. and F. Patterson (2010), 'Investigating the role of proactive personality, innovation potential and leader–member exchange in employee innovation', paper presentation at the Division of Occupational Psychology Conference, Brighton, UK.

Kenny, D.A., N. Bolger and D.A. Kashy (2002), 'Traditional methods for estimating multilevel models', in D.S. Moskowitz and S.L. Hershberger (eds), *Modeling Intraindividual Variability with Repeated Measures Data: Methods and Applications*, Mahwah, NJ: Lawrence Erlbaum, pp. 1–24.

Kim, K.H. (2005), 'Can only intelligent people be creative?', *Journal of Secondary Gifted Education*, **16**(2–3), 57–66.

King, L.A., L.M.K. Walker and S.J. Broyles (1996), 'Creativity and the Five-Factor Model', *Journal of Research in Personality*, **30**(2), 189–203.

Kwang, N.A. and D. Rodrigues (2002), 'A Big-Five personality profile of the adaptor and innovator', *The Journal of Creative Behavior*, **36**(4), 254–68.

MacKinnon, D.W. (1962), 'The nature and nurture of creative talent', *American Psychologist*, **17**(7), 484–95.

Madjar, N.A., G.R. Oldham and M.G. Pratt (2002), 'There's no place like home? The contributions of work and nonwork creativity support to employees' creative performance', *Academy of Management Journal*, **45**(4), 757–67.

Martindale, C. and A. Dailey (1996), 'Creativity, primary process cognition and personality', *Personality and Individual Differences*, **20**(4), 409–14.

Mascitelli, R. (2000), 'From experience: harnessing tacit knowledge to achieve breakthrough innovation', *Journal of Product Innovation Management*, **17**(3), 179–93.

Mayer, J.D. and P. Salovey (1997), 'What is emotional intelligence?', in P. Salovey and D. Sluyter (eds), *Emotional Development and Emotional Intelligence: Implications for Educators*, New York: Basic Books, pp. 3–31.

McCrae, R.R. (1987), 'Creativity, divergent thinking, and openness to experience', *Journal of Personality and Social Psychology*, **52**(6), 1258–65.

McCrae, R.R. and P.T. Costa Jr (1999), 'A Five-Factor theory of personality', in L.A. Pervin and O.P. John (eds), *Handbook of Personality* (2nd edition), New York: The Guilford Press.

McNeil, T.F. (1971), 'Prebirth and postbirth influence on the relationship between creative ability and recorded mental illness', *Journal of Personality*, **39**(3), 391–406.

Merten, T. (1993), 'Word association responses and psychoticism', *Personality and Individual Differences*, **14**(6), 837–9.

Mohan, J.L. and M. Tiwana (1987), 'Personality and alienation of creative writers: a brief report', *Personality and Individual Differences*, **8**(3), 449.

Mumford, M.D. (2003), 'Where have we been, where are we going? Taking stock in creativity research', *Creativity Research Journal*, **15**(2), 107–20.

Nicholson, N. and M. West (1988), *Managerial Job Change: Men and Women in Transition*, Cambridge, UK: Cambridge University Press.

Oldham, G.R. and A. Cummings (1996), 'Employee creativity: personal and contextual factors at work', *Academy of Management Journal*, **39**(3), 607–34.

Parker, S.K., H.M. Williams and N. Turner (2006), 'Modeling the antecedents of proactive behavior at work', *Journal of Applied Psychology*, **91**(3), 636–52.

Patterson, F. (1999), *The Innovation Potential Indicator, Manual and User's Guide*, Oxford: Oxford Psychologists Press.

Patterson, F. (2002), 'Great minds don't think alike? Person-level predictors of innovation at work', in C.L. Cooper and I.T. Robertson (eds), *International Review of Industrial and Organizational Psychology 2002*, Chichester: John Wiley and Sons, pp. 115–44.

Patterson, F. and M. Kerrin (2009), 'Innovation for the recovery', Chartered Management Institute, Research Reports, pp. 1–32.

Patterson F., M. Kerrin, G. Gatto-Roissard (2009), 'Characteristics and behaviours associated with innovative working in organizations', *NESTA Research Reports*, London: NESTA.

Preckel, F., H. Holling and M. Wiese (2006), 'Relationship of intelligence and creativity in gifted and non-gifted students: an investigation of threshold theory', *Personality and Individual Differences*, **40**(1), 159–70.

Rank, J. and M. Frese (2008), 'The impact of emotions, moods, and other affect-related variables on creativity, innovation and initiative in organizations', in N.M. Ashkanasy and C.L. Cooper (eds), *Research Companion to Emotion in Organizations*, Cheltenham, UK and Northampton, MA, USA: Edward Elgar Publishing Ltd, pp. 103–19.

Rank, J., V.L. Pace and M. Frese (2004a), 'Three avenues for future research on creativity, innovation, and initiative', *Applied Psychology*, **53**(4), 518–28.

Rank, J., N. Boedker, M. Linke and M. Frese (2004b), 'Integrating proactivity concepts into innovation research: the importance of voice and initiative', in S.K. Parker and C. Collins (Chairs), Proactivity: Enhancing Understanding of Self-started and Dynamic Action within Organizations, Symposium Conducted at the Meeting of the Academy of Management, New Orleans.

Rickards, T. (1996), 'The management of innovation: recasting the role of creativity', *European Journal of Work and Organizational Psychology*, **5**(1), 13–27.

Runco, M.A. (2006), 'Introduction to the special issue: divergent thinking', *Creativity Research Journal*, **18**(3), 249–50.

Russ, S.W. (2000), 'Primary-process thinking and creativity: affect and cognition', *Creativity Research Journal*, **13**(1), 27–35.

Salgado, J.F. (1997), 'The Five Factor Model of personality and job performance in the European Community', *Journal of Applied Psychology*, **82**(1), 30–43.

Sauermann, H. and W. Cohen (2008), 'What makes them tick? Employee motives and firm innovation', Working Paper No. 14443, Cambridge, MA: National Bureau of Economic Research.

Shalley, C.E., J. Zhou and G.R. Oldham (2004), 'The effects of personal and contextual characteristics on creativity: where should we go from here?', *Journal of Management*, **30**(6), 933–58.

Shin, S.J. and J. Zhou (2003), 'Transformational leadership, conservation, and creativity: evidence from Korea', *Academy of Management Journal*, **46**(6), 703–14.

Silvia, P.J. (2008a), 'Another look at creativity and intelligence: exploring higher-order models and probable confounds', *Personality and Individual Differences*, **44**(4), 1012–21.

Silvia, P.J. (2008b), 'Creativity and intelligence revisited: a latent variable analysis of Wallach and Kogan (1965)', *Creativity Research Journal*, **20**(1), 34–9.

Simonton, D.K. (1984), 'Artistic creativity and interpersonal relationships across and within generations', *Journal of Personality and Social Psychology*, **46**(6), 1273–86.

Simonton, D.K. (2003), 'Expertise, competence, and creative ability', in R.J. Sternberg and E.L. Grigorenko (eds), *The Psychology of Abilities, Competencies and Expertise*, New York: Cambridge University Press, pp. 213–40.

Snijders, T.A.B. and R.J. Bosker (1999), *Multilevel Analysis: An Introduction to Basic and Advanced Multilevel Modeling*, London: Sage.

Sosik, J.J., S.S. Kahai and B.J. Avolio (1999), 'Leadership style, anonymity, and creativity in group decision support systems: the mediating role of optimal flow', *The Journal of Creative Behavior*, **33**(4), 227–56.

Spearman, C. (1923), *The Nature of 'Intelligence' and the Principles of Cognition*, London: Macmillan.

Sternberg, R.J. (1982), 'Nonentrenchment in the assessment of intellectual giftedness', *Gifted Child Quarterly*, **26**(2), 63–7.

Sternberg, R.J. (1997), *Successful Intelligence: How Practical and Creative Intelligence Determine Success in Life*, New York: Plume Books.

Sternberg, R.J. (1999), *Handbook of Creativity*, Cambridge, UK: Cambridge University Press.

Sternberg, R.J., and T.I. Lubart (1991), 'An investment theory of creativity and its development', *Human Development*, **34**(1), 1–31.

Sternberg, R.J. and L.A. O'Hara (1999), 'Creativity and intelligence', in R.J. Sternberg (ed.), *Handbook of Creativity*, Cambridge, UK: Cambridge University Press, pp. 251–72.

Tierney, P. (2008), 'Leadership and employee creativity', in J. Zhou and C.E. Shalley (eds), *Handbook of Organizational Creativity*, New York: Lawrence Erlbaum Associates.

Tierney, P. and S.M. Farmer (2002), 'Creative self-efficacy: its potential antecedents and relationship to creative performance', *Academy of Management Journal*, **45**(6), 1137–48.
Van Dyne, L. and J.A. LePine (1998), 'Helping and voice extra-role behaviors: evidence of construct and predictive validity', *Academy of Management Journal*, **41**(1), 108–19.
Weisberg, R.W. (2006), *Creativity: Understanding Innovation in Problem Solving, Science, Invention, and the Arts*, Hoboken, NJ: John Wiley and Sons.
West, M.A. (2000), 'State of the art: creativity and innovation at work', *Psychologist*, **13**(9), 460–64.
West, M.A. and J.L. Farr (1990), *Innovation and Creativity at Work: Psychological and Organizational Strategies*, Chichester: John Wiley & Sons.
Williams, W.M. and L.T. Yang (1999), 'Organizational creativity', in R.J. Sternberg (ed.), *Handbook of Creativity*, Cambridge, UK: Cambridge University Press, pp. 373–91.
Wolfradt, U. and J.E. Pretz (2001), 'Individual differences in creativity: personality, story writing, and hobbies', *European Journal of Personality*, **15**(4), 297–310.
Woody, E. and G. Claridge (1977), 'Psychoticism and thinking', *British Journal of Social and Clinical Psychology*, **16**(3), 241–8.
Zhou, J. (2008), 'Promoting creativity through feedback', in J. Zhou and C.E. Shalley (eds), *Handbook of Organizational Creativity*, Boca Raton, FL: Taylor & Francis, pp. 125–46.
Zhou, J. and J.M. George (2003), 'Awakening employee creativity: the role of leader emotional intelligence', *Leadership Quarterly*, **14**(4/5), 545–68.
Zibarras, L.D., R.L. Port and S.A. Woods, 2008, 'Innovation and the "dark side" of personality: dysfunctional traits and their relation to innovation potential', *Journal of Creative Behavior*, **42**(3), 201–15.

8 Management education for organizational and managerial innovation
Renu Agarwal, Roy Green and Richard Hall

INTRODUCTION

Recent theory, research and policy development has increasingly highlighted the significance of the organization as the site at which innovation needs to be facilitated, fostered and inculcated, as well as realized in practice. This is helpful in the sense that it gives sharper focus to the meaning of innovation in practice, without detracting from the notion that state policy and the institutional milieu remain vital in shaping the broader macroeconomic environment for innovation.

In addition to emphasizing the importance of managerial and organizational innovation, the recognition that organizations, their behaviour and management, are central to stimulating innovation directs attention to the role of management education and business schools. Management education encompasses on the job, in-house and informal training and development undertaken by firms. It also includes the management and leadership training and development undertaken by business schools in their undergraduate, postgraduate, MBA and executive education programmes, increasingly expected to have a significant impact on organizational management capability and its capacity to facilitate and drive innovative practice.

This chapter critically considers the role of management education in managerial and organizational innovation with a particular emphasis on the way in which business schools in the future might be better able to develop management competencies and attributes that encourage innovation in, and of, organizations. Any consideration of the relationship between management education and innovation must bring together two fields of research and enquiry that have had little history of engagement. On the one hand, innovation theory is relatively well developed and has traditionally focused on the identification of different types of innovation, the factors associated with innovation capability and the organizational and societal outcomes of innovation. On the other hand, work on management education has not normally been theoretically developed, with the possible exception of work concerning pedagogy and adult learning theory, and has understandably had a strongly practical, policy-oriented and institutional focus. It is also the case that any analysis of management education needs to be contextualized – management education undertaken by business schools (the key focus of this chapter) occurs in specific historical and national-institutional contexts. For these reasons, a review of the role of management education in managerial and organizational innovation needs to engage with a number of relatively distinct domains of enquiry: the state of managerial and organizational innovation theory and research, the contemporary institutional and policy context in which management education occurs, and the current state of management education and business school practice. In the absence of an extant body of theory and research on management education for innovation per se this suggests the need for some synthesis of the findings and implications of these different domains.

In this chapter some of the key themes in managerial and organizational innovation theory are first examined in order to identify the ways in which management education might potentially contribute to innovation. In order to provide a contextual setting for the analysis of management education some of the major policy forces impacting (or potentially impacting) on management education in Australia are then briefly detailed in the second section. Australia provides a particularly interesting case as there have been significant recent initiatives in both innovation policy and higher education policy. The role and purpose of business schools has recently been the focus of considerable debate and widespread rethinking around the world, but especially in the USA and UK in recent years. The evolving consensus is that business schools need to change and play a much stronger role in developing capabilities required for innovation, creativity and managing organizational change, in addition to the development of technical and core business skills that has traditionally dominated their approach. All of these forces and factors – the implications of what we know about managerial and organizational innovation, innovation and higher education policies, and the implications of the critical debate about the role of business schools – throw management education for innovation into sharp relief and place business schools under significant pressure to rise to the innovation challenge. In the final section we consider two promising directions for management education – integrative and design thinking, and practice-based learning. In conclusion we consider the implications of this analysis for managerial and organizational innovation theory and research.

THE ROLE OF MANAGEMENT EDUCATION IN MANAGERIAL AND ORGANIZATIONAL INNOVATION

There is a wealth of research acknowledging the vital role of management capability in boosting productivity and performance at both the enterprise and macroeconomic levels. Alexopoulos and Tombe (2009) suggest that not only do tangible technologies such as machinery and new products influence productivity, but so do intangible technologies such as management techniques and new processes. Kale and Singh (2007, p. 995) regard management capabilities as 'higher-order capabilities that help a firm extend, modify, or improve its ordinary or operational capabilities that are relevant to managing any given task'. Management capabilities involve the execution of management practices that are a collation of 'processes that use resources – specifically the processes to integrate, reconfigure, gain and release resources to match and even create market change' (Eisenhardt and Martin, 2000, p. 1107). Thus, changes in workplace organization, team structures, communication and managerial leadership all affect productivity at the firm level and workforce efficiency (Black and Lynch, 2001), thus making human resource management, as well as skills and education, critical for organizations (Agarwal and Green, 2011). Research on management practices and its influence on productivity (Bloom and Van Reenen, 2007; Green et al., 2009) has recently gained prominence, but their impact on innovation is still not clearly understood.

Innovation, and to a lesser extent, managerial and organizational innovation, have been the subject of intense theoretical interest and extensive research in recent decades. However, relatively little is known of the potential and actual role of management education in promoting innovation in general, and managerial and organizational innovation in particular. There are good reasons to suspect that management education should be critical to the encouragement of innovative practices in organizations: as noted above, managers are key decision-makers controlling resources, influencing behaviours and cultivating distinctive cultures in ways that may or may not be conducive to innovation (Bloom and Van Reenen, 2007). While there has been some informative research and work on the skills associated with innovation (Bell and Pavitt, 1997; Arthur, 2007; OECD, 2011; Toner, 2011), there has been little that directly considers exactly what managers (can) do to facilitate managerial and organizational innovation. This kind of research and theoretical reflection would at least provide a key lead for the broader question of the role of management education.

MANAGERIAL AND ORGANIZATIONAL INNOVATION

Much of the innovation literature has been concerned with the definition and delineation of different forms of innovation (Tidd et al., 2005). Beyond the classic distinction between product and process innovation (Bessant, 1992) lies a range of closely related forms of innovation: service innovation (Gallouj and Weinstein, 1997), strategic innovation (Hamel, 1998), business innovation, managerial innovation (Birkinshaw and Mol, 2006) and organizational innovation (Damanpour and Evan, 1984). 'Organizational innovation' is potentially very broad and might encompass any innovation (in 'product', 'process', 'position' or 'paradigm' (Tidd et al., 2005, p. 10) introduced in an organization. More recently, management innovation has been expressed as 'invention and implementation of a management practice, process, structure, or technique that is new to the state of the art and is intended to further organisational goals' (Birkinshaw et al., 2008, p. 825). What is core is how management innovation can enhance, foster or inculcate innovation capability in organizations, thus increasing their productivity and competitiveness. For example, in the context of service value networks, Agarwal and Selen (2009) have empirically validated the existence of several higher-order competencies including 'collaborative innovative capacity', and have also demonstrated the process of dynamic capability building leading to elevated service offerings – 'service innovation' (Agarwal and Selen, 2011a) – for collaborating service organizations.

In focusing specifically on management innovation, Birkinshaw et al. (2008) contrast institutional, fashion, cultural and rational perspectives. Institutional perspectives focus on the socioeconomic and institutional conditions conducive to innovation and are often macro and cross-national (e.g., Guillen, 1994). Fashion perspectives examine how management thought leaders influence, and are influenced by, managers (e.g., Abrahamson, 1996). Cultural perspectives consider how organizational power, behaviours and cultures mediate management innovations (e.g., Zbaracki, 1998). Both fashion and cultural perspectives might have some relevance for the identification of management behaviours that might facilitate managerial innovation. However, rational perspectives, which see management innovations as purposive (if not necessarily successful) attempts to improve organizational performance, are probably most oriented to a concern with managerial agency. Indeed, Birkinshaw et al. (2008) argue that one of the weaknesses of most theoretical approaches to management innovation has been their failure to give due weight to the role of human agency in effecting innovation. If they are right, then a key factor such as management education and training, which presumably shapes (to some degree) the agency of managers in the context of organizational innovation, is likely to be important. Others, from a 'rational' perspective, have argued that innovation is key to organizational prosperity, even survival (Drucker, 1985). These perspectives assume then that innovation can indeed be managed. But the key theoretical and practical question for management education is how?

PROCESS OF MANAGEMENT INNOVATION

Birkinshaw et al. (2008) have developed a detailed model of the process of management innovation that can be utilized to identify some of the most important management skills and behaviours for innovation. Their model envisages the interaction and impact of both internal and external change agents managing the innovation process through the stages of motivation, invention, implementation and theorizing and labelling. In the motivation phase, managers evaluate a problem and verify it through reference to external change agents as a means of agenda-setting. In the invention phase, managers might use trial and error, a problem-driven search or engage in 'idea linking' with external change agents to generate potential solutions. In the implementation phase managers test innovations and evaluate against the original idea, its conceptual validity or the reactions of other employees. In the final phase of theorizing and labelling, managers are seeking to secure the legitimacy of the innovation through a variety of techniques including by linking the success of the innovation to theories and/or previous experiences. In summary, some of the key managerial behaviours associated with these forms of innovation appear to include problem or opportunity identification, the linking of ideas from other sources, domains or organizations to those of the organization, the testing of those ideas and the grounding of the results of the innovation experience in existing theory or prior practice. At a more abstract level, this appears to suggest the importance of learning, experimentation, reflection and communication (within and beyond the organization).

SOCIAL CAPITAL INNOVATION

From another angle, contemporary theories of innovation strongly suggest that social capital is likely to be a critical variable shaping the innovation capability of organizations. According to the social capital innovation theorists, the locus of innovation is no longer seen to be the individual or the firm, as much as the network in which the firm is embedded (Powell et al., 1996). Clegg et al. (2002) advocate the need for an integrated culture between all stakeholders of partnering organizations in order for collaborative alliances and networks to succeed. Social capital is seen by some as the bedrock of innovation (Subramaniam and Youndt, 2005). In one sense the social capital of the organization (and its members) might be seen to be a potentially important determinant of the extent to which managers as change agents can engage in the learning, experimentation, reflection and communication identified above as it shapes the organization's access and exposure to new ideas. More generally, innovation, especially management innovation, can be seen to be the result of the interactions and exchanges of knowledge amongst a diversity of actors (Zheng, 2010). Nahapiet and Ghoshal (1998) identify three dimensions of social capital:

- The structural dimension concerns the number and patterns of connections that organizational members have with people in and beyond the organization.
- The relational dimension refers to the norms and beliefs that people in the social network share.
- The cognitive dimension concerns the narratives, language and codes shared by members of the network.

Generally the research finds that network size, the strength of one's ties with network members, one's centrality to the network (sub-constructs of the structural dimension), high levels of trust and well-developed norms (the relational dimension) and the presence of a shared vision (the cognitive dimension) are all positively related to innovation (Zheng, 2010). The social capital innovation literature therefore suggests that well-developed and reasonably extensive social networks are, typically, highly conducive to innovation, including managerial and organizational innovation. Facilitating networks might therefore be critical to the effective management of innovation in organizations.

IMPLICATIONS OF MANAGERIAL AND ORGANIZATION INNOVATION FOR MANAGEMENT EDUCATION

What might this emergent theory of managing organizational innovation imply for management education? Something of the potential role of management education, and the business schools that provide that education, can be deduced from the management and organizational innovation theoretical literature across four dimensions. First, management innovation theory suggests that managers can play a decisive role as the internal change agents driving organizational innovation as envisaged by Birkinshaw et al. (2008). Management education therefore might usefully focus on developing some of the core skills and capabilities associated with this work: problem and opportunity identification, idea linking, idea testing and reflection.

Second, managers will be in a key position to facilitate innovation by helping create and sustain the conditions under which others in the organization can develop and exercise their own innovation skills: learning, experimentation, reflection and communication. This suggests a range of initiatives: designing jobs with some discretion, autonomy and effective feedback loops; devoting resources and creating incentives for creativity and experimentation; encouraging open communication, discussion and decision-making; and designing reflection and lesson learning as part of projects. The facilitation of social networks is likely to be key here: encouraging members to network and participate in communities of practice as way of ensuring that the organization is open to new ideas, thereby generating improved innovation capability (Francis and Bessant, 2005).

Third, business school faculty, particularly in their roles as executive educators, consultants and research partners, can act as external change agents, as defined by Birkinshaw et al. (2008). In this capacity, faculty can work with internal change agents, helping to identify problems and opportunities, putting (theoretical) ideas into organizational contexts, refining ideas, assisting with idea testing and reflecting on theoretical implications as a result of organizational innovation projects.

Finally, business school research, especially where it is relevant to contemporary business issues, can be a vital source of new ideas, new potential applications for existing ideas, and evidence concerning the features, characteristics, limitations and likely results of various innovation options.

THE INNOVATION AND HIGHER EDUCATION AGENDAS IN AUSTRALIA

In calling for a national proactive response to the stalling of productivity growth, which occurred in Australia in the early 2000s, the Cutler Review (and Report) (Cutler, 2008) of the National Innovation System highlighted the need to rethink Australia's innovation policy. The Cutler Review served to redirect attention from the traditional focus on the stimulation of the *supply side* of innovation – R&D, scientific discovery and research commercialization – to the *demand side* of innovation – the ways in which firms use new knowledge and ideas to better serve the market and meet customer needs. Cutler's model of innovation as a 'dynamic, evolving and learning process' advocates a virtuous cycle of knowledge production (associated with creativity and problem solving), knowledge application (associated with entrepreneurialism) and knowledge diffusion (associated with enhanced productivity and competitiveness). Importantly, Cutler highlights the 'hidden realities of innovation' that occur in the way businesses operate, organize and deliver products, services and value to customers – managerial and organizational innovation. Innovation in this sense happens in businesses and relates to business operations, the ways in which businesses organize their work and utilize their human capital, and their relations with their suppliers, partners and customers (ibid., pp. 26–7).

Competencies for Business Innovation

In addition to foregrounding managerial and organizational innovation, the Cutler Report (2008) identifies a range of competencies and attributes that need to be developed in order to improve business innovation. For example, the Cutler Report endorses Dodgson et al.'s (2008) identification of the competencies needed to lead innovative businesses as including the 'strategic and leadership', 'operational' and 'integrative' competencies summarized in Box 8.1.

Cutler also suggests the need for a range of other competencies and attributes, including skills in entrepreneurship, relationship management, human resource management and business analysis, added with the need for future government support programmes to build innovative organizational cultures and high performance work systems. The Australian Government's response to the Cutler Review, the *Powering Ideas* White Paper, agreed with the emphasis on innovation at the enterprise and organizational level:

> One future focus of the Australian Government's industry and innovation policies will be on building innovation capacity and performance at the enterprise level . . . Government support for business innovation . . . must recognize the complexity of the innovation process and the different forms that innovation can take. (Carr, 2009, pp. 44–5)

The Policy Dimension to Innovation

Along with the earlier reviews of the Australian textile, footwear and clothing industries (Green, 2008), the automotive industry (Bracks, 2008) and the pharmaceuticals industry (McNamee and Pennifold, 2008), the Cutler Review and the *Powering Ideas* White Paper (Carr, 2009) have

BOX 8.1   COMPETENCIES FOR BUSINESS INNOVATION

Strategic and leadership competencies
Ability to respond to changes in the market environment.

Clearly communicating strategic intent and articulating the need for change through innovation.

Nurturing innovative capacity and creativity throughout the organization.

Crystallizing the value that innovation can deliver, and being open to alternative business models.

Openness to learning from failure.

Thinking and acting from a global perspective.

Operational competencies
Evaluating innovation opportunities using formal methods for their analysis, valuation and selection, including market research and risk assessment.

Identifying the challenges in managing innovative activities, acquiring tools to make processes more systematic, and configuring the resources needed to support them.

Reducing the cycle time and cost of innovation by simulating, modelling and using virtual and rapid prototyping.

Creating value from design.

Encouraging employee innovativeness through incentives and rewards.

Protecting intellectual property appropriately.

Auditing and measuring innovation performance in a meaningful way, including the option values it creates.

Integrative competencies
Collaborating effectively with partners, customers and suppliers in the creation and delivery of innovation.

Complying with and developing regulatory frameworks, technical standards and environmental requirements.

Brokering knowledge on innovation across organizational, professional and disciplinary boundaries.

Source: Cutler (2008, p. 33), derived from Dodgson et al. (2008).

contributed to a more coherent innovation discourse. In this discourse business, managerial and organizational innovation includes:

- development and adoption of new business models;
- improved technology absorption and integration;
- agile, engaged, creative, entrepreneurial and collaborative work places;
- fostering of dynamic capability building;
- cultivation of workplace, enterprise and sectoral innovation that is incremental and continuous as well as breakthrough;
- innovation in all sectors and industries – low-tech as well as high-tech services as well as manufacturing, small as well as large;
- openness amongst managers and decision-makers to diverse sources of knowledge and creativity;
- stronger, deeper and broader collaboration, networking and knowledge-sharing between firms, public agencies and educational and research institutions.

Not long after the Cutler Review was released, the Bradley Review (2008) into Australian Higher Education recognized the critical role played by higher education in sustaining economic and social progress and argued that Australia was falling behind other countries in performance and investment in higher education. The review noted that Australia was the only country in the OECD not to increase public expenditure on higher education in the period 1995–2005 and called for a 'significant increase in public investment and funding for higher education' (Bradley, 2008, p. xv). The review also identified problems with quality in the sector arguing that 'there are now clear signs that the quality of the educational experience is declining' (ibid., p. xii).

The government's policy report titled *Transforming Australia's Higher Education System* (2009) presents an ambitious programme for the sector, with an emphasis on improved funding, enhanced access, quality and standards and a student-centred funding model. The research initiatives include an emphasis on Joint Research Engagement focusing on end-user research, 'fundamental to the innovation system', encouraged through improved collaborative networks, 'an area in which Australia performs poorly by international standards' (p. 25).

The higher education agenda that has emerged alongside the innovation agenda in Australia, signals a preparedness to increase funding but also calls on the higher education sector to improve participation rates, enhance collaboration with business and government and work to improve quality. In combination with the innovation agenda, these educational imperatives place even greater pressure on higher education providers and business schools in particular.

BUSINESS SCHOOLS AND MANAGEMENT EDUCATION

Undoubtedly, skills have a crucial role in stimulating productivity growth. According to Laplagne and Bensted (1999, p. 46):

> Labour productivity growth appears to be enhanced by the joint introduction of training and innovation. This is due to the fact that training requires the support of innovation to benefit labour productivity growth. Conversely, introducing innovation in isolation is sufficient to promote labour productivity growth, although its returns are increased by the addition of training.

In this context, several studies have urged for increased focus in workplace training to improve nations' international competitiveness and long-term economic performance and to address the 'skills gap' (Black and Lynch, 2004; Richardson, 2007; Toner, 2007, 2011; O'Hanlon-Rose, 2008–09; Green et al., 2009).

On the other hand, several reports and submissions in recent years have documented considerable employer dissatisfaction with Australian graduate skills (ACCI, 2002; BCA, 2006; BIHECC, 2007). Generally, these claim that graduates lack employability skills, or generic skills, amounting to an inability to satisfactorily apply skills and knowledge in workplace and organizational settings. While there is debate as to these employability and generic skills, communication, teamwork and problem-solving skills are routinely mentioned, as is the ability to manage change and demonstrate dexterity across different business contexts (D'Aveni, 1994; Brown and Eisenhardt, 1997; Hall, 2000; Makadok, 2001; Daghfous, 2004; Helfat, 2007).

The *Management Matters* report by Green et al. (2009) has identified a marked weakness in the comparative performance of Australian managers in respect of 'people management skills'. That survey of Australian managers in manufacturing, benchmarked against equivalent international surveys, found the following:

- Australian management practices are only moderately above average when benchmarked globally.
- Australian management tends to over-rate its own performance against the benchmarks.

- Many Australian enterprises are stronger in operations management than people management; specifically, they lag in advanced
  people management practices including attracting, developing and
  retaining talent, identifying innovative but practical ways of developing human capital to improve performance and add value to
  organizations.

In the context of management skills, Agarwal and Green (2011) echo the
earlier research contained in the Karpin Report (1995) on leadership and
management skills, as well as in interpretations of a series of Australian
workplace employment relations surveys (Alexander and Green, 1992)
that higher skills and education levels, both for managers and their
workforces, are positively and significantly associated with the ability to
develop and deploy superior management practices. The findings of the
study provide a unique insight into the 'intangible' factors at work in the
determination of productivity and performance and that high-performing
management is a key driver in the promotion of more innovative and
productive enterprises. In a recent survey conducted by the Open Forum
for the Society of Knowledge Economics (SKE, 2008), key barriers noted
to the fostering of innovation included: political and business intellect
operating on a short-term basis; under-resourced education and business
infrastructure; and attitudes that were 'risk averse' and 'insurance driven'.
The findings suggested that a change in behaviour and mindset is required
of Australian managers and their workplace environments to optimize
firm productivity and competitiveness.

The series of enquiries, reports and related research undertaken in
Australia in recent years into innovation, higher education, management
skills and management education appear to point to a number of interrelated areas where the need for improvement is clear. Overall, the body
of evidence suggests that there continues to be a need to improve management education in its capacity to develop the following interrelated and
overlapping capabilities and skill sets:

- soft or generic skills including communication, etc.;
- skills for innovation, particularly business innovation;
- leadership skills;
- advanced people management skills;
- strategic and integrative skills.

This is indeed reinforced in the findings from the recent work on
management education by Datar et al. (2010) who reviewed a number
of the Ivy League and best European business schools to map what they

have offered in the past. They then mapped what these schools have subsequently revised and changed in their degree in response to industry requirements and the perceived failings of business leaders in the global financial crisis. Datar et al. identify eight unmet needs across MBA programmes. These unmet needs relate to *knowing* (identify, analyse, explain), *doing* (learn skills needed) and *being* (deeper psychological understanding of self). These unmet needs are the basis on which to innovate and change MBA programmes. The needs are:

- gaining a *global perspective* – understanding and practising economic, institutional and cultural differences;
- developing *leadership skills* – not just about inspiration and vision, but also doing performance reviews, giving feedback, understanding one's own impact;
- honing *integration skills* – diverse and shifting angles to frame problems holistically – building judgement and intuition;
- recognizing *organizational realities* and implementing effectively – getting things done when there are hidden agendas, unwritten rules, coalitions and competing points of view;
- acting *creatively and innovatively* – finding and framing problems – collecting, synthesizing, distilling ambiguous data – generative and lateral thinking; experimenting and learning;
- thinking *critically and communicating* clearly;
- understanding the *role, responsibilities and purpose of business* – financial and non-financial objectives, shareholders' interests and other stakeholder interests; and
- understanding the *limits of models and markets* – questioning risk and underlying assumptions – what might go wrong, understanding the sources of errors that lead to flawed decision-making.

In addition to the need to do better at developing these skills it is also clear that management education providers need to improve quality of their management programmes and enhance their level, span and depth of collaboration with business, government and industry in the design, development, delivery and evaluation of their programmes.

BUSINESS SCHOOLS IN CRITICAL FOCUS

For some years now there has been an extensive debate, particularly in the USA, as to the role of business schools (Ghoshal, 2005; Khurana et al., 2005; AACSB, 2010). Contributions to this debate relate to critiques of existing business school practice (Bennis and O'Toole, 2005; Datar et al., 2010) and a reconsideration of the role of business schools (Bennis and O'Toole, 2005; AACSB, 2010). These debates can be used to inform an analysis of how business schools might better contribute to management education for innovation.

The major themes in the critiques of business schools relate to their increasing tendency to be disconnected from real world business practice, and to their philosophy of being too narrow and insufficiently critical. In this context, Bennis and O'Toole (2005), for example, identify a 'crisis in management education' caused by business schools adopting a 'scientific research model . . . that uses abstract financial and economic analysis, statistical multiple regressions and laboratory psychology' that has had the effect of 'institutionalizing their own irrelevancy' (p. xx). They advocate business schools adopting a 'professional model', in which engagement with businesses, attention to the learning needs of business leaders and enquiry into real world business problems are valued just as much as the scientific rigour associated with publication in leading academic journals.

Another strand to the recent critique of business schools contends that they have come to focus too narrowly on one, short-term aspect of business success – the maximization of shareholder value. As a result, management is constructed not as a profession with a range of duties, obligations and responsibilities, but as an agent of shareholders charged with the sole responsibility of profit maximization. According to Khurana et al. (2005): 'A kind of market fundamentalism took hold in business education . . . The new logic of shareholder primacy absolved management of any responsibility for anything other than financial results' (quoted in Holland, 2009, p. 2). In a similar vein, Ghoshal (2005) has argued that business schools' approach to management is dominated by the twin forces of the 'pretence of knowledge' in which business studies have been elevated as a science, and a particular ideology ('liberalism') that adopts a 'gloomy vision' of individuals and institutions. The former tends to rule out moral or ethical considerations in management theory. The latter has portrayed individuals as self-interested rational actors, *homo economicus*, and the rationale for institutions as being one of dealing with the 'negative problem' of 'preventing bad people from doing harm'. The implication of these twin forces and their translation into the governing assumptions and theories that inform management theory results in a degraded form of management practice:

> Combine agency theory with transaction cost economics, add in standard versions of game theory and negotiation analysis, and the picture of the manager that emerges is one that is now very familiar in practice: the ruthlessly hard-driving, strictly top-down, command and control focused, shareholder-value-

obsessed, win-at-any-cost business leader of which Scott Paper's Chainsaw Al Dunlap and Tyco's Dennis Kozlowski are only the most extreme examples. (Ghoshal, 2005, p. 85)

The critical discourse that has developed around business schools points to a number of very serious failings in their capacity to deliver a more progressive management education. In addition then to the list of skill development demands associated with the innovation imperative discussed above, it is apparent that business schools also need to improve their performance in terms of their capacity to cultivate professionalism in management and to offer a more balanced and critical orientation to business issues. Arguably, these imperatives associated with greater professionalism, a stronger ethical orientation, greater sensitivity to social as well as financial goals and cultivation of an openness to alternative perspectives and approaches are clearly consistent with management education for innovation.

If recent critiques are right, too few business schools cultivate critical thinking, have sufficient relevance for management practice, and develop what might be termed 'management knowledge'. The Advanced Institute of Management Research report on the future of business schools in the UK (AIM Research, 2006) identified four different potential forms that contemporary business schools can adopt: the social sciences school; the liberal arts school; the professional school; and the knowledge economy school. Innovation can obviously be a strong feature of the 'social sciences school' but it typically might not be *business* innovation as much as academic or scientific innovation; the features of liberal arts, professional and knowledge economy schools seem more consistent with the ambitions of cultivating innovation, especially business and organizational innovation.

AACSB International, the leading association representing and accrediting business and management schools around the world, recently commissioned a report on business schools and innovation. This AACSB report (2010) identified three main ways in which business schools might contribute to innovation:

1 Innovation and learning Business schools can develop management innovation by teaching and cultivating key skills associated with the creative application of solutions, entrepreneurship and 'integrative thinking', which encourages thinking across knowledge gaps and domains.

The development of management innovation is central to AACSB's vision for business schools. It notes that as 'innovation activities involve ambiguity, change and risk' there is a great need for the development of skills related to 'applying knowledge, judgement and the ability to adapt and fashion new tools to solve problems creatively' and highlights, in particular, the need to develop 'leadership, communication and collaboration' (p. 22). As the definition of the 'innovation and learning' mission suggests, the development of entrepreneurial skills is also prioritized. Entrepreneurship is seen to be a set of behaviours that can be developed (Drucker, 1985) and the report advocates 'practice and feedback' as the best way of developing these skills, implying the importance of an experiential approach to learning. Focusing on 'innovation and learning' also implies the need for business schools to encourage 'integrative thinking', which, evidently, calls on schools to do more to break down the disciplinary demarcations and 'silos' within which discipline-specific, technical skills are taught. There is no suggestion that this commitment to technical skill development should be compromised. There is, however, a significant need in business for managers with a stronger capacity to think, explore and exploit, as well as work across the disciplinary domains that, after all, define business schools rather than business problems. In order to assist with this process of enhancing the relevance of management education for innovative management practice, schools are urged to correct their tendency to focus more on content than pedagogy when reforming curricula (AACSB, 2010, p. 23).

2   Innovation and intellectual capital development   Management research, including the invention, implementation and diffusion of new ideas, as well as the testing, codifying and organizing of management and other tacit knowledge, can make a vital contribution to innovation. Business schools also have a key role as a hub for research on innovation being well placed to undertake practice-oriented and interdisciplinary research.

The AACSB report (2010) notes that innovation depends not just on 'invention' but also on 'implementation' and 'diffusion' and suggests that too much business school research focuses on scholarly contributions rather than practical contributions that engage with these questions. The report endorses an earlier AACSB report (2008) on the impact of research, which argued that:

> Business schools have an obligation to maintain contact with and contribute to practice, as well as their underlying core disciplines. A business school cannot separate itself from practice to focus only on theory and still serve its function. On the other hand, it cannot be so focussed on practice that it fails to support development insights into principles and theories that serve to increase understanding of practice. (AACSB, 2008, p. 15)

The AACSB (2008) report noted Pfeffer and Fong's (2002) argument that 'discipline-based parochialism' had led to a 'narrowing' of research agendas that militated against the development of 'truly integrative curricula' that might facilitate more effective management education for business innovation. In one sense, this narrowing and the irrelevance of much published research for practising managers is a direct result of the incentives that business school researchers face:

> Publishing theoretically and methodologically sophisticated research in a leading journal often 'counts for more' than an applied article amongst tenure review committees and for annual compensation purposes. Hence faculty members have less incentive to address practice more directly in their research. (AACSB, 2008, p. 21)

The AACSB report (2010) calls for more incentives for practice-oriented and 'high-impact' research. It is apparent, though, that more attention to high-impact, business-relevant research will also require a stronger and deeper level of two-way engagement between business schools and businesses and their managers.

3   Innovation and outreach   Business schools engage with their communities, including the businesses in their region and beyond, through a range of activities including business plan competitions, social entrepreneurship, community-based student consulting projects, convocations and business incubators.

This is clearly an area where many business schools can do much more. What seems to be especially important here is the recognition that outreach means more than just publicizing business school research and teaching into business communities – as important as that is. It means establishing a diverse range of sustained relationships with business, industry, organizations, regulators and policy-makers that facilitates the interplay of ideas; ideas that move from school to business and from business to school in iterative fashion. Obviously this kind of relationship is critical for business innovation. According to the AACSB report (2010) business schools have a particularly important role to play in innovation diffusion. Business schools are very well positioned to bring together diverse groups of stakeholders in business innovation as a means of accelerating diffusion and sharpening the focus on implementation (AACSB, 2010, p. 28).

Several academic scholars have also argued for the need for increased collaboration, as a means of promoting learning that is contextualized and deals with real pragmatic problems (Ekanem and Smallbone, 2007; Agarwal and Selen, 2009; Teece, 2009). Indeed, collaboration is a key driver for organizational learning and building dynamic capabilities (Agarwal and Selen, 2009, 2011b). The mutual trust that can be developed through long-term business and/or social relationships facilitates knowledge transfer and assists in mitigating risk (Ekanem and Smallbone, 2007). This also directly links to further functions of education in developing graduates with 'higher-order' capabilities such as critical reasoning, lateral thinking, problem solving in different contexts, and collaborative teamwork (Candy and Crebert, 1991); and dynamic capabilities (Cepeda and Vera, 2007; Agarwal and Selen, 2009, 2011b; Teece, 2009; Wu, 2010) that exploit collaborative capabilities such as organizational relationship capital, customer engagement, collaborative organizational learning, entrepreneurial alertness, collaborative agility, and collaborative innovative capacity (Agarwal and Selen, 2009).

***

A set of consistent themes emerge from the critical examination of the contribution of contemporary business schools to innovation. With respect to their teaching and learning there is too much relative emphasis on narrow technical skills and too little focus on the more generic skills of leadership, entrepreneurship, innovation, people management as well as attention to ethical issues and the development of integrative thinking skills. With respect to pedagogy, there is too little emphasis on addressing practical business problems and an insufficient use of experiential and lifelong approaches to learning. The research undertaken in business schools is too heavily weighted in favour of relatively narrow, technically sophisticated contributions designed for publication in leading scholarly journals rather than research more clearly oriented to practical business problems and issues. And business schools have also been widely criticized for failing to develop sustained partnerships with business and government that might facilitate a deeper level of mutual engagement.

TOWARD MANAGEMENT EDUCATION FOR INNOVATION

The contribution that different business schools can make to address these challenges will vary depending on their particular strengths and weaknesses, and their institutional and historical context. Nevertheless, we contend that their contribution to building innovation capability might be enhanced by addressing two broad imperatives: the need to cultivate a greater capacity for 'integrative thinking', and the need to promote 'practice-based learning'. In the following subsections these two organizing concepts are used to describe a range of more specific practices and initiatives, which in themselves might be more or less appropriate for different kinds of schools. While both imperatives are most immediately related to teaching and learning content and approaches, they also have implications for business school research and for the kind of outreach and external collaborations that business schools might profitably pursue.

Integrative and Design Thinking

The term 'integrative thinking' has been used by a number of commentators and academics (Martin and Austen, 1999; Martin, 2007) in recent years to mean related, but often different, things. In the context of this chapter, here it is defined as a meta-skill used to denote a range of approaches to thinking about business and organizational problems including design thinking, critical and analytical thinking, creative thinking, cross-disciplinary collaboration as well as 'integrative thinking' as defined by its leading advocate, Roger Martin (2007). Attention to these kinds of approaches and their use in informing curriculum and course design, as well as business school research agendas, will help management education foster greater organizational and business innovation and creativity in graduates, clients and stakeholders.

The demand in business for new approaches to thinking that can help solve novel problems and generate creative ideas and solutions is amply demonstrated by the contemporary success of 'idea entrepreneurs' like IDEO, Jump Associates and Kotter International. In some ways these international companies, and those such as Australia's 2nd Road, have emerged to meet a need left unmet by contemporary business schools that many progressive corporate clients have come to see as too dominated by disciplinary boundaries and traditions, linear thinking, inductive and deductive reasoning and conventional research agendas. Jump Associates, for example, has worked with corporate clients such as GE, NBC, Target and Proctor & Gamble to solve 'highly ambiguous problems' (Segal, 2010). Jump also works with client employee groups to help develop creative problem-solving skills. What is particularly interesting in this aspect of its work is the company's preparedness to use brainstorming techniques, free association, open collaboration, and what might be termed 'upside-down' thinking to generate new ideas and innovations in products, services, delivery methods and marketing strategies. Jump founder, Sev Patnaik, sees these competencies as central to the demands of contemporary management practice and strategy, arguing that management is now less about 'processing data' and more about 'leadership, creativity, vision' (ibid.).

This is not to say that business schools can or should seek to emulate the emerging idea entrepreneurs. Nevertheless, to the extent that creative thinking is an increasingly important part of contemporary management practice, management education needs to complement its development of analytical and critical thinking with a greater emphasis on the cultivation of creative thinking skills.

'Design thinking' on the other hand represents a related approach with considerable potential application to the future of management education for innovation. Design thinking can be defined as 'approaching management problems as designers approach design problems' (Dunne and Martin, 2006, p.512). In simple terms, this approach might be characterized by a commitment to developing a product, service or activity, guided primarily by the needs of a potentially diverse range of ultimate users. For businesses and managers seeking to better respond to the needs and aspirations of clients and customers the appeal is obvious. However, design thinking implies more than simply achieving client satisfaction and it does not simply consign business schools to a future of helping businesses secure happy customers. 'Designers think of themselves as problem finders more so than problem solvers because their solutions start with a deep understanding of the problem requiring a solution' (Bell, 2010). And working toward a 'deep understanding of a problem' is likely to be a space where business school faculty will feel comfortable and can excel.

Design thinking has distinct cognitive, attitudinal and interpersonal aspects (Dunne and Martin, 2006, pp.517–19). The cognitive dimension involves using abductive as well as inductive and deductive reasoning in the problem-solving process. Martin defines 'abductive logic' as the logic of 'what might be' as distinct from the logic of 'what is' (inductive) or 'what should be' (deductive) (Martin, in Dunne and Martin, 2006, p.513). It also implies the use of systems thinking, recognizing that a change in any one part of a system implies changes to other parts of the system. In this way the cognitive aspect compels creative, 'out of the box' imagining, and cognizance of the 'big picture' of whole systems.

The attitudinal aspect implies a different orientation to constraints: whereas more conventional management thinking tends to see constraints as negatives that need to be accommodated, design thinkers welcome constraints as presenting opportunities for innovation or as the 'impetus for creative solutions' (Dunne and Martin, 2006, p.518). This explains design thinkers' appetite for so-called 'wicked problems' (Rittell and Webber, 1973) – novel and complex problems with no known solution – which demand novel solutions or responses in which constraints are reconstructed. One example might be the case of global warming. While the rapidly depleting supply of fossil fuels might be conventionally cast as a constraint, it can, of course, also be seen as an opportunity – an impetus to the development of more sustainable energy sources.

The attitudinal aspect of design thinking also invokes Martin's (2007) idea of 'integrative thinking' – the ability to move beyond 'either/or' propositions to a synthesis in which both, apparently opposed imperatives are accommodated or transcended. This is the central idea of Martin's book, *The Opposable Mind*. For Martin, for example, the case of contemporary corporations being seen to promote short-term shareholder value at the expense of social responsibility cannot be left as an 'either/or' problem:

> There is no reason why it has to be *either* about customers *or* about shareholders. If you are teaching from a design standpoint, those two things are inexorably linked and you have to think about both . . . A designer would say [in relation to privileging shareholder value at the expense of longer-term customer interests] 'Well that doesn't work, that's not sustainable; the people that you are ripping off will eventually find out and get you'. (Martin, in Dunne and Martin, 2006, pp. 516–17)

The interpersonal aspect of design thinking signals a need for managers to be more committed to working with others in two ways. First, by paying more attention to users and user perspectives and second, by collaborating with peers. While these principles might seem straightforward, each is complicated. User perspectives, particularly in the instance of complex problems, are diverse and their interests and aspirations might be apparently incompatible. And when Martin urges collaboration with peers he notes the tendency for many managers to prefer collaboration with like-minded peers. More challenging and more constructive, however, is collaboration with those with different views and from different domains of expertise.

A commitment to developing the capacity for design thinking in students and more so in faculty has significant implications for business schools and their approach to management education. It means designing curricula, learning experiences and assessment that involve the posing of 'wicked problems', requiring diverse groups to work as project teams, understanding user perspectives more deeply, practising abductive reasoning alongside inductive and deductive reasoning, recognizing the systemic implications of proposals and decisions, and collaborating constructively and openly, with people with different views, experiences and assumptions.

While a commitment to developing design and integrative thinking capacity will contribute to forms of management education that more directly promote innovation, teaching integrative thinking in itself might not necessarily make business schools more relevant for business. The innovative solutions students are taught to generate may be little more useful than the knowledge of case studies, experiences in responding to hypothetical scenarios and skill at applying trusted disciplinary algorithms to narrow set problems they currently possess. As a result, we contend that business schools also need to respond to what might be termed the practice-based learning imperative.

The Practice-based Learning Imperative

Many have long criticized the management education typically offered by business schools as too often lacking direct engagement with the actual practice of managing (Mintzberg, 2004; Bennis and O'Toole, 2005; Ghoshal, 2005; Khurana et al., 2005; AACSB, 2010; Datar et al., 2010). One obvious response to this problem is the greater use of learning approaches involving experiential methods, action learning, work-integrated learning and the use of innovation labs, here collectively referred to as 'practice-based learning'. Added to these practise-based learning methods, the role of innovation narratives operating as cultural mechanisms to facilitate structures, processes and practices in sustaining organizational innovation are emerging (Cartel and Garud, 2009).

One relatively long-standing example of a direct application of experiential pedagogy to management education is the University of Central England's (UCE) MSc in Organization Development and Management Learning and its MBA. This programme is based on the use of action learning sets of between six and nine students where teams work on assignments based on real organizational issues and 'situations'. To take one example of a specific assignment, students are asked to undertake a comparative evaluation of an overseas market environment for a particular product or service. The task is undertaken on-site in the foreign location and while the institution organizes travel and administrative arrangements, the teams need to identify the relevant organizations, negotiate access and design, and undertake the necessary market research (Trehan and Rigg, 2007).

Another example of experiential learning in practice concerns the use of 'multi-disciplinary action projects' at the University of Michigan's Ross School, where students learn through placements with organizations. In the last few years, over 600 organizations have sponsored over 1200 such projects (Green, 2010). While resource intensive, programmes whereby students are placed in organizations, working in teams on current organizational problems as action research projects, and reporting back proposals and solutions to the senior management of those organizations, are becoming increasingly popular.

A range of Masters and MBA programmes at many of the leading business schools around the world now seek to combine the qualities of a design thinking approach with the principles of practice-based learning involving sustained business partnerships. Not only that, there has also been a growing interest in allowing students to co-create their MBAs – examples include Stanford, which allows students to choose different levels of functional courses – basic, intermediate or fast-paced, and advanced. Chicago Booth is another example – students select five to seven subjects in any order, undertaken at any time in the course. More examples recently documented by Scott-Kemmis (2010) include:

- The Case Western Reserve University's Weatherhead School of Management MBA where students are required to take a course in either 'Managing Design Opportunities' or 'Sustainable Value' and work with business partners such as Fed Ex Custom Critical, PNC Bank and Sherwin-Williams.
- The Masters in Design and Innovation and Creativity in Industry resulting from the Cranfield University joint venture with the University of the Arts London. Here students learn about management and technology at Cranfield and study consumer behaviour at the Centre for Competitive Creative Design and work with firms including Ford, Proctor & Gamble and Xerox.
- All MBAs at Imperial College London take the Innovation, Entrepreneurship and Design course working on business and design problems in association with BAE Systems, Hewlett-Packard and Proctor & Gamble.
- The MBA at the Rotman School of Management at the University of Toronto includes courses at DesignWorks, the School's learning lab for design-based innovation and education. Corporate partners include Medtronic, Nestlé and Pfizer.

Programmes incorporating practice-based learning as a major part of their experience demand that business schools develop deep partnerships with business and industry. These partnerships need to move beyond simply using organizational case studies to relationships in which students, facilitated by faculty, work with business leaders and managers in the reframing of real business issues and problems and in which solutions and prototypes are evaluated in the context of current business processes and practices. Not only does this require business schools to be open to business, but it requires business to commit resources, information, time and personnel to support student and faculty experiences working with, and inside, their businesses.

CONCLUSION

A core argument of this chapter is that managerial and organizational innovation theory and research will benefit greatly from a more serious and sustained consideration of the actual and potential role of management education and the business schools that provide it. Birkinshaw et al.'s (2008) contribution to the field has been so valuable because it has provided some much needed detail as to the actual processes through which management innovation occurs. In this chapter we have used their process model for guidance as to the management skills and capabilities that might enhance the innovation capabilities of managers and their organizations. Our analysis suggests that management education and business schools can contribute to management innovation capability in four ways:

1. by developing the core innovation skills for managers, enabling them to be more effective internal change agents;
2. by developing managers' capacity to cultivate pro-innovation environments at work;
3. by developing faculty that are well prepared to partner, as external change agents, with organizations; and
4. by increasingly developing business schools as sources of business-relevant ideas and research.

We have suggested that integrative and design thinking approaches, combined with a greater emphasis on practice-based learning, will help management education better meet these challenges. Integrative thinking can enhance the creativity of managers and, in particular, enhance their capacity to identify problems and opportunities, and link ideas from one domain to another – key management innovation skills. Practice-based learning offers great potential in more effectively preparing managers to act as internal change agents by developing their learning, experimentation and reflection skills in real business contexts. But practice-based learning, predicated, as it is, on deeper partnerships between business schools and business organizations, can also enhance the capacity of faculty to act as external change agents working with managers in stimulating practical managerial and organizational innovations.

Recent work on managerial and organizational innovation has been valuable and stimulating. However, we contend that a greater emphasis on the role of management education will serve to sharpen the focus on the actual practice of management innovation and illuminate the range of practical strategies that managers can pursue. By adopting novel approaches to management education that are informed by the innovation imperative we can gain greater purchase on practical strategies for stimulating and sustaining innovation in organizations. In this way good innovation theory can be more often translated into good innovation practice.

REFERENCES

AACSB (2008), *Final Report of the AACSB International Impact of Research Task Force*, Tampa, FL: AACSB International.

AACSB (2010), *Business Schools on an Innovation Mission*, a report of the AACSB International Task Force on Business Schools and Innovation, Florida.

Abrahamson, E. (1996), 'Management fashion', *Academy of Management Review*, **21**(1), 254–85.

ACCI (2002), *Employability Skills – An Employer Perspective: Getting What Employers Want Out of the Too Hard Basket*, Canberra: AGPS.

Agarwal, R. and R. Green (2011), 'The role of education and skills in Australian management practice and productivity', in P. Curtin, J. Stanwick and F. Beddie (eds), *Fostering Enterprise: The Innovation and Skills Nexus – Research Readings*, Adelaide: NCVER, pp. 90–117.

Agarwal, R. and W. Selen (2009), 'Dynamic capability building in service value networks for achieving service innovation', *Decision Sciences*, **40**(3), 431–75.

Agarwal, R. and W. Selen (2011a), 'Multi-dimensional nature of service innovation – operationalisation of the elevated service offering construct in collaborative service organisations', *International Journal of Production Management*, **31**(11), 1164–92.

Agarwal, R. and W. Selen (2011b), 'An integrated view of service innovation in service networks', in H. Demirkan, J.C. Spohrer and V. Krishna (eds), *Service Systems Implementation, Volume 2*, Service Science: Research and Innovations in the Service Economy Book Series, Berlin: Springer, pp. 253–73.

AIM Research (2006), *The Future of Business Schools in the UK: Finding a Path to Success*, Economic and Social Research Council.

Alexander, M. and Green, R. (1992), 'Workplace productivity and joint consultation', *Australian Bulletin of Labour*, **18**(2), 95–118.

Alexopoulos, M. and T. Tombe (2009), 'Management matters', manuscript, University of Toronto.

Arthur, W.B. (2007), 'The structure of invention', *Research Policy*, **36**(2), 274–87.

BCA (2006), *Changing Paradigms: Rethinking Innovation Policies, Practices and Programmes*, Report by the Business Council of Australia, Melbourne.

Bell, S. (2010), '"Design thinking" and higher education', *Inside High Education*, available at: http://www.insidehighered.com/views/2010/03/02/bell; accessed 23 June 2012.

Bell, M. and K. Pavitt (1997), 'Technological accumulation and industrial growth: contrasts between developed and developing countries', in D. Archibugi and J. Michie (eds), *Technology, Globalisation and Economic Performance*, Cambridge, UK: CUP, pp. 83–136.

Bennis, W. and J. O'Toole (2005), 'How business schools lost their way', *Harvard Business Review*, May, 96–104.

Bessant, J. (1992), 'Big bang or continuous evolution: why incremental innovation is gaining attention in successful organizations', *Creativity and Innovation Management*, **1**(2), 59–62.

BIHECC (2007), *Graduate Employability Skills*, Report by Business Industry and Higher Education Collaboration Council, Melbourne.

Birkinshaw, J. and M. Mol (2006), 'How management innovation happens', *Sloan Management Review*, **47**(4), 81–8.

Birkinshaw, J., G. Hamel and M. Mol (2008), 'Management innovation', *Academy of Management Review*, **33**(4), 825–45.

Black, S. and L. Lynch (2001), 'How to compete: the impact of workplace practices and information technology on productivity', *Review of Economics and Statistics*, **83**(3), 434–45.

Black, S.E. and L.M. Lynch (2004), 'What's driving the new economy? The benefits of workplace innovation', *The Economic Journal*, **114**(493), 97–116.

Bloom, N. and J. Van Reenen (2007), 'Measuring and explaining management practices across firms and countries', *Quarterly Journal of Economics*, **122**(4), 1351–408.

Bracks, S. (2008), *A New Car Plan for a Greener Future*, Review of the Automotive Industry, DIISR Commonwealth of Australia, Canberra, available at: http://www.innovation.gov.au/Industry/Automotive/InitiativesandAssistance/Documents/NewCarPlanGreenerFuture.pdf; accessed 23 June 2012.

Bradley Report (2008), *Transforming Australia's Higher Education System*, Canberra: Australian Government.

Brown, S. and K. Eisenhardt (1997), 'The art of continuous change: linking complexity theory and time-paced evolution in relentlessly shifting organizations', *Administrative Science Quarterly*, **42**(1), 1–34.

Candy, R.C. and R.G. Crebert (1991), 'Ivory tower to concrete jungle: the transfer of learning skills from the academy to the workplace', *Journal of Higher Education*, **62**(5), 570–92.

Carr, K. (2009), *Powering Ideas: An Innovation Agenda for the 21st Century*, Canberra: Australian Government.

Cartel, C.A. and R. Garud (2009), 'The role of narratives in sustaining organizational innovation', *Organization Science*, **20**(1), 107–17.

Cepeda, G. and D. Vera (2007), 'Dynamic capabilities and operational capabilities: a knowledge management perspective', *Journal of Business Research*, **60**(5), 426–37.

Clegg, S.R., T.S. Pitsis, T. Rura-Polley and M. Marosszeky (2002), 'Governmentality matters: designing an alliance culture of inter-organizational collaboration for managing projects', *Organization Studies*, **23**(3), 313–37.

Cutler, T. (2008), *Venturous Australia: Building Strength in Innovation*, Report of the Review into the National Innovation System, Canberra: Australian Government.

Daghfous, A. (2004), 'Knowledge management as an organizational innovation: an absorptive capacity perspective and a case study', *International Journal of Innovation and Learning*, **1**(4), 409–22.

Damanpour, F. and W. Evan (1984), 'Organizational innovation and performance: the problem of "organizational lag"', *Administrative Science Quarterly*, **29**(3), 392–409.

Datar, S., D. Garvin and P. Cullen (2010), *Rethinking the MBA: Business Education at a Crossroads*, Boston, MA: Harvard Business School Press.

D'Aveni, R.A. (1994), *Hypercompetition: Managing the Dynamics of Strategic Manoeuvring*, New York: The Free Press.

Dodgson, M., D. Gann and A. Salter (2008), *The Management of Technological Innovation: Strategy and Practice*, Oxford: Oxford University Press.

Drucker, P.F. (1985), *Innovation and Entrepreneurship: Practice and Principles*, New York: Harper & Row.

Dunne, D. and R. Martin (2006), 'Design thinking and how it will change management education: an interview and discussion', *Academy of Management Learning and Education*, **5**(4), 512–23.

Eisenhardt, K. and J. Martin (2000), 'Dynamic capabilities – what are they?', *Strategic Management Journal*, **21**(10–11), 1105–21.

Ekanem, I. and D. Smallbone (2007), 'Learning in small manufacturing firms', *International Journal of Small Business*, **25**(2), 107–29.

Francis, D. and J. Bessant (2005), 'Targeting innovation and implications for capability development', *Technovation*, **25**(3), 171–83.

Gallouj, F. and O. Weinstein (1997), 'Innovation in services', *Research Policy*, **26**(4–5), 537–55.

Ghoshal, S. (2005), 'Bad management theories are destroying good management practices', *Academy of Management Learning and Education*, **4**(1), 75–91.

Green, R. (2008), *Building Innovative Capability*, Review of the Australian Textile, Clothing and Footwear Industries, DIISR Canberra: Australian Government, available at: http://www.teansw.com.au/Curriculum/Textiles%2011-12/Resources/401_TCF%20review_vol1.pdf; accessed 23 June 2012.

Green, R. (2010), 'Changing the world', *Australian Financial Review*, 22 February.

Green, R., R. Agarwal, J. Van Reenen, N. Bloom, J. Mathews, C. Boedker, D. Sampson, P. Gollan, P. Toner, H. Tan, K. Randhawa and P. Brown (2009), *Management Matters in Australia: Just How Productive Are We?*, Canberra: Department of Innovation, Industry, Science and Research, available at: http://www.innovation.gov.au/Industry/ReportsandStudies/Documents/ManagementMattersinAustraliaReport.pdf; accessed 22 June 2012.

Guillen, M. (1994), *Models of Management: Work, Authority and Organization in Comparative Perspective*, Chicago: University of Chicago Press.

Hall, R. (2000), 'What are strategic competencies', in J. Tidd, *From Knowledge Management to Strategic Competence*, London: Imperial College Press.

Hamel, G. (1998), 'Strategy innovation and the quest for value', *Sloan Management Review*, **39**(2), 7–14.

Helfat, C. (2007), 'Relational capabilities: drivers and implications', in C.E. Helfat, S. Finkelstein, W. Mitchell, M. Peteraf, H. Singh, D.J. Teece and S.G. Winter (eds), *Dynamic Capabilities: Strategic Change in Organisations*, Oxford: Blackwell, pp. 65–80.

Holland, K. (2009), 'Is it time to retrain B-schools?', available at: http://www.nytimes.com/2009/03/15/business/15school.html; accessed 24 June 2012.

Kale, P. and H. Singh (2007), 'Building firm capabilities through learning: the role of the alliance learning process in alliance capability and firm-level alliance success', *Strategic Management Journal*, **28**(10), 981–1000.

Karpin Report (1995), *Enterprising Nation*, Canberra: Government of Australia.

Khurana, R., N. Nohria and D. Penrice (2005), 'Management as a profession', in Jay W. Lorsch, Leslie Berlowitz and Andy Zelleke (eds), *Restoring Trust in American Business*, Cambridge, MA: MIT Press.

Laplagne, P. and L. Bensted (1999), 'The role of training and innovation in workplace performance', Productivity Commission, *Staff Research Paper*, December.

Lester, R.K. (2006), *Future of Business Schools in the UK*, Advanced Institute of Management Research Report, AIM Research.

Makadok, R. (2001), 'Toward a synthesis of the resource-based and dynamic-capability views of rent creation', *Strategic Management Journal*, **22**(5), 387–401.

Martin, R. (2007), *The Opposable Mind: How Successful Leaders Win Through Integrative Thinking*, Boston, MA: Harvard Business School Press.

Martin, R. and H. Austen (1999), 'The art of integrative thinking', *Rotman Management* magazine, Fall.

McNamee, B. and C. Pennifold (2008), *Final Report of the Pharmaceuticals Industry Strategy Group*, Review of the Australian Pharmaceuticals Industry, Canberra: DIISR Commonwealth of Australia, available at: http://www.innovation.gov.au/Industry/PharmaceuticalsandHealthTechnologies/PharmaceuticalsIndustryStrategyGroup/Documents/PISG_Final_Report.pdf; accessed 23 June 2012.

Mintzberg, H. (2004), *Managers Not MBAs: A Hard Look at the Soft Practice of Management Development*, San Francisco, CA: Berrett-Koehler.

Nahapiet, J. and S. Ghoshal (1998), 'Social capital, intellectual capital and the organizational advantage', *Academy of Management Review*, **23**(2), 242–66.

OECD (2011), *Skills for Innovation and Research*, OECD Publishing, available at: http://dx.doi.org/10.1787/9789264097490-en; accessed 22 June 2012.

O'Hanlon-Rose, T. (2008–09), 'The skills gap – what is it? How do we fill it?', *VOCAL: The Australian Journal of Vocational Education and Training*, **7**, 10–18.

Pfeffer, J. and C.T. Fong (2002), 'The end of business schools? Less success than meets the eye', *Academy of Management Learning and Education*, **1**(1), 78–95.

Powell, W.W., K. Kenneth and Laurel Smith-Doerr (1996), 'Interorganizational collaboration and the locus of innovation: networks of learning in biotechnology', *Administrative Science Quarterly*, **41**(1), 116–45.

Richardson, S. (2007), *What is a Skills Shortage*, Adelaide: NCVER.

Rittel, H. and M. Webber (1973,) 'Dilemmas in a general theory of planning', *Policy Sciences*, **4**(2), 155–69.

Scott-Kemmis, D. (2010), *Transformative Innovation Spaces and Processes Through Integrating Design, Business and Engineering*, Sydney: UTS.

Segal, D. (2010), 'In pursuit of the perfect brainstorm', *New York Times*, 16 December 2010.

Society of Knowledge Economics (SKE) (2008), *Innovation Attitudes in Australia: The Results of the Online Survey Conducted by Open Forum*, available at: http://www.ske.org.au/download/Innovation_Attitudes_in_Australia_Survey_Report.pdf; accessed 24 June 2012.

Subramaniam, M. and M. Youndt (2005), 'The influence of intellectual capital on the types of innovative capabilities, *Academy of Management Journal*, **48**(3), 450–63.

Teece, D.J. (2009), *Dynamic Capabilities and Strategic Management*, Oxford: Oxford University Press.

Tidd, J., J.R. Bessant and K. Pavitt (2005), *Managing Innovation: Integrating Technological, Market and Organizational Change*, Chichester: John Wiley.

Toner, P. (2007), 'Skills and innovation: putting ideas to work', background paper on VET and innovation for the NSW Department of Education and Training, Sydney.

Toner, P. (2011), 'Workforce skills and innovation: an overview of major themes in the literature', *OECD Education Working Papers*, No. 55, OECD Publishing, available at: http://dx.doi.org/10.1787/5kgk6hpnhxzq-en; accessed 23 June 2012.

Transforming Australia's Higher Education System (2009), Department of Education, Employment and Workplace Relations, Canberra: Commonwealth of Australia, available at: http://www.deewr.gov.au/HigherEducation/Documents/TransformingAusHigherED.pdf; accessed 23 June 2012.

Trehan, K. and C. Rigg (2007), 'Working with experiential learning: a critical perspective in practice', in E. Reynolds and V. Russ (eds), *The Handbook of Experiential Learning and Management Education*, Oxford: Oxford University Press.

Wu, L. (2010), 'Applicability of the resource-based and dynamic-capability views under environmental volatility', *Journal of Business Research*, **63**(1), 27–31.

Zbaracki, M.J. (1998), 'The rhetoric and reality of total quality management', *Administrative Science Quarterly*, **43**(3), 602–38.

Zheng, W. (2010), 'A social capital perspective of innovation from individuals to nations: where is the empirical literature directing us?', *International Journal of Management Reviews*, **12**(2), 151–83.

PART II

INNOVATION AS (PRACTICAL) EMERGENCE

9   Living ideas at work
Arne Carlsen and Lloyd Sandelands

INTRODUCTION

> Men need a purpose which bears on eternity. Truth does that; our ideals do it, and this may be enough, if we could ever be satisfied with our manifest moral shortcomings and with a society which has such shortcomings fatally involved in its workings.
>
> (Michael Polanyi, [1966] 2009, *The Tacit Dimension*, p. 92)

Sometimes, when you work with ideas in organizations, a set of peculiar things happens. Say you have organized a workshop or just engaged in a more informal brain-storming session with colleagues. Inspired by supposed truths that quantity of ideas breeds quality (e.g., Simonton, 2004) you may have tried to generate many and distinctly different ideas. Inspired by advocates of knowledge combination (e.g., Koestler [1964] 1989; Hargadon, 2003) you may have taken great care to bring people with different backgrounds together and systematically used analogues from other domains to further enrich the combinatory efforts. After all the hard work you emerge from what seemed like a wonderful discussion to a prioritized list of ideas. On the wall are all the products of your efforts; the best new ideas listed and labelled, maybe also numbered and visualized. And then, by mystery, right there, seemingly out of nothing, it may all die. It is as if the lively joint creative activities have somehow been frozen, congealed into a nothingness of a list that nobody wants to pursue. It happens quickly if it is hard to see the connections between the rich discussion and the necessarily thin abstractions on the wall. It happens with the speed of light if someone leans back and utters: 'This looks like the list we made half a year ago, there is nothing really new here'. It is over. Let's go home.

At other times when you work with ideas you may have landed on one idea that all in the team are enthusiastic about – what could, for example, be the concept for a new building in a prestigious architectural competition. Let us assume this idea indeed does win the competition. Celebration is due! Then, disappointingly, as the project progresses, enthusiasm is lost. What once seemed so great for the team does not catch on further down the road. The concept is so tightly defined that there is not much more to add for people engaged in the detailed design and drawing. They find it utterly boring. And users of the new building do not relate to or even recognize the intended concept.

At yet other times you may find yourself in a somewhat unrewarding position of trying to manage a system for handling new ideas in your organization. Say you have tried to implement insights from evolutionary theory on creative processes (e.g., Campbell, 1997) by installing processes for variation (local idea generation), selection (screening and prioritizing) and retention (further development of chosen ideas in coordinated corporate efforts) and even combined that with a stage-gate decision approach (e.g., Cooper, 1993). In your carefully designed scheme then, people are encouraged to nominate ideas for new products and services, preferably by email, to a committee of idea screeners who may send it back for further development or pass it on to a development unit (who may or may not include the original idea generators in their work). It is all carefully designed and backed with resources. You may even have created a web application that allows people to comment upon the ideas of others. As you engage in this you discover that the quality of ideas you receive is fairly low and that ideas when passed back to the organization from the screening tend to lose momentum. More troubling, the development efforts that do get realized seem somehow to have done so by circumventing the system. You overhear one person stating harshly: 'If you send your idea in there it is guaranteed to die, it's a black hole, you'll hear nothing in months'. Another openly boasts about achieving success by managing to stay under the radar of the system.

The occurrences described here are not pure fantasy, but taken from a recent research project on 'idea work' (Carlsen et al., 2008, 2012; Coldevin et al., 2011) involving five organizations: an architectural firm, the exploration units of an oil company, a law firm, as well as product development units in a major bank and a trading analysis company. We will revisit this empirical context several times. Here the examples serve to highlight that a starting point for this chapter is both an empirical and theoretical puzzlement: what is really an idea? Or more precisely – how are we best served to think and talk about ideas in organizations? The three empirical vignettes all point to a basic dilemma: as practitioners and researchers interested in innovative efforts in organizations we more or less willingly inherit a language of ideas as nouns. It follows that ideas are typically talked of as varieties of *entities* and *cognitive* manifestations: conceptions, thoughts, principles, beliefs, plans.[1] And ideas are referred to as *discrete* – something one can number, count and represent in one-to-one models, stand-alone images, texts or objects with clear limits to where they start and end.[2] In this chapter we take the position that for ideas to *live* – to engage people inside and outside organizations and have valuable impact – they are better considered not as inert things and settled conclusions, but as forms of being in which we participate with the fullness of our humanity. Ideas are forms of life that we experience and come to understand aesthetically. Idea work is first of all an aesthetic experience. This is to be seen in examples of being passionately engaged in idea generation at work, of noticing something as an idea from within ambiguous fields of input, of being drawn into the ideas of others, and of getting reacquainted with the details and doubts that brought established categories into being. In this, their active living form, ideas are verbs, are what people feel and do. And we suggest that the living of ideas at work is at its most intense when it transcends individuals and organizations and is somehow linked to purposes and questions that bear on eternity; on the many Mysteries of being itself that the smaller mysteries we deal with in organizations may speak into and receive life from.

We shall let our investigation unfold in three stages, all dealing with living ideas at work and cast in the order of intensified life:

1. how ideas die in reification, isolation and dogma;
2. how they live in continued processes of participation and connection; and
3. how ideas live in fields of wonder.

IDEAS DIE BY REIFICATION, ISOLATION AND DOGMA

One clue to understanding why ideas die is found in a line by Neil Young: 'Love is a rose but you better not pick it. Only grows when it's on the vine' ('Love is a Rose', 1974). Once picked, taken out of its context of creation and presented as a listed item on the wall, ideas risk no longer being on the vine. Such a statement may appear intuitively graspable to some and sufficient as such. For others it sounds unsatisfactory as an explanation of what is going on when vivid processes come to a halt. What exactly could 'being on the vine' mean here?

For a deeper explanation let us turn to Mark Johnson (2007) who has provided a forceful contemporary account of how human meaning-making and understanding is inherently aesthetic. Building on the philosophy of John Dewey ([1925] 1958; [1934] 1980), William James ([1890] 1950) and Susanne Langer (1967), as well as more recent research within embodied cognition and neurophysiology, Johnson argues that all meaning is embodied, indeed that what we call reason, mind or ideas are embodied processes by which our experience is explored and transformed.

People come to know something and produce meaning through organism–environment transactions and patterns of feeling from such interactions. First there are the stimuli from bodily movement and sensory-motor engagement in our interactions in situations that occur within ongoing experience (such as a workshop for generating ideas). Some such stimuli (e.g., peak moments in discussions) elicit the complex neural, chemical and behavioural responses one may think of as emotions and that largely take place automatically and outside conscious awareness (Johnson, 2007, pp. 56–7, 61–5). Then, some of this emotional response may be registered as a felt pattern (breakthrough, opening, reversal, movement) of the moment or situation. These felt patterns are consciously experienced bodily processes. All new meanings arise from and lead back to such processes.[3] Moreover, Johnson (2007, Chapters 4 and 5), again closely following Dewey, James and Langer, surmises that new meanings come to us as unifying wholes that are best thought of as *a pervasive quality of a situation*, a pervasive quality that *only later* is discriminated into objects, properties and relations (Johnson, 2007, p. 74):

> An identifiable, meaningful experience is neither *merely* emotional, nor *merely* practical, nor *merely* intellectual. Rather, it is all of these at once and together. We call it *emotional*, after the fact, when we wish to stress the felt quality of its emotional valence. We call it *practical* when we wish to profile its outcome and the interests it might serve. We call it *intellectual* when we are interested primarily in the distinctions, associations and connections of thoughts that arise through the course of the experience.

Following Johnson, we may say that what we call new ideas in organizations always arise as a felt pattern of some pervasive quality of a situation (a workshop, a client meeting, an informal conversation, individual contemplation), but later gets distinguished as an object, an intellectual general proposition of some phenomenon in the world or a new product or service. It is this latter fruit or flower that we tend to preserve as the idea, and doing so, risk taking it from the fullness and richness of its experiential cradle. At worst the understanding of ideas as nouns underpins reified and isolated conceptions that are cut off from their original experiences, stop further imagination and even work against creative efforts. Metaphorically speaking, the farther away the roses are taken from the vine, the more likely they are to die. Such distancing may occur between phases of a project, as when the roses are passed from one group to another (e.g., the experiences of generating a concept in an architectural competition versus the further work on the project and based on that representation, or indeed, the further experiencing of the building by users). Or it may occur in gaps of time, as between the experience of the felt pattern and later work. The example of submitting an 'idea' into a corporate screening mechanism, with the delay in response and the takeover of this 'idea' by others, is an extreme version. Here the roses are ripped from the soil of their cultivation, deprived of nourishment for months, and then thrown into a new pot of questionable fertility.

While the workings of the described corporate scheme for idea generation and selection for many reasons sounds intuitively wrong in terms of shutting down people's engagement, the situation that opened this chapter is much less obvious. The 'ideas' listed on the wall are roses that have just been picked. How can it be that they already seem to die? Again, the insight from Johnson here is that ideas are first of all processes in ongoing experience. What has made it to the wall are not these processes, but the residua or husks of these processes. These objectified and reified remains may lack sufficient openings or indications to recall to the participants the idea processes that bore them. The labels on the wall, regarded apart from their constitutive acts, are dead forms that make for a limited and stultifying idea of idea. These are the forms that can be invited by a scientism that confines ideas to what science can study by empirical means, or by a positivism that confines ideas to what can be defined in ostensive terms, in terms of observables, or by materialism that limits ideas to what is physically present. This idea of idea limits us to the material things of nature that can be observed and studied empirically. And this idea stultifies our thinking, by:

1. directing and confining experiences of the world to the things we've seen before, to the things we can already name and list and catalogue;
2. by closing off wonder and thereby our curiosity about those things in the misbegotten belief that what they are, the fact that they are, and how they came to be is already resolved; and
3. by confirming (1) and (2) as socially validated public facts, as 'what everyone knows'.

Ideas die when their being is forgotten or denied; when things are taken not as appearances of being, but as things themselves.

There is a parallel to this set of insights in Karl Weick's (2005, 2006) work on imagination. Weick insists that imagination and exploration need to be stimulus driven and bottom-up, a continued embodied engagement with the matters in question. Direct acquaintance with 'primary data' of some sort is necessary to involve people's perception and avoid conceptual reification:

> Once people start working with names and concepts for the things that they see, they develop knowledge by description rather than knowledge by

acquaintance, their cognitive processing is now schema-driven rather than stimulus-driven, and they go beyond the information given and elaborate their direct perceptions into types, categories, stereotypes, and schemas. Continued conceptual processing means that people now know less about more ... To design imagination into organizing, we need to slow the upward movement from perceptions toward the naming that begins to compound our abstractions. And we need to hasten the downward movement away from reifications back toward perceptions that can be renamed with labels that are imperfect in new ways. (Weick, 2006, pp.450–51)

According to this thinking, an organization that only deals with finished and reified conceptions would accumulate not only dead roses, but also stoppers of further exploration and idea work. Hydrocarbon exploration is a type of idea work that may be easily driven by such closed models and remnants of frozen understanding if bias, doubt and misconceptions in previous work are ignored (Carlsen et al., 2008). Explorers need to imagine geological processes that took place hundreds of millions of years ago based on what is always insufficient data. Seizing the crutches of models that have worked or been assigned weight in the past is tempting. And, sometimes, what were once vibrant ideas haunt people from the grave. In a geological province with scant data, a senior explorer recently commented upon the peculiar lack of history of the models that had been guiding the efforts for many years: 'we have been searching for some time for where these models [that have restrained imagination and stopped genuinely new search] came from, who produced them. It's really strange: nobody seems to know!'

A related explanation for the death of the labelled ideas at the workshop is that they have no action consequent. Pragmatists like Peirce ([1878] 1958) and James ([1907] 1977) held that the highest level of clarity of ideas is tied to their practical bearings, not their definitions or universal recognition. The real test of whether differences in thinking matter is achieved by looking at consequences for future practice. This is achieved by bringing ideas back to experience and testing their relevance, whether in scientific experiments or everyday action. Thus, ideas that remain labels on the wall without suggestions for further actions, such as some form of testing of a prototype, remain incapable of being brought back, of being reconnected to the vine.

In summary, ideas die by reification, isolation and dogma:

- when cut off from the aboriginal experiences that created them with no trace of their histories and makers;
- when locked in accepted and unquestioned conceptions, monologically championed as dogmatic and closed forms that people cannot contribute to;

- when they fail to brush up against the ideas of others and become stand-alone, isolated from other provinces of knowing that could have filled them with new life;
- when they have no action consequent and nothing is done to them.

IDEAS LIVE THROUGH PARTICIPATION AND CONNECTION

How then do ideas come to be lived at work? A little anecdote by a senior explorer who is also an ardent amateur sailor, may be indicative:

> I believe one of my best sailing friends really has the right kind of attitude: 'I'm not really interested in the weather forecasts', says he. Rather, he really wants access to the raw data, get his hands dirty with all the numbers and tables, and then build his own models of what the weather may be. That's the way we should all do it in exploration. But taking the time to gather all that we have and engaging with the messiness of the data with fresh eyes can be very uncomfortable.

Apparently, this is precisely the kind of open-ended, bottom-up, stimulus-driven approach to exploration that Weick (2005, 2006) advocates. And certainly, the things that keep ideas alive are to some extent the opposite of the items listed above. Ideas live when something is done to them, when people use them, participate in them and when they are connected to the ideas of others within and across the knowledge domain in question. The roses need to be reconnected to the vine or not taken off at all. The ideas need to stay in motion of testing and adaptation in ongoing experience. Building on Shotter (2006) we may say that this shift in thinking amounts to rejecting the idea of ideas as finished representational-referential-monological entities and consider them responsive-dialogical-interactive-understandings that are in the making.

Let's visit two examples. One of the largest discoveries of hydrocarbons on the Norwegian shelf took place in an area with over ten dry wells and massive disappointments (Carlsen and Pitsis, 2008). Encouraged by the proven existence of movable oil in a dry well (a new stimuli), the exploration team painstakingly reprocessed data from all the dry wells in search of an alternative explanation that could explain the data (a new consistent whole), thus breathing new life into the idea process through opening, increased participation and new connections. Likewise, when architects at Snøhetta describe the process of coming up with the winning concept for the Norwegian Opera they emphasize the long, almost endless conversations, with all members of the team jointly looking at all the user requirements, technical-commercial constraints and possibilities and cultural-historical conditions: 'We have very long conversations. [There is] an incredible amount of contextual conditions that we have to talk through again and again . . . circles of conversation . . . a joint walk in references'.

The significance of these examples is not only that people are continuously engaged in the idea work in question, but that they strive to keep a variety of possibilities and interpretations open to nourish a thicker and more robust vine with more roses. The Snøhetta architects refer to it as keeping concepts *generous* in the sense that they (1) can survive and assimilate continuously changing ideas, demands and constraints, and (2) evoke a broad range of interpretations and user experiences. Says one of the senior architects:

> If the project has that quality, that it is so generous to begin with, that it opens up for your own interpretations as you go – and generosity seems to be a very important theme – if you imagine that it is so, then it is as if the project develops itself. That means that you have found something, collectively, the very core of something that is this project's most important development potential.

Generous concepts then may be seen as a temporarily stabilized output from idea work that allows a fruitful interplay between explicit renderings and ongoing processes of ideation. Going back to the insights from Johnson (2007), the key term here is temporary. The point is not to avoid or disregard any descriptive output from idea work but to place and arrange such output so that it is considered unfinished, with traces of its historical making (under which particular situations it was created by which people for which purposes) and its continued development and testing (its action consequents) held within a *temporal contour* that interacts with ongoing experiences. It is this entire set of artifacts, interactions, thoughts, trials and feelings of rightness that takes place in repeated bouts of interaction that we might regard as living ideas: fields of participation and connection.

At this point readers may ask whether there are points in time when one can say that ideas are complete and suitably rendered for unaltered implementation. With William James we find it fruitful to talk about perchings and flights, denoting phases of honing of that which has been created and more radical movements of thinking-doing. It is too limited to think of such processes as having final destinations. This is fairly obvious if one considers the case of understanding a reservoir of hydrocarbons. Even after verification of resources and many years of drilling and exploitation of oil, the reservoir and its workings still remain at least partially a mystery to geologists. More surprising is perhaps the unfinished nature of key ideas in architecture. Craig Dykers, Chief Architect at Snøhetta and leader of the company's New York office, talks about imagining, simulating and producing embodied user experiences rather than buildings, experiences that engender memories and should not be limited by prior intent:

> For me the people are the real things and the buildings are in fact the abstractions . . . and I think the best authors of architecture, are creating a story that has different associations from the reader . . . I never heard anyone walk into a building and go – 'My God, what a great concept'. Never heard it. Even amongst architects. You walk into a building, you go – 'Wow, what a great place', or 'What an amazing room'. . . . In fact, if you look at our competition entry [for the Norwegian Opera], we were talking about things that nobody can even see anymore. A good example is a swan. You know, we're looking at this swan one day, and the shape of the swan, how beautiful it is. And how, when it sits on the water it just seems so majestic. And that shape on the opera, if you look at it from elevation, it goes down and it comes back and it goes back. Nobody can see that. You'd have to tell somebody, and I'm glad that they don't see it, and that they are seeing it in another way. So there's a lot of open-endedness to it.

The gap between an intended concept or user experience and the one realized is not only a noted quality but to some degree a sought-after quality. This is particularly clear in the design of the 9/11 memorial museum, where the goal is to allow dualities of qualities like grief, hope, beauty and ugliness to be present at the site. We may say that by allowing a broad range of user experiences to happen, thus connecting the experience of being there to other experiences people have had in their lives, the architects try to enlist people in participating in the ideas of a building and its placement in the landscape. In this sense, the building is an artifact mediating the overall aesthetic experience of living ideas.

Another dimension of living ideas that we shall only touch upon lightly here is the mere physical engagement of people doing idea work. We first came across this when noting how experienced oil finders, despite the welter of new technology for various forms of interpretation and analysis, emphasized the scribbling on well-logs, sketching together on seismic maps and unplugged interactions in their work (Mortensen et al., 2007; Mortensen, 2013). We have later seen that playing with artifacts is an important element in making qualitative research generative (Dutton and Carlsen, 2011) and in researcher–practitioner interactions (Carlsen et al., 2011). At its most generative, idea work simply gets physical: ways of working that entail moving from over-dependence on electronic media and mental representations towards touching data, jointly sketching emergent understandings, gesticulating and moving while doing idea work. Such ways of working often entail materialization of ideas in models, sketches and images as well as habits of interaction around such artifacts.

In summary, ideas live by participation and connection:

- when they carry with them histories and voices of their making, as well as action consequents, both being contours of temporal movements;
- when they appear open by being somehow unfinished, messy, voluptuous and indeterminate so to invite combination between close or distant analogies, particulars and their wholes;
- when they can be somehow touched, invite gesticulation, co-movement and other forms of playful embodied interaction around artifacts;
- when people do things to them and act upon them.

IDEAS LIVE IN FIELDS OF WONDER

There is a particular kind of participation and connection with ideas that takes place when they are lived the most, when the experiencing of being and participating in a mystery is the most intense, and when the search is connected to larger questions of life. This is the experiencing of wonder – typically evoked by appreciation of some stimuli of beauty or strangeness, feeling surprised, disturbed, unsettled or amazed by something that triggers search (Parsons, 1969; Rubinstein, 2008; Carlsen and Sandelands, 2012). Wonder is the first of all passions, the precondition for people's deep interest in anything beyond self and a primary engine of imagination, appreciation and empathy at work (Fisher, 1998; Nussbaum, 2011). The experience of wonder bears some similarity to flow but it is not self-rewarding and self-limiting. It is self-transcendent and takes place in a series of moments as part of a search journey that may go on inevitably but that may also have its perchings and flights. It is a two-in-oneness of engaging mystery and rational inquiry (Sandelands and Carlsen, 2012) marked by a series of emotive signs such as enchantment, bewilderment, restlessness, deep sense of passion and worry (see Shotter, 2007 for a thoughtful account of worry in wondering, amongst other things).

The experience of wonder underpins extraordinary idea work in many ways (Carlsen and Sandelands, 2012). Exploration geologists express deep reverence for nature and exhilarating joy of finding out how the natural world works – pursuing freedom of thinking and 'flying with the birds'. Lawyers highlight the ability to 'genuinely care for the client' and imagine consequences of choices and strategies in their world. Bankers talk about openness to ideas, impulses and needs of others and 'daring to be in a state of not knowing'. The founders of an (energy) trading analysis company emphasize the generation of fundamental new questions as a prerequisite to keeping ideas flowing and imagining new demand. Architects talk about the importance of attention to beauty, seeing 'pearls in the sand', noticing what 'feels right' and pursuing 'bare-naked honesty' in discussions. And all of them, especially the people who *lead* in idea work independent of their formal positions, are enlivened by being in contact with some larger questions: lawyers about what is right and the making of new law, energy traders about climate change and energy use, explorers about the processes making the energy reserves of the earth as we know it, bankers about how economic risk is dealt with by our institutions, architects with the larger cultural-historical tales and questions of morality that experiencing of major new landmark buildings falls within. They all wonder about questions of being, about what is right, good and true.

Wonder calls attention to the metaphysical aspect of idea work by calling to mind an idea of idea concerned with the being of things. This relates to what Aristotle, in *Metaphysics* ([circa 350 BC] 2002), delineated as the substance and essence of things and with what Aquinas in his *Summa Theologica* ([1265–74] 2003), identified as the existence or 'subsistence' of things in the divine. This is the idea of idea that begins in wonder about what things are, about whether or not they exist, and about how they come into and go out of being. This is the idea of idea that engages not only natural properties and quantitative relations of mathematics that derive there from (e.g., the objects and relations of geometry), but also properties of being that are before and beyond the natural. Included among these are the so-called 'transcendental properties' that reach across categories or species of natural things such as *being* itself, as well as *unity, eternity, immutability, truth, goodness* and *beauty*. Also included among these are the so-called 'pure properties' of being that pertain uniquely to human persons such as *personhood, free will*, and *rationality*. Wonder thus is our uniquely human interest in being; in matters of substance, essence, existence and subsistence. These are the things deeper than science, the things betrayed by its reification and objection, the things that inspire the best and most human in us.

In metaphysical terms, what we have called participation and connection are bound up with the fact that we occupy a special place in creation as the one form of being able to take being into itself (through a process Aquinas called 'adequation') and able thereby to know being as being. According to Aquinas we are made in the image of God, Who is Being itself, absolute and pure, and in Whom substance, essence, and existence are perfected. We come into our always partial and imperfect being – into our partial and imperfect substance, essence and existence – as we participate in His Being, which we do by our actions, by what we feel, think and do. This is to cast wonder's life of ideas as the more or less perfected movements in and through which we come into our (human) being. And this is to cast Johnson's (2007) ideas of feeling and idea into a new light. Where Johnson and others (e.g., Langer, 1967) trace the life of ideas to bodily processes (of neurophysiology and the like), Aquinas and the philosophers of the scholastic tradition trace the life of ideas to our involvement in God's ongoing creation of being. The disadvantage of the former is that it makes a mystery of the process by which body begets mind.[4] The disadvantage of the latter, if it is one, is that it is mystery itself.

All this said, it is important to emphasize that wonder is not necessarily a comfortable experience that brings unambiguous joy and enchantment to people, neither is it a luxury activity of letting the mind wander to whatever larger question we choose to deal with. Heidegger ([1926] 1962, Chapter 5; [1937–38] 1994) emphasizes a darker dimension. Wonder is an in-dwelling that resists final conclusions because it tolerates staying in a 'wound' of understanding. Frantic curiosity or claiming certain knowledge or negating larger questions are ways of running away from the restless un-comfort that wonder can be. In this regard, wonder is a conceptual cousin to what Keats called negative capability (Keats [1817] 2002, pp. 40–42; Dewey [1934] 1980, pp. 32–4), something that seeks and tolerates bewilderment, accepts half-knowledge and allows people to stay and dwell in their inquiry. It is possible that the list of ideas we talked about at the start of this chapter may have represented not vibrant new understandings, but temporary escape routes, labels one clings to when being in the dungeon of not knowing becomes intolerable.

In summary, ideas live in fields of wonder:

- when they arise from appreciation of strangeness or beauty in some occurrence or other stimuli and arouse people and engage them in passionate search;
- when people learn to tolerate ambiguity and bewilderment, resist reaching for premature conclusions and search for truth while accepting it can never be fully reached;
- when they somehow bear on eternity by engaging in the larger questions of being, what is right, good and true;
- when they make people *stay* and *dwell* in inquiry.

EXIT – PARTICIPATING IN THE IDEA OF THE OTHER

What is that which we call an 'idea'? We have argued that ideas are best thought of as processes. Ideas are lived-in dialogically responsive processes of conception/articulation, production/adaptation and use/experiencing by which people interact with artifacts and other symbolic resources to create new understanding. Ideas are subsections in the stream of experiencing that come to us as feelings of some patterned pervasive whole that joins ambiguous elements and that later can be dissected, discriminated and given shape in symbolic resources and artifacts. We have argued further that ideas die by reification, isolation and dogma, that they live in participation and connection and that they live most intensely in fields of wonder. Focusing on ideas as lived-in aesthetic experiences is not just a theoretical exegesis. Rather, it serves to lay the basis for cultivating habits of working that increase the potential for innovation.

We have presented summaries of the argument along the way, so all that is due here are only a few implications. For practitioners interested in the management and practice of idea work in organizations, this chapter poses a challenge: stop thinking about ideas as things. Start thinking about them as processes – as living forms of connecting and participating; as forms of our human social life (cf. Sandelands, 2003). To preserve these living forms that ideas are, we need to heed their histories – which processes they were birthed in and which voices they carry – as well as their futures; what their action consequents are. Keeping ideas alive means not only keeping them visible but also acting on them and testing them in series of small and large experiments. Throughout any such efforts we also advocate a need to listen better to how ideas take seat in our bodies. This means, for example, to learn to appreciate the feeling of being startled that may instigate search and the feeling of wholeness and beauty associated with breakthrough explanations and new unities arising from ambiguous input. It also means letting go of control, letting ourselves be immersed in data or the phenomenon we investigate and tolerate the embodied feeling of restlessness that may accompany idea work. And, ultimately, keeping ideas alive means connecting our everyday concerns to larger questions that bear upon eternity, whether they are about the natural world or social matters.

For researchers interested in work with ideas in organizations, our chapter highlights at least two sets of foci that should be strengthened. One is following in a recent push to see creativity more as collective processes than individual efforts and stable qualities of actors (e.g., Hargadon and Bechky, 2006; Sawyer, 2006). More broadly, our chapter follows in a tradition of research that applies a processual lens (Hernes and Maitlis, 2010) to organization. In a strong process theory (such as in James [1890] 1950), ideas simply do not exist outside their constitutive events. We nevertheless need the concept of ideas as nouns as conceptual referents to our processes. And we still know little about the ongoing dynamics between the residues and artifacts of ideas and their unfolding ongoing processes. Understanding that dynamics necessitates a more wholehearted turn to the aesthetics of knowing (Ewenstein and Whyte, 2007) and the embodied nature of imagination (Johnson, 2007). A crucial aspect here is the interplay between focal and subsidiary attention, and the role of poetic forms in such attention-drawing (Weick, 2010). Poetic forms, like metaphor, have the power to focus attention in a way that implies the subsidiary and invite further participation in ideas.

For both practitioners and researchers, another set of implications may be more fundamental. Rose Montgomery-Whicher (2002) has written a lovely, wise essay on how her engagement with drawing involves a visually embodied attentiveness to the world and seeing things anew. Drawing – or sketching – becomes a corporeal, relational, temporal and spatial activity that also works as a tool for renewing her wonder of places, things and people. When taking a picture of her sister on a bench in the park in front of a wall of yellow roses, Montgomery-Whicher (2002, p. 43) describes the experience of seizing her in the moment: 'I've caught you'. Drawing her sister on a long train ride is a very different experience. Drawing makes Rose wonder how her sister came to be, who she is, what she thinks. It is an experience of letting the embodied mind ask a lingering metaphysical question: 'Is this you?'

The snapshot and the drawing contrast the difference between attending to ideas as reified objects and as responsive-dialogical interactions. It also reminds us that the primary Mysteries of organization are not products or artifacts or services. The primary Mysteries, the ones that should evoke our continued wonder, are irreducibly unique and never must be closed by dogma or reification, are our colleagues, peers, leaders and followers, providers and beneficiaries: the Mysteries of the Other.

NOTES

1. From idea (n.d.), *Collins English Dictionary -- Complete and Unabridged* (10th edition), available at: http://dictionary.reference.com/browse/idea; accessed 25 January 2011: 1. any content of the mind, esp. the conscious mind; 2. the thought of something: *the very idea appals me*; 3. a mental representation of something: *she's got a good idea of the layout of the factory*; 4. the characterization of something in general terms; concept: *the idea of a square circle is self-contradictory*; 5. an individual's conception of something: *his idea*

of *honesty is not the same as yours and mine*; 6. the belief that something is the case: *he has the idea that what he's doing is right*; 7. a scheme, intention, plan, etc: *here's my idea for the sales campaign*; 8. a vague notion or indication; inkling: *he had no idea of what life would be like in Africa*; 9. significance or purpose: *the idea of the game is to discover the murderer*; 10. philosophy: a. a private mental object, regarded as the immediate object of thought or perception, b. a platonic idea or form; 11. music: a thematic phrase or figure; motif; 12. obsolete: a mental image.

2. The idea of ideas as objects is a stubborn one that seems impossible to completely escape, so there are many examples of ontological oscillation even in this text. Borrowings from the conceptual terrain of evolutionary theory when talking about creativity exemplify the pervasiveness of the problem. It is a language of implied objects undergoing processes of variation, selection and retention (see Ford, 2009). Koestler ([1964] 1989, p. 226) gave an early remark on why the analogy has limits: 'The branching of the evolutionist's tree of life is a one-way process; giraffes and whales do not bisociate to give rise to a new synthesis. The evolution of ideas on the other hand, is a tale of ever-repeated differentiation, specialization and reintegrations on a higher level; a progression from primordial unity through variety to more complex patterns of unity-in-variety'.

3. It is interesting to note that this understanding of new ideas or imaginations as felt, all-at-once flashes of holistic insights, has parallels in the work of several philosophers. Merleau-Ponty ([1962] 2002) emphasized that imagination is partly pre-reflective and embodied and that new ideas present themselves as a 'felt sense of rightness'. Peirce suggested that all decisive leaps of imagination – what he famously called abduction – are associated with a 'single feeling of greater intensity', the same emotion as when an orchestra plays well (Peirce, 1931–58, p. 2.643). Polanyi's ([1966] 2009) theorizing of tacit knowing speaks of attending from proximal particulars to a distal coherent whole, this coherent whole being an embodied skill or discovery whose particulars remain in subsidiary awareness during the act of knowing. And Langer (1967) presents a theory of mind as feelings of form that cross a threshold of awareness to become conscious ideas. 'Feeling', she says, 'is a verbal noun . . . To feel is to do something, not to have something' (p. 20). Moreover, 'the phenomenon usually described as "a feeling" is really that an organism feels something, that is, something is felt. What is felt is a process, perhaps a large complex of processes, within the organism. Some vital activities of great complexity and high intensity, usually (perhaps always) involving nervous tissue, are felt; being felt is a phase of the process itself' (p. 21).

4. According to Johnson (2007) an idea or meaning 'arises through embodied organism–environment interactions in which significant patterns are marked within the flow of experience' (p. 273). 'Meaning', he continues, 'emerges as we engage the pervasive qualities of situations and note distinctions that make sense to our experience and carry it forward' (ibid.). There is no telling how material bodily 'organism–environment interactions' become meaningful mental 'experiences' or a 'flow of experience'. The mystery lies in the word 'emerges', which holds the place for a process that has not been and cannot be fully described.

REFERENCES

Aquinas ([1265–74] 1993), *A Shorter Summa: The Essential Philosophical Passages of St. Thomas Aquinas' Summa Theologica* (ed. Peter Kreeft), San Francisco: Ignatius Press.

Aristotle ([*circa* 350 BC] 2002), *Metaphysics* (trans. Joe Sachs), Santa Fe, NM: Green Lion Press.

Campbell, D.T. (1997), 'The experimenting society', in W. Dunn (ed.), *The Experimenting Society: Essays in Honor of Donald T. Campbell*, New Brunswick, NJ: Transaction Press.

Carlsen, A. and T. Pitsis (2008), 'Projects for life. Building narrative capital for positive organizational change', in S.R. Clegg and C.L. Cooper (eds), *Handbook of Macro Organization Behavior*, London: Sage, pp.456–77.

Carlsen, A. and L.E. Sandelands (2012), 'First passion: towards a theory of wonder in organizational inquiry', paper under editorial review.

Carlsen, A., S.R. Clegg and R. Gjersvik (2012), *Idea Work: Lessons of the Extraordinary in Everyday Creativity*, Oslo/London: Cappelen Damm/Palgrave.

Carlsen, A., T. Mortensen and R. Gjersvik (2008), 'Against all odds? Remembered imaginings and enriched identities in hydrocarbon exploration', paper presented at the Academy of Management meeting in Anaheim.

Carlsen, A., G. Rudningen and T. Mortensen (2011), 'Playing the cards. On the aesthetics of making research co-generative', paper presented at the Third International Process Symposium in Corfu, 16–18 June.

Coldevin, G.H., A. Carlsen, S. Clegg, E. Antonacopoulou and T. Pitsis (2011), 'Idea work in organizations', paper under editorial review.

Cooper, R.G. (1993), *Winning at New Products: Accelerating the Process from Idea to Launch* (2nd edition), Cambridge, MA: Addison-Wesley.

Dewey, J. ([1925] 1958), *Experience and Nature* (2nd edition), New York: Dover.

Dewey, J. ([1934] 1980), *Art as Experience*, New York: Perigee Books.

Dutton, J.E. and A. Carlsen (2011), 'Seeing, feeling, daring, interrelating and playing: exploring themes in generative moments', in A. Carlsen and J.E. Dutton (eds), *Research Alive. Exploring Generative Moments in Doing Qualitative Research*, Copenhagen: Copenhagen Business School Press, pp.214–35.

Ewenstein, B. and J. Whyte (2007), 'Beyond words: aesthetic knowledge and knowing in organizations', *Organization Studies*, **28**(5), 689–708.

Fisher, P. (1998), *Wonder, the Rainbow, and the Aesthetics of Rare Experiences*, Cambridge, MA: Harvard University Press.

Ford, C. (2009), 'Prototyping processes that affect organizational creativity', in R. Tudor, M.A. Runco and S. Moger (eds), *The Routledge Companion to Creativity*, London: Routledge.

Hargadon, A. (2003), *How Breakthroughs Happen*, Cambridge, MA: Harvard Business School Press.

Hargadon, A.B. and B.A. Bechky (2006), 'When collections of creatives become creative collectives: a field study of problem solving at work', *Organization Science*, **17**(4), 484–500.

Heidegger, M. ([1926] 1962), *Being and Time*, Oxford: Blackwell Publishing.

Heidegger, M. ([1937–38] 1994), *Basic Questions of Philosophy*, R. Rojcewicz and A. Schuwer (trans.), Bloomington, IN: Indiana University Press.

Hernes, T. and S. Maitlis (eds) (2010), *Process, Sensemaking and Organizing*, New York: Oxford University Press.

James, W. ([1890] 1950), *Principles of Psychology*, New York: Dover.

James, W. ([1907] 1977), 'What pragmatism means', in J.J. McDermott (ed.), *The Writings of William James, A Comprehensive Edition*, Chicago: University of Chicago Press, pp.376–90.

Johnson, M. (2007), *The Meaning of the Body. Aesthetics of Human Understanding*, Chicago: Chicago University Press.

Keats, J. ([1817] 2002), 'To George and Tom Keats', 21, 27 December 1817, in R. Gittings (ed.), *John Keats, Selected Letters*, Oxford: Oxford University Press.

Koestler, A. ([1964] 1989), *The Act of Creation*, London: Penguin.

Langer, S. (1967), *Mind: An Essay on Human Feeling, Volume 1*, Baltimore, MD: Johns Hopkins University Press.

Merleau-Ponty, M. ([1962] 2002), *Phenomenology of Perception*, New York: Humanities Press.

Montgomery-Whicher, R. (2002), 'Drawing to attention', in M. van Manen (ed.), *Writing in the Dark*, Ontario: Althouse, pp.27–47.

Mortensen, T. (2013), 'Unplugged creativity', doctoral dissertation in preparation for defence at the University of Oslo, Department of Psychology.

Mortensen, T., A. Carlsen and R. Gjersvik (2007), 'Unplugged: dialogue objects and imaginative space in exploration creativity', paper presented at the 23rd EGOS Colloquium, 5–7 July, Vienna.

Nussbaum, M. (2001), *Upheavals of Thought: The Intelligence of Emotions*, Cambridge: Cambridge University Press.

Parsons, H.L. (1969), 'A philosophy of wonder', *Philosophy and Phenomenological Research*, **30**(1), 84–101.

Peirce, C.S. ([1878] 1958), 'How to make our ideas clear', in P. Wiener (ed.), *Charles S. Peirce: Selected Writings*, Toronto: Dover, pp. 113–41.

Peirce, C.S. (1931–58), in C. Hartshorne, P. Weiss and A. Burks (eds), *Collected Papers of Charles Sanders Peirce, Volumes 1–8*, Boston, MA: Cambridge University Press.

Polanyi, M. ([1966] 2009), *The Tacit Dimension*, Chicago: University of Chicago Press.

Rubinstein, M. (2008), *Strange Wonder, The Closure of Metaphysics and the Opening of Awe*, New York: Columbia University Press.

Sandelands, L.E. (2003), *Thinking About Social Life*, Lanham, MD: University Press of America.

Sandelands, L.E. and A. Carlsen (2012), 'The romance of wonder in organization studies', paper under editorial review.

Sawyer, R.K. (2006), *Explaining Creativity: The Science of Human Innovation*, New York: Oxford University Press.

Shotter, J. (2006), 'Understanding process from within: an argument for "withness"-thinking', *Organization Studies*, **27**(4), 585–604.

Shotter, J. (2007), 'Not to forget Tom Andersen's way of being Tom Andersen: the importance of what "just happens" to us', *Human Systems: The Journal of Systemic Consultation and Management*, **18**, 15–28.

Simonton, D.K. (2004), *Creativity in Science: Chance, Logic, Genius, and Zeitgeist*, Cambridge: Cambridge University Press.

Weick, K.E. (2005), 'Organizing and failures of imagination', *International Public Management Journal*, **8**(3), 425–38.

Weick, K.E. (2006), 'The role of imagination in the organizing of knowledge', *European Journal of Information Systems*, **15**(5), 446–52.

Weick, K.E. (2010), 'The poetics of process: theorizing the ineffable in organization studies', in T. Hernes and S. Maitlis (eds), *Process, Sensemaking and Organizing*, New York: Oxford University Press, pp. 102–11.

10 Fleshing out everyday innovation: phronesis and improvisation in knowledge work
Erlend Dehlin

INTRODUCTION

Knowledge work can be seen as a process of improvisation, where knowledge is conceived spontaneously in the emerging context of complex practices. Technical rationality represents a kind of closed thinking-before-action, which conceptually opposes the fundamental openness of knowledge creation and innovation.

Seeking to 'flesh out' innovation in everyday knowledge work, this chapter studies, and questions, such either–or distinction between technical rationality and improvisation. From a practice perspective on knowledge it is argued that even if they are conceptually antagonistic, improvisation and technical rationality can be mutually constitutive in the everyday flow of practical knowing and innovation. This may come about as improvised knowledge work makes innovative use of technical rationality through the contextual utilization of tools such as management models, structures and systems to ensure *phronesis* and *workability*. On the normative side I suggest that innovation can be achieved by pursuing, and improving, improvising as a means to act sensibly in the emerging context of which oneself is the co-author. The source of effectiveness and good practice lies in the spontaneously constructed here-and-now, which continuously conveys social and physical elements determining what is workable and not. As a consequence, management models should not be seen as technical-rational restraint jackets, but as tools of improvisation to be used with caution.

IMPROVISING OR MANAGING KNOWLEDGE WORK?

This chapter pursues a crude understanding of innovation as creativity, as associated with the abductive power of human beings to conceive new meaning and create novelty (Wenger, 2004). An equally generic understanding of knowledge work is used, representing any form of work practice where complexity, turbulence and change typically overshadow the mere technical appliance of procedures and routines (Newell et al., 2002). I am deeply critical of a strong division between knowledge work being theoretical and abstract as opposed to practical and concrete. Rather, I assume all knowledge work to be practical, only that it varies in terms of theoretical scope within work branches, occupations, and even within a single work day for some practitioners. For something to become knowledge work, I simply hold that it should be more characterized by mindfulness than mindlessness; of attentiveness and intellectual concentration rather than lassitude and automatic behaviour. But even this is a difficult and overly crude demarcation line to draw.

Brought into the domain of organizational theorists and managers, an immediate question concerns which is the best model for managing innovation and to ensure its flourishing in knowledge work. Does such a model even exist, or do innovative processes emerge from the categorical dismissal of plans and models? Such questions form the basis for my discussions in this chapter, which are structured around the two concepts of improvisation and technical rationality (TR) – concepts that are often seen as dichotomous and mutually exclusive.

Whereas improvisation entails thinking *in* action, TR involves planning first, creating a model for action, and *then* going to action. According to Crossan and Sorrenti (1997), Ciborra (1999) and Alterhaug (2004) some speak of improvisation as a form of inferior action that occurs when planning breaks down, indicating that improvisation is action without preparation or plan. Improvisation is something one should not pursue voluntarily, but a sort of emergency action that skilled and dedicated practitioners shun to the greatest extent possible. As opposed to such focus on the reactive dimension, others speak of improvisation as a more proactive and exceptional art form, involving either pure forms of spontaneity, creativity or both (e.g., Crossan and Sorrenti, 1997; Hatch, 1997, 1999; Weick, 1998, 2001; Zack, 2000). Both the reactive and the proactive approaches seem to portray improvisation and planning as *unrelated* phenomena; that is, there can be *either* planning *or* improvisation, but not both at the same time.

I want to challenge such an either–or logic on the epistemological premise that theory is submissive to practice (Feldman and Orlikowski, 2011). I suggest a view on improvisation that is less concerned with the black-and-white reasoning of theoretical conceptualization, and more in line with the emergent nuances of grey in everyday knowledge work. The main argument is that if improvisation is understood as *spontaneous and hermeneutical sense-making via external action* (Dehlin, 2008), knowledge work can be seen as a process of improvisation in which innovation plays a crucial part. In other words, I offer a theoretical view on knowledge work where improvisation and technical rationality are *not* separate traits, but where improvisation is a cornerstone of all knowledge work, and which in practice might *involve* technical rationality.

WHAT IS TECHNICAL RATIONALITY?

Donald Schön (1987, 1991) conceptualizes technical rationality (TR) as a rule-bound form of action that strictly follows an administrative model or procedure, which many will say is the main characteristic of modern management thinking. Three aspects of TR deserve special attention. First, by the word technical, a form of instrumentality is indicated – a means to achieve a certain end. Second, the end is defined by those means applied to achieve it. The means and the end form an internal bond, which makes the pathway from thought to action *linear*. Third, 'technical' is an adjective used to delimit the more general concept of 'rationality'. This specific and technical form of rationality has greatly informed the way we have come to think about organizations in general, and knowledge work in particular (Styhre, 2003). TR has transcended its epistemic position as one form of rationality out of many, through a transition from concept to paradigm. Such paradigmatic TR can be traced back to the early classics such as the work of Henri Fayol (Urwick, 1934), where the ambition is to create a universal management model from which efficient practice can be effectuated. Since the time of Fayol, TR has succeeded in comprising a language that stretches beyond social, historical and cultural boundaries. The emphasis on ideal conditions of stability and structure and on plan(ning) before execution (thinking before acting), has formed the essence of more recent management thinking that focuses on 'decision-making' (e.g., Simon, 1968; Cyert and March, 1992) and 'control' (e.g., Ouchi, 1979, 1980; Eisenhardt, 1985), and 35 years after the first publication of *Organizations*, James March and Herbert Simon (1993) still argue that its technical-rational assumptions persist, and have not been challenged significantly until the early 1990s.

Donald Schön (1987) claims that TR has become the dominant epistemology in thinking about professions and institutions. From this dominant position in the social sciences, Schön (1991) argues that TR is to blame for an overemphasis on rule-bound forms of organizing where action is supposed to follow strictly from some management model or procedure. Another leading figure in the organizational literature, Edgar Schein (1996, p. 232) argues that what has been missing is:

the anchoring of our concepts in observed reality . . . We have gone too quickly to formal elegant abstractions that seemingly could be operationally defined and measured, i.e., centralization–decentralization, differentiation–integration, power, etc., and failed to link these to observed reality. I say 'seemingly' because in the effort to define such concepts, we often relied on further abstractions, i.e., questionnaire responses, and began to treat the abstractions as the reality. Not only does this create fuzzy theory and research that is made significant only by massaging the data statistically, but the results are often useless to the practitioner.

As indicated by Schön and Schein the ideas of TR have been taken so far so as to be taken for granted and reified into a (management) paradigm of their own (Berger and Luckmann, 1991). In that regard my interest concerns how well the technical-rational model is suited for understanding authentic knowledge work? Whilst the conceptual nature of TR makes it interesting and useful as one model out of many, the practice of knowledge work is more fluid, emergent and complex to be encapsulated by a single model. Thus, to make room for an epistemology of innovation that is as close to practice as possible, I propose to de-reify, not eliminate, TR as a generic model of knowledge management. As the world of practice tends to soften conceptual distinctions, I suggest being less hung up on theory, and more concerned with practice. On a conceptual level a separation between TR and improvisation is useful, but what if in the practical unfolding of knowledge work the two can exist simultaneously and even in harmony? What would the implications be?

PROCESS THINKING AND INNOVATIVE KNOWLEDGE WORK

As noted by Newell et al. (2002) knowledge work tends to refer to practices concerned with theoretical knowledge, something that encourages a skewed image of knowledge workers as human calculators or philosophers. But knowledge work is more than pure abstraction. In my generic understanding of knowledge work it emerges as a complex practice, with concrete and irreversible features. Innovation can thus be seen as a processual characteristic anchored in, and flowing from, that practice. Knowledge work takes place on the inside *and* the outside of individuals, and it evolves as a reflexive process of producing objectives and solving problems, some more vague and ambiguous than others.

From a practice perspective, knowledge work is an *emergent* phenomenon (Mead, 1967), something that implies a change of attention from 'a sociology of nouns towards a sociology of verbs' (Chia, 1996). Shifting the focus from the temporary objects of consciousness to the narrative process that produces them, opens up a rich source of knowledge (Tsoukas and Hatch, 2001). For example, pursuing a quest for the perfect innovation model will always be a somewhat outdated project, as reality has already moved on (Weisbord, 1988). Thus, in the following, knowledge as a noun will be de-emphasized, benefiting the concept of *knowing* as practice, as process.

Process thinking is not abstract, but concrete, as it focuses on authentic ongoing practice: on people meeting and communicating on both a conscious and unconscious level as they are brought together in processes of joint sense-making (Mead, 1967; Blumer, 1969; Lave and Wenger, 1991; Weick, 1995, 2001; Wenger, 2004). They arrive at these processes with certain intentions for the future that are simultaneously influencing and being influenced by everyday actions (Stacey et al., 2000; Stacey, 2001). And if everyday organizational life is a matter of emergence (Mead, 1967), of continuous microscopic change (Tsoukas and Chia, 2002), knowledge work will always differ with context (Purser and Petranker, 2005). Sometimes it will involve planning and routine behaviour; other times calculation and implementation of models; and yet other times it will presuppose genuine spontaneous action and risk-taking behaviour with little anticipation or preparation. All knowledge work is innovative in some respect. It is unavoidable. Thus, as improvisation is defined as sense-making activities targeted at the external sphere (social or not), *knowledge work can be seen as a process of improvisation.*

KNOWLEDGE WORK AS IMPROVISATION

In an extensive review of the field of organizational improvisation Kamoche et al. (2002) hold that a functional concept of improvisation should stretch further than solely serving as a metaphor for phenomena such as jazz improvisation. Indeed, improvisation can be ascribed much more general, and even mundane, characteristics. Cemented in the everyday mash of spontaneity, creativity, emotionality, irreversibility and sociality, improvisation can be defined as *spontaneous and hermeneutical sense-making via external action* (Dehlin, 2008). Implicitly this is a way of focusing on the bond between corporality and contextuality, and on how creativity emerges hermeneutically through these. Improvisation in this view glues itself to all practical situations, even to some extent to routine-like conditions.

Understanding the quality of improvisation in everyday knowledge work presumes taking an interest in the ongoing corporeal and social merger of spontaneity and creativity from which knowledge work emerges. For sure, spontaneity is held to be an important constituent of improvisation by many authors in the organizational field (e.g., Miner et al., 1996; Crossan and Sorrenti, 1997; Hatch, 1997). What has been given little attention, however, is the point that spontaneity can be viewed from different angles. It can, for example, be linked to the notion that each situation in everyday life is somewhat unique, making the human body inevitably *situated* (Gadamer, 1975; Joas, 1993), which again implies a continual spontaneous freshness. Spontaneity, here, emerges through an unbreakable tie between a living body and a present-in-the-becoming (Bergson, 1944; James, 2007). Spontaneity is not an occasional or rare event, but an inextricable feature of corporality: having, or indeed being, a body of bones, flesh and blood (and emotions), presumes spontaneity in one way or the other. Spontaneity is tied to existence as emotion to rationality and body to soul. Spontaneity *is* embodied contextuality.

A second angle can be associated with the contrasting of spontaneity with abstraction – the ability to project scenarios upon an imagined past, present or future and to think logically, a-contextually and metaphysically. In order to think and act spontaneously one needs to go the opposite way of abstracting *from* the present. Spontaneous thinking in this sense is about 'improspection' (Dehlin, 2008), and involves thinking *in* the present *on* the present (Crites, 1971; Purser and Petranker, 2005).

In line with the first angle, the inside of corporality is always burdened with a physical (and social) outside, something that makes spontaneity and difference expected features of knowledge work no matter how abstract the nature of the practitioner's thinking is in a given moment. In line with the second angle, however, the manager is in a given situation *more or less* spontaneous, and when his or her thinking is sufficiently directed at the present it can be qualitatively measured as spontaneous rather than abstract. The practical unfolding of knowledge work can thus be understood through four different modalities of knowing: improspection, prospection, retrospection and abstraspection: whenever the practitioner acts (noticeably) spontaneously, he or she addresses and acts upon what is becoming in the here and now (improspection) more than upon something in the near or distant future (prospection) or past (retrospection), or solely in abstract terms as in the case of formal science (abstraspection). The shorter the perceived interval between cognition and external action, the more spontaneity and improspection stands out; and vice versa, the more thoughts wander into abstractness the less spontaneous any succeeding action (Miner et al., 1996). Unlike Miner et al., however, the intention here is not to measure linear time-lags in quantitative terms. The 'degree' of spontaneity is rather seen as a qualitative and contextual assessment.

In the words of Ciborra (1999): 'improvisation defies measurement and method. It surfaces and vanishes "on the spur of the moment"' (p. 86).

In part, improvisation is subjected to the same logic as spontaneity: the less spontaneous knowledge work is, the less improvisatory it is. Note, however, that there can be no improvisation without the involvement of meaning-making and consciousness (Weick, 2001). Without consciousness one would be reduced to pure spontaneity, to corporality in the animalistic, biological sense (Stacey et al., 2000). This is, for instance, the case with mere 'behaviour' (Nyeng, 2004), which represents a bodily state not delayed by cognition at all. With regard to improvisation, however, the point is that trying to control the body through conscious deliberations potentially creates a delay from thought to action, and the longer the delay the less improvisatory is action.

As corporality is involved in all knowledge work no matter the length of the delay, there is always an element of spontaneity in abstraction, and rather than being categorically separated the two concepts (in practice) emerge together – in shades of grey, as it were. This is in harmony with Ciborra's (1999) argument that improvisation is 'situated performance where thinking and action emerge simultaneously and on the spur of the moment' (p. 78). Philosophically this is a way of saying that knowing is essentially improspective, and is closely related to Purser and Petranker's (2005) term 'deep improvisation'. But it takes more than spontaneity and improspection to label knowing as improvisation; external action is needed, too (Ciborra, 1999). To sum up, improvisation concerns knowing which is more or less spontaneous but never entirely non-spontaneous, as it comes to life as corporeal action inevitably tied to a present in the becoming. Lastly, improvisation concerns the kind of knowing that involves external action, in which case the consequences of that action is physically and socially irreversible (Weick, 1998).

Rather than as an inevitable part of everyday knowing and organizing, improvisation is most often conceptualized in its pure forms, such as in studies of improvisational theatre (Crossan and Sorrenti, 1997), jazz music (Bastien and Hostager, 1988, 1992; Weick, 1989, 1998, 2001; Hatch, 1997; Barrett, 1998; Zack, 2000; Alterhaug, 2004), radical change processes in organizations (Orlikowski, 1996; Orlikowski and Hofman, 1997), radical innovation (Bastien and Hostager, 1988; Cunha and Kamoche, 2001; Kamoche et al., 2002), and projects (Leybourne, 2006). Further, in many studies purity is either associated with spontaneity, creativity or both (for example, Miner et al., 1996; Crossan and Sorrenti, 1997; Hatch, 1997; Moorman and Miner, 1998; Weick, 2001; Kamoche et al., 2002). In these studies the strong focus on purity tends to skew improvisation, discarding less pure forms of spontaneity and creativity as less interesting. Indeed,

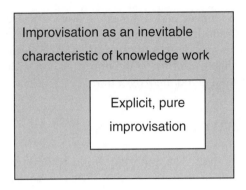

Figure 10.1   Improvising (wo)man

less pure forms are not even considered to be improvisation, thus contributing to the view of improvisation as an either–or phenomenon.

On the contrary, this chapter expands on a practical non-dualistic philosophy where action is per definition creative, and where innovation is persistently measured in terms of context and workability (Dewey, 1929; Joas, 1993, 1996). In the same vein as Ciborra (1999), Petranker (2005) and Purser and Petranker (2005), this inserts improvisation into the core of knowledge work, in contrast to many organizational writers who see improvisation merely as an interesting feature of, say, one particular practice, or as a competence with special value for just a few. Improvisation is more like a *capacity-in-the-becoming* than a competence, as it is an expected feature of everyday human activity that is never repeated exactly the same way. In Strauss's (1993) words: 'Any specific situation in which action takes place will require some if only the smallest adjustment' (p. 194).

The knowledge worker is more like an 'improvising man (or woman)' (see Figure 10.1), than an administrative or economic man. In the everyday and mundane trot of knowledge managers improvisation is a feature of normality, not of rareness. Knowledge work can only come to life as process – as practical knowing performed by spontaneous innovators – and it is hard to see why managing such processes would be any less improvisatory. Even if the practice of knowledge workers varies immensely with respect to theoretical scope, their corporeal origin deems them as improvisers more than calculating machines.

In any given situation a knowledge worker is more or less spontaneous and more or less innovative. By the latter it is indicated that different situations are characterized by different *forms* of creativity, some more genuine, non-technical and in that sense demanding than others. The idea is simple: the less familiar and technical creative processes are, the more genuine they are, and the more genuine creativity is mixed with genuine spontaneity, the purer becomes improvisation. The reason for emphasizing this is to be able to contrast 'pure' improvisation with two other concepts: 'everyday' and 'good' improvisation.

IMPROVISATION AND TOOLS

Weick (2001) says that: 'The important point is that improvisation does not materialize out of thin air' (p. 290). Thus, if you are to improvise you need 'tools', which can be translated as any means or instruments to accomplish certain ends (Dewey, 1929; Schön, 1991). Dewey (1929, pp. 184–6) sees *language* as the most fundamental tool of all, and all tools essentially as tools of language:

> Language is always a form of action and in its instrumental use is always a means of concerted action for an end, while at the same time it finds in itself all the goods of its possible consequences . . . The invention and use of tools have played a large part in consolidating meanings, because a tool is a thing used as means to consequences, instead of being taken directly and physically . . . As to be a tool, or to be used as a means for consequences, is to have and to endow with meaning, language, being the tool of tools, is the cherishing mother of all significance.

Similarly, in the works of Peirce (1966a), Foucault (1981, 1989), Barthes (1991) and Merleau-Ponty (1996) language is seen as a living process of meaning-making in which linguistic signs provide tools (structures) of language. In Mead's (1967) terms 'there neither can be nor could have been any mind or thought without language' (p. 192) and language, the content of mind 'is only a development and product of social interaction' (p. 191). Tools form the fundament for the expression of meaning, and it is the *function* of tools that is accentuated. Tools represent the images or symbols in memory that become part of and define context as they are perpetually *put to use* by knowledge workers. Following Peirce (1966b) tools provide the basis for meaning (both subjective and intersubjective) through 'sufficient similarity'. Thus, the tool does not stand alone; it can only be spoken of as it appears to the individual mind (Blumer, 1969). Any tool is infused with meaning (Joas, 1993), and meaning can only be defined from the practical application of tools, that is, something *is* not meaningful; something *works as* meaningful.

The improvisatory practice of knowledge workers is *nothing but* the intelligent employment and utilization of tools. The nature of improvisation, however, is restricted by the way tools are perceived by practitioners in situ. If they, for instance, are seen as control instruments, the degree of openness in improvisation may be low and action will become more technical-rational. If they are seen as creative points of departure, as more or less usable instruments, improvisation is likely to appear more explicitly.

TECHNICAL RATIONALITY – A TOOL OF IMPROVISATION

According to Schön (1991) the essence of technical rationality (TR) is to create a model for action first, and apply this model on a real-world problem afterwards. Schön's discussion is, however, to a large extent on a philosophical level, and he warns against taking TR for granted as a *societal paradigm*, in which case TR would be reified. A most vivid example would be naive positivism, where language, as opposed to Dewey's (1929) conception, is considered autonomous and ontologically objective.

Conceptually, TR involves disregarding the present from an intention to follow abstract idioms. When these idioms are put into practice, TR reflects an intention of non-spontaneity and non-contextuality. It involves first addressing a (e.g., management) model, and then seeking to apply this model onto the practical world (Schön, 1991). With regard to innovation, TR involves a specific type of *prospection* via *abstraspection* succeeded by *action*, rather than free and open imagination. TR, then, involves the restrictive intention of non-spontaneous prospection that is closed and analytical as opposed to open-ended and imaginative, and when put into action the analytical model controls succeeding action (Schön, 1987, 1991). To the extent that such restrictions are actually pursued, action becomes technical-rational (see Figure 10.2). In principle, TR implies that innovation models work as restricting tools, which are *obeyed* and *followed* a-contextually rather than used creatively and spontaneously.

In the most vivid cases of TR, practitioners display compulsory model-following behaviour, where the *intention* is not to *use* rules and models as tools to create something new, but to *follow* them for the sake of re-producing identical outcomes. This approach involves the pursuit of technical-rational ideals to such extent that models are taken for granted and followed *blindly*, in which case the room for improvisation is marginalized.

It is indeed possible to conclude that improvisation and technical rationality are antagonists, but *this is only true on a conceptual and abstract level*. Conceptually, the technical-rational terms 'abstract' and 'follow'

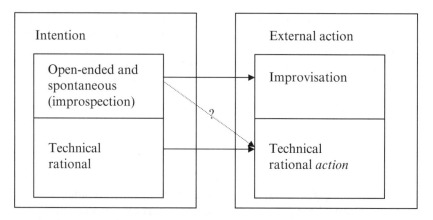

Figure 10.2   A conceptual model of technical rationality

can in the improvisational vocabulary be replaced by 'context', 'create' and 'use'. However implicitly, this creates an interesting opening for *aligning* improvisation and TR. Non-dualistic process thinking collapses the separation between the conceptual and the practical. It gives precedence to practice, and positions concepts merely as tools (Dewey, 1929), including the concept of TR. On a practical level, then, the conceptual difference between improvisation and TR is potentially misleading and false. If practice has precedence, and it emerges as improvisation, context comes first, deeming concepts as temporal and lifeless abstractions (tools) (Ciborra, 1996). This is indicated by the dotted arrow in Figure 10.2; in practice improvisation may collapse the dichotomy between follow and use, as 'use' in a given situation may stand for 'temporarily following'.

No matter how they are perceived in practice, all models are nouns, and as such they are temporal objects in processes of knowing. This coincides with Hatch's (1999) argument that structures are temporal, ambiguous and emotional, Pentland and Rueter (1994) and Feldman's (2000) notes on routines as grammar, and Ciborra's (1999) notes on plans, rules and routines as lifeless objects that must be breathed into practical life. For instance, no particular structure is technical-rational per se, rather TR concerns *a particular manner in which to perceive and make use of structures*. As a result, structures must be chosen anew again and again and adapted intelligently to emerging contexts: they must be *made* to work (Orlikowski, 1996; Orlikowski and Hofman, 1997; Ciborra, 1999; Tsoukas and Chia, 2002). To make knowledge work effective, situations may occur where the practitioner improvises on technical-rational structures. Effective knowledge work is inevitably innovative. It is improvisation.

The dualism of TR and improvisation is merely a linguistic construct. In practice, the question is *how* dualisms are perceived – as tools or as ontological objective entities. For knowledge workers the question is perhaps not so much about TR or not, but about *one's relationship* to TR: is it a *dominant, taken for granted, model for action* or a *tool of improvisation*? Is the model for innovation a restraint jacket to be followed blindly, or an instrument to be used with pragmatic caution?

KNOWLEDGE WORKABILITY – SOME IMPLICATIONS

In knowledge work there is a tight connection between improvisation, workability and perspective. Workability is ensured in the shape of renewed technical measures based on improvisatory evaluations; it is a matter of improvisation. For example, as real life problems in practice may be at odds with established regulations, knowledge managers seek to create new structure and new routines that will fit the new context. For instance, whereas bureaucratic equality and predictability are examples of a-contextual ideals, and constitute the building blocks of bureaucracy for precisely that reason (Weber, 2002), it follows that bureaucracy as a technical-rational system can only vouch for those instances covered by its systemic nature (Schön, 1991). The bureaucracy, and any system for that matter, can only handle what it is defined to handle. In terms of predictability this is functional; it is much like knowing something about the future; having something to trust and take for granted. But *the upside of system is also a possible downside* to the extent that unexpected incidents occur.

Second, workability is a matter of perspective. Taking systemic action might be contextually the right thing to do from the manager's perspective, and might indeed prove to work in line with these considerations. From an employee's perspective, however, the action taken might be perceived as contextually *insensitive*. Some degree of budget control and centralization might be right in one respect, but also be seen as interfering negatively with everyday operations in another. Which is right and which is wrong? Perspective itself is an ongoing and contextual measure (Mead, 1967), something that subdues (technical) workability to improvisation. Thus, some balance between perspectives needs to be negotiated in situ – not as a static one-time decision, but as a living process of determining what is good and functional. In situations of conflict, context sensitivity seems to work both ways, just as shared understanding is not *only* a management concern, but a concern of all those involved in (joint) knowledge work.

Knowledge work is not a question of *either* improvisation *or* technical rationality, but of how different forms of technical rationality are perceived and utilized – as something temporary or as something solid. In a subtle way this contradicts Mintzberg (1973), who says that a plan *in itself* should be adaptive, and that managers should have a collection of alternative plans in decision-tree form, something that resembles Weick's (2001) and Thompson's (2005) view that some structures are more open to creative elaboration than others. Flexibility, however, does not come from within the model alone, or from a number of models, but from the *perception and appliance of* models. Flexibility is found in *the way* models are contextually translated into action. This observation resembles Kotter (1986) and Ciborra (1999), who claim that plans should be *seen and treated as* flexible and context-sensitive tools. Implicitly this suggests the normative message that planning should not be exaggerated; practitioners should plan as far ahead as possible, but *not too far* into ideal futures.

As a verb TR does not exist in 100 per cent pure form. TR in practice, however skilfully, can never fulfil the requirements set by its conceptual ideal. Only as a noun (concept) is TR perfect, but as nouns are temporary and lifeless, this perfection can never be fulfilled in practice. Thus, knowledge work is not so much a matter of *either* improvisation *or* TR, but of how improvisation can make use of TR in specific settings to ensure practical workability and innovation. On the most profound level, everyday knowledge work is improvisation and innovation, not TR. Everyday innovation is essentially a task of defining what is going on in the present and improvising the means to move onwards:

> We would suggest, if anything, a 'small' Copernican revolution: improvisation is fundamental, while structured methods and procedures possess a derived and de-rooted character. A formalized procedure embeds a set of explicit in-order-tos, but the way these are actually interpreted and put to work strictly depends upon the actor's in-order-tos and because-of motives, his/her way of being in the world 'next' to the procedure, the rule or the plan . . . Procedure and method are just 'dead objects': they get situated in the flow of organizational life only thanks to a mélange of human motives and actions. (Ciborra, 1999, pp. 85–6)

TECHNICAL-RATIONAL DOMINANCE AND *NON*-WORKABILITY

TR works better in some instances than in others, and workability is a matter of perspective. Systemic behaviour works well in those contexts where the degree of unpredictability and complexity is low, but elsewhere the complexity of real life context will continually outdate it and make it invalid – even dangerous. It is senseless to clutch on to a fancy management model, which produces a certain output when practical needs never stay the same. There is no single management model that can ensure innovation in all settings. Problems of emergent contextuality are more or less inevitable, as models can never keep up with the flow of everyday events. And this is perhaps not so much a problem of the model or of TR, as a problem with the nature of everyday life. If, however, TR is categorically clutched onto irrespective of the actual surroundings, serious problems may arise.

Whenever TR is taken for granted, it can form a compulsory way of thinking and acting. Creating an inauthentic base from which to act, reification forms a blindness that undermines practical wisdom. Anyone might experience drifting out of the moment and wandering into abstract landscapes, and this merely points to the challenges of maintaining a context-sensitive gaze and improvising (Petranker, 2005). Blind TR, however, is more than drifting away from context; it is systematically forgetting and neglecting context *and from that stance* to act. The message to the practitioner is to always stay attentive to how ingrained TR has become in daily operations.

In Aristotelian terms, a reification of TR can be seen as a blind pursuit of 'techne' (technical expertise) or as an overstated passion for 'sophia' (theoretical knowledge) (Russell, 1995). Going against the stereotypical image of knowledge work as consumed with techne or sophia, however, a more authentic turn could be to unify sophia and techne in a practical ideal of 'phronesis' (practical wisdom). An overweight of sophia or techne is a threat to phronesis. For example, the prevalence of management directives, quantitative measurements, incentives to improve efficiency, top-down control, administrative structures, system implementations and reforms, can form a systemic contextuality for knowledge workers, and as they enact upcoming situations they are 'encouraged' to interpret reality through system lenses. Not to take seriously technical-rational demands might not be a viable option, and as systemic pressure increases, translating systemic demands into phronesis via improvisation becomes more of a challenge. When 'the system' weighs heavily on the knowledge worker's shoulders, the pressure increases of seeing the system in context and subjecting it to practical validation. Increased systemic pressure does not make the practical *how* less complex, but it can make it harder to grasp. In a sense, then, the very concept of phronesis serves as a reminder of why the mainstream view of knowledge work as concerned with theoretical or technical knowledge needs to be balanced with contextual and practical considerations. An understanding of knowledge work as 'good improvisation' might be a step in the right direction.

PURSUING INNOVATIVE KNOWLEDGE WORK THROUGH 'GOOD IMPROVISATION'

It seems reasonable to claim that artistic and innovative improvisation as in the case of idea-storming processes and humour, is epistemically different from emergency action or any form of immediate improvisatory reaction. As a consequence I suggest a division between *positive* and *negative* improvisation, implying that improvisation in knowledge work varies between the more voluntarily chosen action (positive) and the more forced upon *re*action (negative). Hypothetically, one could disregard the often urgent complexity of real life and care little about innovation (Petranker, 2005), in which case there would be no active or conscious intention to improvise. In the case of positive improvisation, however, there can be identified a conscious positive knowledge-attitude guiding spontaneous action, and likewise, in negative improvisation an externally induced urge to innovate.

Also I suggest a separation between 'pure' and 'good' improvisation. For instance, it might be *good* improvisation to employ impure (technical-rational) improvisation, if this is what the knowledge worker perceives to be right and wise, taking the context into consideration. 'Good improvisation' facilitates the theorizing of improvisation as phronesis, as it concerns an innovative challenge linked to how to make technical models *work* in a becoming present. Implicitly this entails a view on phronesis as an improvisational assessment of the present, and implies a fundamental attitude of using physical and mental objects as creative tools rather than as restraint jackets to be followed without question.

Good improvisation only rarely implies breaking contextual parameters and pursuing the unfamiliar and genuine as seen in, say, free jazz (Zack, 2000). This is similar to the views of Crossan and Sorrenti (1997), Ciborra (1999), Petranker (2005) and Purser and Petranker (2005) who regard good improvisation as a process of considering the emerging context at hand and acting accordingly. As implied, this involves less focus on radical innovation and genuine novelty, and more focus on the quality of everyday, improvisatory innovation.

Good improvisation entails intentionally minimizing the delay between thought and action. It means to improspect and get close to the context at hand, not to abstract from it. Practical wisdom in the improvisatory sense is similar to what Purser and Petranker (2005) call 'deep improvisation', which implies thinking and acting *in situ* as opposed to following some kind of rule or ideal blindly. Good improvisation implies performing 'deep improvisation' in practice, and it implies striving for authenticity and spontaneous creativity through improspection. Phronesis can derive

Table 10.1   Good improvisation, authenticity and purity

Proactive/Reactive Intention	Authenticity	Form of Action	Improvisational Purity
Context-sensitivity and improspection,	Authentic	Negative improvisation	Sufficiently pure
i.e., *good* improvisation	Authentic	Positive improvisation	Sufficiently pure
	Authentic	Technical-rational action	Impure
Taken for granted technical rationality	Inauthentic	Blind technical-rational action	Impure

from trial and error, from prior experience, or from immediate reaction, and therefore it is not categorically wise to think before acting, however counterintuitive it may sound.

A subtle message from Table 10.1 is that improvisation in practice is always intended as *good* improvisation; as a way of acting spontaneously and creatively that may ensure practical workability and effectiveness. With reference to Feyerabend (2002) the normative and the descriptive amalgamate in abductive processes, implying that action always presumes *the intention of* action (Skjervheim, 2001). Thought is inevitably guided by a desire, an urge (Dewey, 1929; Feyerabend, 2002), in which case improvisation in practice results from intentions of good improvisation. A second reflection from Table 10.1 is that good improvisation, and thus any form of improvisation, is not always sufficiently pure to be empirically recognized *as* improvisation in practice (positive/negative). For contextual reasons good improvisation can take the form of TR, and when it does, it can be hard to identify it as improvisation *even if it is in fact context-sensitive*. This is why I have chosen to categorize only two forms of improvisation in practice, negative and positive, and to separate these from technical-rational action. Finally, in Table 10.1, 'good' and 'taken for granted' are emphasized, and the point is to show that I see them as antagonists (i.e., Schön 1991). Good improvisation implies *not* taking something for granted. I have therefore separated three forms of authentic and improvisatory action from blind, inauthentic action that flows from taken for granted beliefs.

Improvisation, be it positive or negative, is about creating and applying theories that work in context, which is a fundamentally open process of *abducting* sense. Whereas induction and deduction entail working systematically, abduction concerns the birth of meaning (Dewey, 1929; Peirce, 1966a, 1966b, 1974a, 1974b) within a dialogical self (Mead, 1967).

Abduction entails using tools pragmatically, not following a programme blindly:

> The process (of abduction) itself is not guided by a well defined programme, and cannot be guided by such a programme, for it contains the conditions for the realization of all possible programmes. It is guided rather by a vague urge, by a passion (Kierkegaard). The passion gives rise to specific behaviour which in turn creates the circumstances and the ideas necessary for analysing and explaining the process, for making it rational. (Feyerabend, 2002, p. 17).

Expanding on Feyerabend, the mind works as an open process of defining, of constructing theories and beliefs, not as a closed process of calculation guided by some programme. TR may, however, result from abduction and may at times be very useful in everyday knowledge work. TR is, however, just one of the many possible ways in which to perform innovative knowledge work, not *the* one. In some practical situations management models work and in others they do not, and the process of determining this is contextual and improvisatory.

CONCLUSIONS

Everyday situations in which knowledge workers make sense and act are fluid, emergent and continuously novel, and as a result an improvisatory language provides good tools for grasping the depths of everyday innovation. Knowledge work is more than theoretical abstraction and mindless technological execution. In an improvisatory pursuit of innovation and workability knowledge work involves *defining* problems and *making* spontaneous sense on a perpetual basis. This implies interpreting, interacting with and utilizing ambiguous models, but not following them blindly. Reification of technical-rational formulas, however, implies the substitution of phronesis with sophia and/or techne, in which case there is little room for alternative perspectives to grow and for the continually revalidation of workability.

Seen as nouns all models receive some sort of secondary priority; call it instrumental value, something that reflects the view that mental objects are temporary constructions (Bergson, 1944; Berger and Luckmann, 1991). They are tools and not ends in themselves (Dewey, 1929).

Technical rationality can only come to practical life as a verb, as an improvisatory practice. Thus, innovation in knowledge work is not a matter of either improvisation or technical rationality, but of how the latter can be utilized and breathed into life by the former. And from the perspective of a skilled knowledge worker, a structure is only used and maintained to the extent that it has practical value. An improvisatory view on technical rationality implies that models should not be followed blindly, but used with caution. As a manager one should not shun the use of technical-rational approaches, but keep an open eye even when performing the most simple and pre-planned activity. Innovation has poor conditions under strict technical-rational regimes, but can flourish in a pragmatic milieu of utilizing and contextualizing technical models.

REFERENCES

Alterhaug, B. (2004), 'Improvisation on a triple theme: creativity, jazz improvisation and communication', *Studia Musicologica Norvegica,Universitetsforlaget*, **30**, 97–118.

Barrett, F. (1998), 'Creativity and improvisation in jazz and organizations: implications for organizational learning', *Organization Science*, **9**(5), 605–22.

Barthes, R. (1991), *Mytologier* (*Mythologies*), Oslo: Gyldendal.

Bastien, D.T. and T.J. Hostager (1988), 'Jazz as a process of organizational innovation', *Communication Research*, **15**(5), 558–60.

Bastien, D.T. and T.J. Hostager (1992), 'Cooperation as communicative accomplishment: a symbolic interaction analysis of an improvised jazz concert', *Communication Studies*, **43**(2), 92–104.

Berger, P. and T. Luckmann (1991), *The Social Construction of Reality: A Treatise in the Sociology of Knowledge*, London: Penguin Books.

Bergson, H. (1944), *Creative Evolution*, New York: Modern Library.

Blumer, H. (1969), *Symbolic Interactionism: Perspective and Method*, Berkeley: University of California Press.

Chia, R. (1996), 'The problem of reflexivity in organizational research: towards a postmodern science of organization', *Organization*, **3**(1), 31–59.

Ciborra, C.U. (1996), 'The platform organization: recombining strategies, structures and surprises', *Organization Science*, **7**(2), 103–18.

Ciborra, C.U. (1999), 'Notes on improvisation and time in organizations', *Accounting Management and Information Technologies*, **9**(2), 77–94.

Crites, S. (1971), 'The narrative quality of experience', *Journal of the American Academy of Religion*, **39**(3), 291–311.

Crossan, M.M. and M. Sorrenti (1997), 'Making sense of improvisation', in A. Huff and J. Walsh (eds), *Advances in Strategic Management, Volume 14*, Stanford, CT: JAI Press, 155–80.

Cunha, M.P.E. and K. Kamoche (2001), 'Minimal structures: from jazz improvisation to product innovation', *Organization studies*, **22**(5), 733–55.

Cyert, R.M. and J.G. March (1992), *A Behavioral Theory of the Firm*, Malden, MA: Blackwell.

Dehlin, E. (2008), 'The flesh and blood of improvisation: a study of everyday organizing', doctoral dissertation, Norwegian University of Science and Technology.

Dewey, J. (1929), *Experience and Nature*, London: George Allen and Unwin.

Eisenhardt, K.M. (1985), 'Control: organizational and economic approaches', *Management Science*, **31**(2), 134–49.

Feldman, M.S. (2000), 'Organizational routines as a source of continuous change', *Organization Science*, **11**(6), 611–29.

Feldman, M. and W. Orlikowski (2011), 'Theorizing practice and practicing theory', *Organization Science*, **22**(5), 1240–53.

Feyerabend, P. (2002), *Against Method*, London: Biddles.

Foucault, M. (1981), 'The order of discourse', in R. Young (ed.), *Untying the Text: A Poststructuralist Reader*, Boston, MA: Routledge and Kegan Paul, pp. 48–78.

Foucault, M. (1989), *The Archaeology of Knowledge*, London: Routledge.
Gadamer, H.G. (1975), *Truth and Method*, New York: Seabury.
Geertz, C. (1973), 'Thick description: toward an interpretive theory of culture', in C. Geertz (ed.), *The Interpretation of Cultures: Selected Essays*, New York: Basic Books, pp. 3–32.
Hatch, M.J. (1997), 'Jazzing up the theory of organizational improvisation', *Advances in Strategic Management*, **14**(1), 181–91.
Hatch, M.J. (1999), 'Exploring the empty spaces in jazz: how improvisational jazz helps redescribe organizational structure', *Organization Studies*, **20**(1), 75–100.
James, W. (2007), *The Principles of Psychology*, New York: Cosimo.
Joas, H. (1993), *Pragmatism and Social Theory*, Chicago: The University of Chicago Press.
Joas, H. (1996), *The Creativity of Action*, Cornwall, Ontario: Hartnolls.
Kamoche, K.N., M.P. Cunha and J.V. Cunha (2002), *Organizational Improvisation*, London: Routledge.
Kotter J.P. (1986), *The General Managers*, New York: The Free Press.
Lave, J. and E. Wenger (1991), *Situated Learning: Legitimate Peripheral Participation*, Cambridge: University of Cambridge Press.
Leybourne, S. (2006), 'Improvisation within the project management of change: some observations from UK financial services', *Journal of Change Management*, **6**(4), 365–81.
March, J.G. and H. Simon (1993), *Organizations*, New York: John Wiley.
Mead, G.H. (1967), *Mind, Self, and Society*, Chicago: University of Chicago Press.
Merleau-Ponty, M. (2002), *Phenomenology of Perception: An Introduction*, London: Routledge.
Miner, A.S., C. Moorman and P. Bassoff (1996), 'Organizational improvisation and new product development', unpublished manuscript, Cambridge, UK: Cambridge University.
Mintzberg, H. (1973), *The Nature of Managerial Work*, New York: Harper & Row.
Moorman, C. and A. Miner (1998), 'Organizational improvisation and organizational memory', *Academy of Management Review*, **23**(4), 698–723.
Newell, S., M. Robertson, H. Scarbrough and J. Swan (2002), *Managing Knowledge Work*, London: Palgrave Macmillan.
Nyeng, F. (2004), *Vitenskapsteori for økonomer*, Oslo: Abstrakt Forlag.
Orlikowski, W.J. (1996), 'Improvising organizational transformation over time: a situated change perspective', *Information Systems Research*, **7**(1), 63–92.
Orlikowski, W.J. and J.D. Hofman (1997), 'An improvisational model for change management: the case of groupware technologies', *Sloan Management Review*, **38**(2), 11–21.
Ouchi, W.G. (1979), 'A conceptual framework for the design of organizational control mechanisms', *Management Science*, **25**(9), 833–48.
Ouchi, W.G. (1980), 'Markets, bureaucracies, and clans', *Administrative Science Quarterly*, **25**(1), 129–41.
Peirce, C.S. (1966a), *Collected Papers, VII*, Cambridge, MA: Belknap Press.
Peirce, C.S. (1966b), *Collected Papers, VIII*, Cambridge, MA: Belknap Press.
Peirce, C.S. (1974a), *Collected Papers, V*, Cambridge, MA: Belknap Press.
Peirce, C.S. (1974b), *Collected Papers, VI*, Cambridge, MA: Belknap Press.
Pentland, B.T. and H.H. Rueter (1994), 'Organizational routines as grammars of action', *Administrative Science Quarterly*, **39**(3), 484–510.
Petranker, J. (2005), 'The when of knowing', *The Journal of Applied Behavioral Science*, **41**(2), 241–59.
Purser, R.E. and J. Petranker (2005), 'Unfreezing the future: exploring the dynamic of time in organizational change', *The Journal of Applied Behavioral Science*, **41**(2), 182–203.
Russell, B. (1995), *History of Western Philosophy*, London: Routledge.
Schein, E.H. (1996), 'Culture – the missing concept in organization studies', *Administrative Science Quarterly*, **41**(2), 229–40.
Schön, D.A. (1987), *Educating the Reflective Practitioner*, San Francisco: Jossey-Bass.
Schön, D.A. (1991), *The Reflective Practitioner: How Professionals Think in Action*, Farnham, Surrey: Ashgate Publishing.

Simon, H.A. (1968), *Administrative Behavior: A Study of Decision-making Processes in Administrative Organization* (2nd edition), New York: The Free Press.

Skjervheim, H. (2001), *Objectivism and the Study of Man*, Oslo: Universitetsforlaget.

Stacey, R.D. (2001), *Complex Responsive Processes in Organizations: Learning and Knowledge Creation*, London: Routledge.

Stacey, R.D., D. Griffin and P. Shaw (2000), *Complexity and Management: Fad or Radical Challenge to Systems Thinking?* London: Routledge.

Strauss, A.L. (1993), *Continual Permutations of Action*, New York: Aldine De Gruyter.

Styhre, A. (2003), *Understanding Knowledge Management – Critical and Postmodern Perspectives*, Copenhagen: Copenhagen Business School Press.

Thompson, M. (2005), 'Structural and epistemic parameters in communities of practice', *Organization Science*, **16**(2), 151–64.

Tsoukas, H. and R. Chia (2002), 'On organizational becoming: rethinking organizational change, *Organization Science*, **13**(5), 567–82.

Tsoukas, H. and M.J., Hatch (2001), 'Complex thinking, complex practice: the case for a narrative approach to organizational complexity', *Human Relations*, **54**(8), 979–1012.

Urwick, L. (1934), 'The function of administration with special reference to the work of Henri Fayol', in L. Gulick and L. Urwick (eds), *Papers on the Science of Administration*, New York: Institute of Public Administration, pp. 115–30.

Weber, M. (2002), *Makt og byråkrati*, Oslo: Gyldendal Norsk Forlag.

Weick, K.E. (1989), 'Organized improvisation: 20 years of organizing', *Communication Studies*, **40**(4), 241–48.

Weick, K.E. (1995), *Sense-making in Organizations*, Thousand Oaks, CA: Sage Publications.

Weick, K.E. (1998), 'Improvisation as a mindset for organizational analysis', *Organization Science*, **9**(5), 543–55.

Weick, K.E. (2001), *Making Sense of the Organization*, Oxford: Blackwell Publishers.

Weisbord, M. (1988), *Productive Workplace*, San Francisco: Jossey-Bass.

Wenger, E. (2004), *Communities of Practice: Learning, Meaning, and Identity*, Cambridge: Cambridge University Press.

Zack, M.H. (2000), 'Jazz improvisation and organizing: once more from the top', *Organization Science*, **11**(2), 227–34.

11 Communities of practice: from innovation in practice to the practice of innovation
Emmanuel Josserand and Florence Villesèche

INTRODUCTION

In the quest to explain competitive advantage, the knowledge view of the firm appears to be one of the most topical alternatives to transaction costs economics. The ability to share and generate knowledge is thus considered a key capability (Nonaka and Takeuchi, 1995; Nahapiet and Ghoshal, 1998; Merali, 2000). Beyond the initial fads around technology and IT-driven knowledge management projects (Swan et al., 1999), research points to the importance of cultural (McDermott, 1999; Ndlela and du Toit, 2001) and structural change (Grant, 1996; Buckley and Carter, 2002) to favour openness to learning and sharing. This openness is deemed hard to achieve in bureaucratic organizations (Gupta and Govindarajan, 2000; Ravasi and Verona, 2001).

How do organizations deal with the apparent contradiction between a necessary order that could lead to bureaucracy and the strategic importance of an innovative openness that could lead to chaos? According to Wenger and Snyder:

> today's economy runs on knowledge, and most companies work assiduously to capitalize on that fact. They use cross-functional teams, customer- or product-focused business units, and work groups – to name just a few organizational forms – to capture and spread ideas and know-how. In many cases, these ways of organizing are very effective and no one would argue for their demise. (Wenger and Snyder, 2000, p. 139)

However, these forms are usually formal groups often driven by short-term objectives. Communities of practice (CoPs) – a new name for an old practice – have been theorized since the early 1990s. They are 'groups of people who share a concern, a set of problems, or a passion about a topic, and who deepen their knowledge and expertise in this area by interacting on an ongoing basis' (Wenger et al., 2002, p. 4). Wenger (1998) also described CoPs as emergent spaces where knowledge exchange can take place away from organizational constraints. Would CoPs thus be the ideal solution for practitioners confronted with the dilemma between control and learning? The concept is so appealing that its proponents have had a tendency to underestimate the difficulty of implementing such an emergent and informal organizational form within existing organizational structures and power games (Lave and Wenger, 1991; Fox, 2000; Wenger et al., 2002).

CoPs: An Elusive Concept?

But what exactly are CoPs? Equipped with the broad definition above, the concept is somewhat elusive. Wenger and Snyder (2000) provide defining criteria such as the fact that members are self-selected, that they are bound together by passion, and that a CoP lasts as long as members find interest in it. However, this might not be enough to describe a given group as a CoP, especially as examples found in the literature vary from professional guilds to members of the same department. Another way to better grasp the concept is to rely on the differences between CoPs and other organizational forms, for instance a working group or a project team.

Like project teams or working groups, members of a CoP do not necessarily work with each other every day (Wenger and Snyder, 2000). A key distinction is that CoPs do not have definite beginnings and ends. Indeed, the life-span of a CoP is not predetermined; the CoP lasts for as long as members sustain their interest in the practice and see value in gathering around it. Moreover, the coherence of project teams and working groups comes from the common goal to be attained, while CoPs draw coherence from their very membership (Vaast, 2002). In working groups and project teams, members are mostly chosen by management while in a CoP members are self-selected (Wenger and Snyder, 2000). Further, the activity of CoPs is auto-determined, while in other types of groups goals are assigned. Also, a CoP is not a network, even if a network can be a starting point where members of the future CoP first come into contact (Gongla and Rizzuto, 2001).

CoPs as an Organizational Innovation

CoPs have been considered as an organizational innovation even though one could discuss their novelty – or their lack of such – in a business context. This is symptomatic of what has been called the practice turn in management literature, that is, the development of an interest in what people actually do and not only in the theory of what they are 'meant to be doing'. This practice turn is present in most areas of management literature; 'there is a literature on knowing in practice, formal analysis in practice, and technology in practice, each of which shares a common focus upon the way that actors interact with the social and physical features of context in the everyday activities that constitute practice' (Jarzabkowski, 2004, p. 539). Strategy itself is seen as 'something people *do*' (Whittington, 2006, p. 613).

This interest in practice has combined with firms' interest in knowledge management and innovation. In this regard, CoPs are a good example of a new organizational form around which these different interests crystallize: indeed, by their very definition they are a group of people gathered around a practice; transmission and sharing, but also innovation, can possibly arise from their activity (Wenger, 1998; Adler, 2001).

From Innovation in Practice to the Practice of Innovation

In this chapter, we wish to explore how CoPs, first identified and theorized in works in the field of anthropology, have quickly been adopted as an organizational innovation for intra- and inter-organizational knowledge sharing and creation. However, there appears to be a wide gap between Lave and Wenger's theorization of situated learning and today's operationalization of CoPs. We start by proposing a genealogy of the concept to show how the concept has been taken up in organization and management studies. We then proceed to look at the institutionalization and commodification of CoPs, and comment on the drifting away from their original conceptualization.

Just as the literature points out the difficulty of fitting CoPs into organizations, it also tries to approach the issues of control, power and individual agency that pertain to the role of manager in this tentative organizational innovation (Josserand, 2004; Probst and Borzillo, 2008). There is now 'a consensus that management can play an active role in setting up and supporting CoPs' (Borzillo et al., 2011, p. 15) and thus that organizations need to be actively implicated in making this possible (Brown and Duguid, 2001; Dubé et al., 2006). Indeed, the manager will be at the interface between the organization and a given CoP and will have to find ways of managing this novel form, whether regarding participants, process, or assessing the CoP's outcomes, even if this contradicts some of the defining traits of the original concept.

Further, we argue that the different movements away from the 'original' definition of CoPs have created a new sense by semantic sliding. This linguistic detour is relevant to explaining how new meanings become fixed, which is especially interesting in the case of a concept like the CoP that originally comes from anthropology and not from organization or management theory.

GENEALOGY OF THE CONCEPT

CoPs have been described as a very old organizational form reminiscent of Ancient Greek and medieval guilds or like groups, as well as paradoxically being a very recently nominalized practice inside organizations (Wenger and Snyder, 2000). While this comparison has been criticized (Vaast, 2002), the way CoPs are envisaged today in a business context seems a far cry from anthropologists' description of the phenomenon in the 1990s, and actually quite close to the very formalized and rather rigid norms and hierarchies that were also typical features of Ancient Greek and medieval guilds.

By having a closer look at the seminal works that inspired organization and management studies to adopt the concept, we can identify two distinct orientations from the start. We propose to distinguish between Lave and Wenger's *situated learning* perspective and Orr's *situated innovation* perspective. Though Wenger is more prominent and cited in the field, it appears that it is rather Orr's perspective that has been integrated into management and organization theory, as we will see, for instance, in one of the field-shaping works of Brown and Duguid (1991).

Lave and Wenger: Situated Learning

In their seminal work *Situated Learning: Legitimate Peripheral Participation*, Lave and Wenger (1991) look at different ethnographies of apprenticeship to show how the learning process is actually not one of knowledge transfer from a single master to his or her apprentice, but rather a social process grounded in practice. This situated learning takes place in what they come to call a community of practice.

The concept of communities of practice 'is left largely as an intuitive notion' (ibid., p.42). However, the ethnographies they present (see Box 11.1) clearly show that the apprentice is involved not only in a master–apprentice relationship, but also in a group formed by more advanced apprentices and journeymen. The newcomer thus learns from the group as a whole. This process is coined as legitimate peripheral participation (LPP); this 'peripherality provides an approximation of full participation that gives exposure to actual practice' (Wenger, 1998, p.100). The apprentices are peripheral but nevertheless legitimate participants in the CoP: they are made legitimate by their interest in the practice and by their position as apprentices in a specific trade. Apprentices can gradually move from peripheral to full participation while completing their apprenticeship.

The CoP becomes 'the context in which an individual develops the practices (including values, norms and relationships) and identities appropriate

---

BOX 11.1   LAVE AND WENGER'S EXAMPLES OF COPS

The first community of practice under scrutiny is that of Yucatec Mayan midwives in Mexico. In this particular CoP, knowledge is passed down from mother (and grandmother) to daughter through the daughter's observation and participation from a young age on. In the apprenticeship of Vai and Gola tailors in Liberia, non-kin are integrated into a master's family. There is a similar pattern of moving from peripheral to full participation over time. The third ethnography deals with naval quartermasters. In this specific CoP, the emphasis is on 'the importance for learning of having legitimate, effective access to what is to be learned', that is, to be considered as a member of the CoP. Finally, the apprenticeship of meat cutters is an example where LPP actually fails. Failure is here linked to the commodification of labour, to coercive behaviour by the master or senior members of the CoP (p. 76). In this particular setting, failure arises from the schism between what is taught and what is needed in practice. This prevents the meat cutters from learning 'the full range of tasks once proper to their trade' (p. 79). These four studies in an organizational setting show how all members of a CoP, whatever their level of seniority, need to be implicated for the LPP to lead to eventual full participation of the apprentice. They also draw attention to the importance of culture and context, which impact on the way in which a CoP functions and legitimates members.

---

to that community' (Handley et al., 2006, p. 642). Apprentices learn while the community builds a shared repertoire of resources and knowledge. This building is social, situated and grounded in practice, and 'the repertoire of a community of practice includes routines, words, tools, ways of doing things, stories, gestures, symbols, genres, actions, or concepts that the community has produced or adopted in the course of existence' (Wenger, 1998, p. 83).

The studied situations involve hierarchical and non-hierarchical relations, but do not address managerial roles. This can be linked to another important dimension in the original description of CoPs: the fact that it is driven by the members. Furthermore, a given CoP does have borders, but they are not fixed, as the CoP is not a formal group (Wenger, 2000). What is thus prominent in this perspective on CoPs is their informal, intuitive nature, as well as the fact that members are self-selected but do not necessarily have equal status. Also, the focus is on learning and how it is situated in practice; the CoP of meat cutters provides an interesting example of failure when learning and practice are disconnected.

Orr: Situated Innovation

Julian Orr, another anthropologist, wrote his PhD thesis and later published a book on technicians at Xerox (Orr, 1990, 1996) entitled *Talking about Machines: An Ethnography of a Modern Job*. Orr describes how copy machine repairers gather to share and build knowledge in order to circumvent inefficient and scattered practices. His work illustrates:

> how an organization's view of work can overlook and even oppose what and who it takes to get a job done. Reliance on espoused practice (also referred to as canonical practice) can blind an organization to the actual practices of its members. Actual practices, however, determine the success or failure of organizations. (Brown, 1998, p. 227)

This can be coined as positive resistance: the resistance is directed towards positive outcomes on the organizational level, and becomes a resource for change (Ford et al., 2008). As in Lave and Wenger's definition (1991), these communities are emergent, united around a practice and do not have a formal hierarchy.

Nevertheless, this brief description of Orr's work shows a quite different focus on the role and possibilities brought about by CoPs: we have shifted from *situated learning* to *situated innovation* – which does not, however, exclude learning possibilities. Indeed, the technicians at Xerox meet because individually they feel they do not know enough about how to repair copy machines; they exchange and share expertise to develop a body of knowledge, a common repertoire that is an innovation in the sense that it ends up being more than the sum of individual skills. This type of CoP leading to innovation can also be found beyond a focal organization, as illustrated in Box 11.2.

Adoption of the Term in Organization and Management Studies

One of the earliest and most influential articles adopting and adapting the concept of CoPs to the field of organization and management studies is Brown and Duguid's (1991) article 'Organizational learning and communities-of-practice: toward a unified view of working, learning, and innovation'. While also drawing on Lave and Wenger, they appear to

---

BOX 11.2   INTER-ORGANIZATIONAL COPS AND SITUATED INNOVATION

In their study of four inter-organizational communities of practice, Grima and Josserand (2011) describe how training managers exchange their practices, their doubts, and their knowledge. The four communities studied are part of an association of more than 800 training managers. The training managers gather in small groups of about 20 people, and they meet regularly to compare daily problems and to discover innovative practices. Old-timers bring their experience and networks while younger members, eager, among other things, to prove their value to their respective companies, are more likely to implement new practices and provide feedback to the group. They also discuss more specific situations: for instance, when faced with budgetary cuts and unchanged training objectives, a junior training manager 'crafted a program in which he turned two experienced skilled workers that were close to the end of their careers into trainers' (Grima and Josserand, 2011, p. 303). This programme was presented to the community of practice and was adopted by other companies from the same sector, resulting in the creation of a structure that benefited from EU funding.

---

focus more on Orr's approach. This can be explained by the fact that they are actually:

> writing about improvised new practice, not the reproduction of an existing practice. This may explain why there is little reference to the concept most borrowed by other writers from Lave and Wenger, legitimate peripheral participation. As a consequence, Brown and Duguid's concept of community seems relatively homogeneous, without different levels of participation. (Cox, 2005, p. 530)

This focus on innovation and change in the practice, as well as relative homogeneity in participants, seems indeed more appealing and adaptable to the needs of organizations in their search for new tools to manage and create knowledge.

Hence, from the very start we have two perspectives on CoPs: one is centred on the idea of situated learning, of a practice whose norms and processes are transmitted and also possibly shifted in a social process. The CoP boundaries are delimited by the legitimacy of a given actor in a practice. In this first perspective, learning skills and learning about a tradition is predominant over innovation. The other perspective is concerned rather with innovation in practice made in organizational interstices. In organization and management theory, this second perspective has been far more popular especially as CoPs have widely been identified as being part of knowledge management efforts (Hildreth and Kimble, 2004; Cox, 2005; Roberts, 2006). Wenger himself, in his subsequent work, has concentrated on the second approach (Wenger, 1998; Wenger et al., 2002).

THE ADOPTION OF COPS IN ORGANIZATIONS

This shift, we believe, is a sign of a progressive institutionalization and commodification of CoPs. Indeed, from the ethnographic observation of what CoPs are (Orr, 1990; Lave and Wenger, 1991) to recent managerial articles reframing what CoPs should be (McDermott and Archibald, 2010), there appears to be a clear movement towards fitting the concept to organizations' needs, a movement that of course entails transformation but that can also lead to 'denaturing' the concept to the point where its innovativeness and distinctiveness become questionable.

Institutionalization

The institutionalization of CoPs, that is, their identification and recognition, can be considered as a prominent phenomenon in the adoption of an informal organizational form originally identified by anthropologists. In theory, the conceptualization of CoPs as the place where innovation arises seems to fit contemporary organizations' concern with knowledge management as a key element in the development of a sustainable competitive advantage. Nevertheless, 'the applicability of the concept to the heavily individualized and tightly managed work of the twenty-first century is questionable' (Cox, 2005, p. 527). This reactivates Contu and Willmott's desire 'to invite reflection upon the affinity between the dilution and selective adoption of Lave and Wenger's thinking and its ideological compatibility with dominant managerial values' (2003, p. 284).

In order that the organization can make sense of CoPs and their activity, there is a drive towards the formalization of CoPs that starts by an effort to identify their existence, and thus also identify their members. In the process CoPs can be assigned boundaries and their membership regulated, and often goals are set: whatever practice the community is gathered around, it has to function formally so that its activities can be monitored and aligned with broader strategic objectives. Such formalization of CoPs

– in order for them to be integrated into the organizational structure – can actually impede their potential 'effectiveness' as they are originally defined as non-formal work groups. Modifying one of the founding characteristics of an organizational form means running the risk of modifying the form and losing its intrinsic benefits. As pointed out by Wenger and Snyder, 'it is not particularly easy to build and sustain communities of practice or to integrate them within the rest of an organization. The organic, spontaneous, and informal nature of communities of practice makes them resistant to supervision and inference' (2000, p.140).

Further, depending on the degree of incompatibility with a given organizational culture, community development and innovation capabilities can be annihilated altogether, as the CoPs are 'shaped by the needs and beliefs of the corporation' (Standing, 2009, p.251). If a given firm seeks innovation through an organizational form that is formatted to its current way of thinking, these structures will rely on norms and frameworks that already exist outside of the CoP, and thus are not negotiated by CoP participants. CoPs' boundaries are stiffened through institutionalization and formalization, and the setting of goals by the organization further constrains the possibility of membership, overlooking the fact that innovation and knowledge creation may arise from an unforeseen combination of people and ideas by reaching out of a business unit or even outside a focal organization. Box 11.3 shows an example of both the positive and negative impacts of the institutionalization of the knowledge exchange and the eventual innovative output of CoPs.

Commodification

We also identify a tendency to commodify CoPs. In the original tentative definition, a CoP is informally organized around a practice; it is self-organized and members are self-selected (Wenger and Snyder, 2000). Moreover, one of its main values lies in the fact that it gradually permits a legitimating of members, who are moving from a legitimate position at the periphery (LPP) to full participation. While contributing to the sustainment of a given practice during the whole process (Lave and Wenger, 1991), there are no precise goals in terms of knowledge development or innovation assigned to the members from the start. In today's management conceptualization, CoPs are assigned not only objectives, but also economic value: they need to operate efficiently, and their outcomes have to bring added value (McDermott and Archibald, 2010). Otherwise, their very existence is a loss of time and money. This notion of potential loss of economic value further participates in legitimizing the effort to formalize and control CoPs:

BOX 11.3 THE PROS AND CONS OF INSTITUTIONALIZATION

Josserand (2004) describes the results of the institutionalization of CoPs in a consulting firm. Management decided to create CoPs in order to improve knowledge sharing in a project-oriented, decentralized structure. One of the first effects of the institutionalization was that the topics were chosen by management, and this resulted in the creation of six communities. The first two did not take off since the topics were of no interest to the consultants. Even though membership was on a voluntary basis, a pilot, co-pilot, experts and a mission manager were appointed. The mission manager was supposed to arbitrate delicate matters and could be approached to obtain resources. CoPs had no formal obligations except to meet regularly and to make their outcomes available to the rest of the organization. Of the four remaining CoPs, only the one in which the mission manager stuck to his role was sustained. Another one was transformed by the mission leader into a successful project team. The mission leaders of the third and fourth CoPs became very involved, intervening in a hierarchical mode. Interest in the CoP progressively decreased for consultants who did not see their practical preoccupations addressed. Interestingly enough, this was not all for nothing. One of the CoPs was formed again, this time informally: members started to organize lunchtime debate meetings and to exchange views very actively on the same topics originally addressed by the company-formed CoP.

---

when communities of practice first began to appear, we hailed them as a dirt-cheap way to distribute knowledge and share best practices. We thought they would be relatively self-organizing and self-sustaining, flying below the radar of organizational hierarchy. We thought they would flourish with little executive oversight – a notion that seemed to work well at the time. But as life and business have become more complex, we began to see that to make a difference over the long term, communities needed far more structure and oversight. (McDermott and Archibald, 2010, p. 89)

Interestingly enough, this radical redefinition of what CoPs are and how they should be managed is (at least in part) made by R. McDermott, one of the authors who was once a proponent of CoPs in their original emergent, boundaryless and uncontrolled form (Wenger et al., 2002).

However, this tentative commodification is made at the risk of contradicting the original purpose of CoPs; further, even if the commodification is achieved, the value generated by CoPs seems difficult to assess. Indeed, 'the effects of community activities are often delayed. For another, results generally appear in the work of teams and business units, not in the communities themselves' (Wenger and Snyder, 2000, p.145). Also, Wenger et al. (2002) point out that 'communities of practice are what Ray Oldenberg calls *neutral places*, separate from the everyday work pressures of people's jobs' (p.61), which is clearly no longer the case if CoPs have to deliver results, reach goals within determined time frames and function under managerial supervision.

This commodification also concerns participants themselves: while members were originally self-selected, and were likely to include a wide array of members from novices to experienced staff, most recent consideration of CoP membership in a business setting focuses on expertise as a decisive element for membership, or at least a certain level of responsibility inside the organization, above and beyond passion and interest for a given practice. This is reminiscent of Brown and Duguid's (1991) article, in which the adaptation of the concept of CoP in organizations is drawn rather from Orr's ethnography of a CoP characterized by a relatively homogeneous membership (Xerox technicians) than from the varied membership in Lave and Wenger's examples. The idea of innovation coming from low-ranking 'experts', or more generally people passionate about a given practice, has been lost along the way. The idea of 'positive resistance' has likewise been put to bed. Indeed, if CoPs are institutionalized and commodified, it seems very unlikely that a company will give funding and time to, say, engineers to come up with ways of improving the organization. In short, it is rather incompatible to tell people to find new rules while following existing ones.

Commodification and Consulting Firms

The commodification of CoPs is also an outcome of the mercantile orientation of consulting firms. One approach to knowledge management promotes the conversion of contingent knowledge into objectified and universal practices; the knowledge is codified and synthesized so that it can be applied to an altogether different context (Hansen et al., 1999). Consulting firms thus commodify the knowledge gathered contextually by their consultants (Suddaby and Greenwood, 2001) and can subsequently sell it as a business solution to another organization. Regarding CoPs, this can lead to the most sterile misinterpretation and use of the concept when tools for the implementation of communities of practices are sold with no consideration for social dynamics (see Box 11.4). Commodification is thus

---

BOX 11.4   COMMODIFICATION AND THE FAILURE OF COPS

In her work on an air traffic control organization in Europe, Jouirou (2007) describes the limits of commodification. She provides an account of her observation of the 'implementation' of CoPs in the organization: this was done using IT tools that had been sold to management as a solution for the development of CoPs. Once the tools had been installed, the CoPs had to become active in order to prove the relevance of the investment. Thus, advised by the consulting team, management adopted a 'natural' approach and organized groups: topics were chosen by management and people were told that they were now members of a specific community and that they should participate and contribute. Interestingly, there were a number of pre-existing networks and actual communities of practice, but there was no effort to capitalize on them. Since management was still trying to maintain the illusion of voluntary participation, the pressure to actually participate was moderate. Consequently, individuals rapidly stopped participating in the imposed communities while continuing to participate in previously existing informal structures. Implementation was thus a failure, and the project was abandoned.

---

accentuated by consulting firms, and they are known to be pushing for faster changes in management practices that can often prove counterproductive (ibid.). CoPs can thus also be considered as a management fashion (Abrahamson, 1996; Abrahamson and Fairchild, 1999), that is, a standardized knowledge product for which there has been no consideration of the wider implications of developing CoPs in a given organizational context. It is thus fundamentally because of a need to control processes and outcomes that the initial concept of CoP in anthropological studies gave birth to one more management fad.

COPS: BETWEEN EMERGENCE AND CONTROL

As seen earlier, institutionalization and commodification are two tempting ways to make sense of this organizational innovation, align goals and harness value from CoPs. This creates a tension between the research of organizational innovation such as CoPs, requiring more freedom, and the desire for control. If organizations wish to reap the benefits of CoPs, it thus seems necessary to go beyond the control reflex, as control mechanisms can foster negative resistance and preclude the desire to learn (Argyris and Schön, 1978). There is definitely a challenge to move towards a logic of cooperation (Nahapiet and Ghoshal, 1998). In any case, 'this is only possible with the existence of an autonomy allowing the emergence of some form of creative chaos' (Nonaka, 1994, p. 309).

Organizational and Managerial Control over CoPs

If the challenge of establishing such free spaces is not taken up, organizations lose sight of their own interest in accepting the CoP as an uncontrolled and off-the-radar organizational form. Referring to Orr's work on Xerox technicians still in press at that time, Lave and Wenger stated that 'communities of practice may well develop interstitially and informally in coercive workplaces' (1991, p. 64). Even if organizations do not view themselves as coercive, the rigidity of their structure and their way of controlling the outcomes of knowledge management practices should appear to them as a factor that limits knowledge creation and innovation. CoPs can help them to overcome their own limitations and rigidities by building resilience inside organizations (Josserand, 2004). Furthermore, 'by introducing spaces of freedom and exchange within the organization, they allow an informal free flow of knowledge that can be translated into the evolution of practices' (ibid., p. 307). Following Brown, we can consider that 'the source of innovation lies on the interface between an organization and its environment' (1998, p. 231). The difficulty thus resides in finding ways to support the development and sustained activity of CoPs without constraining their particular dynamics (Thompson, 2005).

The initial concept of a CoP – whether in the situated learning or the situated innovation manifestation – is very different from the institutional establishment where a manager controls a CoP, or when there are leadership positions in the CoP (McDermott and Archibald, 2010). In the original conceptualization of a CoP, differences in role taking (according to seniority for instance) are not equated with establishing formal leadership as regards knowledge sharing. It is a joint enterprise by all members of a given CoP, and the scope and aim of it is continually renegotiated among its members (Wenger, 1998).

CoPs in their original sense therefore appear to be a disturbance to the smooth and controlled running of the modern corporation. Indeed, CoPs 'contribute to organizational complexity more than other approaches to knowledge because they create multiple centres of power based on knowledge' (Wenger et al., 2002, p. 158). They are seen as a threat to the organization's power centre as well as a threat to the manager's hierarchically superior position, as power and superiority include being informed about what is happening in the organization and being able to control these actions. Moreover, for the organization as well as for the manager, it is difficult to encourage without controlling (Josserand, 2004; Borzillo et al., 2011), even if in the case of CoPs this can lead to their failure (Anand et al., 2007). Guidelines developed in the academic and practitioner literature to help managers deal with this issue are giving a framework to such a shift. As argued by Cox (2005), 'the most recent work by Wenger ... marks a distinct shift towards a managerialist stance. The proposition that managers should foster informal horizontal groups across organizational boundaries is in fact a fundamental redefinition of the concept' (p. 527). This redefinition allows a better alignment with existing practices and goals; nevertheless, it can actually prevent innovation from coming out of CoPs, as innovation becomes a mandatory and controlled outcome when it was rather incidental in the original conceptualization of CoPs.

Commodification and Voluntary Participation in CoPs

As organizations try to commodify CoPs, some remain nevertheless aware of the importance of the essential characteristics of CoPs, like the voluntary participation that will trigger, among other effects, a willingness to share. To this end, even when CoPs are created and controlled by management the participation can be voluntary, but will often be strongly encouraged or even mandatory (Dubé et al., 2006). While the mandatory status can preclude CoP success in a rather obvious way, the in-between status of strong encouragement is trickier to get around. Indeed, encouraged participation in a CoP gives an impression of choice: if one joins, it is out of sheer interest, as should be the case in a CoP. However, not acting on the invitation to join is often not perceived as being an option, and this is actually a way for management to downplay the mandatory character of membership 'in order to retain the spontaneous and informal aspects of CoPs' (Borzillo et al., 2011, p. 26). It certainly only retains aspects, and this deceptive voluntary participation in a CoP, where employees can act on their own interests and not only those of the organization, can be described as a 'fictitious decommodification' (Standing, 2009, p. 250). This is again symptomatic of the dilemma between control and freedom, and is yet another sign of the drifting away from the original spirit of CoPs.

DISCUSSION: SEMANTIC SLIDING OF THE CONCEPT OF COP

This dilution of the concept of CoP is nevertheless an interesting phenomenon, as from the outside it can still look like organizations are open to radical change and that they are ready to adopt very innovative organizational forms even if this implies less control and the risk of having no fruitful outcomes in the short or longer term. As seen throughout this chapter, this is clearly not the case, but still the term is used though it appears to refer to a different organizational form. We argue that the adoption of the concept of CoP in organization and management studies, and its subsequent institutionalization and commodification, has resulted in a change to the sense in which we use the term CoP; we observe a semantic slide from the concept of *innovation in practice* to the one of the *practice of innovation*. This linguistic approach of the shifting use of the term is interesting as it can be considered as an outcome of the institutionalization and commodification of CoPs. Indeed, when CoPs are implemented in a given organization, the self-selection of members and the absence of managerial control hardly seem to be among the defining elements. The *signification* of the term 'community of practice' is difficult to shift (CoPs are not project teams; the term and its components cannot be changed – *community* and *practice* – and this clearly distinguishes them from other types of group). Nevertheless, the *meaning* of the concept can be modified within a given discourse and context. The sense given to a term is always subjective and contextualized; commodifying a CoP can thus be considered as a way of making sense of it in a business environment where, unlike in the context of the early ethnographic observations of CoPs, it is difficult to accept the absence of economic justification and control.

This semantic slide does not affect the term 'CoP', but affects the eidetic characteristics of it, that is, the essential elements forming its definition (Roche, 2005, p. 59), and leads to a different semantic fixation in the business context. In eidetic definition making, consensus is not reached around an original definition, but around the identification of eidetic characteristics that are agreed upon in a given context (ibid., p. 60); this helps to explain how definitions can shift when in a different context. It follows that, while CoPs were originally an informal site of potential innovation in practice (i.e., innovation as a situated activity), CoPs are now more likely to be defined as clearly identified groups of people oriented towards the practice of innovation. In Figure 11.1, we use a terminological tree to propose a visual representation of the semantic slide from *innovation in practice* to *practice of innovation* since concepts can be linked by terminological arborescence (Depecker, 2005, p. 10).

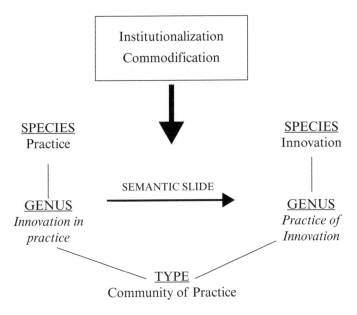

Figure 11.1   Terminological arborescence of the concept of CoP

In the arborescence of Figure 11.1 we can see that the semantic slide implies that CoPs can be linked to a different *species* and *genus* (i.e., greater-order taxonomic categories) depending on the sense that is assigned to the concept; this helps when mapping out the split between the original definition and the current sense in a business setting. Indeed, if, on the one hand, like in the original definition, we talk about CoPs as an example of *innovation in practice*, it means that we are situating our discourse in the species of *practice*, and that, in the spirit of the 'practice turn' in management studies, we are interested in this organizational form as potentially productive of innovation. Further, the adoption of the concept in a business setting can be considered as an organizational innovation as it is grounded in practice vs. theory, and because its structure and functioning are different from other existing organizational forms. On the other hand, if we consider that CoPs are a new organizational form whose purpose is to foster innovation in a novel way, that is, in practice (and not only through brainstorming and so on), and which is managed differently from working teams or project teams to allow for potentially different outcomes, we are seeing CoPs as sites of *practice of innovation*. It follows that the concept of CoP is then situated in a discourse around the species of *innovation*. In the first version we are interested in the way socially situated practice shapes learning and can eventually lead to innovation. In the second version we are interested in innovation, and we want to maximize the chances that it arises from a group of people gathered around a practice. While innovation is incidental and the process emergent in *innovation in practice*, it is programmed and controlled in the *practice of innovation*.

It follows that CoPs matching the original definition of *innovation in practice* are quite rare. Again, this is due to the difficulty of achieving compatibility with the functioning of today's organizations. CoPs understood as a *practice of innovation* can take the form of something close to yet another project team, working group or expert group. They can either succeed in such a different form (even if still called a CoP) or simply fail because the 'in-between status' proves to be unproductive. Hence, semantic slides are not innocent as they result from an exercise of power that drives institutionalization and commodification. The linguistic approach we take in this chapter reveals such exercises of power and can help to better trace the evolution of organizational innovations in particular and managerial discourse in general.

REFERENCES

Abrahamson, E. (1996), 'Management fashion', *Academy of Management Review*, **21**(1), 254–85.
Abrahamson, E. and G. Fairchild (1999), 'Management fashion: lifecycles, triggers, and collective learning processes', *Administrative Science Quarterly*, **44**(4), 708–40.
Adler, P.S. (2001), 'Market, hierarchy, and trust: the knowledge economy and the future of capitalism', *Organization Science*, **12**(2), 215–34.
Anand, N., H.K. Gardner and T. Morris (2007), 'Knowledge-based innovation: emergence and embedding of new practice areas in management consulting firms', *Academy of Management Journal*, **50**(2), 406–28.
Argyris, C. and D. Schön (1978), *Organizational Learning: A Theory of Action Perspective*, Reading, MA: Addison Wesley.
Borzillo, S., S. Aznar and A. Schmitt (2011), 'A journey through communities of practice: how and why members move from the periphery to the core', *European Management Journal*, **29**(1), 25–42.
Brown, J.S. (1998), 'Internet technology in support of the concept of "communities-of-practice": the case of Xerox', *Accounting, Management and Information Technologies*, **8**(4), 227–36.
Brown, J.S. and P. Duguid (1991), 'Organizational learning and communities-of-practice: toward a unified view of working, learning, and innovation', *Organization Science*, **2**(1), 40–57.
Brown, J.S. and P. Duguid (2001), 'Knowledge and organization: a social-practice perspective', *Organization Science*, **12**(2), 198–213.
Buckley, P.J. and M.J. Carter (2002), 'Process and structure in knowledge management practices of British and US multinational enterprises', *Journal of International Management*, **8**(1), 29–48.
Contu, A. and H. Willmott (2003), 'Re-embedding situatedness: the importance of power relations in learning theory', *Organization Science*, **14**(3), 283–96.
Cox, A. (2005), 'What are communities of practice? A comparative review of four seminal works', *Journal of Information Science*, **31**(6), 527–40.

Depecker, L. (2005), 'Contribution de la terminologie à la linguistique', *Langages*, **157**, 6–13.

Dubé, L., A. Bourhis and R. Jacob (2006), 'Towards a typology of virtual communities of practice', *Interdisciplinary Journal of Information, Knowledge, and Management*, **1**, 69–93.

Ford, J.D., L.W. Ford and A. D'Amelio (2008), 'Resistance to change: the rest of the story', *Academy of Management Review*, **33**(2), 362–77.

Fox, S. (2000), 'Communities of practice, Foucault and actor-network theory', *Journal of Management Studies*, **37**(6), 853–68.

Gongla, P. and C.R. Rizzuto (2001), 'Evolving communities of practice: IBM Global Services experience', *IBM Systems Journal*, **40**(4), 842–62.

Grant, R.M. (1996), 'Prospering in dynamically-competitive environments: organizational capability as knowledge integration', *Organization Science*, **7**(4), 375–87.

Grima, F. and E. Josserand (2011), 'The roles of peripheral participants and brokers: within and beyond communities of practices', in E.B. Campos and O.R. Rivera Hernáez (eds), *Handbook of Research on Communities of Practice for Organizational Management and Networking: Methodologies for Competitive Advantage*, Hershey, PA: IGI Global, pp. 297–307.

Gupta, A.K. and V. Govindarajan (2000), 'Knowledge management's social dimension: lessons from Nucor Steel', *Sloan Management Review*, **42**(1), 71–80.

Handley, K., A. Sturdy, R. Fincham and T. Clark (2006), 'Within and beyond communities of practice: making sense of learning through participation, identity and practice', *Journal of Management Studies*, **43**(3), 641–53.

Hansen, M.T., N. Nohria and T. Tierney (1999), 'What's your strategy for managing knowledge?', *Harvard Business Review*, **77**(2), 106–16.

Hildreth, P.M. and C. Kimble (2004), *Knowledge Networks: Innovation Through Communities of Practice*, Hershey, PA: Idea Group Pub.

Jarzabkowski, P. (2004), 'Strategy as practice: recursiveness, adaptation, and practices-in-use', *Organization Studies*, **25**(4), 529–60.

Jouirou, M. (2007), 'Les conditions de développement des communautés de pratiques', PhD thesis, Université Paris-Dauphine.

Josserand, E. (2004), 'Cooperation within bureaucracies: are communities of practice an answer?', *M@n@gement*, **7**(3), 307–39.

Lave, J. and E. Wenger (1991), *Situated Learning: Legitimate Peripheral Participation*, Cambridge, UK/New York: Cambridge University Press.

McDermott, R. (1999), 'Why information technology inspired but cannot deliver knowledge management', *California Management Review*, **41**(4), 103–17.

McDermott, R. and D. Archibald (2010), 'Harnessing your staff's informal networks', *Harvard Business Review*, **88**(3), 82–9.

Merali, Y. (2000), 'Individual and collective congruence in the knowledge management process', *The Journal of Strategic Information Systems*, **9**(2–3), 213–34.

Nahapiet, J. and S. Ghoshal (1998), 'Social capital, intellectual capital, and the organizational advantage', *Academy of Management Review*, **23**(2), 242–66.

Ndlela, L.T. and A.S.A. du Toit (2001), 'Establishing a knowledge management programme for competitive advantage in an enterprise', *International Journal of Information Management*, **21**(2), 151–65.

Nonaka, I. (1994), 'A dynamic theory of organizational knowledge creation', *Organization Science*, **5**(1), 14–37.

Nonaka, I. and H. Takeuchi (1995), *The Knowledge-creating Company: How Japanese Companies Create the Dynamics of Innovation*, New York: Oxford University Press.

Orr, J.E. (1990), *Talking about Machines: An Ethnography of a Modern Job*, Ithaca, New York: Cornell University Press.

Orr, J.E. (1996), *Talking about Machines: An Ethnography of a Modern Job*, Ithaca, New York: ILR Press.

Probst, G. and S. Borzillo (2008), 'Why communities of practice succeed and why they fail', *European Management Journal*, **26**(5), 335–47.

Ravasi, D. and G. Verona (2001), 'Organizing the process of knowledge integration: the benefits of structural ambiguity', *Scandinavian Journal of Management*, **17**(1), 41–66.
Roberts, J. (2006), 'Limits to communities of practice', *Journal of Management Studies*, **43**(3), 623–39.
Roche, C. (2005), 'Terminologie et ontologie', *Langages*, **157**, 48–62.
Standing, G. (2009), *Work after Globalization: Building Occupational Citizenship*, Cheltenham, UK and Northampton, MA, Edward Elgar.
Suddaby, R. and R. Greenwood (2001), 'Colonizing knowledge: commodification as a dynamic of jurisdictional expansion in professional service firms', *Human Relations*, **54**(7), 933–53.
Swan, J., S. Newell, H. Scarbrough and D. Hislop (1999), 'Knowledge management and innovation: networks and networking', *Journal of Knowledge Management*, **3**(4), 262–75.
Thompson, M. (2005), 'Structural and epistemic parameters in communities of practice', *Organization Science*, **16**(2), 151–64.
Vaast, E. (2002), 'Les communautés de pratique sont-elles pertinentes?', paper presented to the *Conférence de l'Association Internationale de Management Stratégique*, Paris.
Wenger, E. (1998), *Communities of Practice: Learning, Meaning, and Identity*, Cambridge, UK/New York: Cambridge University Press.
Wenger, E. (2000), 'Communities of practice and social learning systems', *Organization*, **7**(2), 225–46.
Wenger, E. and W.M. Snyder (2000), 'Communities of practice: the organizational frontier', *Harvard Business Review*, **78**(1), 139–46.
Wenger, E., R.A. McDermott and W. Snyder (2002), *Cultivating Communities of Practice: A Guide to Managing Knowledge*, Boston, MA: Harvard Business School Press.
Whittington, R. (2006), 'Completing the practice turn in strategy research', *Organization Studies*, **27**(5), 613–34.

12 Initiation, implementation and complexity of managerial innovation
Fariborz Damanpour, Holly H. Chiu and Catherine Magelssen

INTRODUCTION

Research on innovation has generally followed a technological imperative, postulating that the development of innovation in organizations is primarily through R&D activities. Hence, the majority of the studies on innovation have focused on technology-based product and process innovations. Whereas economists, organizational sociologists and management scholars have noted the importance of organizational and managerial innovations, conceptual and empirical studies of antecedents and consequences of this innovation type are scarce. Most models and theories of innovation are still based on technological innovation.

Articles by Hamel (2006), Birkinshaw and Mol (2006) and Birkinshaw et al. (2008) have renewed interest in research on managerial innovation. This research interest is long overdue as a firm's prospect to compete and sustain performance requires continuous innovation, which is subject to the introduction of new management ideas and practices for modifying and improving the firm's structure and processes to enable strategic renewal and organizational change. We employ managerial innovation as an umbrella term for administrative, organizational and management innovations and define it as innovations in organizational structure and processes, administrative systems, and management tools, techniques and practices (Kimberly, 1981; Birkinshaw et al., 2008; Walker et al., 2010).

This chapter focuses on the adoption of managerial innovations in organizations. We distinguish between two phases of the innovation adoption process – initiation and implementation – and assess the influence of their attributes on the adoption of two types of outsourcing of the delivery of public services by local governments. We also examine the role of two indicators of innovation complexity – asset specificity and service measurability (Brown and Potoski, 2003) – as antecedents of managerial innovation, as well as moderators of the association between attributes of initiation and implementation and adoption of managerial innovation. Figure 12.1 shows the study's conceptual model.

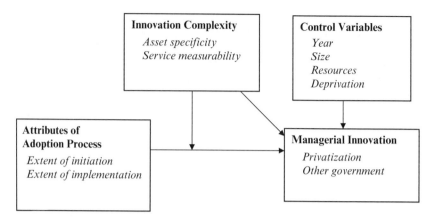

Figure 12.1   The study model

In the following sections we first develop hypotheses and then test them by analyzing the data from a database we formed by merging six different surveys – three surveys conducted in 1997 and three follow-up surveys conducted in 2002. The two managerial innovations we examine are both non-traditional modes of service provision in US local governments – outsourcing the delivery of public service to (1) for-profit firms and (2) other local governments. Outsourcing of services is an innovation attributed to the new public management (NPM) and reinventing government (RG) reform movements to make public service organizations more efficient and effective (Osborne and Gaebler, 1992; Boyne et al., 2005; Schneider, 2007; Walker, 2008). The results of our analysis suggest:

1. attributes of implementation affect outsourcing of services but attributes of initiation do not;
2. only one of the indicators of innovation complexity (service measurability) affects innovation adoption; and
3. the influence of the antecedents depends on the type of innovation.

ADOPTION OF MANAGERIAL INNOVATION

Based on the open systems perspective and contingency theory, the adoption of innovation is conceived as a means of organizational adaptation and change to facilitate achieving the organization's performance goals (Jansen et al., 2006; Birkinshaw et al., 2008; Damanpour et al., 2009). We view innovation adoption as a process that results in the assimilation of a product, process, or practice that is new to the adopting organization (Daft, 1978; Kimberly and Evanisko, 1981; Walker et al., 2011). The adoption process has two major phases – initiation and implementation – that are separated by the decision to adopt (Duncan, 1976; Rogers, 1995; Damanpour and Schneider, 2006). That is, initiation and implementation reflect, respectively, the activities associated with the pre- and post-adoption-decision stages of innovation process.

Managerial innovations are usually defined in distinction from technological innovations. They have variably been called administrative, organizational, or management innovations. The name notwithstanding, they have been defined as non-technological innovations that are related to managerial work (Kimberly, 1981; Hamel, 2006). Contrary to technological innovations, which are directly related to the basic work activity of the organization and mainly produce changes in the products, services, production and operation systems, managerial innovations are indirectly related to the organization's production or operational activities and mainly affect administrative or managerial activities (Damanpour and Evan, 1984). They are innovations in managerial processes, tools, techniques and practices and represent the rules and routines by which managerial work gets done inside organizations (Birkinshaw et al., 2008, p. 828).

Managerial innovations examined in this chapter are alternative types of delivery of public services (also called 'modes of service provision' and 'service production arrangements') in local government organizations. These organizations not only choose which services to deliver within their jurisdictions, but also decide how to deliver each service (Brown and Potoski, 2003). Traditionally, all services were produced completely in-house. Over time, alternative or non-traditional modes of service provision were adopted. We focus on the contracting out or outsourcing of services to for-profit organizations (known as 'privatization') or to other (usually neighboring) local governments (Lopez-de-Silanes et al., 1997; Brown and Potoski, 2003; Levin and Tadelis, 2010). Outsourcing of public services is among the innovations encouraged by the NPM/RG movement to make public service organizations more efficient and effective. It is a strategic decision conceived here as managerial innovation because it can modify the focal organization's rules and routines by changing the role of organizational members in providing or monitoring services, and the role of organizational leaders in contracting, evaluating and controlling the provision of services. This conception of managerial innovation is compatible with both Kimberly's (1981) and Hamel's (2006) definition of managerial innovation as 'what managers do' and 'how they do what they do'. Managers are viewed as decision-makers and managerial innovations as a means of changing 'the nature, location, quality, or quantity of information that is available in the decision-making process' (Kimberly, 1981, p. 86).

ATTRIBUTES OF INITIATION AND IMPLEMENTATION

The process of adoption of innovation in organizations has been divided into a variety of phases (Hage and Aiken, 1967; Zaltman et al., 1973; Rogers, 1995; Klein and Sorra, 1996). We focus on the two general phases of initiation and implementation (Duncan, 1976). *Initiation* consists of activities that pertain to recognizing a need, searching for solutions, becoming aware of existing innovations, identifying a suitable innovation and making decision to adopt (Duncan, 1976; Rogers, 1995). *Implementation* consists of events and actions that pertain to adapting the innovation to organization, acceptance of the innovation by organizational units and members, and use of the innovation until it becomes a routine feature of the organization (Zaltman et al., 1973; Rogers, 1995).

The initiation of an innovation is motivated by internal and external forces such as institutional pressure, fiscal pressure, government regulation, client demands and aspirations of organizational leaders. In public service organizations, for instance, the ongoing management reform has created expectations of improved organizational performance due to revenue-generating activities and more effective organization management through the adoption of new managerial processes and practices. In the past two decades, public organizations have also encountered fiscal pressures as the federal and state governments have continually reduced their financial assistance. Under these external conditions, it is possible to assume that public service organizations have been motivated to adopt new administrative systems and management processes, cost-saving programs, and seek more efficient delivery of their services to their clients (Damanpour and Schneider, 2006). We define the *extent of initiation* as the set of external and internal pressures and inducements to begin the process of adopting new managerial practices in compliance with the NPM movement and propose:

Hypothesis 1:   The extent of initiation will positively affect adoption of managerial innovations.

Compared to initiation or adoption-decision, the implementation phase of adoption process is more difficult to both plan and control for several reasons. First, the innovation may need to be adapted and changed during the implementation process. Second, implementation takes more time, includes more players and involves more tension and conflict. Third, building and maintaining networks of organizational connections and resolving conflicts among units and members is time consuming; hence, top managers' enthusiasm may wane over time, reducing their involvement in the implementation process (Damanpour and Schneider, 2006). Fourth, successful implementation requires buy-in and cooperation of non-managers, acceptance of the innovation by the intended users and its continuous use by organizational members or clients (Klein and Sorra, 1996; Holahan et al., 2004).

Despite these challenges, the innovation adoption process is not complete until the innovation is successfully implemented. Since the intended benefits of an innovation cannot be realized until it is fully assimilated and used, organizations engage in a set of activities to ensure successful implementation. These activities include hiring consultants, trying to influence external constituencies, forming internal committees, resolving conflict among units and members, piloting the innovation and monitoring the implementation process. We capture the extent to which an organization employs these activities by the *extent of implementation* and propose:

Hypothesis 2: The extent of implementation will positively affect adoption of managerial innovations.

INNOVATION COMPLEXITY

Characteristics or attributes of innovation are commonly studied in innovation diffusion research, where the adoption of innovation by individual decision-makers (such as farmers, physicians and consumers) are examined and innovation attributes are measured as perceived by the individual adopter (Fliegel and Kivlin, 1966; Rogers, 1995). Reviews of this research have identified several innovation attributes such as compatibility, relative advantage, observability, cost and complexity that significantly affect innovation adoption across studies (Tornatzky and Klein, 1982; Rogers, 1995). As discussed below, we focus on two indicators of innovation complexity for which data have been publicly available.

The level of analysis of innovation adoption research is often a firm or an organizational unit rather than an individual adopter. Hence, adoption researchers have focused on the environmental, institutional and organizational determinants of innovation and have mostly neglected the influence of innovation attributes. To include innovation characteristics in adoption research, a distinction between innovation primary attributes (characteristics that are intrinsic to an innovation) and secondary attributes (characteristics as perceived by the individual adopter) is necessary (Downs and Mohr, 1976; Moore and Benbasat, 1991; Wilson et al., 1999). That is, innovation attributes can be represented by two constructs: (1) a macro-construct reflecting the characteristics that facilitate or inhibit innovation adoption by organizations within a population; and (2) a micro-construct reflecting the characteristics as perceived by organizational members that facilitate or inhibit innovation use (Damanpour and Schneider, 2009). Since organizational members cannot use the innovation unless it has already been adopted by the organization, we employ a macro-construct and rely on expert ratings of innovation complexity that can be applied to all organizations in the population.

Innovation complexity is defined as the degree to which the innovation is difficult to understand and use by the unit of adoption (Zaltman et al., 1973; Rogers, 1995). Innovation complexity embraces multiple facets of innovation (Gopalakrishnan and Damanpour, 1994); for example, it can represent the intellectual difficulty associated with understanding an innovation, as in differences between marginal and knowledge-based, or low-technology and high-technology innovations (Gopalakrishnan and Damanpour, 1994; Wolfe, 1994), or it can represent the originality (the degree of newness) or trialability (the degree to which an innovation may be experimented with on a limited basis) of an innovation (King, 1990; Rogers, 1995). Innovations that are more original, less trialable, and more difficult to implement are less likely to be adopted by the organization because of higher uncertainty of their successful assimilation and thus lower likelihood of their contribution to organizational conduct or outcome (Tornatzky and Klein, 1982; Rogers, 1995; Damanpour and Schneider, 2009). Therefore, innovation complexity is expected to affect innovation adoption negatively.

Brown and Potoski (2003, pp. 444–66) applied the transaction cost approach (Williamson, 1981) and defined two indicators of the complexity of outsourcing of public services: asset specificity and service measurability. 'Asset specificity refers to whether specialized investments are required to produce the service' (p. 444). Special investments are the 'investments that apply to the production of one service but are difficult to adapt for the production of other services' (p. 466). 'Service measurability refers to how difficult it is for the contracting organization to measure the outcomes of the service, to monitor the activities required to deliver the service, or both' (p. 444). An increase in either asset specificity or service measurability would increase potential risks associated with outsourcing public services, making the decision to outsource more difficult, negatively affecting the selection of either privatization or other government modes of service provision. Therefore:

Hypothesis 3: Innovation complexity will negatively affect adoption of managerial innovations.

In addition to its direct effect, we propose innovation complexity would also influence the associations between the extent of initiation or implementation and the adoption of managerial innovations. As argued above, local governments would be less willing to outsource public services when they presume outsourcing requires more special investments and is more difficult to monitor. The greater the requirement of special investments, the lower the availability of vendors to outsource services (Brown and Potoski, 2003), the less likely that the focal organization is able to outsource. The greater the difficulty to monitor outsourced services, the more time and resources needed to ensure success, the less likely that the focal organization will outsource services. These conditions exacerbate both the extent of initiation and implementation of adopting an alternative mode of service provision. That is, whether due to greater asset specificity or service measurability, initiation of outsourcing of a more complex service would require more pressures or inducements from internal and/or external sources. Successful implementation of outsourcing complex services, on the other hand, would require more management commitment, members' involvement, and greater horizontal and vertical integration. In this vein, we expect that innovation complexity negatively moderate the relationship between both the extent of initiation and implementation with either privatization or other government mode of outsourcing public services:

Hypothesis 4a: Innovation complexity will negatively moderate the relationship between the extent of initiation and adoption of managerial innovations.

Hypothesis 4b: Innovation complexity will negatively moderate the relationship between the extent of implementation and adoption of managerial innovations.

SOURCES OF DATA

We constructed a database by combining data from multiple sources: two reinventing government (RG) surveys administered by the International City/County Management Association (ICMA) in 1997 and 2003; two alternative service delivery (ASD) surveys conducted by ICMA in 1997 and 2002; two censuses of US government surveys conducted in 1997 and 2002; and the results from a survey conducted by Brown and Potoski (2003, pp. 450–52). The ICMA surveys are available on ICMA's website (http://www.icma.org).

We first merged both panels of RG and ASD surveys. Because their samples are not identical, the merged 1997 RG-ASD dataset and the merged 2002 RG-ASD dataset respectively include 725 and 531 organizations (municipalities only) that responded to both surveys. For triangulation and inclusion of objective measures, we then merged the 1997 RG-ASD and 2002 RG-ASD datasets with the 1997 and 2002 censuses of US government surveys. Since the census data includes local governments with populations of 25 000 and more (vs. ICMA's 10 000 or more), the number of cities in the merged 1997 and 2002 RG-ASD-census datasets was reduced to 329 and 261, respectively. Similar to Levin and Tadelis (2010), for the cities that were included in both 1997 and 2002 RG-ASD-census datasets, we used the data from the panel where it was either more recent, contained more complete responses, or both. The resulting dataset used in our analysis includes a total of 473 organizations, 212 cities from the 1997 panel and 261 from the 2002 panel. Sample validity was tested by comparing city population, number of employees and total expenditure of the cities in the sample with those from a proportional random sample of local governments from the census of US government datasets. No significant differences were found (p > 0.05).

MEASURES AND ANALYSIS

Outsourcing of Services

The ASD questionnaires provide a list of public services. Respondents are asked to mark whether or not their organization supplies each of the services, and if so, whether it offers the service by an alternative mode of service provision. We operationalized *privatization* for each local government by the number of public services outsourced to for-profit firms divided by the total number of services provided by that organization. Similarly, *other government* was measured by the total number of services outsourced to other local governments as a percentage of the total number of services provided by the focal organization.

Attributes of Initiation and Implementation

These variables were measured by the data collected via the ASD surveys. Respondents were asked to indicate the pressures and inducements for initiating an alternative service delivery provision from a list of seven pro-vided on the questionnaire (e.g., fiscal pressure, federal or state mandate, citizens' demand). We measured *the extent of initiation* by the proportion of items a manager indicated. Similarly, *the extent of implementation* was computed as the proportion of items that a manager marked from a list of 12 actions taken by the organization to assist successful implementation (e.g., benchmarked outsourced services, hired consultants, implemented on a trial basis, surveyed citizens).

Innovation Complexity

This variable was measured by using the data from a random survey of 75 city managers and mayors conducted by Brown and Potoski (2003). The survey asked respondents to rate the asset specificity and service measur-ability of 64 programs listed on the ICMA's ASD questionnaire on two 5-point scales (ibid., p. 450). Brown and Potoski report the average asset specificity and service measurability ratings for each of the 64 public serv-ices (ibid., pp. 451–2). We used these ratings and calculated four indicators of innovation complexity – *asset specificity for privatization, asset specific-ity for local government, service measurability for privatization* and *service measurability for local government* – for each organization in our dataset. Each indicator was computed by measuring the mean of the average rating of asset specificity or service measurability of the services that the focal organization provides via one of the two modes of outsourcing. For instance, *asset specificity for privatization* was computed by the mean of asset specificity of the services that the focal organization provides via outsourcing them to for-profit firms.

Control Variables

Since we have data drawn from two panels, we controlled for *year* (0 = 1997 and 1 = 2002). In addition, we controlled for three other variables common in the studies of public service organizations. *Deprivation* was measured by a 4-point scale, reflecting the rate of unemployment in the local government's jurisdiction (1 = under 3 percent; 2 = 3–4.9 percent; 3 = 5–7 percent; 4 = greater than 7 percent). *Organizational size* was measured by the number of full-time employees on a 7-point scale (1 = fewer than 50; 2 = 50–99; 3 = 100–249; 4 = 250–499; 5 = 500–749; 6 = 750–999; 7 = 1000 or more). *Organizational resource* was measured via rating of the organization's eco-nomic health on a 5-point scale by city manager/chief administrator (1 = poor; 2 = fair; 3 = good; 4 = very good; 5 = excellent). Table 12.1 includes descriptive statistics and correlations of all variables used in our analysis.

Table 12.1 Descriptive statistics and correlations

Variables	Mean	s.d.	1	2	3	4	5	6	7	8	9	10	11
1. Privatization	7.10	6.11											
2. Other government	4.86	5.88	*0.41*										
3. Year	0.56	0.50	−0.08	−0.18									
4. Size	4.53	1.49	*0.15*	−0.13	*0.13*								
5. Resources	3.30	1.04	0.00	0.05	*−0.20*	−0.07							
6. Deprivation	2.30	0.88	0.03	−0.02	*0.14*	0.09	*−0.35*						
7. Initiation	0.23	0.19	*0.16*	0.06	*−0.18*	0.05	−0.07	0.00					
8. Implementation	0.16	0.18	*0.29*	*0.19*	*−0.10*	0.06	0.04	−0.04	*0.40*				
9. Asset specificity – privatization	2.85	0.33	0.00	0.02	0.00	*0.10*	0.04	0.00	0.02	0.03			
10. Service measurability – privatization	2.42	0.28	−0.05	0.01	*0.14*	0.09	0.01	0.00	0.04	−0.01	*0.59*		
11. Asset specificity – other government	3.30	0.36	0.08	0.02	−0.03	0.10	0.00	0.02	0.03	0.07	−0.06	*−0.19*	
12. Service measurability – other government	2.72	0.31	0.10	*0.19*	−0.09	0.05	0.03	0.03	0.03	0.08	*0.11*	*0.13*	*0.27*

Notes: $N = 343$–473. Numbers in italic are statistically significant at the 0.05 level.

Analysis

We conducted hierarchical and moderated regression analyses for privatization and other government provisions (Table 12.2). We first entered control variables (Models 1 and 2), then, added the extent of initiation and the extent of implementation (Models 3 and 4), the indicators of innovation complexity for each dependent variable (Models 5 and 6), and finally, the interaction effects for each dependent variable (Models 7 and 8). We centered the continuous predictor variables to reduce the occurrence of multicollinearity in the moderating analysis (Aiken and West, 1991). We tested for the effects of multicollinearity using variance inflation factors. These factors for privatization and other government regression models (Table 12.2) were respectively between 1.01–2.36 and 1.01–1.58, less than the threshold value of 10, indicating that multicollinearity is not a major concern (Neter et al., 1985).

RESULTS

Both Models 1 and 2 are significant ($p < 0.05$). Among the control variables, financial resources and deprivation do not significantly affect outsourcing via privatization or other government (Table 12.2). Organizational size, however, influences privatization positively ($p < 0.01$) and other government negatively ($p < 0.05$). This finding suggests that larger public organizations, which provide more services and serve a larger population, outsource the services to for-profit firms that are likely to reduce costs or generate revenue. Smaller public organizations on the other hand contract out the services to neighboring governments perhaps because they do not have the capacity to provide the service in-house, or because the scale of their operation is not sufficiently large to attract private contractors. The negative effect of year on both modes of outsourcing, though weak on privatization ($p < 0.10$), indicates that the adoption of each outsourcing provision has declined from 1997 to 2002. This finding contrasts with the goals of NPM and RG reforms, however, without further confirmation it might not reflect a long-term pattern because our dataset included only two panels.

The extent of initiation and implementation were entered in Models 3–4 (Table 12.2). Hypothesis 1 was not supported as the extent of initiation did not affect outsourcing provisions significantly ($p > 0.05$); however, Hypothesis 2 was supported as the extent of implementation influenced both modes of outsourcing positively ($p < 0.01$). We offer a possible explanation for this finding. As stated above, initiation and implementation

Table 12.2 Results of regression analysis

	Model 1 (PV)	Model 2 (OG)	Model 3 (PV)	Model 4 (OG)	Model 5 (PV)	Model 6 (OG)	Model 7 (PV)	Model 8 (OG)
Year	−0.095†	−0.203**	−0.082	−0.199**	−0.071	−0.178**	−0.055	−0.186**
Size	0.158**	−0.130*	0.148**	−0.137*	0.150**	−0.152**	0.145**	−0.150**
Resources	−0.027	−0.029	−0.032	−0.040	−0.032	−0.042	−0.042	−0.044
Deprivation	0.001	0.001	0.012	0.003	0.009	−0.007	0.004	−0.009
Initiation (II)			−0.034	−0.063	−0.030	−0.062	−0.020	−0.066
Implementation (IM)			0.221**	0.171**	0.218**	0.160**	0.227**	0.164**
Asset specificity – PV (ASPV)					0.031		0.025	
Service measurability – PV (SMPV)					−0.062		−0.067	
Asset specificity – OG (ASOG)						−0.034		−0.030
Service measurability – OG (SMOG)						0.185**		0.179**
ASPV × II							0.050	
ASPV × IM							−0.107	
ASOG × II								−0.025
ASOG × IM								−0.036
SMPV × II							−0.149†	
SMPV × IM							0.057	
SMOG × II								−0.011
SMOG × IM								−0.037
F	2.82*	5.60***	8.67***	5.13***	3.47***	5.24***	3.16***	3.96***
d.f. (residual)	365	318	363	316	361	314	357	310
R^2	0.030	0.066	0.074	0.090	0.077	0.121	0.096	0.127
Change in R^2	0.030	0.066	0.044***	0.024*	0.002	0.031**	0.020†	0.006

Notes: Table entries are standardized regression coefficients; PV = privatization; OG = other government; † $p < 0.10$; * $p < 0.05$; ** $p < 0.01$; *** $p < 0.001$.

are two consecutive phases of the innovation adoption process and are separated by the adoption decision. Innovations are initiated by internal and/or external agents; however, top managers may reject the proposed new ideas and decide not to implement them. Moreover, even if the adoption decision is positive, the organization may not be successful in fully implementing the innovation. In this vein, the implementation phase is the determining phase in the innovation adoption process. That is, the extent of initiation (intensity of pressures and inducements to adopt) is not as crucial as the extent of implementation (intensity of actions to ensure assimilation and use) because without successful implementation the adoption process is not complete.

Asset specificity and service measurability for privatization and other government were entered in Models 5 and 6, respectively. Hypothesis 3, which proposed that innovation complexity negatively influences the adoption of managerial innovation, was not supported for either of the two modes of outsourcing. In fact, service measurability affected other government provision positively ($p < 0.01$, Model 6). Also, when we tested moderating effects of innovation complexity (Hypotheses 4a and 4b), in only one out of eight possible cases we found weak support for Hypothesis 4b: namely, service measurability negatively moderated the relationship between the extent of initiation and privatization ($p < 0.10$, Model 7). Broadly interpreted, these findings illustrate the role of service measurability in the selection of the outsourcing mode. They suggest that when monitoring or controlling of outsourced services is difficult, public service organizations tend to outsource their services more to the neighboring local governments and less to for-profit contractors.

IMPLICATIONS OF THE FINDINGS

This chapter aimed to provide a better understanding of the adoption of managerial innovation in organizations by examining the influence of attributes of initiation and implementation, and the direct and moderating roles of asset specificity and service measurability, two indicators of the complexity of outsourcing public services. We also explored whether these factors affect the outsourcing of services to for-profit versus governmental organizations. The results suggest that:

1. the extent of implementation affects outsourcing of services but the extent of initiation does not;
2. asset specificity does not have either a direct or a moderating effect, but service measurability does; and

3. the direction of the influence of the antecedents depends on the type of managerial innovation.

We discuss the implications of these findings for theory and research on the adoption of innovation in organizations below.

Attributes of Initiation and Implementation

Previous research has relied primarily on a dichotomous operation-alization of adoption-decision (adoption vs. rejection). We conceived innovation adoption as process and distinguished between two phases of initiation and implementation, which respectively represent the pre- and post-adoption-decision phases of adoption process. Our analysis suggests that the attributes of the post-adoption phase have a stronger influence than those of the pre-adoption phase on outsourcing of public services.

Theoretical arguments in support of the association between pressures and inducements (e.g., fiscal pressure, competition, profit motive) and the initiation of innovation have been developed mainly from research on innovation adoption in business organizations. In general, private sector firms face more external pressure than public sector organizations, thus, performance gap, whether real or perceived, might trigger a search for new ideas and stimulate the selection of an idea for adoption more than it might in non-business organizations. Moreover, because of their profit orientation, financial performance is a more critical factor for the survival of business organizations. Hence, they are more responsive to changes in the environment that relate to demands for efficiency and effectiveness in the production and exchange of products and services in markets than public organizations (Scott, 1992; Wischnevsky and Damanpour, 2006). These differences may mitigate the influence of pressures and inducements on the initiation of managerial innovation in public service organizations.

However, one can argue that public organizations may be more affected by institutional factors that relate to demands for conformity to rules and norms in order to obtain legitimacy and resources from the organizational field (Ashworth et al., 2009; Damanpour et al., 2009). For instance, it is possible that management innovations are initiated and decisions for their adoption are made in compliance with the norms of NPM and RG reform movements rather than from active agency and voluntary adoption by individual organizations (Oliver, 1991; Ashworth et al., 2009). Our findings do not support this view, however, we have not examined the distinct effects of environmental versus institutional pressures, nor have we distinguished between internal and external pressures or inducements. Future research can differentiate between types and sources of pressures and inducements, and explore their likely differences on the initiation of managerial innovations in public service organizations.

Contrary to the influence of the extent of initiation, we found that the extent of implementation has a significant impact on outsourcing of services. Institutional pressures, environmental conditions and internal motives for innovation adoption notwithstanding, effectiveness of implementation as the payoff phase of innovation adoption is necessary to enable the organization to realize the intended benefits of the innovation (Klein and Sorra, 1996). Most studies on innovation implementation have been at the level of the individual, and have primarily examined the implementation of a single innovation. Organization-level studies have been scarce, and the few exceptions (Klein et al., 2001; Holahan et al., 2004) have investigated the implementation of technological innovations. Our findings add to this scarce body of literature by showing that the effectiveness of implementation is equally important for the adoption of managerial innovations. Future research may examine in more detail the nuances of the implementation phase, as 'innovation use is a continuum, ranging from avoidance of the innovation (non-use), to meager and unenthusiastic use (compliance use), to skilled, enthusiastic, and consistent use (committed use)' (Klein and Sorra, 1996, pp. 1057–8).

Innovation Complexity

Damanpour and Schneider (2009) tested the innovation complexity–adoption relationship in a study of 25 administrative innovations in public service organizations. Contrary to expectation, they found a non-significant relationship and offered two possible explanations for this finding. First, the innovations they investigated were primarily incremental and thus could not reveal the impact of innovation complexity. Second, theories of innovation characteristics, which are mainly developed for the adoption of a single innovation by individual adopters, may not apply to the adoption of a set of innovations by organizations (Damanpour and Schneider, 2009, pp. 511–12). These authors did not probe the influence of different aspects of innovation complexity.

The definition of innovation complexity provides for multiple types. We distinguished between asset specificity and service measurability – two indicators of innovation complexity that were developed by Brown and Potoski (2003) based on the transaction cost perspective. According to this perspective, the outsourcing of public services resembles a 'make' or 'buy' decision, that is, public organizations select to outsource services based on the relative costs of internal production and costs of outsourcing (ibid.). Transaction costs are essentially management costs associated with 'pre-contract preparation' and 'post-contract oversight' (ibid.). As such, asset specificity (costs associated with special investments) would be more closely associated with pre-contract transaction costs, while service measurability (cost associated with monitoring the contract) would be more closely related to post-contract transaction costs. The pre- and post-contract costs, in turn, are respectively associated with the pre- and post-adoption-decision phases of innovation process. As such, while concerns for pre-contract transaction costs would mainly affect the initiation of an innovation, those for post-contract costs would primarily affect its implementation. Since innovation adoption is a process that unfolds over time, at the time of adoption-decision the pre-contract costs could be more accurately assessed than the post-contract costs. The non-significant effect of asset specificity and the significant effect of service measurability on other governments' mode of outsourcing could be an example of this difference.

This speculative interpretation, however, should be confirmed by additional research. Research on different indicators of complexity can increase our understanding of how and why complex managerial innovations are initiated and implemented. More generally, comparative studies of different attributes of managerial innovations are needed to provide a better understanding of both process and outcome of the adoption of this type of innovation in organizations.

Types of Managerial Innovation

Whereas several typologies of technological innovations (parts vs. system, product vs. process, radical vs. incremental, architectural vs. modular) have been developed and empirically examined (Cohen and Levin, 1989; Henderson and Clark, 1990; Utterback, 1994; Damanpour, 2010), conceptual and empirical models that explain the generation and adoption of types of managerial innovations have not been developed. We distinguished between two types of outsourcing of public services and found some differences in their antecedents. However, it is likely that research on more distinct types of managerial innovations in public service organizations (e.g., outsourcing vs. joint contracting, or outsourcing vs. restructuring) produce more striking differences. Therefore, we recommend more refined research on typologies of managerial innovation, such as organizational form versus procedures, office automation versus administrative change, and radical versus incremental management practices.

A better understanding of the generation and adoption processes and consequences of types of managerial innovation can contribute to research on innovation in organizations in several ways. First, as Hamel observes, some managerial innovations 'can deliver a potent advantage to the innovating company ... Technology and product innovation, by comparison, tend to deliver small-caliber advantages' (Hamel, 2006, p. 74). Second, managerial innovations are often ambiguous and hard to replicate, thus, they could more likely lead to organizational renewal and sustainable competitive advantages (Vaccaro et al., 2008). Third, organizations are systems of individuals and units that work through a hierarchy of ranks and differentiation of activities and responsibilities, yet they pursue common goals through rules and routines that govern units' and members' activities. The adoption of managerial innovation modifies or introduces new sets of rules and routines underlying relationships among individuals and units. Hence, managerial innovations are more organization specific than product or technological innovations, and may need to be differentiated into more fine-grained typologies. Finally, due to the differences between the nature of activities of service and manufacturing organizations, managerial innovations may more heavily influence organizational processes and performance of service organizations, as may technological innovation in manufacturing organizations (Vaccaro et al., 2008; Damanpour et al., 2009).

The globalization of business and prominence of outsourcing, joint ventures and cooperative arrangements among companies in recent decades have augmented the importance of research on the typologies of managerial innovation. Systematic research on the determinants and consequences of managerial innovations in general, and their typologies in particular, is yet to emerge.

CONCLUDING REMARKS

This exploratory study examined the influence of attributes of initiation, implementation and complexity on the adoption of managerial innovation in public service organizations in the United States. Caution should be applied regarding the external validity of the study to business organizations, and even to public service organizations in other countries. Moreover, our dependent variable constituted two modes of outsourcing of public services. It is likely that the results would differ for other types of managerial innovations. Finally, we grounded our arguments on concepts and models from innovation literature developed in the context of business organizations, but tested them on public organizations. Additional tests across other service organizations, both public and private, should add to the conclusiveness of our findings.

Despite these limitations, our study makes several important contributions. It is among the rare multi-innovation, large-sample studies that include attributes of initiation and implementation phases of innovation adoption process in organizations. It shows that attributes of implementation have a more pronounced impact than those of initiation, pointing out that research relying on dichotomous adoption-decision may not truly capture structural and processual conditions that determine innovation adoption in organizations. Our examination of the role of innovation complexity showed that different indicators of complexity could affect innovation adoption differently. The distinction between privatization and other governments, although both represent outsourcing of public services, calls for more attention to research on more distinct types of managerial innovations.

Overall, the study and its findings help advance our understanding of the adoption of managerial innovations. Despite their potential role in affecting organizational conduct and outcome, managerial innovations have not been examined widely by innovation scholars in both public and private sectors. We recommend continuation of this line of research without hesitation. Indeed, future studies of the antecedents, process and consequences of managerial innovations are needed to augment those of technological innovations and advance the state of knowledge on innovation process and outcome in organizations.

REFERENCES

Aiken, L.S. and S.G. West (1991), *Multiple Regression: Testing and Interpreting Interactions*, Newbury Park, CA: Sage.
Ashworth, R., G.A. Boyne and R. Delbridge (2009), 'Escape from the iron cage? Organizational change and isomorphic pressures in the public sector', *Journal of Public Administration Research and Theory*, **19**(1), 165–87.
Birkinshaw, J. and M. Mol (2006), 'How management innovation happens', *Sloan Management Review*, **47**(4), 81–8.
Birkinshaw, J., G. Hamel and M. Mol (2008), 'Management innovation', *Academy of Management Review*, **33**(4), 825–45.
Boyne, G.A., J.S. Gould-Williams, J. Law and R.M. Walker (2005), 'Explaining the adoption of innovation: an empirical analysis of public management reform', *Environment and Planning: Government and Policy*, **23**(3), 419–35.
Brown, T.L. and M. Potoski (2003), 'Transaction costs and institutional explanations for government service production decisions', *Journal of Public Administration Research and Theory*, **13**(4), 441–68.
Cohen, W.M. and R.C. Levin (1989), 'Empirical studies of innovation and market structure', in R. Schmalansee and R.D. Willing (eds), *Handbook of Industrial Organization, Volume 2*, Oxford: Elsevier, pp. 1059–107.
Daft, R.L. (1978), 'A dual-core model of organizational innovation', *Academy of Management Journal*, **21**(2), 193–210.
Damanpour, F. (2010), 'An integration of research findings of effects of firm size and market

competition on product and process innovations', *British Journal of Management*, **21**(4), 996–1010.

Damanpour, F. and W.M. Evan (1984), 'Organizational innovation and performance: the problem of organizational lag', *Administrative Science Quarterly*, **29**(3), 392–409.

Damanpour, F. and M. Schneider (2006), 'Phases of the adoption of innovation in organizations: effects of environment, organization, and top managers', *British Journal of Management*, **17**(3), 215–36.

Damanpour, F. and M. Schneider (2009), 'Characteristics of innovation and innovation adoption in public organizations: assessing the role of managers', *Journal of Public Administration Research and Theory*, **19**(3), 495–522.

Damanpour, F., R.M. Walker and C.N. Avellaneda (2009), 'Combinative effects of innovation types and organizational performance: a longitudinal study of services organizations', *Journal of Management Studies*, **46**(4), 650–75.

Downs, G.W., Jr and L.B. Mohr (1976), 'Conceptual issues in the study of innovation', *Administrative Science Quarterly*, **21**(4), 700–14.

Duncan, R.B. (1976), 'The ambidextrous organization: designing dual structures for innovation', in R.H. Kilmann, L.R. Pondy and D.P. Slevin (eds), *The Management of Organizational Design: Strategy Implementation*, New York: North-Holland, pp. 167–88.

Fliegel, F.C. and J.E. Kivlin (1966), 'Attributes of innovations as factors in diffusion', *American Journal of Sociology*, **72**(3), 235–48.

Gopalakrishnan, S. and F. Damanpour (1994), 'Patterns of generation and adoption of innovations in organizations: contingency models of innovation attributes', *Journal of Engineering and Technology Management*, **11**(2), 95–116.

Hage, J. and M. Aiken (1967), 'Program change and organizational properties: a comparative analysis', *American Journal of Sociology*, **72**(5), 503–19.

Hamel, G. (2006), 'The why, what and how of management innovation', *Harvard Business Review*, **84**(2), 72–84.

Henderson, R.M. and K.B. Clark (1990), 'Architectural innovation: the reconfiguration of existing product technologies and the failure of established firms', *Administrative Science Quarterly*, **35**(1), 9–30.

Holahan, P.J., Z.H. Aronson, M.P. Jukart and F.D. Schoorman (2004), 'Implementing computer technology: a multiorganizational test of Klein and Sorra's model', *Journal of Engineering and Technology Management*, **21**(1–2), 31–50.

Jansen, J.P., F.A.J. Van den Bosch and H.W. Volberda (2006), 'Exploratory innovation, exploitative innovation, and performance: effects of organizational antecedents and environmental moderators', *Management Science*, **52**(11), 1161–674.

Kimberly, J.R. (1981), 'Managerial innovation', in P.C. Nystrom and W.H. Starbuck (eds), *Handbook of Organizational Design*, New York: Oxford University Press, pp. 84–104.

Kimberly, J.R. and M.J. Evanisko (1981), 'Organizational innovation: the influence of individual, organizational, and contextual factors on hospital adoption of technological and administrative innovations', *Academy of Management Journal*, **24**(4), 679–713.

King, N. (1990), 'Innovation at work: the research literature', in M.A. West, and J.L. Farr (eds), *Innovation and Creativity at Work*, New York: Wiley, pp. 15–59.

Klein, K.J. and J.S. Sorra (1996), 'The challenge of innovation implementation', *Academy of Management Journal*, **21**(4), 1055–80.

Klein, K.J., A.B. Conn and J.S. Sorra (2001), 'Implementing computerized technology: an organizational analysis', *Journal of Applied Psychology*, **86**(5), 811–24.

Levin, J. and S. Tadelis (2010), 'Contracting for government services: theory and evidence from US cities', *Journal of Industrial Economics*, **58**(3), 507–41.

Lopez-de-Silances, F., A.R.W. Shleifer and R.W. Vishny (1997), 'Privatization in the United States', *RAND Journal of Economics*, **28**(3), 447–71.

Moore, G.C. and I. Benbasat (1991), 'Developing an instrument to measure the perceptions of adopting an information technology innovation', *Information Systems Research*, **2**(3), 192–222.

Neter, J., W. Wasserman and M.H. Kutner (1985), *Applied Linear Statistical Models*, Homewood, IL: Irwin.

Oliver, C. (1991), 'Strategic responses to institutional processes', *Academy of Management Review*, **16**(1), 145–79.

Osborne, D. and T. Gaebler, 1992, *Reinventing Government: How the Entrepreneurial Spirit is Transforming the Public Sector*, Reading, PA: Addison-Wesley.

Rogers, E.M. (1995), *Diffusion of Innovations*, New York: The Free Press.

Schneider, M. (2007), 'Do attributes of innovative administrative practices influence their adoption? An exploratory study of US local government', *Public Performance and Management Review*, **30**(4), 590–614.

Scott, W.R. (1992), *Organizations: Rational, Natural, and Open Systems*, Englewood Cliffs, NJ: Prentice-Hall.

Tornatzky, L.G. and K.J. Klein (1982), 'Innovation characteristics and innovation adoption-implementation: a meta-analysis of findings', *IEEE Transactions on Engineering Management*, **29**(1), 28–45.

Utterback, J.M. (1994), *Mastering the Dynamics of Innovation*, Cambridge, MA: Harvard Business Press.

Vaccaro, I.G., J.J.P. Jansen, F.A.J. Van den Bosch and H.W. Volberda (2008), 'Management innovation and leadership: the moderating role of organizational size', paper presented at the EURAM 2008, 14–17 May, Ljubljana, Slovenia.

Walker, R.M. (2008), 'An empirical evaluation of innovation types and organizational characteristics: towards a configuration framework', *Journal of Public Administration Research and Theory*, **18**(3), 591–615.

Walker, R.M., F. Damanpour and C.A. Devece (2011), 'Management innovation and organizational performance: the mediating effect of performance management', *Journal of Public Administration Research and Theory*, **21**(2), 367–86.

Williamson, O. (1981), 'The economics of organization: the transaction cost approach', *American Journal of Sociology*, **87**(3), 548–77.

Wilson, A.L., K. Ramamurthy and P.C. Nystrom (1999), 'A multi-attribute measure for innovation adoption: the context of imaging technology', *IEEE Transactions on Engineering Management*, **46**(3), 311–21.

Wischnevsky, J.D. and F. Damanpour (2006), 'Organizational transformation and performance: an examination of three perspectives', *Journal of Managerial Issue*, **18**(1), 104–28.

Wolfe, R.A. (1994), 'Organizational innovation: review, critique, and suggested research directions', *Journal of Management Studies*, **31**(3), 405–31.

Zaltman, G., R. Duncan and J. Holbek (1973), *Innovations and Organizations*, New York: Wiley.

13 Surprising organization*
Miguel Pina e Cunha, Stewart Clegg and Arménio Rego

INTRODUCTION: WHY SURPRISE?

Psychological research suggests that 'people want their lives to be predictable, orderly, and sensible, and they fear chaos, randomness, and unpleasant surprises' (Hogan and Shelton, 1998, p.130). Organizations provide the type of environment that is supposed to guarantee order, predictability and routine. In fact, the theory of organizations can be viewed in historical terms as a campaign in which the protagonists were organizing against uncertainty. Organizations, much as the people that make them, have been regarded as fearful of chaos, randomness and surprise. In fact, surprise and organization are almost antonyms: to be organized is supposed to make us immune to surprise; to be surprised suggests that one was not organized sufficiently to have anticipated something or other.

Fear of uncertainty is unfortunate because all but the most boring of organizations must confront it. Organizational life, when interesting, complex and realistically grasped, is full of chaos (Stacey, 1991), randomness (Taleb, 2004) and surprise (Watkins and Bazerman, 2003). As Farazmand (2009, p.406) argued, 'The age of rapid globalization, information technologies, and nonlinear chaotic changes dictates the prescription of "surprise" as the "most commanding dimension of uncertainty" and hyper-complexity.' It is hardly strange to be surprised as an organizational actor by the random and chaotic nature of events. Indeed, it would be unusual to be unperturbed, to exist in a state of blissful repetition or boring routine – depending on one's predilections.

In this chapter, we focus on surprise. We discuss the notion of surprise from an organizational perspective, the origins of organizational surprises, their implications, namely in terms of management learning and innovation, and the way organizations may prepare themselves to be surprised when they accept surprise as part of the development of any complex system (McDaniel et al., 2003). We commence our analysis with an observation by Meyer that, in our view, has not been tackled with the subsequent vigor it deserves by organizational researchers. Meyer pointed out in the opening of his exemplary paper on environmental jolts

(Frost and Stablein, 1992) that 'environments often surprise organizations' (1982, p. 515). Surprises deserve to be studied directly and explicitly, rather than obliquely, via crises, uncertainty, or seeing it sensemaking. The category of surprise should be a phenomenon of interest in its own right. The study of other processes may help us to understand surprises but only in passing: by doing so in passing we will not make surprise the proper subject of analysis. In this chapter, we argue for the inclusion of surprises in the organization studies agenda.

We organize the chapter around five sections. In the first we discuss the nature and origin of surprises. Next we elaborate the characteristics of surprises. We suggest that surprises challenge or break existing organizational meanings, and that such discontinuity can be problematic to organizations. The third section is dedicated to the discussion of surprises as a discursive genre. The fourth section discusses ways in which organizations can learn and innovate from surprises by playing with the unexpected. The fifth section discusses why organizations may benefit by being attentive to surprises. We do not suggest that organizations can avoid surprises. We rather consider that surprises can be viewed as sources of novelty and incorporated in innovation processes. Instead of adopting an instrumentalist representation of surprise, one that tends to dominate discussions of surprise, seeing it as unpleasant, threatening, or as crisis, we concentrate on two alternative views: (1) surprise management as a power play among competing coalitions that try to impose their own discursive genre, and (2) surprise as a deliberate play with possibilities to facilitate learning through making surprise ordinary. Before turning to these possibilities, however, we need to discuss the meaning of surprise itself.

WHAT ARE SURPRISES AND WHERE DO THEY COME FROM?

The term 'surprise' originated in Middle English from the Old French, via Latin. The original meaning refers to an act of being taken unawares, the act of seizing unexpectedly (Cunha et al., 2006). People may be taken unawares by (1) that which they do not know, (2) by what they do not expect and (3) by what they do not want. Surprise may accompany a lack of attention rather than a lack of knowledge: some surprises are predictable because existing information could have been used to anticipate the events and their consequences but was disregarded (on the characteristics of predictable surprises see Bazerman and Watkins, 2004, pp. 5–8).

The organizational literature stresses the negative implications of organized activity, especially in our risk societies (Beck, 1992), such that we are inured to the unanticipated consequence carrying a nasty surprise, such as the global warming associated with a carbon-intensive industrial civilization. Hence, there has been considerable interest in a range of risky processes, such as emergencies, crises and catastrophes. Boin and McConnell (2007) distinguish risky processes in the following way:

- *Emergencies* refer to the incidents that occur regularly, that are predictable but unforeseen. The blocking of a highway due to the spillage of oil is a case in point.
- *Crises* are breakdowns of the familiar frameworks that make an existing order legitimate. The collapse of a critical infrastructure, such as the electricity grid, exemplifies this concept.
- *Disasters* are crises that imply loss of life and severe damage to property and infrastructure (e.g., Hurricane Katrina). Some disasters are qualified as catastrophic, although the difference between them may be hard to establish.

The reason why threatening surprises of the various types are regarded as important is obvious and organizations often develop scenarios for which responses will be rehearsed in routines of practice built into contingency planning. As we descend the list, contingency planning becomes more difficult. Events may be known by some to be likely but still end up being organizationally surprising, for instance, some individuals may have known what to expect but have not been in a position to be heard. Cases such as Pearl Harbor, 9/11, and the meltdown of the entire financial system in 2008 provide highly salient illustrations of this possibility. In these cases, some organizations would not know, in the sense of not attending to, what some of its members might know, in the sense of being aware of the possibility of some such phenomena. There is a need for research to address the way linkages between processes and levels combine to produce surprises.

Contrary to what is often assumed (King, 1995), however, not all surprises are threatening nor are they surprising. For example, the Y2K bug threat was predictable and was effectively neutralized (Knights et al., 2008). And some surprises can actually be positive. Some accidental discoveries reveal obvious benefits, as shown by new products that were found serendipitously and became massive hits (Cunha et al., 2010). In the same vein, surprising questions asked by customers may reveal untapped new markets, as observed by Starbuck (1993). An umbrella concept (Hirsch and Levin, 1999) of organizational surprises, encompassing both positive and negative ones, is relevant for both research and practice.

Surprise may be defined as any event that happens unexpectedly, or any expected event that takes an unexpected turn. The organizational preference for overestimating control and predictability has led to ignorance about surprises or to the focus on one specific type of surprise, crisis, and within this case, one even more specific type, the major accident, and, even more specifically, the major industrial accident (Perrow, 1984; Roux-Dufort, 2007). Organizational preferences reveal not only ignorance but also forms of knowing reinforced by the fact that many surprises are negligible and have no apparent real impact on organizational activity. Other surprises can have hugely unpredictable results with high impact, strategic implications and serious consequences. As such, surprises should not be taken as dichotomous on/off phenomena but rather be considered as processes of sensemaking of the salience of events.

From little things big things grow: the idea that only big surprises matter may be wrong because, as considered by authors such as Cannon and Edmondson (2005) and Liker (2004), attention to small, unintended deviations may prevent big ones from happening, and the accumulation of small improvements may contribute to competitive advantage through continuous renewal. Inattention to unintended deviations may disable organizations from facing a bigger surprise, as happened to GM. During several decades of ignoring or neglecting small surprises resulting from competitors' actions, the company was barely able to survive when the automotive market collapsed in 2008. As George (2009, p. 78) observed, 'it was too late for GM'.

The perception of surprise is often a matter of impact: small events may have no significance attached to them until they precipitate a big surprise. Some surprises prefigure themselves in the form of warning signals that may go noticed or unnoticed (Sheaffer et al., 1998), while others apparently come without warning (Levy, 1994). Some surprises are subsequently seen as having been analytically inevitable, as in the case of normal accidents (Perrow, 1984), while others could have been avoided – at least when considered ex post (Watkins and Bazerman, 2003). Processes that lead to organizational catastrophes (Shrivastava, 1992), faltering corporate reputations (Fombrun and Rindova, 2000), or vulnerable competitive positions (Provan and Skinner, 1989) can generate surprise. Some surprises can be neutralized while others escalate.

In spite of the relevance of surprises, a systematic and integrative study of organizational surprises is still missing in organization theory. The lacuna may be partly due to the fact that organizations are normally portrayed as 'solid' and managers as agents 'in charge' of the events taking place around them (Uhl-Bien, 2006). Treating organizational surprises as an umbrella concept means one must encompass both favorable (e.g., when a failed invention becomes a successful innovation, as happened with 3M's Post-it notepads; Fry, 1987) and unfavorable cases (as when a tested routine degenerates into tragedy, as happened with the Challenger launch; Vaughan, 1996).

If to be taken by surprise is to be found failing in knowledge or interpretation, surprises will be seen as emerging in interactive fields (i.e., in action settings that result from the interaction between expectations, dispositions and local particularities) in which actors have not been able to manage a correspondence between internal representations and collective actions. Considering that organizational knowledge is always incomplete, and that uncertainty and ambiguity are inherent to complex systems, surprises should be a well-established field of organizational research. Surprisingly, this is not the case.

Given the possible importance of this phenomenon, why has it been given less attention than it deserves? Why has writing about surprises been more descriptive, with little to say about how people react to surprises? We suggest that this may be due to the fact that being surprised is perceived as the opposite of being competent, at least as portrayed in the mechanistic approaches that were at the origin of modern management thinking (Shenhav, 2003). Traditional organizational wisdom, engineering based and rationality oriented, emphasized such features as objectivity and mechanistic functioning. As a result, as noted by Tsoukas (1994, p. 3) 'in our modern societies . . . prevention is deeply valued; we don't like to be taken by surprise'. Organization in this context means predictability, a functioning from which surprising or non-routine qualities have been extracted. Surprise should be viewed as processes that seize attention in an organizational field, despite predictable expectations, instead of being a mechanical process that can be managed with standard 'crisis management' packages.

SOME CHARACTERISTICS OF SURPRISES IN ORGANIZATIONS

Organizational surprises come in multiple forms and shapes. Some are small, others are big; some are good, others are bad or even catastrophic; some result from planning, others emerge from spontaneous lower-order systemic interactions. We consider that what is common to them is the fact that they challenge established organizational patterns of interpretation, potentially acting as 'sensebreaking' forces. They can only do this, however, when the surprise is not just regarded as some extraneous event outside of comprehension but where comprehension is reconstituted in new terms that accommodate the surprise within new and changed ways of making sense. When this occurs they may trigger new sensemaking efforts, facilitate richer interpretations (Beck and Plowman, 2009) and stimulate organizational adaptation. In this way, they can be a formidable ingredient for innovation and change. By questioning existing interpretations, surprises potentially pave the way for innovative approaches to organizational issues. In this section, we discuss some characteristics of surprises in organizations.

Big and Small

Surprises vary in magnitude. There are big ones and small ones. In other words, some surprising processes have obvious and extraordinary consequences; others can pass unnoticed. The September 11, 2001 terrorist attacks are the example, par excellence, of a big surprise. The attacks were shocking and came as something unexpected to most, although there were plenty of precedent clues to their probability, in retrospect. In other cases, surprises are so discrete that they can easily go unnoticed. Customer rage, a micro-organizational process, tends to involve an element of surprise for the organization's representative (Patterson et al., 2009). Other micro-interactions, on the contrary, may be positive. Consider, for example, the comment of a receptionist in a pharmaceutical company, who registered her surprise at the fact that participants in a test of a cardiac drug were showing a more positive mood (Day and Schoemaker, 2008). Not only was this a surprising observation but it was also a happy one, leading to an unexpected development of a new treatment against depression that is now worth millions of dollars. What makes this story so appealing is the fact that in most companies it would not have happened. The receptionist would have censored herself in the first place or, if she did not, the experts would have ignored her observation as non-expert and irrelevant. In other words, the logic of fear and silence that prevails in many organizations (Deming, 1982) would have censored the voices that spoke and that were heard in this story. Being attentive to surprises may therefore be a form of polyphony (Kornberger et al., 2006).

Good and Bad

As the previous examples show, surprises can have positive or negative consequences. They can be catastrophic, leading to loss of human lives, in cases where surprising interactions among the elements of technological systems lead to accidents, or to the systemic failure of the financial system when excessive exposure to financial risk leads to market meltdowns, corporate collapses and evidence of less than regulatory zeal. But surprises can also be positive. The strong demand for cheap mobile phones in India in recent years revealed an unexpected and untapped market in the country's villages and slums. New products such as US$20 mobiles and two-cent-a-minute call rates allowed companies in the sector to sign up more than 5 million subscribers a month in 2009 (Bellman, 2009). Most of these consumers were without service just a few years ago, before the notion of the base of the pyramid was revealed (Prahalad, 2005). The importance of these millions of consumers came as a surprise for established players.

Planned and Emergent

Some surprises unexpectedly unfold from planning, whereas others simply emerge. Competitors may surprise organizations due to strategic moves. Surprises can therefore be planned (Lampel and Shapira, 2001). But, of course, planning may result in surprise. The introduction of the New Coke formula was carefully planned but become a fiasco. On the contrary, other surprises result from the spontaneous interaction among elements in a complex system. Organizational crises often result from the accumulation of imperfections that interact in such a way that they follow new and unexpected paths (Roux-Dufort, 2009). Because of the unexpectedness of those trajectories, they remain invisible to organizational observers until they emerge as threatening.

Sensebreaking

What is common to many surprising processes, regardless of their characteristics, is that they sooner or later cause some form of interruption (Christianson et al., 2009) and may lead to a sensebreaking episode. Sensebreaking can be viewed as the process by which existing patterns of interpretation are disrupted. Such a disruption may be confusing and further reinforce existing interpretations, regardless of their validity for the present case. The phenomenon of psychological escalation provides an illustration of the process. On the other hand, surprises may disturb dominant mindsets and invite organizational members to rethink existing processes. If this is the case, surprises are opportunities to redirect organizational attention, and to avoid the risks associated with dominant modes of thinking. Regardless of their past utility, they may not serve the organization in the face of changing landscapes (Bettis and Hitt, 1995).

Organizations do not often voluntarily engage in the revision of their mindsets and so surprises are stimuli that enable them to reconsider what is not normally addressed. Surprises challenge established worldviews and dominant logics (Bettis and Prahalad, 1995), loosen cognitive information filters, and project a fresh look at the organization in its environment. Consequently, fighting surprise through uncertainty reduction may cause more harm than good. The difficulties organizations often seem to display with change processes partly results from the assumption that change is a property of organization, something that organization does to itself to get from one steady state to another. However, if as Tsoukas (2005) suggested, organization is a property of change, erecting barriers against change in favor of higher levels of control and efficiency may be a form of limiting management innovation and adaptation, as any specific mode of organization becomes an increasingly arrested form of development in the face of constant change.

The implication is clear: organizations should embrace surprise rather than suppressing or ignoring it. Surprises, although potentially uncomfortable, open up new windows for an organization. They invite organizational members to revise established interpretations and to introduce change in response to concrete evidence. One example of an uncomfortable surprise that opened new and bright windows upon organizational flourishing took place in the Beth Israel Deaconess Hospital (Clair and Dufresne, 2007). A tragically surprising death of a baby during birth shook the gynecology/obstetrics department, whose members were proud of the quality of care they delivered. The event led the organization to develop extensive efforts to learn from the occurrence, the result being a 'transformed culture and numerous systemic changes, refocusing the department primarily on patient safety' (p. 64). The organization also had the courage to disclose the event, in a transparent and detailed way, in an American Medical Association article, thus offering the opportunity for other hospitals to learn from the tragedy.

Organizations have to discover how to take advantage of surprises and how to use the unexpected for positive disruption. But how can they do so? We suggest that organizations may become more competent in dealing with surprises by acting in two ways. First, they can learn about surprises by analyzing the stories they tell about what surprises them. Second, they can actually try to trigger small-scale, controlled surprises in a proactive way. In this way they will, perhaps, avoid being taken unawares in the future. We discuss these two approaches in the following sections.

TALES OF THE UNEXPECTED

The scholarly approach to organizational surprises has been mainly prescriptive and instrumentalist (t'Hart, 1993). Surprises have been assumed to be objective facts and treated as such. Hence, there is a proliferation of books on how to deal with the unexpected. In these approaches, unsurprisingly, there is usually one best way to solve the problem confronting the organization. Instead, we assume that different people in distinct organizations will process surprises differently and that there is rarely one best way of dealing with them, as is documented, for example, in Meyer's (1982) paper on organizational jolts.

The importance of language in articulating and understanding crisis, or, we argue, surprise in general, has been considered by t'Hart (1993, p.41) when he noted that 'the most important instrument of crisis management is language. Those who are able to define what the crisis is all about also hold the key to defining the appropriate strategies for resolution.' Surprise management can thus be viewed as a competition between stories as different discursive devices that seek to position alternate obligatory passage points in power circuits (Clegg, 1989). If sensemaking requires good stories (Weick, 1995, pp.60–61), that is, stories that are plausible (Czarniawska, 1999), the group whose plausible story becomes the official representation of the surprise will be able to influence not only the way the surprise will be managed but what it will have been taken to be. The power dimension has been considered by t'Hart (1993, p.41): 'Much of the conflict inherent in crises centers around the various stakeholders' attempts to impose their definition of the situation on others. They do so by employing different languages, selectively exploiting data and arguments and forming "discourse coalitions" with like-minded groups.'

The prevailing story may influence preferential modes of action as well as the resources (including the psychological ones) that will be allocated to face the surprise. In some cases not many resources will be needed. In other cases, the organization may be mobilized to tackle an issue. We imagine four narratives based on two types of narrative choices: (1) do narrators look inwardly or outwardly when trying to make sense of the situation; and (2) do they approach surprise in a defensive or in an offensive way? The four resulting possibilities are displayed in Figure 13.1.

TWO DIMENSIONS, FOUR NARRATIVES

The Investigation Mode

In some cases, the company will look inward in an offensive mode. It will try to find the culprits: who should have been aware of the surprise? Who should have prevented a deviation from amplifying? It is because organizations adopt this mode that people fear being blamed (Zhao and Olivera, 2006) and protect themselves with silence. It is also because of this tendency

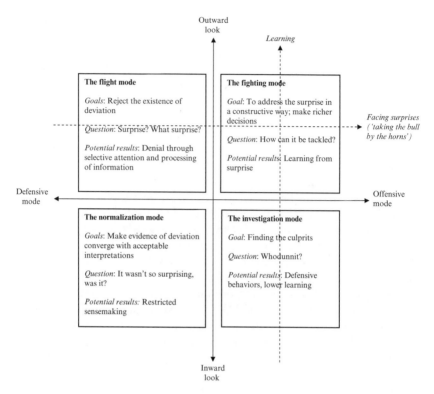

Figure 13.1   Tales of the unexpected: four genres

that Deming argued that deviations/mistakes should be attributed to the system rather than to individual action, a condition that is imperative to 'drive out fear' (Deming, 1982, p. 59). The investigation mode may also be adopted against other company stakeholders. In 2007, Mattel Toys was compelled to recall millions of toys containing excessive lead (George, 2009). Robert Eckert, the CEO, reacted by blaming the Chinese contract manufacturers, neglecting that, since the company's name was on the toys, Mattel was responsible for certifying that the products met safety standards.

The Fighting Mode

A second mode will look to the outside, that is, to the consequences of the surprise for stakeholders rather than to the internal circumstances that caused the surprise. We call this the fighting mode. It aims to discover what can be done to tackle the surprise. The focus on this case will be on the surprise itself rather than its presumable authors. One example of this mode occurred in Medtronic (George, 2009), when, facing a looming crisis in 1993, the company feared that a health care plan proposed by President Clinton would imply mandated price reductions for several company products (e.g., pacemakers, defibrillators). Such reductions would threaten Medtronic's strategies of making high R&D investment and providing extensive support for physicians during implants. The company reacted with massive cuts in product costs, executive benefits, overheads and infrastructure expenses, and seized the opportunity to restructure and simplify itself. In reality, the surprise of the feared price reductions never materialized but the cost cuts and restructuration measures led Medtronic to increased profit margins, greater market share, higher R&D spending, and to achieve better competitive position.

The Normalization Mode

A third mode, defensive and focused on the organization, can be called the normalization mode. In this case, people will find arguments to make the surprise fit existing modes of thinking. All the repertoires of biasing processes can be used to normalize surprises during or after the event. Instead of engaging in sensemaking, actors will follow a process of sense-restricting (Maitlis, 2005). American car-makers adopted this mode and depreciated Japanese and European car quality when their models arrived in the US market (O'Toole, 2008; Collins, 2009). According to George (2009, p. 77), 'For three decades, General Motors management ignored the crises it faced, treating them as short-term events to get through rather than opportunities to transform the company.'

The Flight Mode

A fourth narrative, the flight mode consists in the dismissal of surprise. In this case people will maintain that nothing really surprising actually took place. IBM adopted this mode when, in the late 1980s and early 1990s, its mainframe business showed signs of decline. The disturbing trend was reported by a young executive to IBM's senior leadership, the answer being: 'There must be something wrong with your data.' There was not, as subsequent IBM troubles have shown.

DIFFERENT NARRATIVES, DIFFERENT SURPRISES

The reaction to surprises that is sometimes displayed ('It should not have happened', as Drucker, 1985, p. 68, put it), helps to explain why the unexpected, 'the easiest and simplest source of innovation opportunity', is still denied so frequently. The narratives adopted are influential because they inform what will happen once a surprise is detected. At any surprising moment different organizations will mobilize different resources (Marcus and Nichols, 1999), depending partly on their narratives of choice. Organizations in search of culprits may try to reassure their stakeholders by searching for scapegoats (t'Hart, 1993). Others, in the fight logic, may create teams of people who are 'thrown' at the problem. In some organizations, a variation of these teams are the so-called 'red teams', parallel task forces that aim to explore if the current plans should be abandoned, given new evidence (Schoemaker and Day, 2009). These teams, in other words, are supposed to attack the problem itself. Alternatively, the surprise may be 'normalized', that is, forced to fit in with organizational interpretations, a possibility that is more likely if the decision-makers feel the need to protect themselves from external criticism, as happens in groupthink (Park, 1990). In this case, normalization takes place as people adjust their interpretation so that it can fit the established assumptions of the team. Here, the organization will produce a discourse emphasizing the rationality of the system's functioning that may be satisfactory to stakeholders but that will also harm their capacity to learn. Organizations may also fly away from reality, denying the existence of a surprise by activating interpretive systems that communicate a 'business as usual image', resorting to masking, and creating the impression that there was not such a thing as a surprise (t'Hart, 1993).

We can think of the different narrative devices, when they are organizationally dominant, as forms of institutionalized language games (Wittgenstein, 1968). One such language game is especially powerful.

THE FIGHT GAME

What can organizations gain from openly addressing surprising events through fight rather from denying or normalizing them? Several benefits can be considered. First, a non-defensive approach can create organizational realism and prevent the organization from drifting to fantasy (Starbuck, 2009). Second, by analyzing surprising observations, organizations may create a culture of alertness and an esthetics of imperfection that favors learning. Third, it may counter the hubris that tends to facilitate simplification and pave the way for long-term decline (Miller, 1990, 1993). Fourth, attention and mindfulness may be antidotes to the bureaucratic mechanization that erodes collective heed and interpersonal caring (Starbuck, 2009). Fifth, focus on the unexpected may counter the tendency of people to avoid open discussion of what went wrong. Because surprises challenge the organization's intelligence rather than personal zones of accountability, they may create habits of discussion that transcend areas of individual responsibility, which tend to be defended to preserve one's identity as competent and accountable. Sixth, through openly and courageously addressing surprising events, the organization can transform 'poison' (i.e., negative surprises) into 'medicine' (Clair and Dufresne, 2007) – becoming more invigorated to face competitors and meet the stakeholders' needs.

PLAYING WITH THE UNEXPECTED

In addition to analyzing actual surprises, organizations can generate their own surprises by playing with the unexpected (Schrage, 2000). How can the unexpected be probed to the organization's advantage? While some authors present a number of possibilities (e.g., Weick and Sutcliffe, 2001) we add to these with a number of additional possibilities still marginal to mainstream organizational thinking. These possibilities may facilitate 'imaginization' (Morgan, 1993), the exercise of reimagining the organization through creatively managing it. In an imaginization mode, organizations will be ready to embrace surprise rather than to suppress it. We see many different reasons why organizations should want to play with the unexpected. Organizations may fear surprises because the fact that they are disruptive may present a negative impression of the organization's planning capacity. But in some contrary cases, they may act to let surprise happen. Organizations can sometimes manage to create their own autogenic, self-generated crises in order to avoid complacency (Barnett and Pratt, 2000). The same may occur with regard to surprises – including positive ones. To do so, they may act along two axes: thinking/acting and present/future. Four resulting possibilities for autogenic surprises are presented in Figure 13.2.

Wild Cards

The wild card approach is a methodology aimed at producing anticipatory outlines of major changes and scanning the relevant business and societal landscapes for weak signals, which might anticipate trend-breaking crises. Mendonça et al. (2009) defined wild cards as representing the occurrence of *singular* (idiosyncratic, historically original), *sudden* (abrupt, fast), *surprising* (unexpected, startling) and *shattering* (serious, severe) events. Wild cards refer to one-of-a-kind discrete incidents that arise rapidly, in a way

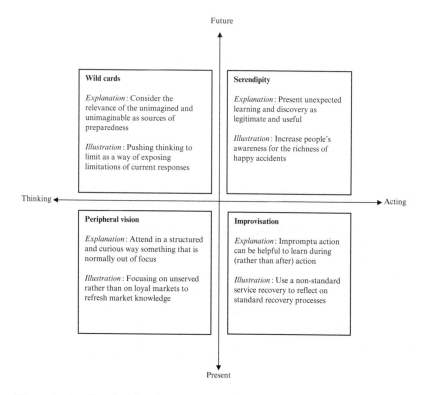

Figure 13.2   Possibilities for autogenic surprises

not fully recognizable ex ante from past information, leading to profound perturbations and alterations in the known state of affairs, not only having a quantitative impact but also transforming the qualitative attributes of the phenomenon, potentially setting new directions for future evolution. Wild cards equip organizations with representations of evolutionary paths that will maybe not materialize. In this sense, they will possibly remain as mere exercises of imagination. However, they confront organizational decision-makers with possibilities that may go beyond their imagination. Preparation for crises may benefit from wild card exercises, but these exercises may also stretch the organization's imagination and invite people to surprise themselves via the structured exercise of gazing at the future.

Peripheral Vision

More than two decades ago, Pascale (1984) pointed out that peripheral vision was central to Japanese companies' strategy: 'They strongly believe that peripheral vision is essential to discerning changes in the customer, the technology or competition, and is the key to corporate survival over the long haul. They regard any propensity to be driven by a single-minded strategy as a weakness' (p. 48). Day and Schoemaker (2004) also applied the notion of peripheral vision to the field of organizations. It refers to the consideration by an organization of areas that are normally outside its horizon of attention. The management literature is replete with concepts that signal the importance of focus, such as specialization, goal setting, segmentation, targeting, positioning. Focus, in itself, has been presented as a source of advantage (Huckman and Zinner, 2007). Focus-reinforcing tendencies contribute to strengthen the dominant logic, creating filters that suppress information that contradicts the prevailing logic. By exploring the periphery, organizations may obtain a different view of themselves and of their action (Cunha and Chia, 2007), and may also identify, beforehand, signals that allow avoidance of organizational decline (Pascale, 1984; Vollmann and Brazas, 1993). Sometimes surprises result from observing reality from a different angle. In this sense, cultivating peripheral vision represents a purposeful way of facilitating surprise.

Improvisation

Organizations may play with the unexpected through improvisation, a sort of real-time foresight. Consider the case of jazz. The beauty of this artistic form is associated, precisely, with its capacity to surprise the audience. Jazz musicians, unlike workers in many organizations, are not simply repeating routines. They are not trained to obey; on the contrary, they strive for novelty in each performance. Structures exist that, in this case, do not to tell people how to work but rather why they should strive to work in a given way. The freedom resulting from this philosophy of organizing can lead to surprising results, as illustrated by Carney and Getz (2009). Improvisation, the conception of action as it unfolds, using whatever available resources (Cunha et al., 1999), indicates possibilities of action that reveal themselves in an impromptu way, in the absence of planning and a future orientation. Baker and his associates' work on the case of entrepreneurs that act upon opportunities by means of improvisation and bricolage indicates how surprises may reveal themselves in the form of windows of entrepreneurial opportunity that could not be planned – they result from chains of actions rather than from analysis (Baker et al., 2003; Baker and Nelson, 2005).

Serendipity

A fourth possibility for triggering surprising discovery lies in serendipity. Serendipity refers to the accidental discovery of something that eventually turns out to be perceived as valuable. Denrell et al. (2003, p.978) define serendipity as 'effort and luck joined by alertness and flexibility'. Serendipitous discoveries may be hard to sell inside organizations because they are unexpected, unintentional and unplanned. Such discoveries are often portrayed as lucky rather than a result of intelligence or diligence and may, therefore, simply be dismissed as irrelevant by those who stumble on them, by their leaders or by the organization's power circuitry. As we discuss elsewhere, serendipity cannot be managed (Cunha et al., 2010). However, some conditions may be cultivated to allow unsought findings possibly to emerge in an unpredictable future. Opportunities for what Meyer (1982) calls bootlegging incidental changes exist while surprising projects unfold but can also be nurtured outside these periods.

BENEFITING FROM SURPRISE

What can organizations gain from experimenting with surprise? We consider that by opening up or 'inoculating' surprises into their processes, organizations may provoke interruptions of standard processes and force people to question what is going on. In this sense, surprises may be triggers for learning, opportunities to confront the mindlessness that tends to be created as routines are practiced, and a means of focusing attention on the 'abnormal' that can facilitate the mindfulness that will increase the capacity to deal with surprise (Farjoun, 2010). Additionally, by training for surprise, organizations may develop more and more varied response repertoires when unexpected events actually occur.

Several literatures, namely on complex systems (Fonseca, 2002) and organizational cognition (Weick, 1993) indicate that early responses have a determinant role in the trajectory of the organization's response to surprise. As such, organizations may gain from having a mindset oriented to the unexpected. Organizations prepared to face the unexpected prefer a flexible, resilient mode, therefore loosening control, broadening information processing, using slack resources (Sutcliffe and Vogus, 2003), to a mindful combination of rigidity and flexibility (Christianson et al., 2009). Such an orientation can help them to avoid automatic threat-rigidity effects, in which rigid responses lead to the centralization of control, narrow processing of information and a preoccupation with the conservation of resources (Staw et al., 1981). We suggest that rigid responses may not only occur in cases of crisis but also when organizations are confronted with unexpected discoveries with positive potential.

Playing with surprises in a deliberate manner may also have other fruitful consequences. For example, it can create a safe space where people will feel encouraged to speak up and expose problems (Edmondson, 1999) that otherwise may be undetected not because they went unnoticed but because they were 'normalized' across the hierarchy (Ashforth and Anand, 2003; Rerup, 2009). In the same way that deviations from ethical conduct are made ordinary through repeated practice and defense mechanisms (Argyris, 1982) that operate through cognitive biasing, surprises may be normalized and therefore become unsurprising. Surprises legitimate 'unorthodox experiments' that may revitalize organizations and open up prospects for renewal that would not be revealed otherwise.

FINAL COMMENT: WILL SURPRISE REMAIN SURPRISING?

It should be clear – we like surprises; we are in favor of them, and we think that organizations that can be surprising and know how to handle surprises will be better organizations. Hence, this chapter is not meant to be read as an aid to neutralize surprises or to reduce, tame and neuter them. Novelty emerges from interactions among the components of complex systems and in this sense it is part of these systems' functioning – rather than something to be neutralized and avoided (see e.g., King, 1995).

We invite readers to think about surprises as part of processes of organizing. In particular, attending to surprises can open windows of opportunity for studying how organizations learn because surprises expose properties less visible in tranquil times (Meyer, 1982). Organizations should consider the value of preparedness rather than the suppression of surprises via anticipation/foresight (Farazmand, 2009). Research on surprise appears to be necessary to increase our understanding of such factors as the micro–macro interactions between elements of the system, the processes through which surprises evolve, namely its tipping points, that is, the thresholds that make a surprising process unstoppable (Gladwell, 2000), and the impact of surprise on sensemaking.

As indicated by Lampel et al. (2009, p.835), 'we are often surprised at the failure of organizations to draw appropriate lessons' from certain types of events, including rare and surprising events. We contributed to the discussion of organizational surprises by showing that they should not be reduced to technicalities that can be addressed with a normative approach. Surprises, we suggested, may be prepared for/anticipated but they should also be analyzed from the perspectives of language/communication, and play/imagination.

How can organizations deal with surprises and what can researchers do to better understand the process? First, as suggested by LaPorte (2007) they can prepare to be 'very surprised' (p. 62). Farazmand (2009, p. 403) also suggested the 'anticipation of impossibilities through "surprise management" knowledge, skills, and attitudes'. He also argued (p. 406) that:

> Surprise management is what we need to develop as a new capacity to managing emergency governance and crises under predatory corporate globalization, a process that tends to produce more crises worldwide as it is obsessed with short-term profits and control over the commanding heights of the world while ignoring long-term strategic issues of our planet and its powerless people.

In other words, if surprise is inevitable, then becoming prepared to be surprised may be viewed as an exercise of prudence rather than as an oxymoronic tip. Being aware of the positive and negative aspects of surprises may facilitate the creation of cultures of alertness and information sharing (Schoemaker and Day, 2009).

Our discussion contributes to the consideration of the role of surprises in organizations. It was based on several literatures, including those on crises and rare events, process-based views of organizations, decision-making and cognition. However, it differs from those views by focusing on surprises per se. By looking at surprises, organizations may discover positive ways of addressing the unexpected, namely by injecting into the organization's fiber a propensity to be surprised, to look for surprise, and to use surprise. While it may be surprising to find openness to surprise a common attribute of most organizations (and organization theorists) today because of the centrality of routine-thinking, we look forward to a time when such routine-thinking would itself be surprising.

ACKNOWLEDGMENTS

We are grateful to our colleagues and co-authors João Vieira da Cunha, Ken Kamoche and Sandro Mendonça for the opportunities for learning that have informed this chapter.

NOTE

*   Parts of this chapter are influenced by or drawn from our previous work on the topics united here under the label 'surprises'.

REFERENCES

Argyris, C. (1982), *Reasoning, Learning, and Action: Individual and Organizational*, San Francisco: Jossey Bass.

Ashforth, B.E. and V. Anand (2003), 'The normalization of corruption in organizations', in R.M. Kramer and B.M. Staw (eds), *Research in Organizational Behavior, Volume 25*, Amsterdam: Elsevier, pp. 1–52.

Baker, T. and R. Nelson (2005), 'Creating something out of nothing: resource construction through entrepreneurial bricolage', *Administrative Science Quarterly*, **50**(3), 329–66.

Baker, T., A.S. Miner and D.T. Eesley (2003), 'Improvising firms: bricolage, account giving and improvisational competencies in the founding process', *Research Policy*, **32**(2), 255–76.

Barnett, C.K. and M.G. Pratt (2000), 'From threat-rigidity to flexibility: toward a learning model of autogenic crisis in organizations', *Journal of Organizational Change Management*, **13**(1), 74–88.

Bazerman, M.H. and M.D. Watkins (2004), *Predictable Surprises*, Boston, MA: Harvard Business School Press.

Beck, T. and D.A. Plowman (2009), 'Experiencing rare and unusual events richly: the role of middle managers in animating and guiding organizational interpretation', *Organization Science*, **20**(5), 909–24.

Beck, U. (1992), *Risk Society*, Newbury Park, CA: Sage.

Bellman, E. (2009), 'India engineers a new market as companies focus on the poor', *Wall Street Journal*, 21 October, 14–15.

Bettis, R.A. and M.A. Hitt (1995), 'The new competitive landscape', *Strategic Management Journal*, **16**(S1), 7–19.

Bettis, R.A. and C.K. Prahalad (1995), 'The dominant logic: retrospective and extension', *Strategic Management Journal*, **16**(1), 5–14.

Boin, A. and A. McConnell (2007), 'Preparing for critical infrastructure breakdowns: the limits of crisis management and the need for resilience', *Journal of Contingencies and Crisis Management*, **15**(1), 50–59.

Cannon, M.D. and A.C. Edmondson (2005), 'Failing to learn and learning to fail (intelligently): how great organizations put failure to work', *Long Range Planning*, **38**(3), 299–319.

Carney, B.M. and I. Getz (2009), *Freedom Inc*, New York: Crown.

Christianson, M.K., M.T. Farkas, K.M. Sutcliffe and K.E. Weick (2009), 'Learning through rare events: significant interruptions at the Baltimore and Ohio Railroad Museum', *Organization Science*, **20**(5), 846–60.

Clair, J.A. and R.L. Dufresne (2007), 'Changing poison into medicine: how companies can experience positive transformation from a crisis', *Organizational Dynamics*, **36**(1), 63–77.

Clegg, S.R. (1989), *Frameworks of Power*, London: Sage.

Collins, J. (2009), *How the Mighty Fall: And Why Some Companies Never Give In*, New York: Arrow.

Cunha, M.P. and R. Chia (2007), 'Using teams to avoid peripheral blindness', *Long Range Planning*, **40**(6), 559–73.

Cunha, M.P., J.V. Cunha and K. Kamoche (1999), 'Organizational improvisation: what, when, how and why', *International Journal of Management Reviews*, **1**(3), 299–341.

Cunha, M.P., S.R. Clegg and K. Kamoche (2006), 'Surprises in management and organization: concept, sources, and a typology', *British Journal of Management*, **17**(4), 317–29.

Cunha, M.P., S.R. Clegg and S. Mendonça (2010), 'On serendipity: metaphors for understanding', *European Management Journal*, **28**(5), 319–31.

Czarniawska, B. (1999), *Writing Management: Organization Theory as a Literary Genre*, Oxford: Oxford University Press.

Day, G.S. and P. Schoemaker (2004), 'Peripheral vision: sensing and acting on weak signals', *Long Range Planning*, **37**(2), 117–21.

Day, G.S. and P. Schoemaker (2008), 'Are you a vigilant leader?', *MIT Sloan Management Review*, **49**(3), 43–51.

Deming, W.E. (1982), *Out of the Crisis*, Cambridge, MA: MIT Press.

Denrell, J., C. Fang and S.G. Winter (2003), 'The economics of strategic opportunity', *Strategic Management Journal*, **24**(10), 977–90.

Drucker, P.F. (1985), 'The discipline of innovation', *Harvard Business Review*, May–June, 67–72.

Edmondson, A. (1999), 'Psychological safety and learning behavior in work teams', *Administrative Science Quarterly*, **44**(2), 350–83.

Farazmand, A. (2009), 'Hurricane Katrina, the crisis of leadership, and chaos management: time for trying the "Surprise Management Theory in Action"', *Public Organization Review*, **9**(4), 399–412.

Farjoun, M. (2010), 'Beyond dualism: stability and change as duality', *Academy of Management Review*, **35**(2), 202–25.

Fombrun, C.J. and V.P. Rindova (2000), 'The road to transparency: reputation management at Royal Dutch/Shell', in M. Schultz, M.J. Hatch and M.H. Larsen (eds), *The Expressive Organization: Linking Identity, Reputation and the Corporate Brand*, Oxford: Oxford University Press, pp. 77–96.

Fonseca, J. (2002), *Complexity and Innovation in Organizations*, London: Routledge.

Frost, P. and R. Stablein (eds) (1992), *Doing Exemplary Research*, Newbury Park, CA: Sage.

Fry, A. (1987), 'The Post-it-note: a case of intrapreneurial success', *SAM Advanced Management Journal*, **52**(3), 4–9.

George, B. (2009), *Seven Lessons for Leading in Crisis*, San Francisco: Jossey Bass.

Gladwell, M. (2000), *The Tipping Point*, Boston, MA: Little, Brown.

Hirsch, P.M. and D.Z. Levin (1999), 'Umbrella advocates versus validity police: a life-cycle model', *Organization Science*, **10**(2), 199–212.

Hogan, R. and D. Shelton (1998), 'A socioanalytic perspective on job performance', *Human Performance*, **11**(2–3), 129–44.

Huckman, R.S. and D.E. Zinner (2007), 'Does focus improve organizational performance? Lessons from the management of clinical trials', *Strategic Management Journal*, **29**(2), 173–93.

King, A. (1995), 'Avoiding ecological surprise: lessons from long-standing communities', *Academy of Management Review*, **20**(4), 961–85.

Knights, D., T. Vurdubakis and H. Willmott (2008), 'The night of the bug: technology, risk and (dis)organization at the fin de siècle', *Management and Organizational History*, **3**(3–4), 289–309.

Kornberger, M., C. Carter and S.R. Clegg (2006), 'Rethinking the polyphonic organization: managing as discursive practice', *Scandinavian Journal of Management*, **22**(1), 3–30.

Lampel, J. and Z. Shapira (2001), 'Judgmental errors, interactive norms, and the difficulty of detecting strategic surprises', *Organization Science*, **12**(5), 599–611.

Lampel, J., J. Shamsie and Z. Shapira (2009), 'Experiencing the improbable: rare events and organizational learning', *Organization Science*, **20**(5), 835–45.

LaPorte, T. (2007), 'Critical infrastructure in the face of a predatory future: preparing for untoward surprise', *Journal of Contingencies and Crisis Management*, **15**(1), 60–64.

Levy, D. (1994), 'Chaos theory and strategy: theory, application, and managerial implications', *Strategic Management Journal*, **15**(S2), 167–78.

Liker, J.K. (2004), *The Toyota Way*, New York: McGraw-Hill.

Maitlis, S. (2005), 'The social processes of organizational sense-making', *Academy of Management Journal*, **48**(1), 21–49.

Marcus, A.A. and M.L. Nichols (1999), 'On the edge: heeding the warnings of unusual events', *Organization Science*, **10**(4), 482–99.

McDaniel, R.R., M.E. Jordan and B. Fleeman (2003), 'Surprise, surprise, surprise! A complexity science view of the unexpected', *Health Care Management Review*, **28**(3), 266–28.

Mendonça, S., M.P. Cunha, J. Kaivo-oja and F. Ruff (2009), 'Venturing into the wilderness: preparing for wild cards in the civil aircraft and asset-management industries', *Long Range Planning*, **42**(1), 23–41.

Meyer, A.D. (1982), 'Adapting to environmental jolts', *Administrative Science Quarterly*, **27**(4), 515–37.

Miller, D. (1990), *The Icarus Paradox*, New York: Harper.

Miller, D. (1993), 'The architecture of simplicity', *Academy of Management Review*, **18**(1), 116–38.

Morgan, G. (1993), *Imaginization: The Art of Creative Management*, Newbury Park, CA: Sage.

O'Toole, J. (2008), 'Speaking truth to power', in W. Bennis, D. Goleman and J. O'Toole (eds), *Transparency: Creating a Culture of Candor*, San Francisco: Jossey Bass, pp. 45–92.

Park, W.D. (1990), 'A review of research on groupthink', *Journal of Behavioral Decision Making*, **3**(4), 229–45.

Pascale, R.T. (1984), 'Perspectives on strategy: the real story behind Honda's success', *California Management Review*, **XXIV**(3), 47–72.

Patterson, P.G., J.R. McColl-Kennedy, A.K. Smith and Z. Lu (2009), 'Customer rage: triggers, tipping points, and take-outs', *California Management Review*, **52**(1), 6–28.

Perrow, C. (1984), *Normal Accidents: Living with High Risk Technologies*, New York: Basic Books.

Prahalad, C.K. (2005), *The Fortune at the End of the Pyramid. Eradicating Poverty Through Profits*, Philadelphia, PA: Wharton School Publishing.

Provan, K.G. and S.J. Skinner (1989), 'Interorganizational dependence and control as predictors of opportunism in dealer–supplier relations', *Academy of Management Journal*, **32**(1), 202–12.

Rerup, C. (2009), 'Attentional triangulation: learning from unexpected rare crises', *Organization Science*, **20**(5), 876–93.

Roux-Dufort, C. (2007), 'Is crisis management (only) a management of exceptions?', *Journal of Contingencies and Crisis Management*, **15**(2), 105–14.

Roux-Dufort, C. (2009), 'The devil lies in details! How crises build up within organizations', *Journal of Contingencies and Crisis Management*, **17**(1), 4–11.

Schoemaker, P. and G.S. Day (2009), 'How to make sense of weak signals', *MIT Sloan Management Review*, **50**(3), 81–9.

Schrage, M. (2000), *Serious Play*, Boston, MA: Harvard Business School Press.

Sheaffer, Z., B. Richardson and Z. Rosenblatt (1998), 'Early warning-signals management: a lesson from the Barings crisis', *Journal of Contingencies and Crisis Management*, **6**(1), 1–22.

Shenhav, Y. (2003), 'The historical and epistemological foundations of organization theory. Fusing sociological theory with engineering discourse', in H. Tsoukas and C. Knudsen (eds), *The Oxford Handbook of Organization Theory*, Oxford: Oxford University Press, pp. 183–209.

Shrivastava, P. (1992), *Bhopal: Anatomy of a Crisis* (2nd edition), London: Paul Chapman.

Stacey, R. (1991), *The Chaos Frontier. Creative Strategic Control for Business*, Oxford: Butterworth-Heinemann.

Starbuck, W.H. (1993), 'Keeping a butterfly and an elephant in a house of cards: the elements of exceptional success', *Journal of Management Studies*, **30**(6), 885–921.

Starbuck, W.H. (2009), 'Cognitive reactions to rare events: perceptions, uncertainty, and learning', *Organization Science*, **20**(5), 925–37.

Staw, B.M., L. Sandelands and J.E. Dutton (1981), 'Threat-rigidity effects in organizational behavior: a multi-level analysis', *Administrative Science Quarterly*, **26**(4), 501–24.

Sutcliffe, K.M. and T.J. Vogus (2003), 'Organizing for resilience', in K.S. Cameron, J.E. Dutton and R.E. Quinn (eds), *Positive Organizational Scholarship*, San Francisco: Berrett-Koehler, pp. 94–110.

Taleb, N.N. (2004), *Fooled by Randomness: The Hidden Role of Chance in Life and in the Markets*, London: Penguin.

t'Hart, P. (1993), 'Symbols, rituals and power: the lost dimensions of crises management', *Journal of Contingencies and Crisis Management*, **1**(1), 36–50.

Tsoukas, H. (1994), 'From social engineering to reflective action in organizational behaviour', in H. Tsoukas (ed.), *New Thinking in Organizational Behaviour*, London: Butterworth-Heinemann, pp. 1–22.

Tsoukas, H. (2005), 'Afterword: why language matters in the analysis of organizational change', *Journal of Organizational Change Management*, **18**(1), 96–104.

Uhl-Bien, M. (2006), 'Relational leadership theory: exploring the social processes of leadership and organizing', *Leadership Quarterly*, **17**(6), 654–76.

Vaughan, D. (1996), *The Challenger Launch Decision. Risky Technology, Culture and Deviance at NASA*, Chicago: University of Chicago Press.

Vollmann, T. and M. Brazas (1993), 'Downsizing', *European Management Journal*, **11**(1), 18–29.

Watkins, M.D. and M.H. Bazerman (2003), 'Predictable surprises: the disasters you should have seen coming', *Harvard Business Review*, **81**(3), 72–80.

Weick, K.E. (1993), 'Sense-making in organizations: small structures with large consequences', in J.K. Murnighan (ed.), *Social Psychology in Organizations*, Englewood-Cliffs, NJ: Prentice-Hall, pp. 10–37.

Weick, K.E. (1995), *Sense-making in Organizations*, Thousand Oaks, CA: Sage.

Weick, K.E. and K.M. Sutcliffe (2001), *Managing the Unexpected. Assuring High Performance in an Age of Complexity*, San Francisco: Jossey Bass.

Wittgenstein, L. (1968), *Philosophical Investigations*, Oxford: Blackwell.

Zhao, B. and F. Olivera (2006), 'Error reporting in organizations', *Academy of Management Review*, **31**(1), 1012–30.

PART III

INNOVATION AS NARRATIVE

14 Managing the Łódź ghetto: innovation and the culture of persecution
Nigel Rapport

INTRODUCTION

'I, Haim Rumkowski: why am I so hated and cast down? Decades after my death at Auschwitz I remain the subject of derogatory portrayals. But who knows me? Does Mr Primo Levi, for instance, that "expert survivor", know me? He describes me as "disturbing": "uneducated", "authoritarian", "despised", "derided". Who will speak for me (who ever speaks for the Jew)? Well, I will. Here I am still. Here I am! Haim Rumkowski is my name. I suffer but I do not flinch and I do not hide.

Figure 14.1   Haim Mordecai Rumkowski

It pains me but I shall remind you of my history. If this is to be Haim Rumkowski's Testament, then let no one say that it did not look history in the face or that it hid away from truth. "So dazzled by power and prestige", Mr Levi describes me, as to forget my "essential fragility" as a human being. Neither dazzled nor fragile, Mr Levi, Sir . . . And you know it yourself: the Jew has no time, no place, to be either dazzled or fragile. In the ghetto of Litzmannstadt even less than other places. The Jew is always bargaining in biased conditions: "How much of what is mine will you let me keep? What do you want from me? My goods, my security, my children, my dignity, my integrity, my life?" And always the Jew has gone on. He suffers: he goes on. The point is to step forward.

In the ghetto of Litzmannstadt, as the Nazis "rechristened" Łódź when they invaded Poland in 1939, I was the "Eldest": the President of the Jewish Council. And I had to manage the ghetto as its dictator, as my little kingdom. For four long years I worked tirelessly and selflessly. I accepted the role of organizing a normal life at any price. The goal was to be attained primarily by productive employment. Therefore, my principal slogan was "Work Is Our Only Way". Through work we might survive the Nazis as we had earlier oppressors. The limbs that were weak – that were too old or too young or too ill or too low and perverted to work – had to be sacrificed that the body might somehow survive. And was I not vindicated? Did not more survive in the ghetto of Litzmannstadt, and for longer, than in any other? Did the "blessed" Adam Czerniaków at Warsaw succeed so well? I think not.

Łódź had been Poland's industrial centre in 1939: a busy modern city, home to vast modern mills, factories, villas, hospitals, parks and squares; the Polish Manchester. People called it ugly, but that was envy: Warsaw and Krakow were yesterday's news. Łódź was not my birthplace: that was Ilino, a village in the district of Wielka Luki in Russia, in 1877. My parents were poor, and besides going to cheder *[Hebrew classes], my formal education consisted of five years of elementary schooling. But I was clever and a hard-worker. "Work is my coin", I always said. Work must ever be the Jew's coin, and coin ever be the Jew's wealth and hope of security. So I worked hard and when my parents moved us to Poland, I became a merchant, and then a manufacturer. I ran a factory in Łódź making velvet: I travelled far to raise money and make trading contacts. I had made a comfortable position for myself but then the First World War arrived and I lost it all. I moved back to Russia where I had better contacts. Again I became wealthy –"Work is my coin" – and then I lost everything again in the Revolution of 1917.*

What was God telling me? The fate of the Jew is to suffer. But why should I be made comfortable and then downcast so? Also, twice happily married and twice widowed; and no children . . . For what was I being prepared? Swallowed by war and then by revolution, like the ordeals of Jonah.

After the 1917 Revolution, with no financial means and no learned profession, I worked at a variety of occupations, became an insurance agent, then moved back to Łódź. There, through donations from business contacts and with funding from the Joint Distribution Committee, as well as my own philanthropy, I set up a Jewish orphanage on a farm at Helenowek, outside the city. I became the managing director, a prestigious and responsible position. Once again I was a respected member of the community, elected to the executive of the Łódź Kehillah [Jewish Council] and a board member of the Zionist Party.

At the outbreak of the Nazi War, I was 62. And again God had plans for me. A position of yet more authority. But a poison chalice'.

***

'In history, success is the only virtue' in the judgment of C.P. Snow (1962, p.215), the assessment of a civil service manager and academic scientist as well as a novelist. Snow's novel, *The Light and the Dark*, considers the possibility of a Nazi-dominated Europe and the impatience that history might show to the losers in such a struggle: what would survive of their perspectives? Snow's conclusion is comprehensive: 'No one is fit to be trusted with power, . . . [no one] ought to be allowed to decide a single human fate [besides his own]' (ibid., p.221).

This chapter has begun with a fictional monologue, imagining my way posthumously into the perspective of a controversial historical figure. I do this not to escape Snow's directive – not to give myself licence to meddle in the fate of Haim Rumkowski's posthumous reputation – but because the distinction that Snow recognizes between the history of facts and the lived perspectives of individual actors is a significant one. The métier of the novel, which includes the might-be and might-have-been of other people's conscious lives, deploying criteria of evidence that extend beyond simple notions of proof, is not divorced from a human science that would sensitize itself to the specificity of individual consciousness as it is lived. A human science might hope to evidence both human generality and individual particularity in a composite or 'cosmopolitan' account (Rapport, 2007). Factual and fictional registers are juxtaposed against one another as one moves between human necessities and individual possibilities.

My project in this chapter is to examine the managerial efforts of a controversial historical figure whose reputation for virtue is difficult to estimate. Haim Rumkowski (1877–1944?) was the Nazi-nominated head of the *Judenrat* or Jewish Ghetto Administration set up after the German invasion of Poland and occupation of the city of Łódź on 8 September 1939. For some four years, Rumkowski mediated between the Nazi military overlords and the Jews, managing a ghetto population initially of some 164000. If he could ensure an obedient and productive workforce, Rumkowski reckoned, then some body of Jewish souls might survive. His 'achievement' was that the Łódź (or 'Litzmannstadt') ghetto, the second largest in Nazi-occupied Poland (after Warsaw), remained in existence longer than any other in Europe besides Theresienstadt: in spite of starvation and disease, and periodic Nazi demands for trainloads of inmates for shipping to extermination camps at Kulmhof and Auschwitz-Birkenau. In August 1944, when the Soviet army reached the edge of Warsaw, some 70 000 Jews were still alive in Łódź (75 miles away) and might have survived had the Soviets not delayed their advance until January 1945. And still an estimated 7000 Jews survived from Łódź: the largest number to survive any Polish ghetto. *Here is management in extremis*: 'managing' a Nazi ghetto when one's military overlords intend the ghettoes to be staging-posts towards a liquidation of the 'Jewish Question' and a 'cleansing' of Europe.

The literature on Haim Rumkowski is large (e.g., Huppert, 1983; Dobroszycki, 1984; Unger, 2004; Rubenstein, 2005). My intention in this chapter is a narrow one: to treat what is known about his work between 1939 and 1944 as a case study in managerial innovation. He was, and remains for many, a hated figure: a collaborator and appeaser, energetic and capable but whose managerial style was despotic, autocratic, Machiavellian, nepotistic, self-serving and capricious. Appropriating the Nazi slogan, '*Arbeit Macht Frei*' ('Work Sets You Free'), and making it his own – 'Work Is Our Only Way' – he believed that an industrialized ghetto, operating 'like clockwork', working 'earnestly' and 'well', might become indispensable to the Nazis. The public proclamation forming the ghetto was made by the Nazis on 8 February 1940; the walling-in was completed on 30 April 1940. Already, on 5 April, Rumkowski had petitioned the Nazis for means by which the ghetto might be productive: manufacture in exchange for food. The Nazis agreed. Rumkowski's vision was a ghetto community accoutred with work, schools, hospitals, currency and mail, and attributes of Jewish culture and nationalism. In Nazi evidence later given at the Nuremberg Trials it is seen that the Łódź ghetto became one of the largest industrial enterprises in the Reich.

My focus is on Rumkowski as an individual innovator of managerial practice in an organizational context of military occupation and ghettoization. I do not consume more of this chapter's brief extent with imagined monologue but I do allow myself to imagine motive ('Rumkowski reckoned . . . '). I am intent on appreciating the *humanity of managerial innovation*, by which I mean how innovation exists amid individual life courses and individual life projects: it is part of a subjective attendance to the world and action upon it. Here is Haim Rumkowski seeking to manage dire conditions – terrible occurrences, daily, for years without relief – and proceeding onwards by way of decision-making that combines personal energy and vision (and fantasy) with social institutionalism and routine.

The fulcrate point of the chapter is the issue of responsibility. The Nazis appointed Rumkowski 'Elder of the Jews' ('*Älteste der Juden*'): Chairman or President of the Litzmannstadt *Judenrat* or *Ältestenrat* (Jewish Council of Elders). The Nazi regime was murderous and arbitrary. What space is there here for responsible, creative and planned individual initiatives? Nietzsche reminds us, however, that:

> Ultimately, the individual derives the value of his acts from himself for he has to *interpret* in a quite individual way even the words he has inherited. His interpretation of a formula is personal, therefore, even if it is a formula he does not create. As an interpreter he is still creative. (Nietzsche, 1968, p. 403; emphasis original)

Managing his situation, initiating policies, Rumkowski becomes more than a mere conduit of institutional forces and structures. He is the source of social processes whose consequences are moral as well as practical.

I proceed in three stages. First I outline more of the history of the ghetto and specifically Rumkowski's work as manager within it (courtesy of the careful research of Melvyn Conroy).[1] Then I consider history's judgement of Rumkowski, through prominent commentary such as that of Primo Levi and Hannah Arendt. Lastly, I address Rumkowski's history through the lens of managerial innovation.

A HISTORICAL OUTLINE

'Who here is the *Älteste* [the Eldest or Chairman]?', the Nazis are reputed to have asked of the Jewish Council after their military occupation of Łódź in 1939. Rumkowski answered that he was, either out of bravery or out of ignorance and pride, misunderstanding the German to mean 'the oldest'. The episode as such might be apocryphal, and evidence of the ambiguity surrounding Rumkowski's reputation. What is clear is that soon after the Nazis' arrival, with many erstwhile leaders of the Jewish community either escaped or murdered and with existing institutions and hierarchies dissolved, Rumkowski was appointed *Älteste der Juden* and ordered to form an *Ältestenrat* (Council of Elders) under the scrutiny of the Gestapo. Rumkowski himself assumed a wide array of personal powers in many aspects of the daily lives of the Jewish population, even if not of their ultimate fates; he managed individual destinies.

The Nazis occupied Łódź on 8 September 1939; by 13 October Rumkowski was *Älteste der Juden*; and by 30 April 1940 the ghetto of 164000 Jews was walled in, with the population stripped of its property and assets. Rumkowski reported to the Nazi ghetto administration (*Gettoverwaltung*) and its head, the erstwhile industrialist Hans Biebow. But day-to-day life inside the ghetto, as long as there was order and the boundaries were not breached, was Rumkowski's affair. Beyond the walls, in the city now named Litzmannstadt and incorporated into the Reich, the Nazis began an Aryanization of language and population, resettling over the next five years some 80 000 '*Volksdeutsche*'.[2] As the new *Oberbürgermeister* of Litzmannstadt, Franz Schiffer, wrote to Rumkowski:

> I further charge you with the execution of all measures . . . necessary for the maintenance of an orderly community life in the residential district of the Jews. In particular you have to safeguard order in economic life, food supply, utilization of manpower, public health, and public welfare. You are authorized to take all measures and issue all directives necessary to reach this objective, and to enforce them by means of the Jewish police under your control.

Save a small number who were dragooned into forced labour camps beyond the walls, the Jews of Litzmannstadt came to be completely isolated in their urban ghetto. Their existence depended on their becoming economically productive: work for a ration of food that they had no means of procuring directly themselves. Very early, Rumkowski petitioned the Nazis for production outfits to be established in the ghetto employing Jewish labour: workshops that might fulfil the orders of outside institutions and companies (who would supply the necessary raw materials). The wages due the workers would be used for food and other essentials of survival. 'Survival through work' became Rumkowski's managerial strategy: a repeated exhortation over the years to come that a programme of 'work and peace' was the route to continued existence. The logic of cheap Jewish labour for profitable goods seemed incontestable. Could and should Rumkowski be criticized for not recognizing the ulterior Nazi policy of 'liquidating' the ghetto, 'cleansing it of Jews', en route to the Final Solution (*die Endlösung der Judenfrage*)? His productivist strategy was upheld by his immediate Nazi superiors, too, to the very end (Horwitz, 2008).

By 13 May 1940, Rumkowski could already report that he had assembled a register of 14 850 names of skilled workers (including children and the old aged), capable of producing more than 70 items. On 21 May the number had increased to 18 195, and Rumkowski eagerly sought orders for production. On 25 May, Hans Biebow responded, giving the order for factories or 'work sections' (*Arbeitsressorte*) to be set up in the ghetto. By September 1940, 17 such *Arbeitsressorte* had been established, by July 1941 there were 45 (and 40 000 registered workers), and by January 1943, 96 (employing 78 946). More than 90 per cent of production was for contracts from Reich authorities –mainly military – for uniforms, shoes and knapsacks. The remainder of the contracts came from department stores for civilian clothing, textiles and furniture.

Figure 14.2 Rumkowski testing soup

Rumkowski managed the ghetto as a site (and a mode) of production in a manner that combined efficiency with ruthlessness and megalomania. 'Overnight I erected factories and created a working town', he explained in a speech of 15 May 1941, 'I have carried out my tasks alone, by force. Dictatorship is not a dirty word. Through dictatorship I earned the Germans' respect for my work. . . . My ghetto is like a small kingdom, with all the good and the bad'. If Rumkowski was subject to the abuse of Biebow and the Nazi regime, then a very definite hierarchy took its place within the ghetto, from Rumkowski as *Älteste* at the top, through administrators and policemen he appointed, to workers and finally the unemployed and unfit. A person's position in this hierarchy determined their lifestyle, dictated the quantity and quality of their rations, ultimately their chances of survival. 'King Haim', as he came to be called, retained every significant decision for himself, never appearing to doubt his views or need the experience of others. He received the homage of his acolytes, accepted that his image be hung in every ghetto office, that his signature appear on the ghetto version of the German currency (nicknamed 'Rumkies' by ghetto inmates), that his likeness should appear on proposed ghetto postage stamps, or that sycophants praise his wisdom in congratulatory poems, scrolls or paintings on public occasions. His hand was in everything, from hiring and firing theatrical performers, and editing the content of the shows, to conducting wedding ceremonies and editing the marriage contract.

It appears that Rumkowski believed he was destined to achieve more than simply saving the Jews of Łódź: he was convinced that ultimately he would lead the Jews of all lands to their own homeland, where his position as King would be instated.

We know of Rumkowski's managerial style and ethos in part from the diaries of those in Łódź (and also the Warsaw ghetto, which he visited) who met and heard him. Israel Milejkowski, a Warsaw doctor, recorded that Rumkowski's basic premise was that the ghetto form still enabled those in positions of leadership to do something creative for the Jews: whatever the fate that had condemned them to live there, the ghetto walls might be justified by a 'spiritual pragmatic'. According to Adam Czerniaków, Head of the Warsaw ghetto: 'The individual does not exist for Rumkowski . . . He is replete with self-praise, a conceited and witless man. A dangerous man too, since he keeps telling the authorities that all is well in his preserve' (1983, p. 183). For Emanuel Ringelblum (also at Warsaw), the 70-year-old Rumkowski was 'extraordinarily ambitious and rather odd': 'God's anointed' who recites the marvels of his ghetto, a Jewish state there that has more than 13 000 civil servants, including 400 policemen and three gaols, a Ministry of Foreign Affairs, seven hospitals, seven pharmacies, five clinics, 47 schools and a House of Culture (1988, p. 137).

We also know of Rumkowski because he authorized the foundation of the 'Łódź Ghetto Archives' as a section of The Department of Population Records. This would preserve archival material relating to pre-war Jewish communities and institutions but also be a repository of ghetto history: orders, proclamations, bulletins, texts of speeches, statistical data, photographs and more. From January 1941 a Chronicle of the Łódź ghetto was prepared, presenting mundane details in a factual manner – albeit subject to Rumkowski's censorship and hence with constant reference, in glowing terms, to him and his actions.

The feudal character of Rumkowski's fiefdom manifested itself at first primarily in the matter of work and food. There was a dread of losing the work that supplied the 'Rumkies' that were to be spent in the ghetto stores that supplied the food rations (some 800 calories per day). Rumkowski appeared to control not only who worked (and ate) but the stocks in the stores: a capricious and inequitable distribution of food was a source of constant grievance against the administration and even of strikes. Rumkowski's response, however, was uncompromising; organizers of protest were arrested or else sent from the ghetto to forced labour. As he proclaimed in relation to a hospital strike in December 1940: 'And now, only force will be used. No one is going to deal with the nurses but me. I will break them. . . . I have no intention of teaching people'. By the spring of 1941, most opposition to Rumkowski had dissipated, as had underground movements opposing the Nazis themselves.

But a new and even more painful chapter was about to begin. The Nazis had begun deportations from the ghetto in December 1940. Until early 1942 these had been to forced-labour camps, but in December 1941, Rumkowski was ordered to draw up lists of 'general candidates' and on 16 January 1942 the mass deportation began of Jews to the extermination camp at Kulmhof (Chełmno). Rumkowski tried in vain to reduce the number of deportees and was ordered instead to select persons to fill the quota.

It is questionable whether Rumkowski initially realized the full implication of what 'deportation' to Kulmhof meant. He formed the 'Deportation Committee' to provide names and to listen to appeals against selection. More than ever, Rumkowski's administration would become the visible target of ghetto hatred. Meanwhile, he promised, based on statements of the Nazi authorities, that 'resettlement' did not mean a tragic fate, nor even imprisonment, but farming: 'I guarantee with my own head that the working people will be subjected to no injustice; and I am saying this not only in my own name, but my statement is based on the promises of qualified, competent persons'.

By 29 January 1942, 10 003 Jews had been deported, and by May 55 000, and also 5000 gypsies who had been housed in the ghetto. But even as orders for deportations were first being issued, and as if to underline his belief in a positive outcome, Rumkowski had decided to marry for a third time, Regina Weinberger, a lawyer 30 years his junior, and to adopt a son, Stanislaw Stein (who was to celebrate his Bar Mitzvah in the ghetto on 1 January 1944).

In September 1942, another major deportation was ordered: 20 000 infirm Jews must be given up. It occasioned perhaps Rumkowski's most infamous public act, a speech delivered to the ghetto on 4 September that has come simply to bear the title: 'Give me your children'. Here, in large part, is the text:

A grievous blow has struck the ghetto. They are asking us to give up the best we possess – the children and the elderly. I was unworthy of having a child of my own, so I gave the best years of my life to children. I've lived and breathed with children, I never imagined I would be forced to deliver this sacrifice to the altar with my own hands. In my old age, I must stretch out my hands and beg: Brothers and sisters! Hand them over to me! Fathers and mothers: Give me your children!

I had a suspicion something was going to befall us. I anticipated 'something' and was always like a watchman: on guard to prevent it. But I was unsuccessful because I did not know what was threatening us. The taking of the sick from the hospitals caught me completely by surprise. And I give you the best proof there is of this: I had my own nearest and dearest among them and I could do *nothing* for them!

I thought that would be the end of it, that after that, they'd leave us in peace, the peace for which I long so much, for which I've always worked, which has been my goal. But something else, it turned out, was destined for us. Such is the fate of the Jews: always more suffering and always worse suffering, especially in times of war.

Figure 14.3   Rumkowski delivering a ghetto address

Yesterday afternoon, they gave me the order to send more than 20 000 Jews out of the ghetto, and if not – 'We will do it!'. So the question became, 'Should we take it upon ourselves, do it ourselves, or leave it to others to do?'. Well, we – that is, I and my closest associates – thought first not about, 'How many will perish?', but, 'How many is it possible to save?'. And we reached the conclusion that, however hard it would be for us, we should take the implementation of this order into our own hands. I must perform this difficult and bloody operation: I must cut off limbs in order to save the body itself. I must take children because, if not, others may be taken as well – God forbid.

I have no thought of consoling you today. Nor do I wish to calm you. I must lay bare your full anguish and pain. I come to you like a bandit, to take from you what you treasure most in your hearts! I have tried, using every possible means, to get the order revoked. I tried – when that proved to be impossible – to soften the order. Just yesterday, I ordered a list of children aged nine – I wanted at least to save this one age-group: the nine to ten year olds. But I was not granted this concession. On only one point did I succeed: in saving the ten year olds and up. Let this be a consolation to our profound grief.

There are, in the ghetto, many patients who can expect to live only a few days more, maybe a few weeks. I don't know if the idea is diabolical or not, but I must say it: 'Give me the sick. In their place we can save the healthy'.

I know how dear the sick are to any family, and particularly to Jews. However, when cruel demands are made, one has to weigh and measure: who shall, can and may be saved? And common sense dictates that the saved must be those who *can* be saved and those who have a chance of being rescued, not those who cannot be saved in any case. . . .

I understand you, mothers; I see your tears alright. I also feel what you feel in your hearts, you fathers who will have to go to work in the morning after your children have been taken from you, when just yesterday you were playing with your dear little ones. All this I know and feel. Since four o'clock yesterday, when I first found out about the order, I have been utterly broken. I share your pain. I suffer because of your anguish, and I don't know how I'll survive this – where I'll find the strength to do so.

I must tell you a secret: they requested 24 000 victims, 3000 a day for eight days. I succeeded in reducing the number to 20 000, but only on the condition that these be children under the age of ten. Children ten and older are safe! Since the children and the aged together equals only some 13 000 souls, the gap will have to be filled with the sick.

I can barely speak. I am exhausted; I only want to tell you what I am asking of you: Help me carry out this action! I am trembling. I am afraid that others, God forbid, will do it themselves.

A broken Jew stands before you. Do not envy me. This is the most difficult of all orders I have ever had to carry out at any time. I reach out to you with my broken, trembling hands and beg: Give into my hands the victims! So that we can avoid having further victims, and a population of 100 000 Jews can be preserved! So, they promised me: If we deliver our victims by ourselves, there will be peace!!!

There are shouts from the crowd, calls for other options, refusals to let the children go alone:

These are empty phrases!!! I don't have the strength to argue with you! If the authorities were to arrive, none of you would be shouting! . . .

You may judge as you please; my duty is to preserve the Jews who remain. I do not speak to hot-heads! I speak to your reason and conscience. I have done and will continue doing everything possible to keep weapons from appearing in the streets and blood from being shed. The order could not be undone; it could only be reduced.

One needs the heart of a bandit to ask from you what I am asking. But put yourself in my place, think logically, and you'll reach the conclusion that I cannot proceed any other way. The part that can be saved is much larger than the part that must be given away![3]

Between 5 and 12 September, the 20 000 were sent to Kulmhof: patients in the ghetto's hospitals, the elderly, and children under the age of ten.

On 30 March 1943, a transport with the critically ill was 'resettled': while many sick people went into hiding, those with active tuberculosis were taken to Central Gaol in horse-drawn carts. Between 23 June and 14 July 1944, a further 7000 Jews were transported to Kulmhof, leaving only 68 561 alive in the ghetto. Then, because of the rapid advance of the Soviet Army, in early August the Nazis decided to complete the liquidation forthwith: from 3 August 1944, 5000 people were deported per day, and now to Auschwitz-Birkenau.

But before this end, when rumours of the worst were almost inescapable, what did Rumkowski know of the fate of the mass deportees? It is unclear. Deportation to forced-labour camps he had long used as a threat and punishment:

> I assigned for deportation that element of our ghetto which was a festering boil. And so the list of exiles includes members of the underworld and other individuals harmful to the ghetto. . . . Now, when I am deporting all kinds of connivers and cheats, I do it fully convinced that they asked for this fate. . . . Only work can save us from the worst calamity. (17 January 1942)

And:

> After painful deliberation and inner struggle, I've decided to deport the people on relief [unable to work]. (2 March 1942)

And:

> I will remove troublemakers and agitators from the ghetto not because I tremble for my life, but because I fear for you all. (17 October 1943)

At first Rumkowski could have believed that a strategy of buying the right to live through work could save the ghetto population. As the Nazis demanded deportees in increasing numbers his rhetoric changed, as we have heard, to saving as much as possible of the 'Jewish body' even at the expense of its 'limbs'. Even on 15 August 1944, on a poster bearing his signature, Rumkowski asked the populace to volunteer for the transports bound for Auschwitz-Birkenau so as to 'make your own departure easier'.

Rumkowski's own precise fate remains obscure. But on 28 August 1944, a final transport left the Łódź ghetto for Auschwitz-Birkenau and probably among the deportees were Rumkowski, his wife and adopted son, his brother and brother's wife.

THE JUDGEMENT OF HISTORY

On his return from Auschwitz after liberation, Primo Levi found a 10 mark coin in his pocket, inscribed with the Jewish Star and the words, '*Getto*', '1943' and '*Der Älteste der Juden in Litzmannstadt*': it was a 'Rumkie'. The story of the coin leads Levi to consider the case of Rumkowski: a 'compendiary figure' whose fate clamours for a neat deconstruction that is difficult to effect (1996, p.48). Levi's essay argues that Rumkowski epitomizes a moral 'grey zone', which may be a human constant but which an 'infernal system' such as Nazism exacerbates due to the extreme pressures that it places on people through its dehumanizing and anti-human institutions, such as the ghetto and extermination camps. One does not confuse the murderers and their victims – this is 'a moral disease or an aesthetic affectation' (ibid., p. 33) – and one does not fail to note the 'paroxysm of perfidiousness and hatred' that forces the victims to become complicit in their own persecution – the Jews who put other Jews into the oven, the sub-humans who 'bow to any and all humiliation' (ibid., p. 35). Notwithstanding, one observes how Nazism degrades its victims also by making them more like itself. The space between victims and persecutors is not empty, then, but filled with pathetic and obscene figures, the prisoner-functionaries, held together by the wish to preserve and consolidate their privilege vis-à-vis those without privilege. Here is 'a grey zone, with ill-defined outlines that both separate and join the two camps of masters and servants (ibid., p. 27).

Rumkowski epitomizes the grey, ambiguous person who is fatally provoked by oppression and whose case confronts us with an *impotentia judicandi*.[4] Who was Rumkowski? His four years of dictatorship at Łódź represent 'an astonishing tangle of megalomaniac dream, barbaric vitality, and real diplomatic and organisational skill' (ibid., p. 45). He was a small tyrant, impotent regarding those above – despised, derided and humiliated by his Nazi overlords – and omnipotent regarding those below, someone who became corrupted by power and progressively convinced himself he was a messiah. A passionate love of authority made him an ideal dupe for the Nazis: a fool with an air of respectability. The histrionics of his oratorical style – reminiscent of a Führer's – evidence a distorted world-view: a dogmatic arrogance coupled with a need for adulation, intoxicated by command while having contempt for the law.

But then how many possess the solid moral armature necessary to protect themselves against the totalitarian? The tragedy of Rumkowski's 'half-conscience' is also ours: 'we are all mirrored in Rumkowski, his ambiguity is ours' (ibid., p. 50). The adornments of authority cast dangerous distortions, Levi famously concludes:

> Like Rumkowski, we too are so dazzled by power and prestige as to forget our essential fragility: willingly or not we come to terms with power, forgetting that we are all in the ghetto, that the ghetto is walled in, that outside the ghetto reign the lords of death and that close by the train is waiting. (Levi, 1996, pp. 50–51)

***

In her description of the trial in Jerusalem of Adolf Eichmann, the so-called 'architect of the Holocaust', Hannah Arendt (1963) reaches conclusions that are commensurate with Levi's, in part. Her tone, however, has seemed to some to accord more blame to the victims than their persecutors. The 'darkest chapter of the whole dark story' of the totality of moral collapse effected by the Nazis, Arendt suggests, was the pathetic and sordid 'role of the Jewish leaders in the destruction of their own people' (ibid., p. 117).

In Amsterdam as in Warsaw, in Berlin as in Budapest, Jewish officials compiled trusty lists of persons and of their property, distributed the Yellow Star badges, secured money from the deportees to defray the expenses of their deportation and extermination, kept track of vacated apartments, supplied police forces to help seize Jewish victims and get them on trains, finally handing over the assets of the Jewish community in good order for final confiscation. They issued Nazi-inspired but not Nazi-dictated manifestos that showed how they enjoyed their new power: 'The Central Jewish Council [of Budapest] has been granted the right of absolute disposal over all Jewish spiritual and material wealth and over all Jewish manpower.'

We know the physiognomies of the Jewish leaders, Arendt continues, because, like Haim Rumkowski, they often saw fit to engrave their portraits on currency and postage stamps. (Rumkowski rode around his Łódź fiefdom in a broken-down horse-drawn carriage). And we know the mindset of Jewish officials who became instruments of murder: captains of sinking ships who can bring them safely to port only by casting overboard a part of the precious cargo; wardens who must sacrifice a proportion of their charges so as to save a larger proportion.

Arendt's conclusion is damning:

> Wherever Jews lived, there were recognized Jewish leaders and this leadership, almost without exception, cooperated in one way or another, for one reason or another, with the Nazis. The whole truth was that if the Jewish people had really been unorganized and leaderless, there would have been chaos and plenty of misery but the total number of victims would hardly have been between four and half and six million people. (Arendt, 1963, p. 125)

***

But 'Jewish people who were unorganized and leaderless' would not account for the historical circumstance of an ethnic group that had, perforce, carefully managed its continued separation from overwhelming majorities over centuries. It was by way of a combination of organized otherness, of compliance and stubbornness, that Jewishness had survived until Nazidom. Despite tiny numbers, excluded from many of the rights of the surrounding majority, periodically preyed upon by crippling taxation, by the abduction of its children and by fatal pogrom, survival had been assured over the centuries of diaspora by a kind of organized introspection. This took the form of social endogamy, cultural secrecy, psychological distantiation or irony, and spiritual transcendence. Suffering itself became a kind of spiritual value: an aspect of worldly status quo that evidenced God's special treatment: a testing of His Chosen People. The state of persecution was something from which only He could and should deliver His People, at a messianic time. To resist the Gentile other than by compensating for his tyrannous demands through 'ceaseless and feverish' productive activity (Finkielkraut, 1994, p. 50), was not only counter-productive but impious.

This argument is not my main concern, however. What can the chapter conclude concerning Haim Rumkowski as manager? What perspective is offered on the man if his story becomes a case study in managerial and organizational innovation?

THE LENS OF MANAGERIAL INNOVATION

Managing the Nazi ghetto is undoubtedly an extreme scenario, a limiting case, but it brings the managerial role into stark relief. One manages a situation that one hopes will follow historical precedent: the domineering Gentile will ultimately be satisfied or become distracted. At what point does one recognize that one is entering a grey zone where routine expectations do not apply: that the very structure of man management may itself be morally corrupt: that any leadership and organization lends weight to a policy that is nihilistic and murderous? This was the dilemma facing the *Judenräte*, and their chairmen in particular. Czerniaków's suicide did not save the Jews of Warsaw; Rumkowski's philosophy of production ('We have only our production to thank for our survival'), and the sacrifice of the unproductive and uncooperative, occasions the survival of only a small minority of the Jews of Łódź. At what point does one recognize that complying with the gradual destruction of the populace fatally challenges personal, moral and communitarian integrity? Does one accept a position of determining the fate of anyone else? There is no black or white, no wholly correct or incorrect, response, as Levi intimates.

My intention in the remainder of this chapter is to take Rumkowski's philosophy of production at face value, however. 'Our children and our grandchildren will recall with pride the names of those who gave us the opportunity to work and the right to live': albeit that in hindsight Rumkowski's claim appears deluded, let me assume that this is not sophistry, that he believed his listeners *would* have children and grandchildren. Let me assume that his philosophy developed as more than a rhetorical contrivance: he believed that the right to live *could* be assured through the opportunity of work. From within the confinement of the ghetto, and within a short period of time, he established a society –government, industry, social services, commerce, entertainment – among disoriented refugees and upon the ruins of the institutions, the places and the habitualities that the Nazi army of occupation had torn down. There was a vacuum: a diverse assemblage of refugees from a life before military occupation. One imagines them as strangers, erstwhile industrialists, professionals, artisans and traders, cosmopolitan, apathetic, pious, traumatized, fatalistic. Rumkowski's managerial and organizational innovation was this: to imprint his personality – and his alone – on all aspects of a new ghetto society.

'History', in Donald Creighton's (1972, p. 19) well-known epigram, 'is the record of an encounter between character and circumstances.' History is characterized by the way in which an individual *attends* to environing conditions and so makes the circumstance of his or her life. The necessity of being-in-the-world, in Jean-Paul Sartre's (1997, p. 46) elaboration, of having to labour and to die there, represents a kind of universal and objective resistance to human action. But there is also a particularity, a subjectivity, to the way the individual meets this resistance: individuals inscribe themselves into the material world by virtue of the particular way in which they relate to (recognize, interpret) what is around them. It is *their intentionality that produces the circumstance of their lives out of the conditions of their lives.* Alongside what one might call the 'structural potency' of that which encompasses an individual is the 'existential potency' to determine how that encompassment will be taken up by the individual and deployed in the enacting of a life-project (Rapport, 2003).

Rumkowski's managerial career, I shall say, was animated by a particular existential potency: there was a particular way of being-in-the-world, or 'world-view' (Rapport, 1993), that characterized his actions and led him to embody a forceful personal narrative and project a forceful managerial and organizational model upon what lay around him. I might sum this up by saying that Rumkowski enacted a powerful *mimesis*. He would accommodate himself and his community to the Nazis, make Jewish Litzmannstadt indispensable, by serving up to his overlords a version of themselves, in particular their industry, their efficiency and their ruthlessness. If the 'sub-race' could mimic the organizational effectiveness of the Aryan super-race then would not the complementarity be indisputable? Rumkowski set himself to translate a Nazi managerial and organizational ethos into the ghetto and so mirror the Nazis back to themselves: a compliment that could be life-saving. Hence do his infamous words from September 1942 urge a pragmatism, a *military* self-control: against traditional Jewish familism, emotionalism and other-worldliness must be set a timely 'common sense', 'logic' and 'reason'.

There can be nothing conclusive in such a supposition. But I return to his words from May 1941: 'Overnight I erected factories and created a working town. . . . Through dictatorship I earned the Germans' respect for my work.' Reviewing his infamous 'Give me your children' speech, moreover, one finds a mimicry of another kind. It might be described as Rumkowski seeking to bargain with the Nazi overlords as the Biblical prophets bargained with God. In particular, I find resonances between Rumkowski's rhetoric and those Old Testament passages concerning sacrifice where Abraham, the Father of the Chosen People, is confronted with God's demands. When Abraham is told to sacrifice his son, Isaac (Genesis 22, 1–24), God relents because Abraham is prepared to comply: to 'withhold nothing from Him, not even an only son'. But preceding this there is the account of God's destruction of Sodom and Gomorrah (Genesis 18, 16–33): Abraham bargained progressively with God (albeit ultimately unsuccessfully) that He would not destroy the whole sinful metropolis if 50, then 45, then 40, then 30, then 20 and then finally ten righteous men (the quorum needed for Jewish religious observance) could be found within. Rumkowski was, we know, an Orthodox Jew, religiously observant, also a fervent Zionist. What has been called Rumkowski's 'messianism' (Friedman, 1980, pp. 333–52), took the form, I suggest, of his mimicking the Biblical patriarch who is fated to play a decisive role in Jewish life. Here he is, interceding on behalf of Jewish Litzmannstadt and parleying over the number of human victims, that it might be left relatively alone. He appears before his ghetto audience as a 'broken Jew' and a 'bandit', but the sacrifice of the 'best they possess' might be the deliverance of the community to an independent Jewish life.

Rumkowski described himself as 'both a fascist and a communist': he would mirror back whatever the style of Gentile domination insofar as it enabled him to retain patriarchal control over 'his' people, representatives of a 'new population'. In the fullness of time, amid a New European Order, the ghetto might then transit to a model state of production and property on land of its own.

The potency of Haim Rumkowski's managerial career, I suggest, turned on the *innovative way in which he appropriated to himself two established discourses of management and organization and used them as the mediums of his own intentionality.* He would attend to the world around him as if a messianic patriarch: 'Give me your children', he proclaimed, after the Biblical '-וְהַעֲלֵהוּ שָׁם לְעֹלָה' ('Bring Isaac for a burnt-offering'). And he would attend to the world around him as if a Nazi philosophy of work were conducive to Jewish longevity: 'Work is our only way', he proclaimed, after '*Arbeit Macht Frei*'.

One does not talk of 'success' in this grey zone, but Rumkowski's mimicry, his translation of encompassing discourses and tropes into the context of his personal world-view and management plan – in such a way that an unlikely accommodation occurred between a murderous Nazi regime and a destitute Jewish population – accompanied a delay in the liquidation of the ghetto of Litzmannstadt and the survival of some 7000.

ACKNOWLEDGEMENTS

Anthony P. Cohen commented on a draft of this chapter and emphasized how management entails a social context: to know Rumkowski's achievement is also to imagine the capabilities and liabilities engendered by the world-views of his contemporaries. Andrew Irving's commentary emphasized Rumkowski's complex intentionality: how one needs to imagine Rumkowski as possible strategist, fatalist, utilitarian and entrepreneur at once.

NOTES

1. http://www.jewishgen.org/yizkor/terrible_choice/terrible_choice.html.
2. People of German language and culture living outside Germany.
3. See http://agentsofsocialchange.wordpress.com/2011/11/11/chaim-rumkowskis-give-me-your-children-speech, among others.
4. Inability to judge.

REFERENCES

Arendt, H. (1963), *Eichmann in Jerusalem*, Harmondsworth: Penguin.
Creighton, D. (1972), *Towards the Discovery of Canada*, Toronto: Macmillan.
Czerniaków, A. (1983), *Dziennik getta warszawskiego* (*Warsaw Diary*), Warsaw: Państwowe Wydawnictwo Naukowe.
Dobroszycki, L. (1984), *The Chronicle of the Lodz Ghetto 1941–1944*, New Haven, CT: Yale University Press.
Finkielkraut, A. (1994), *The Imaginary Jew*, Lincoln, NE: University of Nebraska Press.
Friedman, P. (1980), *Roads to Extinction*, New York: Jewish Publication Society.
Horwitz, G. (2008), *Ghettostadt*, Cambridge, MA: Harvard University Press.
Huppert, S. (1983), 'King of the ghetto: Mordecai Haim Rumkowski, the elder of Lodz Ghetto', in L. Rothkirchen (ed.), *Yad Vashem Studies, Volume XV*, pp. 125–57.
Levi, P. (1996), *The Drowned and the Saved*, London: Abacus.
Nietzsche, F. (1968), *The Will to Power*, translated by W. Kaufmann and J. Hollindale, New York: Random House.
Rapport, N. (1993), *Diverse World-Views in an English Village*, Edinburgh: Edinburgh University Press.
Rapport, N. (2003), *I am Dynamite: An Alternative Anthropology of Power*, London: Routledge.

Rapport, N. (2007), 'An outline for cosmopolitan study, for reclaiming the human through introspection', *Current Anthropology*, **48**(2), 257–83.

Ringelblum, E. (1988), *Kronika getta warszawskiego 1939–1943* (*Chronicles of the Warsaw Ghetto*), Warsaw: Czytelnik.

Rubenstein, R. (2005), 'Gray into black: the case of Mordecai Chaim Rumkowski', in J. Petropoulos and J. Roth (eds), *Gray Zones*, Oxford: Berghahn, pp. 299–310.

Sartre, J.P. (1997), *Existentialism and Humanism*, translated by P. Mairet, London: Methuen.

Snow, C.P. (1962), *The Light and the Dark*, Harmondsworth: Penguin.

Unger, M. (2004), *Reassessment of the Image of Mordechai Chaim Rumkowski*, Yad Vashem, International Institute for Holocaust Research, Göttingen: Wallstein Verlag GmbH.

Internet Sites

Ackerfield, L. (ed.) (2006), 'Chaim Mordechai Rumkowski', JewishGenInc, available at: http://www.jewishgen.org/Yizkor/terrible_choice/ter005.html; accessed 3 December 2009.

Holocaust Education & Archive Research Team (2007), 'Chaim Mordechai Rumkowski', Carmello Lasiotto (ed.), available at: http://www.holocaustresearchproject.org/ghettos/rumkowski.html; accessed 3 December 2009.

Wikipedia.org (n.d.), 'Rumkowski', available at: http://en.wikipedia.org/wiki/Rumkowski; accessed 3 December 2009.

15 Innovating professionalism in a communication consultancy
Kjersti Bjørkeng and Katja Hydle

INTRODUCTION

The idea of organizational innovation, renewal and change in ways of managing, ways of organizing and ways of producing have become a leading start in today's business world. Leaders who 'implement change' are viewed as strong leaders – before they are themselves changed for the next best changer on the market. The concept of organizational innovation has many interpretations; it is used to describe a process as well as a product. Twisting the idea of organizational innovation as a process driven by an intentional mastermind we focus in particular on the processual innovations unfolding in much professional service work (Carlsen et al., 2004). More specifically, we are focusing on the changes and innovations that occur from the bottom-up in an organization, a complex process of change created by a collaborating workforce.

In the knowledge economy, with its changing environment of communicative technology and knowledge demands, organizational innovation abilities are increasingly viewed as a key factor to sustained competitive advantage (Tushman and O'Reilly, 1996; Dess and Picken, 2000). This chapter presents organizational innovation in a professional service firm (PSF) (Løwendahl, 2005). Exploring innovations in knowledge-based organizations is particularly challenging because of the social, ambiguous and constantly evolving nature of knowledge (Anand et al., 2007). Professional services are subject to slow continuous evolution through prospective as well as retrospective sense-making processes (Weick, 1995), and defining such services as 'new' and 'old', and consequently as innovations is an ambiguous task.

The study of innovation as real-time processes of development is frequently called for, but hardly answered (Lam, 2005), as such innovations are rarely planned and researchers' presence is thus serendipitous (Cunha et al., 2010). This chapter presents empirical material gathered from a rare opportunity to see organizational innovation unfold in real time. During a five-year period we had access to all internal webpages and databases used to perform work. In addition we performed three periods of ethnographic fieldwork.

In research, the determinants of organizational innovation are described through differentiated means, typically through leadership, managerial levers and business processes (Crossan and Apaydin, 2010) with little cross-fertilization between these different means of exploring and understanding organizational innovation. However, in the real-time study presented here leadership, managerial levers and business processes did not surface as separate drivers of innovation. Instead, what we have interpreted as an entangling of professional, personal and private contexts, a constant negotiation of norms, and the consultants' means of reclaiming of power in the client–consultant relationship are important drivers of the organizational innovations taking place.

We collaborated with a Scandinavian communication consultancy called CommCorp for more than five years, and the empirical material allows us to identify changes in organizational practices over time. In this chapter we explore *how* such differences occur; the drivers of organizational innovation. We unfold a negotiation of professionalism that is narrative in mode. We use as a starting point particular instances of written storytelling gathered from an intranet news page and provide thick descriptions of the effects these stories have on organizational innovation. We interpret the narratives of organizational members from a practice perspective, enabling a discussion of how a narrative mode of thought is not primarily representative, but constitutive, of reality (Bruner, 1991; Weick, 1995). The narrative mode of thought involves making sense of things past and also projecting images to make sense of the future. Such narrative sense-making is thus constantly engaged with and involved in creating something new (Bergson, 1911). Analysing the storytelling as a means of constructing and reconstructing the codes of conduct of practice, we suggest the stories share three common mechanisms of organizational innovation: entangling contexts, negotiating norms and reclaiming power.

Starting with a theoretical section discussing innovation in codes of conduct in professional service firms, this chapter proceeds through three stories from CommCorp's intranet, Gesticulate, and the negotiations of professional codes of conduct unfolding in the wake of these stories. The three particular stories from Gesticulate presented are embedded in a researcher-produced narrative of the contexts in which they were written, read and recalled. These researcher-constructed narratives are assembled as a description of events unfolded, however, such narratives are essentially a partial and biased picture of a context and should be treated as such. Focusing on commonalities in these narratives, we discuss three mechanisms involved in the processes of organizational innovation: entangling contexts, negotiating norms and reclaiming power. Finally, we discuss the narratives and practical particularities of these mechanisms as important contributors in the continuous organizational innovation that CommCorp depends on.

We contribute first to the literature on organizational innovation by providing an in-depth qualitative study of organizational innovation in a PSF (Greenwood et al., 2005; Løwendahl, 2005; Anand et al., 2007). Second, to the literature on PSF, from a micro-perspective providing a study of the construction and reconstruction of professional codes of conduct.

THEORY

PSFs are often understood to be extreme examples of knowledge intensity and models for a knowledge-based economy (Maister, 1982, 1993; Empson, 2000; Teece, 2003; Løwendahl, 2005; Gardner et al., 2008; von Nordenflycht, 2010). Such firms are described as highly successful examples of organizations whose abilities to manage knowledge are critical to their success (Empson, 2001; Løwendahl, 2005; Anand et al., 2007; Awuah, 2007). PSFs include firms such as accounting and auditing companies, advertising agencies, engineering and design firms, law firms, management consulting companies and communication consulting firms (Maister, 1993; Newell et al., 2002; Greenwood et al., 2005; Løwendahl, 2005; Brock, 2006). PSFs can be defined 'as those whose primary assets are a highly educated (professional) workforce and whose outputs are intangible services encoded with complex knowledge' (Greenwood et al., 2005, p. 661). PSFs are by definition service oriented and knowledge intensive, and service provision is based on the application of professionals' expertise (Løwendahl, 2000).

In this chapter, we pay particular attention to the incremental steps that are part of the continuous development of codes of conduct in CommCorp. Professional codes of conduct and limits of expertise are often safeguarded by professional and vocational organizations such as national and international associations of lawyers. However, there are many professionals within professions such as management and communication consultancies that are not guided by vocational codes of conduct. In such professions, there are neither institutions to provide licences to consult nor are there organizations with exclusive rights to supervise consultants and establish professional codes of conduct (Løwendahl, 2005; von Nordenflycht, 2010). For professionals not belonging to vocational organizations, the established system of peer review, the construction of codes of conduct and ethical behaviour presumably occurs throughout work and within firms (Anand et al., 2007).

Our research is positioned in practice-based studies (Schatzki et al., 2001; Nicolini et al., 2003; Gherardi, 2009; Orlikowski, 2010). Such a practice perspective is called for as the most promising way of combining micro- and macro-levels of theorizing organizational innovation (Crossan and Apaydin, 2010, p. 1178), a call we humbly respond to. Practice-based studies have received considerable attention in organization theory in recent years, including special issues in *Management Learning* (2009), *Organization Studies* (2010) and *Society and Business Review* (2009). As Gherardi (2009) points out, practice is a polysemic term, and practice-based studies are by no means a unified discipline. Practice-based studies, however, do share a common starting point. What has been labelled 'the practice turn' in social sciences was initially a reaction to structuralism and a reintroduction of agency in social theory (Ortner, 1984). Furthermore, the social order established by practice is viewed as a constitutive entanglement of agency and structure (ibid.).

The literature on organizational innovation has hitherto been concerned either with agency through managerial intentions and the implementation of innovations (or lack of such) or with the determinacy of organizational structures in shaping organizational innovations – and thus with a lack of agency involved in the success or failure of organizational innovation (Lam, 2005). A practice perspective, however, allows a dual perspective, exploring both agency and structure, thereby enabling a wider understanding of organizational innovation.

Recent research shows how the core characteristics of professions translate into specific organizational effects at the level of the professional firm (Malhotra and Morris, 2009). The core characteristics of professions are referred to as the nature of knowledge being used, jurisdictional control and the nature of the client relationship. These in turn affect the firm's structure, the team's structure and the global network in use (ibid.). In this chapter, we start from the other end; from a micro-perspective we explore the practices of the involved professionals. We identify personal and private experiences as intertwined with the professional, and further discuss how such experiences have an effect at the organizational level, innovating organizational practices and the codes of conduct by which the consultants work.

Regardless of whether professionals have membership of a vocational organization or not, there are several professional norms within PSFs, which are described as core norms. First, having responsibility towards the client by protecting their interests is referred to as altruistic service (Løwendahl, 2005) or trusteeship (Greenwood et al., 2005). Second, the preference for autonomy is another norm (Alvesson and Karreman, 2006). Although the literature discusses the implications of workforce professionalization (Alvesson and Karreman, 2006; von Nordenflycht, 2010), the importance of professional codes of conduct (Løwendahl, 2005; von Nordenflycht, 2010) and how common educational and professional backgrounds facilitate the establishment of common norms (Løwendahl, 2005), no current research highlights how professional codes of conduct are formed, established and then used within firms. Our material highlights the formation of norms and ethical behaviour in PSFs when no vocational organization is involved.

The establishment of codes of conduct is important within PSFs because the preference of professional workers for autonomy is strong. Hence, there is distaste for control, supervision and formal organizational processes (Greenwood and Empson, 2003; Løwendahl, 2005; von Nordenflycht, 2010). Direct supervision is of little use in PSFs because the manager may know less than the other participants (Løwendahl, 2005), in which case direct instructions are fruitless. Thus, informal management processes may be more useful (von Nordenflycht, 2010). Managing people that make their own decisions is referred to as the challenge of 'herding wild cats' (Løwendahl, 2005, p. 69). The challenge resides in retaining and directing these professionals. Several responses to the cat herding challenge have been identified, such as firm ownership, incentive systems, informal management systems and muted competition (von Nordenflycht, 2010). Instead of focusing on firms' responses to this challenge, we draw attention to the professionals and their actions facing the same challenge. Little has been said in the literature on PSFs about how professionals form and construct the firm through their actions and interpretations of what they and others are doing (Czarniawska, 2008). In other words, we highlight the innovating practices within the firm and discuss the establishment of codes of conduct as a processual ongoing accomplishment in practice.

The particular empirical material we focus on is the storytelling unfolding on the company intranet. Narrative as a constitutive part of organizational sense-making has previously been described (Orr, 1995; Brown and Duguid, 2001), however, the process through which narratives provide coherence and flexibility in social interaction during the innovation process remains understudied (Bartel and Garud, 2009). Bartel and Garud (ibid.) discuss how innovation narratives enable coordinating challenges during innovation. Contrary to the stories thus discussed the stories presented in this chapter are not retrospective stories of practice, but stories unfolded in practice, seemingly about anything but practice, and nevertheless an important means of changing (and stabilizing) this practice.

In organization studies, stories and narratives have come to be interpreted as synonyms (Polkinghorne, 1988). Polkinghorne (ibid., p. 44) equates story with narrative; his lead opened an all-encompassing definition of narrative, including any meaningful text (Gabriel, 2000). However, the stories we explore in this chapter align to Gabriel's narrow definition of narrative. Stories are:

> narratives with plots and characters, generating emotion in narrator and audience, through poetic elaboration of symbolic material. This material may be a product of fantasy or experience, including an experience of earlier narratives. Story plots entail conflict, predicaments, trials and crisis, which call for choices, decisions, actions and interactions, whose actual outcomes are often at odds with the character's intentions and purposes. (Gabriel, 2000, p. 239)

Gabriel (2000) uses this narrow definition to explore such stories as sustaining and generating meaning. Stories thus can be viewed as means of sustaining and innovating the organization. This storytelling practice is interpreted with the longitudinal changes in practice as the main interpretative horizon (Gadamer, 1976). We explore the writings on a news page on which the company consultants present an abundance of 'news': odd comments on public events, thoughtful curiosities and strong personal opinions. Like most stories, these news stories are open to a multitude of interpretations and engage responses from others in the company. We interpret this storytelling as contributing to organizational innovation by continuously questioning, constructing and reconstructing a professional code of conduct in CommCorp.

MAKING SENSE OF PRACTICE

CommCorp labels itself a 'Strategic Communication Consultancy'. There are approximately 70 CommCorp consultants located in Norway, Sweden and Denmark, with their head office and largest group of consultants in Oslo. CommCorp provides clients with advice on strategic communication, crisis management and public relations. Its work is project based, and the formal hierarchical structure of the company can be described as flat. The majority of consultants own shares in the company.

CommCorp's services involve what has been labelled knowledge work (Alvesson, 2001, 2004) and professional service work (Carlsen et al., 2004), displaying all the characteristics of ambiguity that describe such work. This particular practice may be labelled an extreme case of such professional service work: 'professional' only refers to the receiving of financial return for work performed, not indicating that they are conforming to the technical or ethical standards of a learned profession. The work practice can be interpreted as ambiguous 'all the way down': there are few vocational rules and regulations on how the practice should be performed. The work is highly dependent on constant input from outside sources, and it depends on and delivers to a constantly changing world of news. The work is inherently innovative and learning intensive. Every project aims towards creating a novel take on an organization or a public controversy, and every project deliverable involves the creation of news stories for its clients. Furthermore, the meaning and impact of this output are continuously negotiated. Media entries, political responses, and, not to forget, the clients' abilities to live the story, are fed back to CommCorp. At CommCorp, the work essentially entails focusing more or less public attention on a certain case compared with that which might otherwise have been, which is a forever unknown quantity. Within this world of change, organizational innovation becomes a dual process of establishing and communicating the particularities of the services provided, while these particularities are also renewed and reinvigorated at all times. Organizational innovation thus becomes a question of stabilizing a practice enough to communicate it as some*thing*, while at the same time changing it so that it is a different some*thing* than the competitors provide.

In this work of constant change we found practitioners that actively engage in creating and recreating the codes of conduct of their practising. As exposed on the company's websites, two statements relate the services of CommCorp to more or less formal vocational organizations. First, there is an explicit statement of adherence to the 'Code of Ethics' of the Norwegian Press Association. CommCorp is not a member of the Norwegian Press Association; on the contrary, CommCorp's role as an advocate of stories that pay money to get attention is often regarded as unethical by this very association. Despite this, CommCorp claims to adhere to these ethical standards. In addition, CommCorp has chosen to distance itself from the national board of communication consultancies. With this position, it is also taking an active attitude against what it labels as an inherent lack of seriousness in the industry. This implies a differentiation from the codes of conduct of the class of consultants of which they are regularly considered to be a part. Simultaneously, CommCorp borrow such codes from a different vocational tradition, a tradition with established codes of conduct that CommCorp finds more valuable (be this because of the ethical content or the communication value inherent in such borrowing and differentiation). CommCorp thus actively engages in a debate on codes of conduct and positions itself in relation to competitors as well as more established industries.

By distancing itself from its vocational organization and borrowing from another, we see that CommCorp is actively and publicly engaged in negotiating its own code of conduct. As promised, this chapter focuses particularly on such negotiation processes as they unfold in the everyday life of the organization. On CommCorp's intranet, one particular function is frequently used. This is an ordinary internal news function named Gesticulate, with an abundance of 'news' that consultants write. In many respects, Gesticulate resembles a shared blog in which all the consultants at CommCorp are possible authors. It predates blogging, however, because Gesticulate has been in use since 1997, long before blogs became state of the art.

The literal content of the news stories presented on Gesticulate can be twisted stories of public events, reflections of particular personal experiences, or rebellious outbursts concerning internal affairs. The contributions also offer meta-stories on methodologies, tools and techniques, and project accomplishments. The news stories dissolve traditional boundaries between the private, personal and professional. The contributions are often long, well formulated and to the(ir) point. Good contributions gain attention and are discussed in the canteen, in the open plan areas and during project meetings. Some of the contributions are also given public access by being linked to CommCorp's external web pages. A large portion of the news is written as a reaction to happenings within the organization, involving discussions of strategic importance – and often as a reaction when an author's voice has previously been silenced.

In the following, three narratives will be presented, including excerpts from three contributions to Gesticulate. The narratives include observational descriptions of situations prior to the posting of the story, an excerpt of the story, and material pertaining to the retrospective sense-making of the story made by the author and other consultants. Though abridged, the excerpts are presented at some length with the hope that the reader gets a better feel of the distinctness of Gesticulate. The postings presented were chosen because they are typical of the stories on Gesticulate. They challenge established truths, play with words and meanings, and often make the reader laugh and (re)think prejudices.

Sleep Deprivation and Monster Communication

The author of this story, a specialist in crisis communication, had been off work for six weeks of paternity leave. He looked exhausted upon returning to work. He was frequently late for work, but stayed at night working long hours. His office was located in a hallway intersection through which all consultants had to pass on their way to three of the main meeting rooms, and his exhaustion was obvious. Colleagues repeatedly asked what they could do to help. After a couple of months back at work, and now with a skin tone of a healthier person, the author posted a much-noted story on Gesticulate. The story was originally a layered story in which we are introduced to a larger gallery of persons, but the excerpt suffices to get a feel for the style of the entry:

As my beloved daughter Fanny (11 months) for the fifth night in a row kept my wife and me awake, I remembered the story Said told me. This little child had total control of my life. I was deprived not only of sleep but also of parental power. I was thinking of Said, and of Shin Bet.

Self-proclaimed expert on children and author Anna Wahlgren places the label 'Nightclub Queens' on girls with Fanny's behaviour. 'Monster!' more precisely described my attitude when her crying woke me up for the tenth time during the same night – at approximately the time when the human body's temperature, including the brain, is at its lowest and we find ourselves in our most primitive mode. Such monster-babies believe sleep, in particular parental sleep, is ballyhooed. And they loudly express this all night long. After three consecutive months of sleep deprivation, my wife and I were quite exhausted. If turning my mum in could give me sleep, I would turn her in. Everyone who knows us has noticed the strain. We have communicated like victims for months. To no avail. The demonstration of power proceeded.

Oslo 16th December 2005: 'You have reached Åge Kaurin Johnsen at the Insomnia Clinic, please leave a message. Piiip . . . !' – 'This is Harry Hanson. I have a daughter. She has kept us awake for months. Can you please help us? We are desperate!' Some days later, we are at the sleep specialists. On the table are packets of earplugs and napkins. Kaurin Johnsen turns out to add to his psychology speciality a considerable communication talent. After a thorough sense-making process, he lets us know that Fanny is lodging at a five-star hotel with ditto service: 'You are communicating that Fanny can serve herself from the top shelves', he says. 'Unless you communicate the opposite the awakenings will continue!' The psychologist nominates me to be sleep-general and communication director, works out a communication plan, casts mum as an outlaw, and expels her from the bedroom (women producing milk are apparently not trustworthy communicators – the kids smell the milk and suddenly we are way beyond what communication can accomplish).

The psychologist painted bright pictures and gave striking examples. From now on we were ordered to communicate consistently and consequently: Fanny was to move to a shelter. Hot mother's milk in the parental bed was replaced by dad's serves of lukewarm water in the crib. Our slipper-tripping circling around the cot and our loving and resolute engagement at any sound was to be displaced by my much delayed, very sluggish replies, preferably through a closed door. Physical contact was only to happen at adrenalin inducing cries and only in a very businesslike manner. We were quite simply ordered to provide service in the worst thinkable manner.

I appointed Basil Fawlty of *Fawlty Towers*, the all-time world champion of worst service provision, to be my mentor. In the sleep specialist's communication plan, it was emphasized that we should make the hours after awakening as boring as altogether possible for the little girl. I consequently start my days with a loooong shower, placing my daughter in a chair in the bathroom, far away from any fun. I would not even talk to her. She is getting it now. Sitting parked and ignored in a chair waiting for ages for dad to shower is no good reason to wake up. 0400 turned into 0500 and 0600, and now Fanny wakes around 0700!

The communication cure has been sensationally effective. I could feel it change power to my advantage and prepare my eyelids for blessed reunion. Communication moves power. Also parental power – Quad Erad Demonstrandum!

As we can see, this story is highly personal. The story is one where the narrator's voice reaches us from a first person view, and the literary theme of the story is drawn from the realms of the personal – even the sphere of the private, some might say. The particulars of the story portray the family life of the author, his wife, their little daughter, and the struggles faced when she deprives them of sleep. Interviewing the author of this story just after writing it, he explained that he suffered from too little sleep, knew his co-workers had been on the receiving end of much of his sleep-deprived distress, and figured Gesticulate was a way to let off some steam, let them know how life had been, and put some humour into it. While the author did not initially suggest a critique of CommCorp's work practice as the reason for writing the story, in later conversations he believed it also offered an important contribution to the ongoing discussion about the ethics and responsibilities involved in client–consultant relationships.

At the time the story was posted, CommCorp had a cumbersome project with a volunteer sector organization because of internal disagreement on how to interpret the relationship between the client and CommCorp. 'Sleep Deprivation and Monster Communication' became an important point of reference in the discussions concerning this client relationship. The issue in the project was to whom CommCorp had the final responsibility: the managing director or the volunteer sector organization she was leading? The story was retold and used from a variety of perspectives, as the client's managing director, her organization and CommCorp's role rotated through the registry of actors in this story.

Busy-busy-busy

The second contribution was written with an almost tactile embodied engagement. Prior to the consultant's posting of the story, the administrative staff had sent several emails concerning the lack of up-to-date invoicing of hours worked. The economic situation in the company was tense. CommCorp's only income is billing workable hours, and a lack of invoicing instantly affects the economy. Two days before writing and posting the story, the author had a project meeting in an open plan area at the headquarters. Much to the other consultants' amusement, he spilled coffee all over the project papers as he gesticulated while telling a story:

Busy-busy-busy
clientbusy
projectbusy
crisisbusy

writingtenderbusy
losingtenderbusy
writingtenderbusy
fuckingprinterbusy
fuckingcopymachinebusy
fuckingvideocanonbusy
goddamnPCbusy
goddamnCCbusy
goddamnBCCbusy
seniorbusy
specialadvisorbusy
sowonderfultohaveaprojectmanagerbusy
Ireallymustcallhomebusy
Iwillbeverylatebusy
ohamIstillherebusy
importanttopeebeforemeetingbusy
tipovermycoffeebusy
veryhotcoffeeonmywee-weebusy
ButatleastIhavetimetowritetheinvoicesheetseveryfuckingdayyoubloodymorons
thatdontbusy!

In Gesticulate, this was one of the entries that received most responses. It got lots of attention in the canteen and the open plan areas, and was presented on the following Monday Morning Meeting for all to engage with. The story was attended to as surprising and funny, with the theme of busyness obviously recognizable for the consultants.

While we were not at CommCorp the day it was posted, the entry was emailed to the researchers with a big smiley attached to it. The sender was not the author, but a fellow consultant that wanted us to see the work of a good story-maker. The consultants at CommCorp label themselves 'story-makers'. This is simultaneously an exclusive and inclusive denotation. Descriptions of what story-makers are and do are told in almost mythical terms, stated as a character trait as much as a competency, and described as a unique exclusive capability that only some possess. Interestingly enough, all consultants interviewed place themselves in this unique exclusive position, independent of their formal status or education. While interviewees all include themselves in the 'community of story-makers', they do not include all employees at CommCorp in this group. The community is both exclusive – only a few people with magical character traits can do it – and inclusive, as all consultants subscribe themselves to the group. A handful of consultants, though, are consistently referred to as good story-makers by the others. The author of 'Busy-busy-busy' is now in this exclusive group.

There is no apparent change in invoicing – or lack thereof – after the entry. However, there is more careful attention to cups of coffee, particularly by the author of the story.

No More Heroes

This is a story that comments on one of five communication archetypes, the hero, in the framework used in the accomplishment of CommCorp's projects. In an interview prior to writing 'No More heroes', the author laconically said that a discussion about how to use the 'heroes' archetype was long overdue. She suggested that the 'hero' role was a disservice to any client. Heroes were seldom in need of communication advice and the role would be too hard to live up to for any ordinary person. She insisted that ascribing such a role in most instances would be a disaster waiting to happen – even inviting the disaster to come – as journalists would screen any hero story for cracks in the polished surface.

The story was posted shortly after the author raised concerns about a particular project accomplishment in a Monday Morning Meeting. The author heavily disagreed with the choice of communication platform presented to the client, suggesting that the choice resembled the emperor's new clothes – a story without substance that would ultimately fall through if presented to the media. In the Monday Morning Meeting, her critique was decisively shouted down. The leader of the meeting, who is also the firm's founder and number one 'rainmaker', interrupted her. He insisted that CommCorp could produce heroes wherever they wanted and demonstratively moved to the next slide on his PowerPoint presentation, introducing a new topic. Below is a small excerpt of the story.

> On Saturday, I was on a hen night. During the evening, we had a loud debate about our time, our heroes, and the lack of them. I joined those holding that all good heroes are either dead, retired, or several generations too old. Where is today's Erik Bye[1]? Gunnar 'Kjakan' Sønsteby[2]? Or at least a new, young, fresh Gro[3]?
>
> Looking at the abundance of historical hero stories at the movie theatre lately (*Lord of the Rings*, *Matrix* trilogy, *300*), not only my friends but also the Zeitgeist are obviously ready for grand heroes. But leaving the movie theatre, we are left with Valgerd, Kristin, Kjell Magne and Jens on radio[4], and Ivar Dyrhaug with his singing amateurs on TV.
>
> In order to decide whether Norway has any heroes we had to bring out the encyclopaedia to investigate what a hero really is.
>
> The word is Greek, and its etymological ancestry comes from protection and serving. 'Hero' is tied to self-sacrifice. A hero drives a story by his or her ability to act, his or her will, his or her guts. And he or she is also willing to sacrifice his or her own needs for another. And out went all sporting heroes, everything close to a hero in Norway. The Captain of MV *Tampa*[5] stood out as a single, shining example of a hero of today. Where are all the others?

Again, the narrator's voice speaks from a first person's point of view, discussing events covered at a party. This narrative is, however, more directly connected with the particularities of everyday work than was 'Sleep Deprivation and Monster Communication'. While the author takes a backseat position as the teller of a tale only, the story simultaneously exposes a strong voice battling in practice, passionately engaged in a dialogue on the boundaries between participation and pacification. The story can be read as a direct counterstrike to the silencing of the author in the Monday Morning Meeting and as a frame narrative used to introduce the ambiguity of both the concept of a hero and the different interpretations of it.

Initially, the story was not given much notice, receiving only a few comments. Several months after this entry on Gesticulate, CommCorp received a lot of media attention for a project that disastrously failed to deliver. Discussions in CommCorp bounced between several explanations: very poor project management, an impossible communication strategy and a lack of critical insight when accepting the project (the second and third points potentially being explications of the first).

Heated discussions unfolded on how CommCorp could ensure the viability of stories designed. Despite the time lag between the incident and the story on Gesticulate, the story was reintroduced at a Monday Morning Meeting discussing this project. A consultant other than the author introduced it. At this point, the story became repeatedly used as a reference point throughout a wider discussion considering the viability of archetypes. 'Hero' still has its place among the five communication archetypes in CommCorp. However, by now the label is seldom used as a framing of a communication plan for clients, but more often as a metaphoric antagonist while suggesting communication archetypes anticipated to better suit the client.

ANALYSIS

Only imagination constrains the potential ways of analysing these stories and their roles in the social life of the practice in question. We explore the stories as material traces of the continuous negotiations of norms unfolding in any practice (Bjørkeng et al., 2009). In the following section, we will present three mechanisms driving changes in the codes of conduct that the consultants work by. We suggest these mechanisms are characteristic of the ways in which consultants innovate their practising more generally and we add examples from the overall practice to illustrate this. We proceed by first discussing the entangling of contexts displayed in the stories as well as practice, from private and personal to professional. Second, we discuss how consultants constantly negotiate norms, thus contributing to a proc-

Table 15.1   Summary of empirical categories and modes of explanation

	Narrative	Practice
Entangling context	The private, personal and professional spheres are mixed in the written narratives	Participants from the dispersed practices that the practitioners engage are all engaged if they are assumed to be helpful for the performance of practice
Negotiating norms	The surprising forms and content of the narratives challenges accepted notions of appropriateness, as well as potential interpretations of the vocabulary by which work is performed	The most salient negotiation of norms unfolds in client projects, with media, public opinion and client performance all being constitutive parts
Reclaiming power	The narratives are presented, and evaluated by the other practitioners only. The client is no longer the executor of the story, and the media and public opinion is no longer the judge. The evaluation of particular performance of practice is withdrawn from a public sphere, and performed inter-practice	Differences in past, present and future ways of performing practice is established through creating events in which the new and the old is pictured and thus differentiated. A differentiation not evident in the processual innovation occurring on a day to day basis

essual innovation of practice. Finally, we discuss how consultants are reclaiming power over practice, both for the individual professional and for the firm. This reclaiming of power stands in contrast to much of the work on organizational innovation in PSFs, where tight integration with clients is made primary for successful innovations (Anand et al., 2007).

Entangling Contexts

The stories presented all entangle contexts from different spheres and practices in the authors' lives. The authors engage in professional, personal and even private themes in their stories. The stories all make room for multiple voices, including experts, friends, families, co-workers and self – a self that is often not in control of the story, but works as a messenger only. Such entangling of contexts is present not only in the stories on Gesticulate, but also in the overall practice at CommCorp.

Most striking in these stories is the combination of their contents and the fact that they are offered on the company's intranet. About 70 consultants from three countries have access to these as they are posted. As we have seen, consultants willingly offer stories of a personal (some more correctly described as private) nature, with an unfolding of affairs that does not immediately spring to mind as professional.

This entangling of context shows how there is a blend of private and personal in the professional sphere. It stands in stark contrast to the PSF literature where the main focus is on the professional, and blending in the private and the personal is often viewed as unprofessional (Løwendahl, 2005; von Nordenflycht, 2010).

The entangling of contexts that we have unfolded in the CommCorp consultants' storytelling is also very much a feature of their everyday work. They invite and engage a range of actors in most project work. In practice, the consultants do not discriminate between these actors by the perceived role they attain in the consultants' networks (be it professional or private), but by the ability these actors have to deliver attention, specific expertise, or other value to the project. The consultants do not create strict boundaries between professional and private – neither for themselves nor for their clients. One consultant, renowned and admired for having strong client contacts, noted the birthdays of all the clients' wives and was sure to remind his clients of these events. This engagement is far outside the boundaries of expected practising and shows the thin line between intrusiveness and welcomed organizing; thus, the consultant is cherished for his ability to elegantly perform this balancing act.

In PSFs, the cat herding challenge (Løwendahl, 2005) is described as a major challenge for management, however, the literature does not discuss how professionals deal with this challenge. Our example suggests that they engage a range of actors in performing work and that the boundaries between the private and professional are blurred. The gang of cats that the managers are expected to herd is thus continuously growing – unless, of course, the idea of herding cats is at the outset flawed. The cats seem to do a pretty good job of herding themselves.

As the consultants all have strong individual autonomy and as they are in need of freedom to act and decide in order to provide the services, we find that they manage by blending and fusing the private, personal and professional. Such practising opens up continuous innovation as the range of possible ways of managing particular situations expands with the additional resources to draw on provided by the use of personal and private networks. At the firm level, such entangling of contexts amplifies the ambiguity involved – there are more cats to herd. At the personal level, however, this might reduce ambiguity because there are no strict lines between different spheres of life and fewer identities to juggle. Thus, it is crucial for the firm and the management to accept and take part in the ambiguity in order to sustain organizational innovation through such practices while maintaining firm stability. As the challenge of cat herding refers to retaining professionals within the firm and directing them when in need, we suggest that firm stability is obtained partially by letting such innovating practices unfold.

Negotiating Norms

The stories presented here all breach expectations with respect to the possible uses of concepts and accepted codes of conduct. Common to all the stories on Gesticulate is that they are caught in a language-of-practice with which the authors and their collectives of practitioners are all familiar. The authors use concepts and styles from the particular language game they use at work to describe people and situations not usually associated with the concepts and styles of this language game. The authors offer unexpected themes, unexpected forms, or marginalized voices.

While some stories are constructed in order to engage in a discussion of practice, others instigate such reactions independent of any authorial intentions. Let us exemplify. According to the author, 'Busy-busy-busy' was written for fun. He laughed about it to himself, got a good idea, jotted it down and posted it without further reflection. The tone is witty, the style is poetic, the theme is private – some suggest too private – the message is ambiguous; all in all, not an easily definable piece. To other consultants, the contribution was reasoned to be (1) a scolding of those not completing their invoices on time, (2) an ironic comment on the administrative staff begging for such invoices when project work takes over all time and energy, (3) a critique of the massive workloads, or (4) a genuinely fun, creative take on work with no particular meta-message.

The stories are part of sense-making processes that exceed any individual's potential intentions. We suggest that they amplify ambiguity by opening the potentialities of acceptable actions and thus fuel the process of continuous organizational innovation. There is no one established way of interpreting the stories on Gesticulate, as the interpretations change with the context. In Bruner's (1991) words, it is the very sensitivity of the narrative that introduces and sustains the multitude of meanings negotiated in it.

As we have seen, the stories presented herein all touch the borders of appropriateness, thus simultaneously questioning and contributing to establishing the codes of conduct in the organization. The form and content of 'Busy-busy-busy' can be interpreted as a negotiation of 'appropriateness' – breaching the boundaries of possible, accepted and interesting topics, themes and forms. By allowing the contribution room on the intranet, this mode of communication is implicitly legitimized, further broadening the scope of possible action.

There are similar patterns of negotiating norms in the other stories presented. The author of 'Sleep Deprivation and Monster Communication' labels his 11-month-old daughter a 'nightclub queen' and a 'monster'. These are hard-boiled dysphemisms, breaching the expectations of appropriateness, and calling out for interpretation. In addition the author describes 'meticulous sense-making', 'communication plans', 'communication directors and experts', 'the monster role', 'the victims', and 'the moving of power in favour of the parents', and also introduces the issue of 'credible communication'. These are integrated parts of CommCorp's language game, figures that exist in the client typology, names of particular processes in the consultant–client interaction, or ways of describing communication roles. The shared language works as a narrative device that opens the stories for multiple readings and contributes to amplifying the equivocality in concepts and codes of conduct.

The same kinds of mechanisms of negotiating norms found on Gesticulate are also found in the storytelling modus operandi at CommCorp. Denoting its way of working as 'communication fundamentalism', it embeds the rebellious juggling of expectations and surprise as its trademark. The core competency at CommCorp is to narrate realities for its clients and also – as exposed in this study – for itself. The successful completion of projects involves creating stories for its clients. Particularly successful or landmark projects are often recognized by a surprising and provoking combination of form and content. Other non-project-related practising also shares the same style. Consultants creatively experiment with playful constructions of realities in Monday Morning Meetings. They actively seek out media to give rebellious and unexpected comments on news. They also arrange grand rites of passage, big parties where their own old work patterns are mortified in an Opus Dei-like fashion. Their clients – who have paid for these now-dead services – are invited and do attend these parties. The stories presented and the consultants' overall practices share a mark of surprise in the combination of form, theme and vocabulary. There is an element of aesthetics here in the balancing act where the borders of the appropriate are constantly challenged – a balancing act that keeps equivocality alive, and themselves and their surroundings engaged and alert.

However, at the same time these narratives stabilize practice; they create a gravitational force illustrating and using the vocabulary of practice in a multitude of settings, thus instantiating this vocabulary as 'how we do things around here' and creating the codes of conduct by which they work. We suggest the consultants constantly expand the boundaries of what may be inside/outside, good/bad and appropriate/inappropriate practice in and by the entries on Gesticulate as well as their wider practising of breaching expectations. The stories on Gesticulate contain meta-stories on methods and ways of doing, and meta-narratives that are metaphoric, ambiguous and in need of enacted interpretation. Therefore, methods are not portrayed as stable entities, but are enacted and accomplished through practising, both on Gesticulate and in the overall practising. Through Gesticulate, and the constant negotiation of codes of conduct, ethics, concepts and methods that are materialized in the posted stories, a constant becoming seems a fitting description of the practising at CommCorp. The codes of conduct are not constituted by following norms, but their equivocality is amplified by the continuous play with breaching expectations.

Reclaiming Power

Work and profession are important contributors to personal and professional identity and reputation (Løwendahl, 2005; Alvesson and Karreman, 2006; von Nordenflycht, 2010). At the same time, the services and their reception among clients and media contribute to the continuous construction and reconstruction of the services performed (Anand et al., 2007). However, through the services delivered, consultants only have meagre control over the final product: in the stories they create, the client is at any time the teller of the story or the one that fronts CommCorp's story in the news world. In interviews and in small talk, the consultants emphasize a lack of control concerning their clients' abilities and willingness to tell and live the stories created for them. The organization and the work of the consultants are thus more visible in the public eye than in most other kinds of work, while at the same time control over the quality of this work is restricted. Organizational image and reputation is in many respects more volatile and floating than it is in most organizations.

However, on Gesticulate this lack of control is greatly reduced, as the client is no longer the storyteller. Consultants can be interpreted as practising imagery and developing reputation; they are experimenting with language, membership and norms, namely they are experimenting with what could be. Through this experimenting, this practising, they constitute what is legitimate. According to Wittgenstein (1953), the practising of imagery is a collective endeavour and the evaluation of 'rightness' can only be preempted by particularities in use. The consultants reclaim the power of their imagery; by constructing the stories on Gesticulate, they construct pockets of practising disentangled from their clients, pockets serving as the particularities by which 'rightness' is negotiated and judged. Through Gesticulate, the power to judge the quality of story-making is no more solely the attention of the general public, but reclaimed; a small zone of power over quality is now placed at the judgement of the consultants alone. Such judgement is performed in the 'safe haven' of the organization. We suggest this active experimentation with the limits of the appropriate, with the context of meaning and language use, and with the private, the personal and the professional is also a way of experimenting with and developing, or practising, what is right and wrong, good and bad. Thus, it is a way of innovating organizational practice that is in the hands of the collective.

Gesticulate can be interpreted as a place in which consultants perform parts of practice, and through this performance the aspects of what counts as good, bad and relevant practice are constituted. Reclaiming power thus involves a certain detachment between the quality of work and quality of practice. This detachment is also visible in client projects through a certain detachment related to the client's ability to live the stories told. Consultants explicitly denounce a responsibility for the clients' presentation of the story. In the words of one senior advisor, a member of the board of advisors: 'We have to accept the client's judgement that they are able to deliver a particular story. We can't quality control this, we are not business developers.' It is important to note that we do not suggest Gesticulate as a place to rehearse or learn to perform work, or that practice is somehow an established set of performing. On the contrary, we suggest that the consultants produce a way to evaluate the quality of practising that is out of reach of work accomplishment. This shows a deep engagement with work and practice – particularly a passion for storytelling that crosses the conventional expectations of work and conceptions of 'appropriate', 'professional', and 'rational' under an instrumental business rationality, and introduces the personal and even the private. This interpretation emphasizes the situatedness of a practical rationality. It makes sense to be practising, and there is no difference between 'what' and 'why' in the immediateness of performing.

DISCUSSION

While we have emphasized the stories on Gesticulate that amplify ambiguity, these stories also reduce some aspects of the ambiguity apparent in work. Antonacopoulou (2009) describes the difference between practising and practicing, where the former, practising-with-an-s, is explicitly concerned with testing, negotiation, finding, and becoming a practice as well as a practitioner (Antonacopoulou, 2009). This is the type of practising we find on Gesticulate. The stories weave the private, the personal and the professional into one tight picture, exposing how codes of conduct are not merely professional, but constructs of the practitioners in their day-to-day practising. The stories on Gesticulate contribute to answering the pressing questions about 'who we are' and 'what we do'.

Organizational innovations are, in a practice perspective, not only about creating something new, but just as importantly about establishing something as old. In a processual view of continuous incremental change, organizational innovations are those differences that make a difference. Our interpretation of the storytelling as well as the overall practice unfolding in CommCorp is guided by practice theory. Insights from Wittgenstein's (1953) concept of language games are particularly useful for our purpose. Wittgenstein insists that 'the meaning of a word is its use in the language' (ibid., §43). Furthermore, the concept of language games 'bring into prominence the fact that speaking a language is part of an activity, or a form of life' (ibid., §22). Viewed from this perspective, all practices can be viewed as a form of language, and such practices as a normative social accomplishment. It is through practising that we continuously constitute meaning, the content of words, and other meaningful symbols. In professional service work, where ambiguity is the norm not the exception, and where symbolic analytic manipulation is at work, organizational innovation unfolds as we have seen as a continuous process of small incremental steps continuously changing these norms, and as acts of engagement attempting explicit negotiations and stabilization within these continuous changes.

Wittgenstein's influence on practice-based studies predominantly unfolds through explanations of rule following, or normativity, in practice (Nicolini et al., 2003; Schatzki, 2005, 2006; Nicolini, 2009). That is, how it is that practices are stable, and the same rules are followed again and again. However, the examples discussed here draw attention to the inherent potential for renewal and change underlying Wittgenstein's elaboration of language games. According to Wittgenstein (1953), rules are *infinite*: they can never be exhaustively defined or described. This infinite nature of the rules implies that any performance is also always a suggestion of stability or renewal; all practising involves a negotiating of norms. Under such a perspective, organizational innovation becomes a continuous process in which the establishment of 'what is', 'what has been', and 'what may become' are interdependent acts of innovating practice. We thus interpret the stories presented on Gesticulate as a dual sense-making device that provides uniqueness and normativity. Our interpretation implies narrative as both means of making sense that are individually enacted and acts of communication that await a response (Mead and Morris, 1934).

Interpreting the narrative sense-making unfolding on Gesticulate from a practice perspective has enabled an explanation that creates room for the creative enactment of senses that amplifies as well as reduces ambiguity in practice. The playful creativity exposed on Gesticulate thus is explained in terms that also resonate with the consultants' experience of playfulness and fun – as a creative surge rather than a pure drive to reduce ambiguity. Following Weick (1995) and his inspiration from Bruner (1991), we suggest that the narrative mode of thought is not representative, but constitutive, of reality (Bruner, 1991; Weick, 1995). This narrative mode though is not solely constitutive of reality as in making sense of things past or by projecting future perfect images to make sense of the future. Such narrative sense-making is also engaged with and involved in creating something new (Bergson, 1911). In Bergson's (1911) words: 'Every human work in which there is invention, every voluntary act in which there is freedom, every movement of an organism that manifests spontaneity, brings something new into the world' (p. 239). In addition to actualizing a reality, narrative sense-making also creates potentiality and organizational innovation.

CONCLUDING REMARKS

Through this empirical material, three particular mechanisms involved in establishing codes of conduct in CommCorp are explored. First, consultants are actively engaged in *entangling the contexts* of which they are part. They juggle their embodied self, families, friends, wider networks and time off work in their storied sense-making processes as well as in the particular of practice. Second, *negotiating norms* is described as a core sense-making mechanism in the practice at CommCorp. With passion and drive, consultants engage in storytelling that celebrates breaching the expectations of the appropriate. They playfully combine concepts and gallery and style and form, and amplify ambiguity as well as potentiality for the storyteller and attendees. Third, the same storied sense-making processes that amplify ambiguity also contribute to reducing it. Storytelling practice is not only acts of accomplishing work, but also acts of accomplishing practice. Through Gesticulate, consultants practise imagery and reputation, enabling a *reclaiming of power* to negotiate their own competences. These three particularities, of entangling context, negotiating norms and reclaiming power, enable the continuous construction of professionalism at CommCorp. Through the practices and storied sense-making processes, the construction of both individual- and firm-level codes of conduct unfolds. Professionalism thus, is not primarily an institutional constitution in CommCorp, but it is enacted by individuals in a collective, constructing and innovating social norms and the particulars of organizational practice.

Previously, the PSF literature has discussed the construction of norms from an institutional perspective only. We have shown how individual consultants engage in the construction of codes of conduct in one particular firm in an industry not guided by vocational norms. We suggest that exploring professional service work guided by vocational norms from a practice-based perspective will expose negotiations of similar kinds to those exposed here. Such explorations will enable a better understanding of the differences between PSFs under the same vocational norms – differences that are necessary to view in order to understand how such firms develop their particular competitive advantages.

For further research on innovation, we welcome more exploration of how the private and the personal influence innovation in a professional context. As we have shown, narratives introduce changes in established organizational and professionally used norms. Future research should delve into exploring how narratives drive innovation and change while maintaining stability.

For practitioners, we hope that more organizations acknowledge the blend of the private and personal with the professional that is an enhancer of innovation. Further, using narratives for both stabilizing and changing existing methods, power relations and customer relations might be fruitful.

Acknowledging that research too is professional work, and thus that language both enables and constrains our research practices, it becomes particularly important to reflect on the ways in which we are constructed by and construct research, and how this research can be practised so that it is relevant and rigorous across the particularities of practices and the language games that we engage in. Obviously, CommCorp has a sophisticated view of what language can perform, how language constructs realities, and thus also of its expectations of what research performed in and on language may accomplish. Future research should go further regarding the situations of interaction that meetings between practitioners and researchers could constitute. Instead of anticipating a neutrality in the researcher–practitioner meetings, we should assume our responsibility, accept that we make an impact on practice and work towards making this impact good. Situations of interaction give the 'object of study' means of engaging with the researchers' interpretations of their work, and thus also give them the possibility of contributing to discussing, validating, changing and adjusting these interpretations. Furthermore, such situations of interaction can be made situations of prospective character that also involve the discussion of what could be. While all situations in which researchers engage in organizations involve some elements of change, we

too seldom engage in real dialogue. Within a representationalist paradigm, such situations of collaboration would be unheard of. However, we
claim that by constructing possibilities for situations of collaboration in
the researcher–practitioner axis the relevance of research can be simultaneously constructed and scrutinized, while potentially enabling innovation
in the organization.

Bergson (1911) describes intellect and intuition as a constitutive entanglement of consciousness. Our intellect is so ordered that it differentiates,
cuts and slices, and presents us to things rather than to changes and acts.
Intuition, by contrast, 'the impetus of life, of which we are speaking,
consists in a need of creation' (Bergson, 1911, p. 251). This implies that
understanding organizational innovation involves more than understanding only the nature of knowledge used, or the professional belonging of
the practitioners, or the intellectual exercise of service provision. Where
organizational innovations may be seen as a mechanism of intellect only,
ordering reality into sequences of differences, the interpretation of the particulars of sense-making instead suggest including intuition in the equation:
the dual forces of reducing and amplifying possible meanings unfold the
role of creativity, will and passion for potentialities unfolding in innovating
practice. Exploring organizational innovation from a practice perspective,
we see that organizational innovation unfolds as the practitioners engage
as whole persons; they blend the private and personal with the professional,
they engage creativity and normativity, and they construct norms of practice that are engaged internally as well as externally. The organizational
innovation unfolding starts when individuals give themselves. And enjoy it.

ACKNOWLEDGEMENTS

We would like to acknowledge the kind sponsorship of the Norwegian
Research Council through the BIP projects KUNNE Balance and
Ideawork. We also acknowledge the contribution and involvement of
our industry partner; your openness and honesty throughout the research
project have been an exemplary basis for research collaboration. Helpful
comments on the chapter were provided by Stewart Clegg, Arne Carlsen
and Roger Klev.

NOTES

1. Norwegian journalist and media personality known for his commitment to the weak and
    the wary.

2. Norwegian World War II resistance fighter.
3. Gro Harlem Brundtland, first female Norwegian Prime Minister, and also former leader of the WHO.
4. Norwegian politicians of today.
5. Norwegian vessel salvaging nearly 500 refugees and refusing to leave Australian waters before Australian authorities agreed to rescue the refugees and provide them with shelter.

REFERENCES

Alvesson, M. (2001), 'Knowledge work: ambiguity, image and identity', *Human Relations*, **54**(7), 863–86.
Alvesson, M. (2004), *Knowledge Work and Knowledge Intensive Firms*, Oxford: Oxford University Press.
Alvesson, M. and D. Karreman (2006), 'Professional service firms as collectivities', in R. Greenwood and R. Suddaby (eds), *Research in the Sociology of Organizations: Professional Service Firms, Volume 24*, Oxford: Elsevier, pp. 203–30.
Anand, N., H.K. Gardner and T. Morris (2007), 'Knowledge-based innovation: emergence and embedding of new practice areas in management consulting firms', *Academy of Management Journal*, **50**(2), 406–28.
Antonacopoulou, E.P. (2009), 'Impact and scholarship: unlearning and practising to co-create actionable knowledge', *Management Learning*, **40**(4), 421–30.
Awuah, G.B. (2007), 'A professional services firm's competence development', *Industrial Marketing Management*, **36**(8), 1068–81.
Bartel, C.A. and R. Garud (2009), 'The role of narratives in sustaining organizational innovation', *Organization Science*, **20**(1), 107–17.
Bergson, H. (1911), *Creative Evolution*, London: Macmillan.
Bjørkeng, K., S. Clegg and T. Pitsis (2009), 'Becoming (a) practice', *Management Learning*, **40**(2), 145.
Brock, D.M. (2006), 'The changing professional organization: a review of competing archetypes', *International Journal of Management Reviews*, **8**(3), 157–74.
Brown, J.S. and P. Duguid (2001), 'Knowledge and organization: a social-practice perspective', *Organization Science*, **12**(2), 198–213.
Bruner, J. (1991), 'The narrative construction of reality', *Critical Inquiry*, **18**(1), 1–21.
Carlsen, A., R. Klev and G.v. Krogh (eds) (2004), *Living Knowledge. The Dynamics of Professional Service Work*, London: Palgrave.
Crossan, M.M. and M. Apaydin (2010), 'A multi-dimensional framework of organizational innovation: a systematic review of the literature', *Journal of Management Studies*, **47**(6), 1154–91.
Cunha, M.P., S.R. Clegg and S. Mendonça (2010), 'On serendipity: unsought discovery in organizations', *European Management Journal*, **28**(5), 319–31.
Czarniawska, B. (2008), *A Theory Of Organizing*, Cheltenham, UK and Northampton, MA, USA: Edward Elgar.
Dess, G.G. and J.C. Picken (2000), 'Changing roles: leadership in the 21st century', *Organizational Dynamics*, **28**(3), 18–34.
Empson, L. (2000), 'Merging professional service firms', *Business Strategy Review*, **11**(2), 39–46.
Empson, L. (2001), 'Introduction: knowledge management in professional service firms', *Human Relations*, **54**(7), 811–7.
Gabriel, Y. (2000), *Storytelling in Organizations: Facts, Fictions and Fantasies*, Oxford: Oxford University Press.
Gadamer, H.G. (1976), *Philosophical Hermeneutics*, Los Angeles: University of California Press.

Gardner, H.K., N. Anand and T. Morris (2008), 'Chartering new territory: diversification, legitimacy, and practice area creation in professional service firms', *Journal of Organizational Behavior*, **29**(8), 1101–21.

Gherardi, S. (2009), 'Introduction: the critical power of the "practice lens"', *Management Learning*, **40**(2), 115–28.

Greenwood, R. and L. Empson (2003), 'The professional partnership: relic or exemplary form of governance?', *Organization Studies*, **24**(6), 909–33.

Greenwood, R., S.X. Li, R. Prakash and D.L. Deephouse (2005), 'Reputation, diversification, and organizational explanations of performance in professional service firms', *Organization Science*, **16**(6), 661–73.

Lam, A. (2005), 'Organizational innovation', in J. Fagerberg, D.C. Mowery and R.R. Nelson (eds), *The Oxford Handbook of Innovation*, New York: Oxford University Press, 115–47.

Løwendahl, B. (2000), 'The globalization of professional business service firms – fad or genuine source of competitive advantage?', in Y. Aharoni and L. Nachum (eds), *Globalization of Services – Some Implications for Theory and Practice*, London: Routledge.

Løwendahl, B.R. (2005), *Strategic Management of Professional Service Firms* (3rd edition), Copenhagen: Copenhagen Business School Press.

Maister, D.H. (1982), 'Balancing the professional service firm', *Sloan Management Review*, **24**(1), p. 1529.

Maister, D.H. (1993), *Managing the Professional Service Firm*, New York: The Free Press.

Malhotra, N. and T. Morris (2009), 'Heterogeneity in professional service firms', *Journal of Management Studies*, **46**(6), 895–922.

Mead, G.H. and C.W. Morris (1934), *Mind, Self, and Society: From the Standpoint of a Social Behaviorist*, Chicago: University of Chicago Press.

Newell, S., M. Robertsen, H. Scarbrough and J. Swan (2002), *Managing Knowledge Work*, Basingstoke: Palgrave.

Nicolini, D. (2009), 'Zooming in and out: studying practices by switching theoretical lenses and trailing connections', *Organization Studies*, **30**(12), 1391–418.

Nicolini, D., D. Yanow and S. Gherardi (2003), *Knowing in Organizations : A Practice-based Approach*, Armonk, NY: M.E. Sharpe.

Orlikowski, W.J. (2010), 'Practice in research: phenomenon, perspective and philosophy', in D. Golsorkhi, L. Rouleau, D. Seidl and E. Vaara (eds), *Cambridge Handbook of Strategy as Practice*, Cambridge, UK: Cambridge University Press, pp. 23–33.

Orr, J. (1995), *Talking About Machines*, Ithaca and London: Cornell University Press.

Ortner, S.B. (1984), 'Theory in anthropology since the sixties', *Comparative Studies in Society and History*, **26**(1), 126–66.

Polkinghorne, D.E. (1988), *Narrative Knowing and the Human Sciences*, Albany, NY: State University of New York Press.

Schatzki, T.R. (2005), 'Peripheral vision: the sites of organizations', *Organization Studies*, **26**(3), 465–84.

Schatzki, T.R. (2006), 'On organizations as they happen', *Organization Studies*, **27**(12), 1863–73.

Schatzki, T., Knorr Cetina, K.D. and E. von Savigny (eds) (2001), *The Practice Turn in Contemporary Theory*, London: Routledge.

Teece, D.J. (2003), 'Expert talent and the design of (professional services) firms', *Industrial and Corporate Change*, **12**(4), 895–916.

Tushman, M.L. and C.A. O'Reilly III (1996), 'Ambidextrous organizations: managing evolutionary and revolutionary change', *California Management Review*, **38**(4), 8–30.

von Nordenflycht, A. (2010), 'What is a professional service firm? Toward a theory and taxonomy of knowledge-intensive firms', *Academy of Management Review*, **35**(1), 155–74.

Weick, K.E. (1995), *Sense-making in Organizations*, Thousand Oaks, CA: Sage.

Wittgenstein, L. (1953), *Philosophical Investigations*, translated by G.E.M. Anscombe, Oxford: Blackwell Publishing.

16 Storytelling in transforming practices and process: the Bayer case
Patrick Thomas and Richard Northcote

BACKGROUND

Large organizations, for the most part, are complex. The larger the organization, the wider its sphere of activities and the greater its geographical reach, the more complexity is added to the structure and, specifically, to the role and effectiveness of a leader.

There are many reasons for complexity in organizations and there appears to be a consensus in academic and business thinking that leadership can suffer as a result of over-complex structures. But, true leadership must find routes through the levels of complexity, breaking down barriers and bursting through blockages to ensure that messages are heard by those who need to receive them.

In time, complexity can be removed, but there are often many well-justified reasons why it exists in the first place. Often it is a result of merging organizations or cultures; or a historical legacy of growth or diversification. But sometimes it is even more ingrained; a result of market dominance, reward and recognition, fast growth or geographical expansion. More than likely, however, it is a result of many of these factors and sometimes all of them.

In reality, the more complex an organization becomes, the more leadership roles there are to fill. Within an organization, cells or teams are formed that require strong leadership. The result of this leadership can often lead to the creation of sub-teams that begin to evolve a culture and direction of their own. This result is only natural and should be welcomed as a method of focusing attention on the various tasks that must be achieved for ongoing success. However, problems can quickly arise if the leadership at the top of the organization is not focused on ensuring that all the various elements of strategy are aligned and contributing to the common good of the one single entity that matters above all: that is, the corporation.

Our philosophy is that the role of a business leader is to ensure an organization ends up somewhere other than where it was headed. Simply put, the leader must ensure that a corporation continues to grow and prosper in order to deliver its commitments to the various stakeholders rooted to the success of a corporation. Shareholders, employees, customers, suppliers and many other interested parties need to be assured of ongoing success in order to maintain their interest and commitment to a business.

Business cycles are such that they cannot sustain constant growth. Basic economic theory quickly shows that even the most successful of corporations will ultimately fail if they simply allow a typical business cycle to run its course. It is the intervention of leadership through realignment of strategy that ensures the ongoing success for all stakeholders. Ensuring this is even more critical in an era of huge change in socio- and political economics. Making the right decisions – and sharing them effectively with stakeholders – is one of the most critical elements of leadership.

A leader must influence so many people; none more so than the corporate employees who will ultimately implement the plans and ensure the sustained success of a business. The leader therefore must not only impart huge influence, but have the necessary vision, commitment and motivational powers needed to change direction. The leader must also have the vision and the will to implement innovative solutions to organizational problems and management philosophy.

INTRODUCTION TO BAYER

The Bayer Group has a proud and successful history of innovation and growth. The company's culture is deep-rooted in traditional European business thinking. Like other extremely successful German giants, Bayer has grown from small seeds planted more than 150 years ago in North Rhine Westphalia, the German industrial heartland, to become a global corporation focused on three main areas of activity: health, agriculture and materials.

Through its three business divisions: Bayer HealthCare, Bayer CropScience and Bayer MaterialScience, the corporation employs some 109000 people in 316 subsidiaries to generate around €33 billion of revenue. Based in Leverkusen, in what was once a small hamlet located on the Rhine between Cologne and Düsseldorf, the company has grown to become an industrial giant that contributes much to the local, German and global economies.

Despite its long and distinguished history in Germany, more recent activity has led to a major demographic change in its employees. Acquisitions and divestments in recent years, coupled with internal reorganization in the divisions, has delivered a mix of cultural challenges that demand focused change management activities to ensure cohesion and ongoing internal participation in corporate understanding.

Bayer MaterialScience, the polymers business of the Bayer Group, has a strong tradition of invention. The business focuses on two main areas of chemistry: polycarbonates and polyurethanes, both of which are widely recognized as being invented by the company. Its products are found in a multitude of everyday objects ranging from DVDs to cars and from mobile phones to furniture.

The company currently has much of its research and manufacturing situated close to its Leverkusen base in North Rhine Westphalia. But as the global markets for its products shift, the company is expanding its operations in other parts of the world, notably the Far East.

RECOGNITION OF HISTORY . . . NEED FOR CULTURAL UNIFICATION

It would be an inexperienced leader that would simply walk into a corporation or business and expect to impose his or her ideals on it. This is particularly true when the leader is coming in from the 'outside' and the organization is already hugely successful and steeped in decades of innovation and success. However, there is always a reason a particular leader has been chosen to lead and invariably the choice is based on a necessity to refocus an organization or to harness the experience and vision of this particular person.

In corporate speak, leadership is often mistaken for communication. And, while communication plays a major role in the leadership of a chief executive or president, there is much more to the role. A good leader must master a range of skills and be able to use each of these skills to maximum effect to create the followers that will ultimately deliver the intended results. Communications plays a major part in achieving the desired success as it touches all of the other skills needed and is the key to understanding, motivation and adapting to change.

In order to communicate effectively, however, a leader must understand to whom he or she is communicating. A deep understanding of the corporation's history, its people, its cultures, its needs and wants, as well as its fears and aspirations, are all fundamental research for any aspiring leader. Only when all of this is understood, should a leader start to communicate the vision and transformations that are about to be experienced.

Establishing a sense of belief in the organization is critical to success and being inclusive in terms of teamwork creates a strong level of identity. There are many examples of individuals operating within an organization who do not see themselves as part of the bigger entity, simply a cog in a smaller machine that contributes to a sub-team's success.

While there are occasions when this divisiveness or silo-thinking can be engineered deliberately, often it is not. In general terms, employees are keen to be part of a team and if they cannot see how they are part of a bigger good, they seek opportunity to be part of something smaller. Again, this can be beneficial, but only if each of these smaller units is moving in the same direction as the greater entity and if individual success contributes to the good of all the stakeholders.

So herein lies the challenge for leadership, ensuring integration of the organization, in terms of culture and strategy, yet also allowing for teams to be innovative, and have a voice. Creating a banner for employees to follow becomes critical. It is also easier said in theory than done in practice; particularly when the transformation of the organization requires breaking habits from the past and innovating practices and processes. Addressing the flaws that may have been seen in the past is a core ingredient to starting the leadership journey to take an organization 'somewhere other than where it was headed'.

In the case of Bayer MaterialScience, the initial banner created was simple. We are 'One Business – One Team'. This message swept across the Bayer MaterialScience world and could be heard uttered in Shanghai, Pittsburgh or Leverkusen, the three regional hubs for the business and its three Business Units: Polyurethanes, Polycarbonates, and Coatings, Adhesives and Specialties.

Using a variety of channels the message was repeated at every opportunity in order to encourage employees to question certain behaviors and decisions that appeared not to correspond to the idea of 'one team'. The more the subject was discussed, the more employees questioned and the deeper the motto engrained itself in the culture of the business. Leaders throughout senior management adopted the slogan and team meetings, town hall meetings and internal interviews all carried the same message. While the words became part of the culture, actions did not always align and later in this chapter we will explore further tactics that were employed to help change behavior.

THE NEXT STEPS – STORYTELLING

A mix of diversity and culture necessitates a simple method of communication. And, to ensure various changes are understood and implemented in such a scenario, demands a common understanding of what are often complicated messages. Storytelling is a critical process in not only sustaining but also transforming organizational practices and processes. When art is used in the storytelling process it can be a powerful and effective tool of change; particularly where there is cultural diversity, and disparate actors. The vast majority of Bayer employees are non-English native speakers and, for this reason, illustrative messaging came to the fore. Simple, straightforward messages that explained what was happening, the rationale behind it and necessity of delivering it, all needed to be captured in much the same way Paleolithic cave paintings give us a great understanding of prehistoric practices.

By basing internal change communications on storytelling through illustration, images could be used to work across cultures and successfully transmit multiple messages with a common interpretation. By focusing change on a changing landscape, audiences around the world were encouraged to harness the historical strength of innovation to focus on delivering modern solutions to new challenges.

At the same time, the idea of a journey was being imparted to audiences and through the introduction of an annual cartoon, the business's position was clearly defined. At the same time, it was suggested that the series of cartoons would not end too quickly; perhaps five or six would be needed to complete the set, delivering a strong message to all that this was not going to be a quick or simple process. Each cartoon carries both an element of real progress in achieving change and an element of aspiration for the future.

THE FIRST CARTOON

For obvious reasons the first in the series of cartoons carries the title 'One Business – One Team', serving as a reminder to all of the aspirations of the leadership, as well as the vast majority of employees (Figure 16.1). The cartoon showed the business moving away from traditionalism (illustrated by the image of Leverkusen in the distance) on a cart pulled by an ox and being led by blue 'change agents' from within the business.

The ox carries new CEO Patrick Thomas and pulls the cart containing a group of green 'traditionalists' looking back with some concern to what they appear to be leaving behind them. At the same time, a group of red 'resistors' is trying to sabotage the plan while a group of grey 'bystanders' watch the scenario from a safe distance. The colour coding was an important step in creating the band of characters in the mind of the viewer as these colours would continue to grace future cartoons in the series.

A small but significant element of the picture is a small sign in the

Source: © 2012, Bayer MaterialScience AG.

Figure 16.1   'One Business – One Team'

bottom left-hand corner. The simple sign, bearing the word 'Market' is a poignant reminder of why the business is embarking on its journey of change. Like many large organizations, there is always a danger of becoming too internally focused. Success in business, however, does not come simply from within, but also from providing the materials that the market needs or demands. For this reason, we must get closer to the market.

While the imagery used is comic, the messages are strong and well understood throughout the hierarchy and across various cultures. A copy of the cartoon was presented to the senior management (some 80 individuals) at their annual meeting and then further communicated through the company's intranet and internal publications to ensure all employees were given the chance to see it and understand the messages first hand.

BUSINESS STRATEGY

There is no doubt that the main message delivered in the first cartoon is one of change and the internal power struggle that lies ahead for the business. In some quarters, there was concern around the openness of the cartoon, but the leadership was committed to painting the picture as it was. Only by showing an honest view of what was ahead, could the leadership ensure that the business was in a strong position to tackle the issues.

At the heart of the problem was a series of independent strategies that were being developed, defined and fine-tuned: corporate strategy, business unit strategies, functional strategies, sector strategies, marketing strategies and customer-specific strategies. The independence afforded each of these strategic developments had, over time, led to confusion in the bigger picture and contributed in part to the evolution of various leadership positions. Bringing the alignment together under the 'One Business – One Team' philosophy was a prerequisite of future success.

Also, the admission that there were areas of the business that needed to be more market focused was a brave step. Steeped in its history of innovation and invention, there is an underlying current of thought that suggests that whatever the business generates has a place in the market. By employing a strategic review of business activities, this was proven to be a false belief and therefore a strong refocusing on innovation needed to take place. The market became the driving force in decision-making and customers became a stronger part of the R&D process.

At the same time as the change was being addressed the business was going through a period of strong self-analysis. Many of the popular beliefs of the past were proving to no longer hold true in the ever-changing markets and shifting economic power. External forces were driving a reality check that in turn was driving the business to change its approach to the markets and to its core area of expertise: innovation.

THE CHALLENGE OF CHANGE

Change became the focus for the business as it set about delivering a number of strategic thrusts that would help ensure it ended up 'somewhere other than where it was heading'. There was a growing acceptance of the fact that change was inevitable if the business was to maintain its position in the various market sectors it had traditionally led.

A large number of projects were started, each aimed at simplifying business processes and reducing the complexity that often clouded reality and acted as barriers to open and honest communication. However, as obvious as the need for change might be, the willingness of the human mind to always accept change can pose significant challenges.

Acknowledging the resistance in many areas was one of the key challenges for the leadership. Understanding why it existed and bringing the issues out into the open became a fundamental part of the change strategy. New messages focusing on the human reaction to change were crafted and delivered throughout the organization at every opportunity; the same strategy that had delivered the 'One Business – One Team' philosophy.

The communication strategy played on the fact that there was nothing wrong with change. The need for change does not suggest that there was failure in previous thinking or previous models, simply that the world was changing. As a business Bayer had long been innovative in process technology and product development and now it had to add a third leg to the stool: innovativeness in its business model and strategy.

This message struck home at various levels of management and the simple logic used in creating the messages was widely understood throughout the business. To assist the analogy, an imaginary competitor was created. This competitor drew on the best of Bayer MaterialScience as well as its competitors and became the benchmark for measuring ongoing success. Closing the gap on the imaginary competitor become a top management challenge and further projects were set in motion to address the inequalities that were evident.

Using an old Chinese proverb 'When the wind of change blows, some people build walls, but others build windmills' a new cartoon was created 12 months after the first one (Figure 16.2). This image focused on the same characters from the previous offering, though the scenario had changed. The wind is evident and traditionalists can be seen cowering from it behind makeshift shelters.

The change agents are building a windmill to harness the wind's energy and the resistors are seen attempting to scupper the plans. The bystanders remain adrift from the action on a river that supports a number of boats; each named after one of numerous change projects.

Once again the cartoon was widely distributed as the second part of an ongoing story. Its success was measured and results were encouraging.

THE CRISIS AND BAYER'S FOCUS

By the time the world was shaken by the economic crisis of 2009, Bayer was steadily moving forward with its change strategy. The impact of the crisis on the business, however, was severe and a number of major decisions had to be taken and implemented very quickly.

A number of production facilities were mothballed as its two key market sectors, automotive and construction, felt the full force of the economic impact. Once again, leadership played a crucial role in stabilizing the business in the midst of global turmoil. Quick, decisive actions proved

Figure 16.2 *'Wind of Change'*

to be extremely well received by all stakeholders. Once again, facing the reality of the situation openly and honestly, proved to be a critical element of stabilizing the boat.

To caption this third cartoon in the series (Figure 16.3), Bayer initially used the Chinese characters for crisis, though Japanese and Korean versions of the cartoon were also created by the teams in these countries. *Wei-ji* as it is pronounced in Mandarin, refers to a situation that has reached an extremely difficult or dangerous point. The first character (*Wei*) means danger, while the second character (*ji*) suggests a critical point in time. There are some suggestions that the character can also mean opportunity, and indeed there can be opportunity if a business moves quickly enough at this 'critical point'.

However, the use of Chinese characters served a purpose other than highlighting the crisis the world was facing. It gave a strong indication as to where Bayer's attention had turned as the mature markets of the West had failed to respond to the economic stimulus packages implemented by various governments. In contrast, the Chinese government's stimulus packages were having a dramatic effect on Bayer's business and providing a well-appreciated lifeline in these troubled waters.

Figure 16.3 '*Crisis – Risk and Challenge*'

This is symbolized through the use of the characters and the illustration of the Chinese dragon boat being paddled by rowers symbolizing Bayer's key base materials that were keeping it moving.

The centerpiece of the image is an ark. Unlike the ark of biblical times, however, the Bayer vessel is carrying innovators and products that will ensure its success in the years ahead. A result of a strong market focus in the preceding year, Bayer's product development is being 'saved' at a critical time. Again, this reflects its commitment to R&D and highlights the fact that despite the effects of the economic crisis, Bayer maintained its previous year's budget in this area.

What by now have become 'the usual suspects' are still in evidence: the ox is safely on board with the change agents and the resistors have taken a new guise as they try and sink the ship in troubled waters. The traditionalists still gaze back towards the days of the past while a smaller number of bystanders now find themselves marooned on a melting iceberg. Bayer's projects are now out in the open water and are keeping it focused on what lies ahead. New projects have been added and those completed removed from the image.

POST-CRISIS – A BOOMING BUSINESS

What came as a surprise to many industry observers and professionals was the speed at which Bayer emerged from the financial pressures of 2009. At the start of the year much debate centered on the shape of the economic curve facing the industry in 2010. While doom mongers focused on a long flat 'L' curve, those slightly more upbeat predicted a slight rise before the next collapse: a 'W'. The more upbeat projections focused on a 'U' scenario; where the industry would eventually return to its previous peak after a rather protracted stay in the doldrums, while few, if any, predicted the fast return signified in the 'V' scenario.

However, while debates raged across the industry and between economists, it was very apparent that whatever the outcome, there was a dramatic shift in economic activity that would not revert. The markets had shifted east and a new strategy was needed to defend positions of strength in the mature economies, while unleashing a new approach to quickly benefit from growing opportunities in Asia.

The challenge facing the business was to face up to reality and quickly shift its base of knowledge and experience to tackle the new and constantly evolving global reality. A balance of messaging was required to explain the heightened activity in the new markets, while focusing on the strength that was greatly evident in Europe and North America.

The cartoon that was used focused on a center of learning where large numbers of 'students' travelled from Asia to gain the knowledge and experience of Western 'lecturers'. The regions were symbolized by the towering structures of Asia facing the classic architecture of the West.

The picture is filled with information and the clusters of change characters still grace the stage. There are a far larger number of blue change agents heading towards Asia, defending the mature markets and receiving 'diplomas' from the Chief Executive. A number of resistors continue to attempt to halt the change strategy by destroying the books of knowledge and thereby retaining the keys to success. The green traditionalists, while still retaining the traditions of the past, which is symbolized by their traditional dress, have arrived to impart their knowledge, while an even fewer number of bystanders peek out of the foliage to see what is happening.

The image is filled with internal messages that had been delivered during the last year: a three-horse race symbolizing the neck-and-neck positions of the USA, Europe and China as they vie for the number one market position; the windmills strategically located in the mature markets still seek and harness the wind; the ark and boats of previous cartoons still play

Figure 16.4 *'Growing Together'*

their part; and the ox and cart of the first cartoon are now resting as the journey ends its first chapter.

Other notable elements of this picture include the statue of Justicia, which is depicted holding the scales of justice to symbolize Bayer's commitment to compliance, while wearing protective clothing to show its commitment to safety. Dragging the caption of 'Growing Together', which signifies Bayer's commitment to growth in global markets and as individuals, is Solar Impulse, the solar-powered plane being developed in Switzerland by Bertrand Piccard and André Borschberg to circumnavigate the world on solar power alone.

As a partner in the Solar Impulse project, the plane has come to symbolize Bayer MaterialScience's commitment to developing solutions to tackle the issues that will inevitably occur as the world is impacted by the global megatrends. This is the future for Bayer MaterialScience and for the people who are attracted to work for the organization.

THE FUTURE

The cartoons are now widely anticipated by management and staff alike as they convey a story that involves everyone in the company. While we have focused much attention on this first series of cartoons, there is much more that leaders must deliver. Not least of which is the development of other leaders, not just followers.

Each of the disciplines of leadership, regardless of who selects them, prioritizes them or implements them, must be understood to be crucial at all levels of a corporate society. The need for profound, simple communication is paramount to their success, yet it is often observed that too little effort is expended in gaining this understanding.

Employees need to understand why resources are being deployed in certain areas and not others; for this they must understand the basics of the business strategy. They must also have a sense of direction and be clear on the goals of the leadership. They must also feel part of a team and of a culture, while seeing for themselves the behaviors they expect to be demonstrated.

Employees must engage and be motivated by a leadership that listens and coaches, for this all leads to an energy that grows into commitment. But above all, employees want to deliver as individuals and as teams. If they see leaders delivering, they will strive to achieve as well and then the organization will end up somewhere other than where it was headed.

Bayer MaterialScience will embark on a new series of cartoons to deliver the next stage of the business's ongoing development. At the time of writing, it is too soon to say what direction the cartoons will take, but the story will be such that everyone will understand it.

And so, the story continues . . .

Index